DR. A.P.J. ABDUL KALAM

Memories Never Die

DR. Y.S. RAJAN & DR. APJM NAZEMA MARAIKAYAR

Translated by:

SRIPRIYA SRINIVASAN

PRABHAT PRAKASHAN

Published by
PRABHAT PRAKASHAN PVT. LTD.
4/19 Asaf Ali Road,
New Delhi-110 002 (INDIA)
e-mail: prabhatbooks@gmail.com

ISBN 978-81-961590-7-8
DR. A.P.J. ABDUL KALAM: MEMORIES NEVER DIE
by Dr. Y.S. Rajan & Dr. APJM Nazema Maraikayar

Edition
2025

Price
₹ 800 (Rupees Eight Hundred only)

Printed at
R-Tech Offset Printers, Delhi

Tamil Publisher Note

APJ Abdul Kalam is among our nation's priceless possessions, nurtured by time and moulded by history. Born in the island of Rameswaram, he became a boon to this great nation of Bharata.

As a pioneer of the Indian space revolution, this Missile Man of India took an oath to safeguard her on all frontiers. As a creative and a critical thinker, he worked diligently to empower her. He became a leader and a role model to Indian youth and children.

Following the footsteps of great leaders like Mahatma Gandhi and Jawaharlal Nehru, he led a simple life, full of humility and patriotism. This book is about the life story of this great son of India, Abdul Kalam, who led a pious life and paved the way for future generations. Serving as the President of India with compassion and dedication, Kalam verily became her cherished crest jewel.

Symbolising poet Kamban's 'Truth of all truths', just as the ambrosia of rain water purifies the land, this great man's story filled with truth and honesty raises the hope and upholds the promise of sanctifying this land.

Abdul Kalam's autobiography Wings of Fire discusses only a portion of his life. Biographies written by those who have seen him from afar have also been published. There are a few other works that are more fiction and imagination than fact.

This book has the privilege of being written by people who have observed Kalam at close quarters and have walked alongside him. Without doubt, it surpasses previous biographies of Kalam, for it honestly brings out his heart and mind with great authenticity.

The noted scientist Dr. Y. S. Rajan, who closely worked with Kalam and followed him like a shadow, has portrayed Kalam's life notes truthfully and holistically. Kalam's brother Muthu Meera Maraikayar's daughter Dr. Nazema Maraikayar has beautifully written about his birth and adolescence. Intertwined like nail and flesh, the life experiences shared by these two great people brings out Kalam's life in an all-round manner.

The lead author of the present work, Dr. Y. S. Rajan, is a space scientist who has worked for the Indian Space Research Organisation (ISRO). He worked under some of the pioneers of Indian space research such as Dr. Vikram Sarabhai, Dr. Brahm Prakash, and Dr. Satish Dhawan, and earned their appreciation. He served as Scientific Secretary of ISRO. He served as the Founder-Executive Director of the Technology Information Forecasting and Assessment Council (TIFAC), and Principal Advisor of the Confederation of Indian Industry (CII). He was a Member-Secretary of the Scientific Advisory Committee to the Cabinet (SACC). He was trained in National Aeronautics and Space Administration (NASA). Dr. Rajan—the closest friend and confidante of the hero of this work, Dr. Abdul Kalam—has co-authored books like India 2020, Beyond 2020, and The Scientific Indian, among others. He is also a gifted poet. He became an inseparable member of Kalam's family.

The co-author of this work, Dr. Nazema Maraikayar is Kalam's niece and holds a doctorate in Tamil literature. A worthy successor of Kalam's genius, she is an author and publisher; she reproduces memories through her skill of language.

The two authors have closely observed and recorded Kalam's innate qualities that were not brought about by others earlier. Circumventing over their close ties as a friend and a relative, they have introduced this book's protagonist true to his nature.

Arutchelvar N. Mahalingam Translation Institute (AMTI) had published the Tamil translation of Dr. Kalam's Beyond 2020 as their first release after taking his permission. At the time of the book release, however, we had already lost Kalam. We had decided to publish Kalam's biography back then. We would like to sincerely thank Dr. Y.S. Rajan and Dr. Nazema Maraikayar for fulfilling our endeavour with utmost commitment. No one else could have done greater justice to Kalam's biography.

There are some special features of this book which talks about the eternal memories of Kalam.

This book was written by people closest to Kalam, and therefore all episodes in this work are authentic with little scope for imagination and fiction.

Episodes from Kalam's childhood have been portrayed for the first time the way they happened. These were carefully collected and presented by his niece.

What are the steps that lead up to a great man in the making? How well has he progressed with his hard work, dedication, and commitment by adjusting to the circumstances and people around him? These questions are answered in this book.

Working beyond scheduled hours with sincere predisposition and by carefully employing the tools of intelligence and wisdom, Kalam was given a free hand at his work and he had earned recognition and acclaim from stalwarts like Dr. Vikram Sarabhai and Prof. Satish Dhawan. Kalam's remarkable work ethic has been portrayed in this work.

The positive spirit with which Kalam handled the occasional negative narratives from some of his co-workers while working at ISRO and Defence Research and Development Organisation (DRDO), which worked to his benefit ultimately is for the first time revealed in this book.

The manner in which Kalam exhibited his humane nature throughout his life is explained in this work.

The fact that success in administration is a collective team effort brought forth by embracing everyone involved has been portrayed through various real life events in this book. The way in which Kalam humbly embraced his failures can also be seen here.

Born in the family of boatmen, how Kalam sailed to become India's Bharat Ratna has been showcased beautifully by the authors.

Kalam's food interests, favourite music, and his love for nature have also been given importance in this book.

The influence of the Qur'an, Thirukkural, and the writings of Mahakavi Subramania Bharathi, which helped in shaping up Kalam's life are also brought to light here.

Episodes of Kalam's sense of humour are equally pleasing to us.

There were times when Dr. Y. S. Rajan was not working alongside Kalam. In order to fill in the gaps, he has adopted a novel technique. He collected essays from those who were with Kalam at the time. Scientist Sivathanu Pillai who worked under Kalam for the Brahmos missile programme, noted scientist Prahlada, and Kalam's personal secretary H. Sheridon have given their narratives on Kalam. There is no place for intermission in this biography on Kalam.

Most people would not have heard of Kalam's religious leanings. Kalam's participation in Foundation for Unity of Religions and Enlightened Citizenship (FUREC) that aims to bring together various religious inclinations and his camaraderie with religious leaders across communities bears testimony to his unifying spirit. Mrs. Sudhamahi Reghunathan has beautifully penned her experience here in this book, which deserves special mention.

The fame, respect, and popularity earned by Kalam overseas have been narrated by Dr. Rajan who had the opportunity to accompany him abroad.

The present work is a masterpiece that enlightens the readers about many such life moments of Kalam.

Arutchelvar N. Mahalingam, after whom our translation enterprise is named, was a very close friend of Kalam. We would like to thank our head Dr. M. Manikkam who felt that it would be apt to bring out this book through our enterprise and encouraged us to do so.

We would like to thank Dr. Y. S. Rajan and Dr. Nazema Maraikayar for fulfilling our commitment.

We would like to thank Mr. M. Hariharasudan, the correspondent of Shakti Education Group and N. I. A. Educational Institution's Secretary Dr. C. Ramasamy for appreciating this publication.

Special appreciation to Hashmedia Shankar for designing a fantastic cover page, and our office assistant V. Balasubramaniam. Our thanks to Professor Kirungai Sethupathi and Giri Prasad for proof reading this work.

Let us celebrate this great leader Kalam with a quote from his most favourite Thirukkural.

"Noble people are like benevolent clouds as they do their duty without expecting anything in return."

–Sirpi Balasubramaniam

Translator's Note

Prof. Joseph Campbell, the renowned mythologist and author famously said, "Follow your bliss and the universe will open doors where there were only walls." This is one of my favourite quotations and I have experienced it in my own life.

I had the good fortune of visiting Dr. Y. S. Rajan at his residence in December 2021. Later, he asked me if I would be interested in translating into English 'நினைவுகளுக்கு மரணமில்லை' (*Ninaivugalukku Maranamillai* – literally translated as 'Memories don't die'), a Tamil biography of the former Indian President A. P. J. Abdul Kalam. Dr. Y. S. Rajan had written the book along with Kalam's niece Dr. Nazema Maraikayar. He might have wanted to check with me if I was interested in translating his book because earlier I had prepared a Tamil translation of his book '*Scientific Indian.*' I readily agreed.

Memories Never Die is a self-complete, thorough, and honest revelation of the phenomenon that was Abdul Kalam. From his early childhood till he breathed his last, this book covers all major episodes of Kalam's life, both personal as well as professional. Dr. Nazema Maraikayar has fondly recounted precious moments since Kalam's childhood days, while Dr. Y. S. Rajan has revealed the professional side of Kalam holistically and truthfully.

The manner in which a small-town boy from Rameswaram rose up to the highest echelons of the Indian political world; his struggles, successes, and failures; his achievements; his supporters and detractors; and his scientific and spiritual leanings have been portrayed holistically and truthfully in this book.

It is my firm belief that if some episodes from this book are introduced to high school students in their textbooks, they will imbibe the values of inquisitiveness, steadfastness, and consistency in their pursuit of knowledge. Dr. Rajan has beautifully introduced the history of Indian rocketry as well as the precursors to a few S&T advancements of the modern day. He has also highlighted the key role played by the industrial sector in the manufacture of indigenous products and the need to integrate it with the latest S&T innovations to help empower the nation.

His invaluable inputs regarding modifications to be made to the current system of administration in India in order to cope up with changes in political and geo-political scenarios is worthy of consideration.

The present work has been authored by two persons closest to Kalam—one connected through his bloodline and the other a witness to some of the most crucial incidents that shaped his life; needless to say, it will serve as an inspiration to the readers.

I have retained poems from the *Blossoms of the Heart* collection as such in my translation. The rest of the poem translations in this book were done by me and later edited by Dr. Rajan. For the names of various persons, I have referred to Abdul Kalam's autobiography *Wings of Fire*. Dr. Rajan shared his inputs with regard to the names and designations related to Kalam's professional field. He also drew my attention to some of the key terminologies employed in the Indian Administrative System.

I feel fortunate and blessed that I got an opportunity to take up this wonderful assignment for which I am eternally thankful to Dr. Y. S. Rajan. In addition to giving me this exciting opportunity, he thoroughly reviewed my translation and offered invaluable suggestions.

I am grateful to my friend Shri Hari Ravikumar who dedicated his time to review my translation despite his busy schedule.

The following lines of Mahakavi Bharathi best describe Kalam:

Thoughts and aims must come to pass;
And the mind shall think only good.
A stout and sturdy heart I seek,
And a clear, lucid intellect.

– Sripriya Srinivasan

Contents

Memories of Dr. Kalam Recounted by Kalam's Elder Brother's Daughter Dr. Nazema Maraikayar

Early Childhood

A father's dream! Jain Maraikayar had a deep respect for studies and scholars. Even though he couldn't study much, he patronised his children to pursue their studies. His elder children couldn't fulfil his dream. His youngest son was his only ray of hope. Having seen his relatives work as lawyers, government servants and railway employees, he wished that his son too would become like them and earn a dignified status in the society; that son is the hero of our story.

He lives in the hearts of millions of people across the globe. He is my father's younger brother APJ Abdul Kalam. This is his story.

Avul Pakir Jainulabdeen was born in a prestigious family. His brother is Mohammed Ibrahim and his sisters are Sulaihamma and Ayishamma.

After his father's death, Jainulabdeen took care of his brother and sisters. He showed great respect to his mother. Following the footsteps of his grandfather Avul Ambalam, and his father Pakir Ambalam, Ambalam Jain Maraikayar took part in proceedings of the Panchayat in his home town Rameswaram which is famous for the renowned Ramanathaswamy temple.

He actively participated in decision making, advising his townsmen whenever they needed his counsel. He was supported and surrounded by his friends and relatives all through his life.

Jain Maraikayar got his sisters married at the right age. He too got married to his uncle's daughter who unfortunately died during her pregnancy. Meanwhile, he got his brother married as well. At his mother's request, Jain Maraikayar got married to his younger uncle's daughter Asiamma.

Soon after, the house was decorated by a colourful array of children. Asim Zohara, Mohammed Muthu Meera Lebbai, Mustafa Kamal, Hajaramma, Kasim Mohammed were all born and brought up in this house.

Asiamma gave birth to a son on October 15, 1931. He was named "Abdul Kalam" after freedom fighter Abul Kalam Azad. They would have never known that this little infant would one day make his mark in world history.

Asiamma was very affectionate towards her son Kalam. Whereas all her other children grew under the care of her mother and mother-in-law, Asiamma fed, sang lullabies and caressed this child all by herself.

The child grew and started saying his first words 'Appa' and 'Amma' . Soon after he was taught to speak Arabic words like 'Alef', 'Be' and so on by his mother.

At the right age, this little boy wearing a small dhoti, cap and slippers, was sent to learn the Holy Qur'an from Alimsa at the local mosque. Soon after, he started his education at the local school popularly referred to as 'The Shrine.' The head teacher was a strict disciplinarian. He encouraged all children to come to school only after their morning bath. This early morning ritual became an integral part all through Kalam's life which made him energetic and active throughout the day.

After learning basic alphabets at the local school, he was sent to the government school to receive formal education. Reciting the Holy Qur'an, going to school and playing in the evening with friends became his daily routine.

"Teach him if you can the wonders of books, but also give time to ponder the extreme mystery of birds in the sky, bees in the sun and flowers on a green hill." US President Abraham Lincoln wrote these words in a letter to his son's school teacher. Jain Maraikayar seemed to have practised these words. On the weekends, he would take his son Kalam to roam around trees and plantations. After this, they would pass by the seashore. Birds flying freely flapping their wings in the vastness of the sky became a treat to Kalam's eyes.

Kalam especially enjoyed watching the rain clouds. While his father rushed him to get back home before torrential rains, Kalam would while away the time waiting for the first set of raindrops to fall on the earth. He loved the aroma of fresh water droplets on land. He used to think that rain drops poured down only to cleanse the street. Whether these rain drops would also cleanse one's mind from anger, hatred and jealousy were beyond the scope of this young boy's imagination!

When his father and brothers were outside, he enjoyed playing in the rain till he was dragged back into the house by his mother and grandmother. His mother rushed with a towel and his grandmother Hasanachiyar made him inhale balsam lest he should catch a cold. But all this lasted only till the next rain! When he suffered from fever, they would make him drink fresh concoction made from the indigo plant.

Kasim Mohammed was older than Abdul Kalam by four years. These two were very affectionate towards their elder brother's wife Ahmed Kanima whom they called as 'Machi.' They had deep regard for her and she too treated them like her own sons. One day while the two boys were playing in the backyard, Abdul Kalam accidentally hit Kasim Mohammed with a spade. Hearing the commotion, Ahmed Kanima rushed to the scene. After plastering the wound, she patiently advised Kalam, "These things happen while playing. But in future play carefully so that there is no bloodbath. Alright?" Kalam felt very guilty. She advised them not to complain about this incident to the elders. Kasim Mohammed had forgotten all about her advice. He pointed a finger at Kalam when the elders asked about the injury. However, Kanima pacified them by saying that the boys were too young and that they should be forgiven. Kanima never spoke a word confronting the house elders. When Kalam saw how supportive she was towards him, his respect for her grew manifold.

One day while his teacher was taking classes in the afternoon, he was saying, "You need to run with the flow." Kalam asked him back, "Sir, if we run with the flow, wouldn't our legs hurt?" The teacher was not at all angry. He patiently explained, " Dear Kalam. What I meant was that you should be able to tackle all situations in life. Besides, this is your age to run and never stop!" This incident had left a lasting imprint on him and he felt deeply for the patience and humility inherent in all men.

While Kanima gave him coconut water one day, surprised by its sweetness, he asked her, "How come this coconut water is so tasty?" to which she replied, "This coconut is from Karaiyur." Kalam was curious to learn more. He wanted to find out how coconuts from different parts within a town tasted so differently. The next day he accompanied his elder brother Chinna Maraikayar to the coconut grove. "Welcome, employers!" acknowledged the Karaiyur elders. While drinking the coconut water, Kalam saw how actively the workers were climbing up the coconut trees which were skinned later on. Looking at Kalam's inquisitive look, Chinna Maraikayar asked, "What's the matter, dear?" Kalam asked, "This morning Machi gave me coconut water from these trees. I wanted to know the reason behind its sweetness." After making him sit down, his elder brother explained, "Till 1480, Rameswaram was a part of the country's mainland. However, after a severe storm, it became an island surrounded by sea water on all sides. To the south of this island, the regions from Karaiyur till Nambu Nayaki Amman temple are enriched by the Devakuli river. The soil here is very fertile and the water here is very tasty. Coconut trees grow in abundance here. The coconuts are pulpy and their water is also sweet. It is now time for us to get back home."

Chinna Maraikayar continued explaining on the way, "To the north of Rameswaram Pancha Kalyani river runs from Poovarasankulam till the first sector of Narikuzhy. In these forests only tamarind trees grow in abundance. In the northern region since hard rocks lay buried underground, coconut trees are scanty. Also, the coconuts are too small and their water is not very sweet. This is because of the nature of the soil."

The daily routine continued. Abdul Kalam started thinking deeply, "If even within our small town, there could be so much difference in soil quality, what could be the nature of soils across India? What could be obtained from all over the place?"

❑

Change of Place

Kalam visited the grove with his brother on many occasions. He was enchanted by the strange sounds made by a variety of colourful birds. Multi-coloured birds! Some birds cooed sweetly while some others shrieked loudly. Kalam was enthralled! Identifying different birds with their colour and sound was perhaps the reason behind why in his later years Kalam sought out the 'Jonathan Livingston Seagull' book written by Richard Bach.

Kalam grew up to become a lover of nature, a good student, and a responsible individual, supported at home. He actively engaged in other useful activities. He had great affection for his cousin brother Samsuddin. Samsuddin was the distributor of the newspaper '*Dinamani*' in Rameswaram. People fondly called him 'the newspaper man.' Kalam accompanied him to the railway station every morning to collect the newspapers. After sorting them out, Kalam would distribute them to various houses before going to school. Kalam punctually did this every morning since he loved reading. His brother Samsuddin gave him small incentives for his help.

Arabic studies, school studies, prayer and sports became his daily routine. Kalam was a strict vegetarian from a young age. So, his grandmother, mother and Kanima used to prepare spinach, onion sambar, tamarind sambar and papad specially for him. He came back from school everyday at 4.30 in the evening. He loved green gram laddus which was the staple snack of all his family members. His mother prepared these and gave 3-4 pieces to him after school everyday. After relishing them, he would sit down and complete his school work. His friends would call him out to play. He would carefully inspect to check whether his mother was around. After that, he would climb up to retrieve a handful of laddus from the vessel hanging on top. He would tell Kanima not to tell his mother about this and give away the laddus to his friends. Kanima admired Kalam's attitude of sharing with others.

Kalam inherently had a lot of good qualities. He believed strongly in *Kaniyan Poongundranar*'s words, "We belong everywhere. We are all interrelated." His friends from school, Sivaprakasan, Aravindan, and Ramanadha Sastry were all from different backgrounds. On account of their good conduct, they grew up to become his intimate friends.

Kalam completed his early schooling in his hometown. However, in order to complete his higher secondary education, he had to travel to Ramanathapuram. His family members decided to send Kalam and his aunt's son Noordeen to Ramanathapuram to complete their studies. The children were hesitant initially to leave behind their family and friends. Since education is the way to success, their local school teachers advised them to pursue higher education.

Asiamma was upset at this separation. However, she felt relieved that Kalam was going to fulfil his father's desire. Asiamma and Ahmed Kanima made arrangements for Kalam's departure. They packed his laundered clothes. Kalam's relative Mustafa Kamal Kaaka fondly remembered as 'Nallakaaka' filled his suitcase with notebooks, pen and ink bottles.

Kalam was to depart in the early morning express. Chanting 'Bismillah' Ahmed Kanima filled a bronze vessel with the well water covering it with betel leaves on top. Kalam's grandmother, mother, father, his sisters, his sister-in-law Kanima, and other young children of the house waited at the front hall to bid farewell. Kalam's elder brother Chinna Maraikayar handed over an unbroken turmeric tuber to his father Jain Maraikayar who dipped it in the bronze pot and wrote the Qur'an verses, "Innal lazee farada 'alaikal Qur-aana laraaadduka ilaa ma'aad..."on the wall. *"Verily, He Who has given you the Qur'an will surely bring you back to your house of residence." (28:85, 86)*. After writing these verses, Jain Maraikayar made Kalam recite them and begged their protector to protect his son. Others said 'Ameen' and bid farewell.

Hugging her son tightly, Asiamma gave him money for his trip. After saying his goodbyes to those around him, Kalam said 'Bismillah' and proceeded on his journey. Every step he took forward on that day was to propel Bharat forward. This seemed to be God's intention!

Abdul Kalam started his education in Schwartz Higher Secondary School in Ramanathapuram. New friends, huge buildings, talented teachers, and disciplined hostel life—everything here was a whole new experience for Kalam. In a way, all these triggered his inquisitive mind.

The teachers were very responsible and would make a genuine effort to guide each and every student. Kalam remembered his father's golden words that one should always respect and obey their teacher. Kalam approached all his teachers with utmost respect and devotion. He became the favourite student of Iyadurai Solomon. Kalam enjoyed studying under him. Solomon used to advise his students that the future belonged to innovators and creative achievers. Kalam used to proudly talk about Solomon sir to his father and brothers. They too started admiring him and made it a habit to pay their visits to Solomon sir whenever they came to Ramanathapuram. Their bonding became so strong that Solomon sir became a member of their family. He visited the Maraikayar family with his wife and children whenever he was in Rameswaram.

When Kalam was in the school playground one day, his friends said that he had a visitor. It was his brother Chinna Maraikayar's close friend Periya Karuppan Ambalam who was fondly called as 'Mona Pena' by his family members. He brought special snacks from the Ervadi Santhana Koodu festival for Kalam.

Abdul Kalam read about Mahatma Gandhi in newspapers and developed a strong sense of affinity and admiration towards him. Gandhi's involvement in procuring national independence in a non-violent passive way imbibed patriotism in Kalam.

India became independent on 15th August, 1947. Solomon sir announced this to his students and also talked about Pandit Jawaharlal Nehru's address to the nation over radio the previous night. In his speech, Nehru had mentioned about his involvement in the freedom struggle with Gandhiji. He said that when he was in prison, he had written a book titled *Discovery of India*. Kalam felt excited listening to Solomon sir about India's independence. He admired Nehru for writing a book in spite of the harassment he faced while in prison. 'How well Nehru made use of his time! Independent India needs such great men!' These thoughts crossed Kalam's mind and he promised himself that he would read Nehru's book one day.

The following day India got her independence. Kalam read the news in the *Dinamani* newspaper. The picture of Nehru hoisting the national flag in Red Fort became glued to his heart.

He also read about the religious conflicts and Gandhi's foot march to Naokhali. That was when he decided that all Indians should follow Gandhi's footsteps and work tirelessly for our nation.

It was lunch time at *Schwartz High School*. It was a hot summer day. Periya Karuppan Ambalam came rushing to Abdul Kalam. After hearing from Chinna Maraikayar that school fees were due, he had come directly from the collection. Kalam was surprised to see Ambalam rush to the spot to help his friend's family member without expecting any reward. Such is the value of friendship! Kalam realised the importance of cordial relationships that day.

Abdul Kalam completed his higher secondary education. Every time on his way to and from Ramanathapuram, Kalam would see hundreds of tourists. All of them were from different sections of the society who wished to visit the sacred pilgrim site Rameswaram at least once in their lifetime. Distance, duration and weather hardly mattered to them. They recited God Rama's name with utmost devotion. Kalam felt proud of India's rich cultural heritage. He used to recollect episodes from the Ramayana that were narrated by his mother when he was young. He would recall the epic's great messages like devotion to parents, brotherly affection, kindness, humility and humanity.

Kalam greatly valued the teachings of *Prophet Muhammad (Peace be upon him). "Heaven lies beneath the feet of your mother (Book: Ahmed)." "The father is in the middle of the gates of Paradise. If you wish, you can squander this gate or keep to it." (Book: Al-Tirmidhi)*

All religions glorify and worship parents. Kalam felt thankful to his parents for taking care of all his needs and their selfless contribution towards his growth and upliftment. He developed deep respect towards his parents and regarded them with gratitude.

❑

Kalam as a College Student

Kalam's aunt's son and sister's husband Ahmed Jallaluddin had earned his living in Colombo, Sri Lanka. Colombo nurtured his innate modern thoughts. He learnt English there. He enjoyed discussing politics, weather, science news and world economics after reading the newspaper. One evening, while they were walking along the seashore, Ahmed Jallaluddin advised Kalam to pursue his higher studies with due vigour.

Kalam was fond of reading books. He enjoyed reading from the collection of his brother Mustafa Kamal's friend S. T. R. Manikkam. These books were a treasure-house of knowledge. "All that mankind has done, thought, gained, or been; it is lying as in magic preservation in the pages of books." Kalam advocated these golden words of Carlyle.

Kalam's father Jain Maraikayar wanted him to complete his intermediate course next. The French priest, Father Fodale, who learnt Tamil at the local church and served there, was his good friend. Heeding his advice, Kalam's father got a recommendation letter from him and admitted Kalam to *St. Joseph's College*, Trichy.

Soon after Kalam got admitted in the college hostel. His roommates Sampath Kumar and Alexander were kind by nature. The three of them became mutual friends and maintained a cordial relationship.

Kalam had studied in a Tamil medium school. In college however, the medium of instruction was in English. Initially, he struggled a lot to learn and understand English. Attracted by his teachers' command over the language, Kalam worked hard. Finally, his efforts paid off. He became fluent in reading, speaking and writing English. He enjoyed reading literary classics by Tolstoy and Hardy.

Kalam was now able to read 'Discovery of India' by Nehru which was recommended by Solomon sir earlier. In the book, Nehru had written extensively about the diverse languages, religions and racial groups of India and how nationality brought in a sense of unity among the Indians. This aspect made the book especially attractive to Kalam.

From a young age, Kalam was fond of Tamil books and literature. In school, everyday he was taught quotes from the Thirukkural.

"The depth of water dictates the length of the stem of a water flower,
Likewise, the spirit of the mind dictates the success of a man."

Such two-lined quotes of Thiruvalluvar ingrained wisdom inside Kalam.

Mahakavi Subramania Bharathi became Kalam's guide and best friend. He read all works of Bharathi with great enthusiasm. Scientific inquisitiveness of Bharathi had left behind a lasting impression on Kalam. 'Learn astronomy' is one of the sayings of *Bharathi* in his '*Puthiya Aathichudi*.' This further broadened Kalam's mind who grew up as a 'skywatcher' from his early days.

In one of his poems from his magnum-opus *The Oath of Draupadi* Bharathi prays to *Sarasvati*, the goddess of learning and wisdom:

"The physicists say that atoms whirl ceaselessly;
the astronomers opine that the orbs gyrate for ever and ever
If it be but natural for the things of globe to work ceaselessly,
O Mother of Arts! Should not my heart, I pray,
function ceaselessly, made one with thy Grace?"

These words of Bharathi that were filled with scientific inquisitiveness made a deep impact on Kalam. He wondered if there was a genre untouched by this great poet.

He brought his favourite books to Rameswaram during vacation and would spend his time productively by reading them. During lunchtime, he would monitor their shops so that his elder brothers Mustafa Kamal and Kasim Mohammed could go home for lunch. They eagerly waited for Kalam's visits and would return back to their shops leisurely after lunch.

Kalam made it a point to recite and learn verses of the *Holy Qur'an* while he visited home for vacations. He wanted to improve on his pronunciation and asked his father to recommend a suitable instructor. Accordingly, his father asked him to learn from 'Asanbhava' who was the husband of Abubaker Ravuthar's sister. He ran his business in Malaysia and he too had come to Rameswaram for vacation. After Jain Maraikayar had requested him, he taught verses of the *Holy Qur'an* to Abdul Kalam. Kalam clarified all his doubts from his teacher with earnestness.

Abdul Kalam continued his college studies. His brother Chinna Maraikayar's friends Periya Karuppan Ambalam and Pazhanivel Nadar helped with the tuition fees. Pazhanivel Nadar accepted the repayment, whereas it was difficult to persuade Periya Karuppan Ambalam to take back his money. Such was the generosity of our family friends!

❑

Kalam as an Engineer

Soon after his college studies, Kalam got a job offer from *Dr. Zakir Husain College* in Ilayangudi. However, studying aerospace engineering had been Kalam's lifelong dream. With his father's blessings, he sent his application to the *Madras Institute of Technology* (MIT).

The Rameswaram Maraikayar family maintained cordial relations with the Sethupathi kings of Ramanathapuram since time immemorial. Jain Maraikayar mentioned about his son Kalam's application to MIT when he visited his friend King Shanmuganatha Sethupathi in Madras. "Why have you travelled all the way to convey this? You could have conveyed this through my secretary in Ramanathapuram district. Don't worry! Your son will surely secure a place in MIT," blessed the king. Soon after, Kalam got an offer letter to pursue his studies at MIT.

He had secured a seat. However, the tuition fee was enormous! Periya Karuppan Ambalam who always came to their rescue was also not in town at the time. They were perplexed. When everybody was discussing this issue, Kalam's elder sister Asim Zohara mortgaged her golden bangles and asked them to pay his fees. Her timely help made it possible to pay the tuition fee at the right time.

Kalam's mother, father, sisters, brothers, Machi, children and all his relatives were there to send him off to college. Kalam, the skygazer, now set out to study 'aeronautical engineering.'

"*Scaling across the wind, let us reach for the sky.*"

These words of Bharathi were echoing in Kalam's heart. He felt grateful to his sister for making his dream come true.

"Even a tiny help rendered at the rightful moment becomes a gift that surpasses the world."

Kalam was reminiscing over these quotes of Thiruvalluvar as he recalled his sister's timely help.

Kalam enjoyed studying at MIT, Chromepet. He subscribed to Tamil magazines like *Ananda Vikatan* and *Kalaimagal* out of his interest for Tamil.

He enrolled for an elocution competition held by the *Tamil Sangam* in MIT. He won first place for his essay "ஆகாய விமானம் கட்டுவோம் (Let us build our own aircraft)." He received his prize from the chief editor Mr. Devan of the *Ananda Vikatan* magazine.

On rare occasions, he went to the movies with his classmates where he relished groundnuts sitting on the ground. Kalam thoroughly enjoyed his college life.

Kalam was glued to his studies. His professors were distinguished and scholarly. They taught their students all that they knew with great enthusiasm. "Do not think too deeply into the future; lay down a strong foundation for whichever discipline you want to pursue." These were Kalam's favourite professor Dr. E. Sponder's words. With his wisdom, hard work and discipline, Kalam earned a good name in college.

Kalam completed his engineering course by securing good marks. His first job was at *Hindustan Aeronautics Limited* (HAL), Bangalore. In his job, Kalam was a disciplined worker. At home, he was humble and polite to everyone. During vacation, he rushed to his home in Rameswaram to be with his parents and other relatives.

Kalam settled his sister's debt from his salary. He gave a huge portion of his earnings to help his family.

Kalam's job opportunities equally supported his good intentions. His next job was as a rocket engineer in the *Indian Space Research Organisation* (ISRO).

❑

Training at NASA

Kalam had to travel to the USA to get trained at the *National Aeronautics and Space Administration* (NASA). Before leaving, he visited Rameswaram to seek the good wishes and blessings from his family members.

His family flocked around to read his letters from the US. In the letters addressed to his father, he wrote about what all he saw there. In one such letter, he had written about the missiles used by the Mysore ruler Tipu Sultan to attack the Britishers in war. He had described elegantly a war portrait of Tipu Sultan taken along with his missile soldiers that he saw in one of the US research centres. Reading this, his family members started discussing his letter. His Machi Ahmed Kanima praised Kalam's patriotism and said that even when he lived abroad, all his thoughts were about his motherland India.

Along with his six months training course, Kalam also learnt the strength of hard work, toil and determination. He returned back to India to serve his motherland.

He returned with a box of chocolates and gave money to buy silk sarees for his sister and Machi. Silk and terlin clothes were purchased for all children. His mother Asiamma donated her money to charity.

Now that Kalam had secured a good job, his parents wanted him to get married. On account of his educational qualification and job status, they were finding it difficult to get a suitable bride among their relatives. They found a suitable girl with a postgraduate degree in their hometown. Kalam's parents visited the girl's parents and they too visited Kalam's house. They wanted to see the bridegroom. However, Kalam couldn't come on the promised date due to excessive workload.

Several months rolled by. Once again, his parents started looking for a suitable bride. During his visit to Rameswaram, Kalam indicated to his mother using hand gestures that he preferred to marry an educated girl. Many relatives approached Kalam's family. However, none of the girls were suitably qualified. Kalam's parents had no other option but to reject all proposals.

Kalam's mother Asiamma who was very fond of him was desperately trying to get him married to a suitable girl. Whenever she visited marriage ceremonies, she pictured Kalam as a bridegroom. Everytime a proposal knocked on the door, Kalam either was not in town or it became impossible to travel due to his job situation.

When Asiamma was reading a wedding invitation one day, she saw two crows sitting together on a drumstick tree nearby. She wondered when her beloved son Kalam would find a suitable life partner. She said to Kanima, "Look at all these birds flying together! Doesn't your brother-in-law Kalam look at all this?" Kanima thought to herself, "Well, of course! However, Kalam's thoughts would be on how these birds could fly!" She pacified her mother-in-law, "Yes, of course! He would have noticed them."

Months rolled into years.

Kalam loved music. During the festival season in Rameswaram, Kalam sat with his friends on the first row listening to sweet carnatic music. He knew all Telugu compositions by heart! Even while he was engrossed in his work, he enjoyed listening to good music. He bought a radio especially to listen to carnatic music. He passionately described it to his brother's daughters. Seeing their eagerness, he promised himself that he would buy one for the children at home. During his next visit, he brought with him a black 'Phillips' radio and taught them how to operate it. The children Arabu, Meharaj and Asiyat Jamila were thrilled to receive their new gift from Kalam uncle.

Hearing the loud noise from the radio, Kalam's brother's little daughter Nazema woke up. Kalam highlighted the value of radio to the little one. He said that sitting at home one could listen to current local news, music, drama, weather and world news. He asked her to study well and blessed her to participate in radio programmes. The children of the house were overcome with joy.

This was the first electronic instrument in their house. To the grownup girls who couldn't get out of the house, radio became their best friend. It covered a wide range of topics from science to spirituality.

❑

Ahmed Kanima: An Epitome of Kindness

Whenever he visited home, Kalam would hand over the books which he had finished reading to the children of the house. He would bring magazines he purchased in the railway station as well.

Ahmed Kanima was reading the *Kalaimagal* magazine brought home by Kalam that day. Her thoughts were all about Kalam. She was reminiscing the day she first stepped foot in her in-laws' house. She recalled how Kalam had climbed with the newly-weds inside their palanquin. Kalam's composure and how he kept glancing at her expecting her to look back at him at least once made her think that this child would become a great man one day. Looking at Kalam now, she was glad that her prayers had been answered.

Her thoughts went back to her first day at the Maraikayar house. When Asiamma welcomed the newly-weds with the ceremonial '*arathi*', when they were given milk and fruits and when Kanima was asked to touch salt, rice and other grains in the kitchen, Kalam looked with bewilderment. He kept asking his mother to explain these rituals. His mother would have probably told Kalam that Kanima was now a member of the Maraikayar family and that with her golden touch she would make this house prosper. "But Kalam was still too young to understand the underlying meaning behind these elaborate rituals," thought Kanima to herself.

After completing the rituals, Kalam's mother introduced him to Kanima. She said to him that Kanima was his elder brother Chinna Maraikayar's wife and that from now onwards he should call her as 'Machi'. Kalam was delighted. With excitement, he kept calling out to his Machi and showed her around the

Maraikayar house. Whenever Kalam was around, Kanima forgot all about her four younger brothers and two elder brothers with whom she grew.

Kalam and Kanima became very friendly. His mother had warned him not to go out in the dark. Earlier, his mother accompanied him. After Kanima's arrival, he called out to his Machi to accompany him. Kanima would take a hurricane lamp and go with him. The members of the Maraikayar family appreciated Kanima's kindness.

Reminiscing over the past, Kanima wished for Kalam to find a suitable life partner. Her thoughts of him continued...

❑

Bonding with the Rameswaram Temple

Kalam always accompanied his father outside. He was curious to find out answers to many questions. He got his answers to a few of them.

Following the footsteps of his grandfather and father, Jain Maraikayar built rafts for the ceremonial float festival at the Rameswaram temple. His workers constructed the boats. Kalam went to the construction site right after school on such days. He would carefully watch every stage of the boat construction. After coming home, he would narrate everything to his Machi. His realistic narration would make Kanima visualise the scenes transforming her to another world.

On the day of the festival, Kalam was enchanted looking at the beautifully decorated colourful boat. Everyone in town crowded around to watch the luminous display. Fire-crackers added to the magic.

After the float festival, temple authorities welcomed Jain Maraikayar to receive his due respects. Kalam accompanied his father. As they approached the sanctum sanctorum, Jain Maraikayar handed over pieces of silk clothes to the temple official. In return, the official gave him a plate which contained three silk sarees, five dhotis, flowers, fruits, coconut, and money knotted inside a piece of silk cloth. Jain Maraikayar returned home with his workers.

He distributed two-thirds of the money and all the *dhoti*s to his employees. He handed over the silk sarees to his wife Asiamma. Opening his eyes widely, Kalam described to his Machi all that had transpired on that day.

Every night, Kalam sat down to talk with his mother. Asiamma would convey messages from the Holy Qur'an and the Hadith. She would also describe episodes from the *Ramayana* and the *Mahabharata*. Kalam always enjoyed these conversations. On that day, Kalam was curious to find more about the float festival.

Kalam waited till she finished her night time Isha prayer. She asked him if he had completed his studies. After answering her, Kalam asked all about the float festival.

Asiamma started narrating. "This happened at the time of your grandfather Avul Ambalam. During the ceremonial boat procession of the Rameswaram temple, the boats carrying the sacred idols of the Gods would go around the lake. On one such occasion, the boat toppled and all idols submerged underwater. Hearing about this, your grandfather Avul Ambalam took with him a few of his employees and the fishermen from Sangukuli and arrived at the scene. On his command, they jumped inside and retrieved back the sacred idols. Thanking God, Avul Ambalam safely handed over the idols to the temple authorities. The temple authorities invited him for a discussion the next day. They discussed building a raft for the procession. Your grandfather suggested that it would be possible to build one by tying small boats and mounting wooden planks. The temple authorities asked him to take up the job. After that, the employees headed by Avul Ambalam designed the festival boats annually. During the Diwali and the Pongal festivities, the Maraikayar family received rice, coconuts, jaggery, fruits, betel leaves and betel nuts from the Rameswaram temple. Ambalakarar (Maraikayars) took some for themselves and distributed the rest to their workers."

The next day, he shared what he had heard from his mother with his Machi. He silently thanked his elders for respecting the sentiments of all religions. He widened his vision and outlook as he listened to such stories.

Kalam had been a naughty boy since childhood. He was as much a prankster as he was peaceful. However, he made sure that he hurt no one with his pranks.

When his Machi became pregnant, Kalam couldn't help but think about Lord Ganapathi. He mocked her, "Why has this Ganapathi's belly enlarged so much?" Everyone in their house laughed at his joke.

Once Kalam accompanied his mother Asiamma, his cousin Samsuddin's mother Alima and a few other ladies of the house. They went out to look at a prospective bride for Samsuddin. When Kanima asked him about her, Kalam replied, "I saw her Machi. She is very fair. She has tiny dots all over her face." He gestured to his description. His paternal grandmother Sultan Beevi Fathima asked him, "Grandson! What are you saying?" To this, Kalam's mother replied that the girl had recently had measles and that was the reason behind the marks on her face. Kanima was impressed with the way Kalam had described these marks as tiny dots.

Kanima knew that like all other boys his age, Kalam too was youthful and energetic. His thoughts were however emancipated and very different from the rest.

Kalam's cousin Mohammed Abubaker's wife Muthu Qureshi who used to play with Kalam when they were children, recalls her memories of Kalam here. "Externally, Kalam resembled all other children of his age. However, his sense of humour and his dedication to fulfil his promise set him apart from the rest. When I was young, I wanted to look around the temple premises. Kalam showed me around. I also recall how Kalam would carefully collect tamarind seeds and get money for household use from the shops. He also liked to share his food with those around him.

He always enjoyed looking at the sky and the fluttering birds in them. Birds like sandpipers, wagtails, treepies, pigeons and cuckoos were bought from hunters and used to be cooked at home in those days. Sambars made out of them became the side dish for chapatis. However, Kalam felt sorry for the birds. He was upset to see how people captured these birds and cooked them for their culinary pleasures. His mother Asiamma would pacify him, "God is the creator. He alone controls birth and death. In one way or another, he takes back all that he created. Imagine what would happen to this earth if those that were created stayed on forever." Kalam would nod his head. However, he was never convinced.

❑

College Life—From the Memories of a Friend

Kalam's college friend, Mr. Sampath Kumar, a resident of Coimbatore is a close family friend. Here he recounts his memories of Kalam in *St. Joseph's College*, Trichy.

"Myself and Alexander were roommates of Kalam. Irrespective of the weather, Kalam always woke up early in the morning, had his bath, and recited his prayer. He then organised his books according to that day's time table. After this, he went around the college campus. He greatly enjoyed looking at the trees, flowers and shrubs. By the time I wake up, he would be sitting in the verandah reading the newspaper. Alexander would be the last one to wake up. Alexander would then quickly get ready to go to college.

Kalam was kind and always treated us with great respect. Kalam always encountered people with a pleasant smile.

Kalam would ensure that everyone got everything when he was made in-charge of the hostel vegetarian mess.

In addition to the college books, he also read library books. He read with vigour all the Tamil and English weekly and monthly magazines. I have never seen him get angry or loud. On the contrary, Kalam had a good sense of humour.

Gaiety Talkies was a famous cinema hall at the time. We would be given permission to go for the morning show during weekends. As I enjoyed watching Hindi movies, all my friends would accompany me. Dilip Kumar, Raj Kumar, Nargis, and Nazema were the famous movie stars at the time. Kalam probably selected the name 'Nazema' for his elder brother's last daughter after the movie star Nazema.

Kalam was a student of Physics. He also showed great passion towards Tamil and English. The founder of 'Konar Notes', Sri Ayyam Perumal Konar was our Tamil professor. He had the habit of singing the poetry verses while teaching. There was pin-drop silence in the campus when he sang the verses from *Kamba Ramayanam*. Even other professors who were teaching at the time, would maintain silence. Myself and Kalam became the favourite students of Professor Ayyam Perumal Konar. This was the reason behind Kalam's dedication towards the epic *Ramayana*.

We celebrated Diwali in our hostel. We would get our supplies of oil, hot water and shikakai powder from a hostel near our college campus. After completing our ritual bath there, we bought fire-crackers which we burst after our morning meals in our hostel. This became the norm for Diwali. During our third year of college, we were given separate hostel rooms. In spite of this, all three of us stayed together. We were returning back to our hostel with fire-crackers after completing the ritual bath that year. Inside our campus, it was flooding. So we decided to burst crackers outside on an elevated place and did so. Suddenly, the water level was rising up. When we were about to fall over the spot accidentally, Kalam tried to stop the crackers from bursting by making use of the rain water. He signalled to us to go forward. We came back to the hostel dripping wet. The manner in which Kalam rescued us still remains fresh in my memory.

This flood incident had made a lasting impression on me. When I heard about the floods in Kalam's hometown Rameswaram in 1964, I decided to offer assistance to the people who were suffering. I was working in the *South Indian Viscose Company* in Mettupalayam at the time. We had arranged for a programme at the recreation club in our office. It was a dance programme by Ponmana Chelvi Jayalalitha, the former chief minister of Tamil Nadu who passed away recently. She had come with her mother for the programme. We collected fifty thousand rupees, which was given to the flood victims of Rameswaram. I felt thankful.

Our friend Colonel Alexander retired after his service in the US military. When Kalam was the President of India, the three of us met at the Presidential house. We cheerfully discussed episodes from our college and hostel life. Truly memorable days indeed!"

❑

Memories of My Beloved Chinnappa

Nuclear scientist and missile man Abdul Kalam was my father's younger brother. I addressed him as Chinnappa. Since he was older to me by several years, I have shared information gathered about him from my father, relatives and other friends so far.

Now I would like to share my personal experiences with him since my childhood. As a daughter, I feel truly blessed to have been the recipient of this great man's kindness and affection.

Abdul Kalam had come home for his vacation. He saw a little girl inching towards him making tiny baby steps. Machi told him that the little baby was hers. Everyone was surprised to see Kalam lift up the little one since he had never carried babies all his life. As he was lifting the baby up, Machi was saying that the baby was eight months old and that it has been ten months since Kalam last visited them. Kalam asked her, "What is her name?" Machi replied that they haven't named her yet. Kalam wanted to call her Nazema to which everyone happily nodded. Every time Kalam visited them, this little girl would come near him addressing him as 'Chinnappa.' Kalam would make her sit on the front porch alongside him.

I am that girl Nazema writing about the memories of my Chinnappa Kalam.

I vividly remember memories of my Chinnappa from my first grade. Mother told me that he was there. One day he asked me where I studied. Hearing my reply, he said, "It is the number one school here. I have also studied there."

"But I have never seen you there?" I replied.

"Oh no no no! I used to study there long back," Chinnappa said.

"Oh! Okay."

Chinnappa was resting in an easy chair reading a book at the time. He left back after his short visit.

Once when I had returned home for lunch, I heard a weird noise. Having come in the afternoon train, Chinnappa wanted to shave before his bath. As I had never seen an electric razor, that noise was new to me. "Have you come home for lunch?" he enquired. When I returned home after school on that day, Chinnappa asked, "So what did you learn in school today?" I showed my writing board. "You have nice handwriting!" Chinnappa appreciated it.

"Now, I shall visit your grandparents. You too come with me," he said. (My grandfather Jainulabdeen, grandmother Asiamma, my father's younger brothers, their wives, daughters and sons were residing near the local mosque at the time).

Kalam always stayed at our house when he visited Rameswaram. He enjoyed the food cooked by my mother Ahmed Kanima. My mother (Umma) would spread out two separate mats, one for sitting and the other for serving the prepared food items. There were special mats for Chinnappa in our house. Since Chinnappa did not eat fish, mom avoided making dishes made out of fish when he was around. In my house myself, my second sister and another Chinnappa too do not eat fish. So, all of us would be looking forward to his visits. During these days, the aroma of curries made out of fresh veggies would envelope the house.

Chinnappa asked me to sing the national anthem standing up. He enjoyed listening to it.

"What was today's lesson?" Chinnappa asked.

"Picture story, Chinnappa!"

"Okay! Narrate it to me," he said.

I started. "Four cows were grazing the fields. A hungry lion attacked them. Together, all four cows chased him away. The lion hatched a plan to separate them. Everyday, he would go to the cows separately and complain about the other cows. This caused animosity and hatred among the four cows. The cows started grazing separately. The lion called out to one of the cows. Once it was all alone, he pounced on the poor cow and ate him up. In this same way, the lion ate up all four of them. All other forest animals lamented over the plight of the poor cows. Our teacher told us that we should always stay united."

"What do you think, dear?" he asked.

"Yes, Chinnappa. Our teacher is correct. Unity is strength," I replied.

"So then tell me how will you stay united?" he questioned me. "I think that we should not fight with others," I told him.

"Yes, you are absolutely right. You have listened attentively to your teacher," Chinnappa appreciated me. I felt so happy.

Chinnappa had come to Rameswaram another weekend. He asked me about Gandhiji. "Do you know who Gandhi is?" he asked. "Yes, Chinnappa. Gandhi is the father of our nation. India became independent because of his freedom struggle." "When you think of Gandhi, what thoughts cross your mind?" he enquired further. "Do you know about Satya and Ahimsa?"Chinnappa asked me. "Satya means speaking the truth and ahimsa means not hurting others. This is what I have read in my book," I replied.

One evening, Chinnappa said,"I am going to test you today."

"What test?" I asked eagerly.

"Supposing I were to give you four 25 paise coins, what would you do with them?"

"I will give one to my mother,"I said.

"Why to your mother?" he asked.

"I have to definitely give it to my mom. With another 25 paise coin, I will get paper and pencil. I will put the next one inside my collection box (Hundi). With the last 25 paise coin, I will get good snacks and distribute them to everyone."

Chinnappa asked, "What will you buy?" to which I replied, "Puffed rice and groundnuts."

The local vendor was selling mixture and boondi at the time. I told Chinnappa that I will buy one of those and distribute. That night, Chinnappa asked me, "Did you get mixture or boondi?" I replied, "Since all children preferred the mixture I bought it and distributed it. I wanted to give you some as well. However, mom told me you were busy reading. So I did not want to disturb you."

Chinnappa cheerfully said, "Okay, dear. You have passed my test."

"How Chinnappa?" I wanted to know.

"Be like this always," he said.

I was too young to understand anything at the time. Should I ask my mother? Will she be angry as she was busy with her chores? Maybe I did nothing wrong in spending all four 25 paise coins. Such thoughts crossed my mind at the time. As I looked around, I saw my mom grinding fresh cardamoms and green grams to prepare laddus for my Chinnappa. Other than special occasions like Ramadan and Bakrid, they made these laddus only when Chinnappa visited us. Laddus were packed in an empty Horlicks container for him to take to his college hostel.

It was time for Chinnappa to get back to his college. My mom gathered water from the well and covered the lid of the vessel with a betel leaf. My grandmother Asiamma brought a small cup containing water into which she had dipped an unbroken turmeric tuber. Chinnappa covered his head with a small kerchief. The other male members covered their heads with caps. My dad started to write the Arabic verses on the wall from the Holy Qur'an using the turmeric tuber...

"Innal lazee farada 'alaikal Qur-aana laraaadduka ilaa ma'aad..."

After this, my grandmother gave Chinnappa a glass of milk to drink. Then my grandmother and grandfather gave him travel money. Chinnappa gave each of us a one rupee coin and then left for his college.

The next time Chinnappa came to Rameswaram was when my grandfather Jain Maraikayar was sick. Chinnappa rushed to his father's residence near the mosque. We too had gone there with my parents. Chinnappa worried looking at his father's condition. The doctor was called. He administered a few tablets and other medicines.

After spending the day with his father, Chinnappa returned to our house in the evening. Chinnappa was perhaps relieved after discussing his father's condition with the doctor. He continued from where he left. "Did you go to school today? Do you know *Thirukkural*?" he asked me. "*Agara mudhala ezhuthellam...*," I started reciting. "That is the first verse, dear. Do you know some other verse?" he asked me. As I was thinking, he started reciting,

"Vellathanaya malar neettam, maandhar tham

Ullathanayadhuyarvu."

("Just as the depth of water dictates the length of the stem of a water plant,

The greatness of men is dictated by the depth of their mind.")

"Did you know that this is a great verse from the *Thirukkural*? You should read *Thirukkural* frequently," he told me.

Soon after his father's health condition improved, Chinnappa left.

War broke out at the Indian frontier. Owing to Chinnappa's advice to read books and also since I had a natural inclination towards reading, I went through all columns related to the war in various newspapers. I would discuss everything with my elder brothers and sisters. On account of all this, I had enrolled in the elocution competition that year. The topic was about war heroes.

All my school seniors talked about the historic Cheras, Cholas, Pandyas, Pallavas, and Ashoka. It was my turn next. It was my first elocution competition. Abdul Hameed was a soldier who had fought in the recent war at the frontier. I had collected all the information for my speech from the daily newspapers and other local magazines. I was able to speak fluently in the competition. I bagged the first prize along with two others. I wanted to share this great news with my Chinnappa.

When Chinnappa came home for his annual vacation, I conveyed this to him and showed him my prize. He was very happy to see it. He asked me if I could repeat my speech in the evening. As soon as I finished, he called out to my mom happily, "Look at this excellent speech by your daughter, Machi." He gave me ten rupees that day.

Due to the encouragement from my Chinnappa and my elder sisters, I took part in many such school competitions and won prizes. All my elder sisters stopped their schooling soon after puberty. However, my mom and dad wished that I continued my schooling. Allah's mercy!

My grandfather Jain Maraikayar's health condition deteriorated. He would sit on the outside portico. Then, he would get back inside to sleep. My father along with Mustafa Kamal Nallappa made it a point to visit my grandfather everyday before and after their five sessions of prayer.

It became a routine for Chinnappa to visit us all more frequently. In spite of his heavy workload, he made it a point to visit his parents and spend time with them.

Life is a race. It is possible to scale great heights with the passage of time. However, what matters the most is the way in which we treat our parents and siblings even as we have climbed up the ladder. Chinnappa became a guide and a role model to all of us.

My dad wrote letters to Chinnappa informing him about their father's health condition. He wrote about ceremonies that were to happen in our relatives' houses. He would also write about the ailments of a few others. Whenever Chinnappa visited us, he would give money for gifts to my father. He would enquire about those who were suffering from ailments as well. He even visited them personally at times. My Chinnappa was a benevolent man.

Our discussion continued. One day he asked me, "After completing your schooling, what are you planning to study in college?"

"Can I study literature?" I asked.

"Why not become a doctor?" he responded.

To this, I simply nodded my head. He did not say anything after that.

❑

Turbulence—Inside and Outside

Mr. Sampath Kumar runs the '*Save our Daughters*' charitable organisation. Girls drop out of school at a young age owing to various societal, family and financial circumstances. The primary aim of this organisation is to identify and bring such girl children back to school. Here they even try to arrange for suitable jobs after schooling is complete. The inaugural ceremony was conducted in a simple way with Kalam as the chief guest.

Sampath Kumar who was regularly in touch with Kalam till the end was shocked to hear about his sudden death. He is a true friend and deeply cherishes his memories of Kalam. His relationship with Kalam serves as a good testimony of friendship.

Dhanushkodi is a place situated to the southeast of Rameswaram island. It is a sacred pilgrim spot and it used to be a harbour until it was completely destroyed overnight. During the second world war, Dhanushkodi port was used to safeguard India's southern borders.

Soon after the midnight of December 22, 1964 at about 12.30 AM, Dhanushkodi was swept over by a storm that approached it at 120 km/hr. Fishermen used to describe Palk Bay as a peaceful place. Quite unexpectedly, waves that were 20 feet tall arose from Palk Bay and entered forcefully into Dhanushkodi. All buildings inside Dhanushkodi were completely destroyed. One kilometre of landmass in southern Dhanushkodi got submerged underwater. There was an enormous loss of life and property.

All boats on Rameswaram port were thoroughly destroyed on account of the storm. Dead bodies of people and poultry were lying all over the place. All modes of communication were lost. Railway transport got paralysed since the girders in Pamban bridge were cut off by the storm. Rescue operations started after the storm. The port office had arranged for motor boats.

Kalam rushed to the spot in a motor boat to see his parents, relatives and neighbours. He enquired about the nature of the storm. Life had come to a sudden standstill. Kalam gave financial assistance to repair and reconstruct the boats after discussing with his father and brothers. He gave some money to his mother to take care of the house. He then took leave from everyone to get back to his job.

Time flew. Kalam's family members were searching for a suitable bride. However, there was no progress. This was because Kalam was unable to visit whenever he was called. His father Jain Maraikayar was becoming old and weak. A leg sore he had developed caused him great pain. Kalam offered to take him to Chennai. However, he refused. His younger son Mustafa Kamal took good care of him.

Marriage was fixed between Chinna Maraikayar's son Shahul Hamid and his sister Asim Zohara's daughter Mehboob. Kalam's parents and brother were approached by their sister's husband and their family friend Ahmed Jallaluddin. Kalam came home two days before the ceremony. He blessed the couple and gave them presents. Everyone started pestering Kalam about marriage. He too nodded his head and left.

Jain Maraikayar's health deteriorated. Kalam would rush to look after his father. His Machi Ahmed Kanima would remind Kalam about getting married. He would always nod his head and leave.

In spite of his stressful career, Kalam would always visit his parents to take care of them. Jain Maraikayar breathed his last one evening.

The day had dawned like every other day. However, it ended on a sad note. After his morning prayers at the mosque, my dad visited his father. He picked up my mom hurriedly and left back to my grandparents' place. My grandfather welcomed them with a smile. However, he had become frail and weak. His condition worsened in the evening. He couldn't eat the food prepared by my mom either. He looked at me deeply and closed his eyes.

Shortly after us, my aunts too arrived in a horse carriage. Even before the evening prayer, my grandfather had left all of us. Chinnappa arrived the following day. He cried profusely. I was afraid to go near him. We stayed there in the afternoon after burial. We returned home in the evening. Chinnappa's eyes had turned blood red after all the crying. When I approached Chinnappa, he held my hands tightly. He did not speak. Next day, he went back to work.

My father wrote the verses from the Hayat on the wall which were usually written by my grandfather while sending Chinnappa. Chinnappa repeated the verses. My mom filled the vessel covering it with a betel leaf as usual.

Chinnappa's grief struck me. He continued to visit us in Rameswaram.

Jain Maraikayar's death was a huge loss to all of us. He had lived a great life for 102 years with good memory power. He monitored everything at work. He had earned great respect from his townsmen. He belonged to a great lineage.

Kalam was deep in thought. The memories of his father since childhood came back to him. The efforts taken by his father to send him to college, and his father's encouragement at every stage of his development enveloped his mind. Without his knowledge, Kalam would exclaim, "Vaappa!" Everyone around tried to console him. They continued to look after their mother.

The last rites of Jain Maraikayar were performed by his sons properly. They recited the Holy Qur'an on all forty days and prayed to God for his eternal peace in paradise. They prepared food and distributed it among their relatives, townsmen and the poor.

Abdul Kalam came frequently to look after his mother. Asiamma became quiet after her husband's death. We all felt that she probably interacted with her husband silently.

With the passage of time, we lost our beloved friend, guide and uncle Ahmed Jallaluddin who was also my aunt Asim Zohara's husband. On a peaceful afternoon, he left his mortal coils leaving behind his only daughter, son-in-law, granddaughter, grandson, wife, brothers and mother.

Kalam was shocked to hear about the death of his childhood friend and his sister's husband. He participated in his last rites.

As time went by, Kalam's mother Asiamma's health condition was deteriorating. Kalam frequently visited her in spite of his tiring research work. Asiamma's sons, daughters-in-law, and grandchildren would call out to her standing by her bedside. Asiamma would slowly open and close her eyes.

Kalam had come to visit his mother. Ravuthar Ali's son Alauddin used to call out to Asiamma to enquire about her health. He suggested that we should keep some money under her pillows so that she could distribute it to people in need. "Allah might reduce her misery," he suggested. Heeding his advice, Asiamma's sons kept some money under her pillow. Many people visited her. Asiamma would identify those deserving money and would take a bunch of notes and hand it out to them. "May God bless you!" They praised her gesture wholeheartedly.

Asiamma wasn't feeling well since morning on that day. Her cousin brother Ibrahim Maraikayar who had relocated to Sri Lanka had come with his wife and children to visit her. Holding her hands, he cried, "Raatha (sister)!" Asiamma was happy to see her brother. She smiled softly and closed her eyes.

The following morning, she breathed her last. Her daughter, sons, and daughter-in-law had gathered around her. Message of her death reached Abdul Kalam who rushed to Rameswaram to take one last look at his mother. He came in the night express. He cried uncontrollably at the loss of his affectionate, beloved mother. His siblings hugged and consoled him.

As he was about to leave, Kalam was surprised to see his maternal uncle Ibrahim Maraikayar enter the house. Kalam was happy to see him after a long time. During his childhood days, uncle used to be a regular visitor to their house. However, he had relocated to Sri Lanka. In his letters, his uncle always encouraged Kalam to pursue his studies. Both of them were engrossed in their past memories.

Kalam had to return urgently since he had taken up a major role at the space research centre. He asked his elder brother to complete the last rites of their mother.

As he was about to leave, he looked at his Machi Ahmed Kanima who took great care of his mother with tear-filled eyes. He recalled his mother's statement. One day, when Kalam was talking to his mother, she said, "Come here, Kalam. My time is about to end. From now onwards, you must treat your Machi as your mother. She is a kind woman." He bade goodbye to his Machi one more time before leaving.

"May Allah protect you! May you prosper!" Saying these words, Kanima performed the usual ritual. She brought the vessel filled with water and covered it with betel leaf. Kalam touched the water. 'Bismillah' chanted his Machi. Kalam left the house for work.

His brothers accompanied him to the railway station. His uncle Ibrahim also joined them. He started talking with Kalam. "Look here, Kalam! You have remained a bachelor for so long. You must think about getting married now. That would be the only way to fulfil the last wish of your parents," uncle Ibrahim advised. Kalam replied, "Yes uncle. Sure." Kalam left in the train.

Kalam became engrossed in thoughts about his mother. By nature, Asiamma was short-tempered. However, she never got angry at Kalam. 'Does that mean that I was a good boy?', thought Kalam to himself. Like all other humans, Kalam did have a few flaws. But his mother never shouted at him.

His beloved mother's love and affection, the way she narrated stories while Kalam was lying down on her lap, punctuality in her prayer routine, reciting the Holy Qur'an, all these thoughts of her crossed Kalam's mind. His mother usually handed him the cap to go to the mosque. After he returned, she would feed him. At the time of the second world war, there was an acute food shortage. His mother would give her share to Kalam. When Kalam came to know of this from his elder brother, Asiamma would pacify him saying that a growing child needs more nutrition for the brain to work. Kalam wouldn't know how to convince her. Kalam was grief-stricken. His heart felt heavy.

Kalam's thoughts were all about his parents till he reached Thiruvananthapuram.

❑

Futile Marriage Efforts

Kalam was engrossed in his satellite project. This turned his thoughts away from his mother's departure. He prayed for her soul to rest in peace. He had made arrangements with his brother for the recital of the Holy Qur'an on all forty days. Asiamma's last rites were completed by her family members.

Chinna Maraikayar (Mohammed Muthu Meera Maraikayar) consulted his wife Ahmed Kanima, his younger brothers Mustafa Kamal and Kasim Mohammed, and his elder sister Asim Zohara to fix Abdul Kalam's marriage. He decided to meet Kalam personally in Kerala to discuss marriage. He sent a message to Kalam that he would be visiting him along with his son Shahul Hamid. They left for Thiruvananthapuram. Kalam gave them a warm welcome. He had arranged a place for them to stay. He asked them to get refreshed and said that he will come back after work.

After lunch, he took them to the ISRO space station in Thumba and showed them around the place. After dinner, Chinna Maraikayar discussed marriage with Kalam. Kalam agreed. He said that he will be visiting them the following month. He asked them to proceed with the arrangements. Kalam was really glad to see his brother. He took them to all places in Thiruvananthapuram. They visited the Beemapalli mosque near the sea. Chinna Maraikayar went along with Shahul Hamid everywhere. Wherever he went, his thoughts were with Kalam. "Dear God, please bless my brother with a good wife."

After showing them around the place, Kalam bought Kerala special Banana chips and fruits and sent them off.

The hunt for a suitable bride was in full swing. They found a good match. Even though Kalam had told them that he would come, he couldn't make it. They informed this to the girl's family. One after another, Mustafa Kamal and Kasim Mohammed approached Kalam.

Kalam visited us in Rameswaram. Kalam distributed his share of the ancestral wealth (houses, shops and groves) equally among his brothers and sister. "Please keep at least one house in your name," begged Chinna Maraikayar. Kalam simply nodded his head. However, Kalam wrote it off to his younger brother. Kalam did not keep anything for himself. He left back to his workplace.

While leaving, he approached Ahmed Kanima and asked her to find suitable alliances for her daughters. "What about your marriage?" she asked. "Let us take care of this first," Kalam replied back and left.

This seemed to be God's wish as well. Suitable alliances from a place called 'Pudhumadam' were fixed for Chinna Maraikayar's two daughters and his younger son. Kalam received the message. At that time, he was busy with the SLV-3 project. He came one day before the marriage. He brought with him sarees, watches and other presents for the girls. "Are you all ready to get married?" he asked them cheerfully.

Whispering amongst themselves Arabu Nachiyar and Meharaju smiled at their uncle Kalam. He asked them what they were discussing. "When we were small, at the time of piercing our ears, you used to imitate us crying even before we started. We got reminded of that incident," they replied. Ahmed Kanima who was familiar with her brother-in-law's pranks from childhood burst out laughing. Kanima's thoughts rewinded to that day. The way Kalam imitated crying had made the two girls laugh that they forgot all about their ears getting pierced. Kanima was thinking about Kalam's gentleness and kindness. She prayed intently, "Ya Allah! Kalam is also like my child. Please bless him with a suitable life partner."

❑

Incessant Work and Unbearable Losses

Mahatma Gandhi's autobiography 'The Story of My Experiments with Truth' was a great motivation for Kalam. Kalam wanted India to become a pioneer in space technology. He worked hard to achieve his goal.

1981 was an important year in Abdul Kalam's life. He was the recipient of the 'Padma Bhushan' award that year. Having worked at ISRO (Indian Space Research Organisation) for eighteen years, he was now shifted to DRDO (Defence Research and Development Organisation). Having been inspired by his intellectual genius, nuclear scientist Dr. Raja Ramanna recommended Kalam for the job.

As a first step, Kalam wanted to get rid of old defence bases and set up modern missile bases that could help the Indian defence force. Accordingly, he and his team members started designing the 'Integrated Guided Missile Development Programme' (IGMDP) after getting formal approval from the then Defence Minister Dr. R. Venkataraman. After six months of hard work, their efforts became fruitful.

Marriage had been fixed for Chinna Maraikayar's daughter Asiyat Jameela in Rameswaram at the time. Kalam wasn't sure how he would make it to the function at such short notice. Dr. Arunachalam informed the defence minister about Kalam's situation. His wish was fulfilled. He travelled to Chennai in flight, came to Madurai in the military helicopter and at last reached Rameswaram by train. He reached right on time for the wedding of Asiyat Jameela who was like his own daughter to him. He blessed her and showered her with presents. In spite of his incessant work, Kalam cheerfully attended our family function. He left back to work shortly after the marriage. His mind was perhaps racing through millions of innovations at the time. However, he was able to allot time for his family members. Chinnappa's selfless caring attitude makes him special and unique.

Kalam couldn't have possibly celebrated Ramadan and Bakrid every year by wearing new clothes. However, he would send money without fail during festive occasions to his eldest brother who would then distribute it among his siblings. When Kalam came to visit us he would ask everyone young and old, "How was the celebration this year?"

Kalam would send money during Ramadan to help the poor and the needy. Porridge would be served at the local mosque everyday during Ramadan at the time of breaking the fast. Kalam would send money to serve that purpose too.

Kalam's next visit was to attend the wedding ceremony of his second brother Mustafa Kamal's daughter Rasheeda Begum. He blessed the bride with presents and left back to work.

For the next few years, Kalam was immersed in his job. In order to integrate and test the missile programme, he had identified a place called 'Imarat Kancha.' He was working day and night to make the mission successful. After obtaining approval and finance from the government, several scientists and technicians took part in the programme.

Kalam never forgot his family even during such exhaustive times. Whenever he visited us, he would donate money towards charitable causes to honour his parents and ancestors. He attended the wedding ceremonies of Chinna Maraikayar's granddaughter Jehara Begum (daughter of Thangarani), and Chinna Maraikayar's son Sarbudeen which happened on the same day. Kalam blessed them and showered them with presents.

Kalam's elder sister Asim Zohara died unexpectedly. Kalam participated in the last rites and consoled her daughter, son-in-law, and grandchildren. He asked his elder brother to complete all rituals and would keep in touch with him regularly.

Kalam would never let go of his duties.

The short range surface-to-surface missile Project Devil, which was a precursor to the Prithvi missile, was tested that year. This proved India's competence in space technology to world nations. Prime minister Smt. Indira Gandhi arrived at the *Defence Research and Development Laboratory* (DRDL) to inspect the project. All members of Kalam's family had great regards for Mahatma Gandhi who got us independence, and Jawaharlal Nehru who became the first Indian Prime Minister engaged in leading the nation towards development. Likewise, his family members greatly admired Prime Minister Smt. Indira Gandhi's leadership qualities.

Kalam has mentioned about the Prime minister's visit to the DRDL in his autobiography *Wings of Fire* –

"On 19 July 1984, Shrimathi Gandhi visited DRDL. Prime Minister Indira Gandhi was a person with a tremendous sense of pride-in herself, in her work and in her country. I deemed it an honour to receive her at DRDL as she had instilled some of her own pride into my otherwise modest frame of mind. She was immensely conscious that she was the leader of eight hundred million people. Every step, every gesture, every movement of her hands was optimised. The esteem in which she held our work in the field of guided missiles boosted our morale immensely."

Kalam was shocked to hear about the sudden demise of his third elder brother Kasim Mohammed. He was in the midst of his space missile programme at the time. Kalam's heart sank as he heard news of the death of his sister and brother one after the other. He recalled their childhood memories together. He consoled his brother's family members and went back to his project. Kalam knew his goal and the right path to achieve it. He focussed on his work accordingly.

He became instrumental in conducting the Rohini, Trishul and Prithvi missile launch programmes successfully.

Prime Minister Smt. Indira Gandhi felt it necessary to make India self-reliant in technology and to release her from the clutches of the world sovereigns. She gave all her support in enhancing technological skills. One such endeavour was the 'Agni' missile programme.

The Agni missile was indigenously developed and launched successfully in 1989. The name and fame of 'Abdul Kalam' spread far and wide after that. The citizens of India came to realise that India has now become capable of protecting her frontiers with her own indigenously developed technology.

Kalam was honoured with the 'Padma Vibhushan' award in 1990 for his competence and excellence.

Kalam attended the wedding ceremony of his brother Kasim Mohammed's daughter, Rahmat Thunisa Nizamuddin and blessed her.

Kalam was escorted by his security guards. His Machi Ahmed Kanima felt thrilled to note that her beloved brother-in-law has now become a symbol of national pride.

Kalam stayed with us for a few days. He slept in the front hall with his brother Chinna Maraikayar. His bodyguards guarded the entrance. Suddenly, they heard a strange noise from inside the house. As they looked around, they saw that Kalam's pillow had accidentally hit a stool nearby. Kalam asked them to get some rest. Kalam's bodyguards appreciated his kindness.

The next day, Kalam was gathering water from the well for his bath. All of them surrounded Kalam and offered assistance. Kalam asked them to leave. He smiled and thought to himself, "This well and this water are not new to me. I have been doing this since I was a child."

It was breakfast time. Kanima had prepared hot idiyappam. Kalam had it with sugar and coconut milk. He enquired, "Machi! Do we have enough water in our well?" Kanima replied, "Yes, of course. During the rainy season, the well is completely full. It is an ancient well, isn't it!"

Kalam spent the morning with his family.

It was now lunchtime. Ahmed Kanima had prepared a feast for her brother-in-law. Onion sambar, brinjal fry, drumstick leaves fried in ghee, cluster beans, banana pudding, pumpkin puree, drumstick sambar, curd, tomato rasam, coconut rice, plain rice, lemon pickle, and papad-this was the lunch menu. Everyone relished the pure vegetarian food.

Kalam recalled his childhood memories. His father's mother Sultan Beevi Fathima was a stout, kind-hearted, affectionate lady. His mother's mother Hasanachiyar was a gentle, patient and a caring lady. As soon as he returned home from school, she would offer him delicious sweets. People belonging to the older generation were always tranquil and serene. His brother Chinna Maraikayar saw him brooding over the past. He too recalled his childhood. Ahmed Kanima endorsed the culinary skills of Hasanachiyar, "The smell and taste of her pepper tomato gravy seems to be floating all over the house." The brothers too felt the same way and reminisced over their past.

Their conversation shifted to great men like Periya Karuppan Ambalam and Pazhanivel Nadar who had helped them financially when they were young. Kalam asked, "What is Kandasamy doing now?" Chinna Maraikayar replied that Kandasamy has become frail and weak and so his family did the laundry work these days. "Oh, I see! Kandasamy is a good man," said Kalam. Kandasamy's family were professional launderers. Kandasamy used to launder Kalam's clothes when he went to school and college.

That evening, Kalam joyfully spent his time with all family members, especially children. He answered all their questions.

He had to leave by the night train. Ahmed Kanima had prepared idlis, coconut chutney and brinjal sambar for him. Kalam relished the food. She had packed green gram laddus in an empty Horlicks jar for Kalam. He took it with him while leaving.

They performed the traditional family ritual while Kalam was leaving. Kalam waved his hand and left in the train.

Abdul Kalam was to retire in 1991. He wanted to run a school for poor children with his friend Dr. B. R. Rao. However, God had planned otherwise. Kalam and Rao were requested to continue their government jobs. Kalam dedicated his time to the missile programme.

The wedding invitation of his uncle Mustafa Kamal's daughter Lathifa reached Kalam. Mustafa Kamal's first wife Lathifa lost her first child. Unable to bear the loss, she too died shortly after that. “It is hard to reconcile that such a great lady is no longer with us, Kaaka. Please console yourself. Everything happens as per God’s wish,” remarked Kalam to his brother. Mustafa Kamal Kaaka married a second time. In loving memory of his first wife, he named his daughter Lathifa. Kalam asked his brother Chinna Maraikayar to make all necessary arrangements for Lathifa’s marriage.

Years rolled by. Chinna Maraikayar’s wife Ahmed Kanima died unexpectedly. Kalam was grief-stricken to hear the news. He conveyed his sorrow in his letter to his brother. “I grew up as her son,” Kalam had mentioned in the letter. Kalam took part in the fifteenth day Fatiha ritual held for his Machi. He consoled his brother and his family. “My Machi was gentle and tolerant. All of you are her children. You must be like her and must fulfil all her wishes,” he told us. His eyes welled up with tears. He consoled Kanima’s children, siblings, and all the children who were there.

Our conversation continued as usual. “What are you planning to do after your schooling?” he asked me. “Can I study literature?” I asked him. “Why not become a doctor?” Kalam Chinnappa said. I simply nodded my head.

I studied literature. My mother died unexpectedly. I was deeply touched by Chinnappa’s letter following her death. He came home and conveyed his condolences to my dad Chinna Maraikayar. He gave his contribution to perform the last rites. At that time, I was conversing with my father. Chinnappa saw this and remarked, “I am surprised to see that you speak boldly to your father.” He patted me on the back and said, “My Machi used to take good care of my brother. I was wondering who would take care of him now that she is no more. I have now realised that you would support your father well.”

Kalam regularly called on his brother from Delhi. He would ask him if he needed anything to which Chinna Maraikayar’s response would always be negative.

“When parents do not know how to bring up children, they make crucial mistakes. However, in my Machi’s family, everyone was brought up well. Even when she did not know much about the outside world, she tried to innovate and contribute productively to the family. In every situation, good or bad, his Machi always felt that God would guide them in the right direction.” These were Kalam’s words about his Machi.

❑

Chinnappa Becomes the President of India

Dr. Kalam had to travel around on account of his job. On September 30, 2001, he had to travel to Pogra village in Jharkhand to visit the mining factory. At the time of descent, his helicopter met with a crash. He listened patiently while the pilots were explaining the situation to him. He then jumped off the copter. By the grace of God, he had escaped the accident.

News of the crash spread all across India. When Chinna Maraikayar heard about it, he immediately asked his daughter to contact Kalam's personal secretary. He then spoke with Dr. Rajan as well. Even after both of them informed that Kalam was safe, Chinna Maraikayar insisted that he wanted to speak with Kalam. This was informed to Kalam in Jharkhand. Kalam was at a programme in Jharkhand at the time. After the function, he spoke with his brother. Thanking God for protecting his brother, Chinna Maraikayar performed charity.

After his job as the primary scientific consultant for two years, Kalam decided to fulfil his lifelong dream as a college professor now.

Kalam conveyed to his brother that he would be retiring from his research work and would be taking up the role of a professor shortly. Chinna Maraikayar prayed to God that all dreams of his younger brother be fulfilled.

In December 2001, Kalam joined the faculty at Anna University as an honorary professor of technology at the social renaissance department. Kalam stayed inside the campus in the room allotted to him. He would give his lectures to the students everyday during the slots allotted to him. Whenever he got the time, he would speak with his family back home.

On June 10, 2002, Kalam informed his brother that he could become a possible candidate for Indian Presidency. He wanted to know his brother's opinion. Chinna Maraikayar was grateful to God. He told Kalam that he should definitely take up this role and fulfil his duty to his motherland and all the people. He told Kalam that God will be with him always and blessed him.

The forthcoming days became fantastic moments of our lives. Kalam was announced as a presidential candidate. Media flocked around Rameswaram. Chinna Maraikayar celebrated by distributing chocolates and cotton candies to everyone. "My father was a president in this town, I was a president in court, my brother Kalam is a President of this nation," he cheerfully told everyone.

After his candidacy was announced, Chinnappa Kalam visited us with Professor Rajan to seek the blessings of his brother. After having lunch with his friend Rajan, they left back to Delhi. After they left, Chinna Maraikayar told everyone, "Vajpayee is a good man. Pramod Mahajan who is the correspondent for my brother is working tirelessly. My brother Kalam would definitely become the Indian President."

When Kalam took his oath as the Indian President, his brother cheered for him from the front row. After that, everyone was taken to the Rashtrapati Bhavan where Kalam was garlanded. As Kalam approached his brother to seek his blessings, Chinna Maraikayar's eyes were filled with tears of joy. He thought that he would see Kalam with the garland during his marriage ceremony. Looking at him now being garlanded as the Indian President, Kalam's brother hugged him tightly. He thanked God for being kind to them.

It was now time for Chinna Maraikayar along with his friends and relatives to get back to Rameswaram. Kalam came all the way till the entrance reception to send them off. On their way back, Chinna Maraikayar saw that everyone was celebrating the event by bursting fire-crackers. Soon after he returned home, people started calling him "The President's brother."

The north Indian pilgrims who visited Rameswaram would inquire about President Kalam's house and come there. Some would like to know the place where he was born inside the house. Some others came all the way till the backyard to see the well used by Kalam. Chinna Maraikayar said to Kalam during his phone conversation, "Today there were too many people in our house. Our house has become special because you were born here."

Chinna Maraikayar and Kalam arranged the marriage ceremonies of the children of their deceased brothers Mustafa Maraikayar and Kasim Mohammed Maraikayar.

In December 2005, Kalam made arrangements for the Haj pilgrimage of his brother Chinna Maraikayar along with his daughter Nazema and his grandson

Gulam Haja Moinudeen. As per his brother's wish, Kalam allowed him to visit the holy site as an ordinary citizen. However, he never forgot to call us everyday. In a way, it could be said that he too travelled with us mentally. His brother prayed for Kalam in Mecca and Madina. The Haj pilgrims received a warm welcome back in Rameswaram by their friends and relatives.

It was the summer vacation of 2006. Chinna Maraikayar was accompanied by everyone in their family from his son Shahul Hamid to his deceased brother Kasim Mohammed's son Jagubar along with their spouses and children to Delhi. Abdul Kalam had made arrangements for their stay at his own expense. There were fifty one members from the family. For each family, a separate room had been allotted in the Rashtrapati Bhavan. Everyone in Rashtrapati Bhavan, from officers to staff members, treated Kalam's family with utmost respect. Kalam's hospitality to his family members never declined, even though he was very busy fulfilling his duties as the Indian President.

Kalam's brother wanted to visit the Ajmer mosque. Accordingly, Kalam made suitable arrangements with his friend Mr. Salwan who was a native of Ajmer. Everyone was delighted to see the holy place.

Kalam had arranged two special buses and had made arrangements for his family to visit all famous places. He handed envelopes with money to all of them and asked them to purchase whatever they wanted.

Kalam participated in the Maghrib prayer every evening with his family.

Kalam's favourite spot in the Rashtrapati Bhavan is the 45 acre Mughal garden. Here he had constructed a thinking hut and a divine hut. Kalam had mentioned to his brother that he used the 'thinking hut' while contemplating on his books and the 'divine hut' while contemplating on national issues. He then took his brother to banana groves, biological eco garden and herbal garden.

One evening, Kalam took all his relatives to the Mughal garden. Everyone was made to sit in front of the fountain. Suddenly, the place dazzled with bright lights. The water in the fountain danced according to the tune made by pre-recorded music. They even danced to a live orchestra. Out of his passion for music, Dr. Kalam had integrated technology and had designed this masterpiece. Everyone young and old enjoyed this musical garden.

Kalam had organised a celebration for the return of the Haj pilgrims and his brother's diamond jubilee in the garden. In that special event, when night had turned into day with all the floodlights, people shared their experience of the Haj pilgrimage. The Holy Qur'an was distributed followed by dinner.

It was now time to leave. Everyone's heart was filled with gratitude over their unforgettable experiences during their pleasant stay at the *Rashtrapati Bhavan*. Kalam handed them shawls and fruit baskets while leaving. He waved the children goodbye. Those were unforgettable memories.

Only a great man like Abdul Kalam could have accomplished all this.

Once they reached Chennai Egmore, Chinna Maraikayar's eldest son Shahul Hamid departed with his wife and daughter to Bengaluru. Everyone bade them farewell.

The following month, Shahul Hamid passed away. Kalam had requested his grandson Sheikh Dawood who was living in Bengaluru then, to leave for Rameswaram along with his aunt (Periamma), sister and the mortal remains of his deceased uncle (Periappa). All relatives and friends rushed to Rameswaram. People from all over gathered to pay their last respects to their President Kalam's brother's son Shahul Hamid.

Thoughts about the marriage of his brother's son and sister's daughter crossed Kalam's mind at the time. He consoled his brother and sister's daughter in Rameswaram.

He conversed with his family regularly.

Three months before he had to retire as the Indian President, Kalam was asked to compete for one more term. However, since Kalam had already decided to educate and empower India by 2020, he politely declined the offer.

July 25, 2007 was Kalam's last day as the Indian President. In his address to the nation, he boosted the confidence of the Indian citizens. He said that he will work hand-in-hand with them in order to empower India by 2020.

Kalam was offered the job to serve as an honorary professor from all over India. He received job offers from Anna University, Bengaluru, Hyderabad, Ahmedabad, Delhi, Gorakhpur, Banaras Hindu university and so on. He was offered placements in foreign universities as well.

❑

Post-retirement

The central government had allotted No. 10, Rajaji Marg, New Delhi to Kalam post retirement. He liked this place since it was easy to commute from here. The architect who designed the *Rashtrapati Bhavan* also stayed here.

The house was surrounded by a beautiful garden. Kalam's personal secretary Mr. Sheridon and his operative secretary Mr. R. K. Prasad continued to work under Kalam by establishing their office rooms inside the house itself. Major General Swaminathan whom Kalam regarded as his guide and mentor, after having worked for more than 30 years under Kalam continued his work in No. 10, Rajaji Marg.

Even after his retirement, Kalam worked tirelessly. He enjoyed conversing with the students and the youth of India. He continued to visit us in Rameswaram. He attended his brother's grandson Gulam's wedding in Ramanathapuram.

Kalam asked his brother to send his grandson Saleem who had finished his MBA to Delhi. When Saleem was a small boy, he used to sit in the verandah outside the house. Kalam would carry him on his shoulders. Chinna Maraikayar thought that Kalam was perhaps inviting his grandson out of affection.

Saleem was sent to Delhi. He took care of Kalam's administrative work. While going on their regular walk, they would call their family in Rameswaram. He would update his brother of the happenings in Delhi.

Next, Kalam attended the wedding of his brother's grandson Sheikh Dawood in Trichy. He invited his brother and his grandsons over to Delhi. Chinna Maraikayar went to Delhi with his family. He continued to visit Kalam in Delhi annually.

Kalam would make all necessary arrangements for his brother's stay in his house. He would sit and chat with him for hours. He would take his brother for a walk and would show the different varieties of birds like parrots and mynahs in his garden. They would sit together and eat. Chinna Maraikayar who was usually hesitant to go outside, enjoyed his annual visits to Kalam's house.

Chinna Maraikayar would prepare Kalam's favourite sweets like green gram laddus and poli. He would invite Kalam over to Rameswaram. Kalam visited them at least twice annually. Chinna Maraikayar would take great care of their ancestral house where Kalam was born.

When a friend of Kalam from America suggested that the ancestral house be preserved and that he would make arrangements for his brother to stay elsewhere, Chinna Maraikayar blatantly refused the offer in a phone conversation with Kalam. He told him that as he is now almost 90 years old, he would like to continue residing in their ancestral house. He also informed Kalam that a new house would be built with the earnings of his children. He asked Kalam to politely refuse his friend's suggestion. Kalam liked his brother's attitude of not receiving favours from outsiders.

Kalam's friend Dr. Sivathanu Pillai who had worked on the Brahmos missile project with him had organised a gallery showcasing Kalam's various achievements from his school days. Students can view the gallery after getting prior permission. It was a carefully protected place.

Kalam wanted to make similar arrangements for people who came to visit his ancestral house. His brother's daughter Nazema suggested that after demolishing their hundred year old house, they could build a new one. She suggested that the family could stay on the ground floor and the first floor could be allotted for Chinnappa's gallery. Kalam and his brother approved her suggestion.

Till completion of the new house, Chinna Maraikayar's third daughter Meharaj Begum invited her family to stay with her. They temporarily shifted to her place with all their belongings.

The ancestral house was demolished in 2010 and the new house was built in 2011. Chinna Maraikayar and his family stayed on the ground floor. Kalam's gallery is located on the first floor. Episodes from Kalam's life starting from his school days till his presidency decorate the gallery. Photographs of Kalam's school, college and work life, the degrees and accolades he received within and outside India, his souvenirs, his poems, model of Tipu Sultan's cannon, models of Kalam's Padma awards as well as a model of his Bharat Ratna award are all neatly displayed in the gallery.

Known as the 'APJ Abdul Kalam Mission of Life Library', this gallery was inaugurated by Abdul Kalam. He had come with his friends Dr. Y. S. Rajan, Dr. Sivathanu Pillai and personal secretary Mr. Sheridon for the event.

Tourists, school and college students frequent this gallery. Electricity is generated from solar power as per Kalam's arrangement.

Kalam's brother's daughter Nazema is the manager of the gallery. His brother's two grandsons (including Sheikh Saleem who stayed with Kalam in Delhi) maintain the gallery.

Kalam attended Sheikh Saleem's wedding ceremony in Ramanathapuram in 2013.

Kalam visited Rameswaram with his personal secretary Mr. Sheridon in June, 2014 for rehearsing his brother's 100th birthday which was in 2016. Grandson Haroon recited verses from the Holy Qur'an first. Kalam presented a silk dhoti and a towel to his brother next. Then he asked all his relatives to speak about his brother Chinna Maraikayar. It was a fun-filled day when all family members conveyed their respects, regards and affection towards Chinna Maraikayar. Kalam asked his brother to distribute money to those who had gathered there next. Special biryani had been arranged for lunch. Vegetarian food had been prepared in the house for Kalam. Post lunch, as per Nazema's request, Kalam and his brother released two books written by her. One was on Avul Pakir Jainullabiddin's family tree titled 'Aalavrutcham' (Tamil word for banyan tree) that she wrote following Kalam's request. The other one was her postdoctoral research work. Sweets were distributed. Chinna Maraikayar blessed and prayed for everyone.

Kalam spoke frequently over the phone. He would enquire about the temperature and weather conditions in Rameswaram. During winter, he sent shawls and blankets for his brother.

Kalam visited Rameswaram in February, 2015 and took photos with his family after dining with his brother.

Kalam invited his family to No. 10, Rajaji Marg, Delhi in May, 2015 for their annual vacation. He welcomed his brother with a bouquet of flowers. This time he spent his time mostly sitting, chatting and dining with his brother. He sent Nazema and others to visit the famous Akshardham temple. He then had tea with his brother.

He asked his secretary Mr. Sheridon, and assistants Mr. Chellappa and Mr. Das to decorate the house for the birthday celebration of Sheikh Dawood's son Aseem Ahmed on May 21, 2015. They had decorated the place with balloons and banners and had ordered Aseem's favourite chocolate cake. At the time of the cake cutting, Kalam seated Aseem between himself and his brother. He then asked him to feed the cake to his granddad. Kalam asked Chellappa and Das to distribute the cake to everyone including his personal bodyguards. Everyone sang the birthday song and blessed Aseem.

Kalam took a picture with his brother under the hundred year old tree in his garden which he had named 'Arjuna.'

It was now time to leave. Kalam came up to the car to send off his brother. He was very fond of his brother. When, like his mother Ashiyamma, his brother began losing his hearing abilities, Kalam advised him to go to a doctor. He wanted to purchase a hearing aid machine for his brother. However, even after repeatedly asking Chinna Maraikayar refused to wear one. Kalam made it a habit to sit close to his brother while speaking. During their phone conversations, Kalam missed this proximity with his brother.

❑

Some More Memories of Chinnappa

Chinnappa had invited his brother to attend the Bharat Ratna award ceremony. Chinna Maraikayar went along with his grandsons Sheikh Dawood and Sheikh Saleem, and his brother Kasim Mohammed's son-in-law Nizamuddin. Chinnappa had arranged for their stay. There he introduced them to his friend Dr. Y. S. Rajan and his family members. Chinnappa used to talk about Rajan sir and so his name had become very familiar to all of us. My father Chinna Maraikayar, Sheikh Dawood, Sheikh Saleem, Nizamuddin, Rajan sir, his wife Koma madam, their sons Vijay, Vikram and daughter-in-law Anu attended the Bharat Ratna award ceremony.

My father's health began deteriorating after he returned back. Our family doctor Kalilur Rahman had gone to Chennai to pursue higher studies. Under the guidance of his friend Dr. Joseph Rajan who worked part time at the pioneer hospital in Ramanathapuram, we admitted my father there.

Kalam had asked his personal secretary Mr. Sheridon to note down the details of my dad's doctors. Mr. Sheridon would constantly communicate with us. He is a cheerful and friendly person. I had given Dr. Joseph Rajan's number to Sheridon. One day, while the doctor was inspecting my father's health, he told us, "Your father has no health issues. He would become better if he took all the medicines. However, his brother seems to worry a lot. Please inform him that your father is getting better." I know that my Chinnappa cared deeply for his brother. I was overwhelmed to learn about his concerns over my dad's health.

We wanted to replace our front portico with a verandah and install a gate in our house. I chose the name 'House of Kalam' for the house. This was to ease the search of several tourists who wanted to see Kalam's house. At the time of construction, a brick fell on my father's hand and he was injured. We took him to Dr. Ravichandran (Ortho) in Ramanathapuram. He was admitted for fifteen days there and it took two months to heal. I gave the doctor's number to Chinnappa. After speaking with the doctor, Chinnappa seemed to be relieved. He advised me not to worry even though he seemed far more concerned than me.

Chinnappa visited us with Dr. Rajan the following month. With his long beard and penetrating eyes, Rajan sir reminded me of a modern saint wearing a shirt and trousers. When Kalam introduced me to him, he instantly recognised me. Since Kalam had spoken a lot about each other, I never felt Rajan sir as a stranger. He had become a part of our family. After dining with us, Chinnappa left with Rajan sir. From that day on, Rajan sir became my good friend.

Rajan sir is a straight forward person who directly conveyed his mind through his speech. Like Chinnappa, he stayed in touch with all of us. Rajan sir would talk about the things he saw, heard, admired and of some others that made him think and contemplate. He encouraged me to write more and more. Rajan sir is a great mentor and a wonderful guide. Whereas my Chinnappa was kind and affectionate, Rajan sir is strict and caring.

I had registered for post doctorate degree in Islam and Islamic Tamil at the *Madurai Kamaraj University*. I took this decision after consulting my former professor Dr. Gandhi Mary along with support from my friend Rajeswari. Chinnappa and my father encouraged me to pursue further studies.

"Why did you choose this line for your doctorate degree?" Chinnappa asked me.

"You always used to tell me that if you wanted to learn about something fully you must be a part of it," I replied.

Chinnappa smiled at my reply. "On which topic should I research?" I wanted to know Chinnappa's suggestion. "Science should be good," he suggested. After speaking with my research consultant Dr. Ajmal Khan, I chose 'Scientific components in the Holy Qur'an.' Chinnappa was surprised and thrilled to know this. He encouraged me to pursue my line of research.

Chinnappa would send books related to my research topic. He would monitor my progress regularly. Rajan sir would constantly enquire whether I have found all materials needed for my research. He wanted to know when my work would be complete.

When his candidacy for the presidential election was announced in 2002, Chinnappa came to visit us with Rajan sir. As he was about to leave after lunch, I called out to him. Chinnappa said that he would get in touch with us as soon as results were announced. Streets were crowded with people at the time.

On the day the results were announced, Chinnappa called us. "I passed!" he said proudly to me. He invited all of us to Delhi to witness his oath-taking ceremony. He bought us all the train tickets. He had made excellent arrangements for our stay in Delhi. Fresh hot vegetarian meals were prepared and served. We all visited Rajan sir's house and had a feast. Those days would never come back!

Chinnappa became the eleventh President of India. After taking part in the oath-taking ceremony, we were invited to the Rashtrapati Bhavan. We received a warm welcome there as well. Then we returned back to our home.

We thought that my Chinnappa's calls would become less frequent now since he has now become the Indian President. However, Chinnappa never changed. He would talk to us and enquire about the day-to-day happenings in town. He liked to share all that he had seen, heard and read.

When he was admitted in the hospital over a stomach ailment, all of us were very worried. When we called Sheridon, Chinnappa himself picked up the phone and asked us not to worry.

One day he called us. He said to me, "Have you heard the news? Tsunami has attacked Tamil Nadu." Only after hearing from him, we saw the news and were horrified.

He called us again. "Even Rameswaram lies along the seashore. I am hearing that the Tsunami could approach there as well. What are you all going to do?" I told him that we would go to the rooftop. I asked him not to worry about us. He seemed convinced with my answer.

Streets were getting crowded with people. Those who lived near the seaside were now shifting to safer areas. Special buses were operated for free from Rameswaram to Madurai and many people started to evacuate. Since people saw on TV that Kadalur, Velankanni and Chennai were affected by the Tsunami, they started evacuating to safer zones. Our place became completely silent within a few hours. When I informed my father about Chinnappa's concerns, he said that God knows best and went to perform his prayer.

Mr. Ashokkumar Das who worked as the Superintendent of Police at the Ramanathapuram police station approached my father. Mr. Ashokkumar Das, his wife Mrs. Tejaswini and his children had great regards for Abdul Kalam. They were very affectionate towards my father. My father regarded them as our own family members. He asked my father to come with him to Ramnad. When my father wanted to know the reason, he simply said that he was worried about the Tsunami. My father smiled and replied back that if he could make arrangements for all the people in our town, he too would accompany them. Hearing this, the SP laughed heartily and left.

Next, people from the corporation office also approached us. We received an invitation from Dr. Joseph Rajan to stay with him. My elder sister Arabu Nachiyar who was with her husband Mubarak in Ramanathapuram at the time also invited us to her place. My father did not want to go anywhere. He prayed for the Tsunami victims and remained silent. Chinnappa was happy to note my dad's concern for others and he called us frequently to get regular updates.

It was monsoon in Delhi and there was heavy rain. One day, Chinnappa said that he had injured his arm and that he was going to get admitted to a hospital. He asked us not to worry. When we contacted Mr. Sheridon explained the situation in his beautiful Nagercoil Tamil accent. He said that after the rains, Chinnappa had stepped out to walk and had accidentally slipped over a wet spot. He had a mild fracture. Kalam had informed us personally so that we wouldn't panic by listening to the news on TV. In spite of his severe pain, Kalam wanted to inform his brother first. Kalam always placed others' concerns before his own. This increased my affection and regards for my Chinnappa. He asked us not to visit him now owing to the weather and to pray for him to get better.

Chinnappa had made arrangements for our Haj pilgrimage. We had to leave from Chennai. Chinnappa had come from Delhi to send us off. He presented a pocket book of the Holy Qur'an to my father. He asked me to take good care of him. "You are a little boy and you are accompanying my brother to the haj pilgrimage," he gleefully told grandson Gulam. "In case you need anything, please do not hesitate to contact me. After you return from the Haj pilgrimage, we will meet again," he told us.

True to his words, he invited our entire family, 56 of us, at his own expense to Delhi. We received a warm welcome and great hospitality.

At the end of the year, I suffered from high fever. Dr. Joseph Rajan said that I was anaemic and I had a lump in my stomach that needed to be surgically removed. Chinnappa spoke with me. "You take care of everyone, but you forgot to take care of yourself," he told me. I was admitted to the *Madurai Meenakshi Mission Hospital*. Chinnappa got my reports from Dr. Joseph Rajan and consulted with other doctors. Dr. Y. S. Rajan informed Kalam that a similar surgical procedure was performed on his wife as well and asked him not to worry. At that time, Chinnappa was the President of India. Even amidst his busy schedule, he would frequently contact me to know about my progress. After I got discharged, professor Rajan sir told us, "He asked you not to worry. But he was more scared than you." Chinnappa later spoke with me and said, "Your father is concerned over your health. Please take good care of him."

Rajan sir would encourage me to write a lot. One day he told me, "Your father seems to know a lot about herbs and their medicinal qualities. You must consult with him and bring out a book on that." Rajan sir had informed Kalam as well. "What happened to herbs?" my Chinnappa would ask me over the phone.

After consulting with my father, I wrote a book in Tamil titled 'Our family medicines' and sent it to Rajan sir. Rajan sir informed us to go to Ooty and that our book is going to be published by J.S.S. College of Pharmacy in Ooty. The book launch was presided by JSS College professor Suresh sir. My father and Chinnappa were very proud of me. That was my first book which got published! An unforgettable event for all of us.

I had sent a copy of my research report for the post doctoral degree in Madurai Kamaraj University to my Chinnappa Kalam. He appreciated my work.

I got my doctorate degree. Chinnappa wanted to know everything from when I left home till I got my doctorate degree. He then said, "So you have now become a doctor after all!" From then onwards, he started addressing me as Dr. Nazema.

I have seen Chinnappa since my early years. I could easily communicate and correspond with him. We talked about family matters, literature, and science. Chinnappa never gave away his mind. However, he always achieved what he wanted. He would absorb bad qualities like anger, jealousy, hatred, deceit, and remorse to himself. He never opposed anyone. But whenever anyone came to him for consolation, his smile would be his reply.

After he retired as the Indian President, he invited his brother annually to visit him in his Rajaji Marg house in Delhi. He would make all necessary arrangements for his brother's stay and would be eagerly awaiting to receive him. He used to run a thorough check over everything. He checked whether hot water was coming for bathing and he would ensure that the bathroom floors weren't slippery. He would buy fresh bed sheets, blankets, and doormats everytime.

Mr. Chellappa who belonged to the Indian military force used to work under Kalam. Kalam was affectionate towards all his employees. Mr. Chellappa told us about Kalam's excitement to receive us. He said that Kalam would be running around the place to ensure that his family received the best hospitality.

Kalam would also enquire about food during his phone conversations. "What was the recipe today?" he would ask me. "My friend would like to speak with you. Can you teach him the recipe for your Papaya vegetable sundal?" he asked me. That friend was his head cook. Chinnappa was always careful not to hurt anyone with harsh words. He treated everyone with kindness. He called me later and told me that I had guided his friend well and that my recipe was amazing.

When Sheikh Saleem stayed with Chinnappa in Delhi, he taught the kitchen staff how to prepare our special home food like onion sambar, brinjal raita, tamarind rice and so on. Kalam would tell me, "Your nephew seems to be a wonderful chef! His wife is really lucky!"

Kalam attended the wedding ceremonies of Ghulam (son of sister Arabu Nachiyar), Sheikh Dawood and Sheikh Saleem (sons of brother Jainulabdeen), Risalat Ali (son of sister Meharaj), and Asfar Khan (son of sister Rasheeda). Kalam and his brother blessed all the newly married couples. They would advise the brides of their grandsons to be happy, responsible and caring. When good news of their pregnancy reached Kalam, he would bless them heartily. When anyone visited him in Delhi at that time, he would send sweets and fruits. Occasionally, he would send parcels too. One time, he even sent a parcel containing raw mangoes.

To be continued in the last few chapters of this book...

❑

From the Memories of Kalam's Friend Prof. Dr. Y. S. Rajan

Frozen Friendship

July 25, 2015; Saturday.

It was like any other day. The letter 'A' was displayed on my phone. Kalam had called me as usual at 4.30 PM. After speaking for a minute or two with me, he asked me to hand over the phone to my wife Koma. Very rarely did he do this. Normally, we would converse for an hour. I was to be prepared to receive his call around 3.30PM everyday. In case I was on a flight, the next day, Kalam would jokingly say, "What happened, sir? Where did you go? I heard a lady's voice on your phone saying that you were busy!"

I was surprised that he wished to speak with my wife Koma. Her full name is Gomathi. As she was born and brought up in Gujarat, people started calling her 'Goma' which became 'Koma' in Kalam's colloquial Tamil.

He spoke with Koma for more than half an hour that day. She was giving him some cooking tips. As she was about to keep the receiver down, Koma was saying, "Are you sure? Everytime you keep telling us that you will come to our house. But then you hurriedly eat a few snacks and leave." Kalam must have convinced her over the phone. Koma was saying, "August, September, for sure? Ok, please wait! Let me hand over the phone to your friend." Then, she handed over the receiver to me. Kalam spoke with me for some 30-40 minutes.

He told me, "Yesterday, your sons were here. We spoke for hours together. We all had a grand feast. Your grandsons have grown tall." My sons Vijay, Vikram, daughter-in-law Mahalakshmi (Anu), and my grandsons Aditya and Ashwin were at Kalam's house the previous day. At that time, Vikram was working in Delhi. He had a job transfer to Jakarta and he wanted to receive Kalam's blessings before leaving. My other son Vijay's family also had to leave for the USA in two days. So, they had all gone together to visit 'Kalam uncle.' Kalam had rescheduled a few of his appointments to accommodate them. Even though Kalam usually ate his dinner at around 11.30 PM, he advanced his dinner time for them.

Kalam continued, "We had a grand feast and took some photos. I have informed Koma amma that I would be coming to your house for lunch some day in August or September. We have discussed the menu already. She was upset that I usually leave in a hurry. This time I have promised her. You also please be there. I am planning to commence my Bengaluru trip after having lunch with all of you this time."

I had greatly reduced my travel frequency (to four times a month). I am younger than Kalam by twelve and half years. However, Kalam never reduced his travel. I normally advised Kalam. "Why are you travelling non-stop? Is it to show everyone that you are still young and agile?" I would tease him thus. In order to avoid my advice, Kalam would turn it around and say, "Sir, you don't keep travelling all the time. Alright?"

We would talk about confidential matters as well. It would start at one point and lead on to many others. Finally he would exclaim, "Oh, look! We forgot about the central topic under discussion," to which I would reply, "You started discussing other topics in between. I am only replying to you. Now let us come to the crucial point of discussion." After this, I would give him my advice. "Ok, sir. I will do as suggested by you," he would say and hang up the phone.

At times, I would advise him to change his stand with regard to something. In order to escape the discussion, he would say, "Sir, can I call you after five minutes?" This meant that he wouldn't call me back. However, the next day when he called, our argument would continue.

July 25, 2015 was my last conversation with Kalam. My wife informed me that Kalam would be visiting us in August-September. She described in detail the lunch menu-rice, vegetable, sambar, pickle, chutney and so on.

My daughter-in-law shared the individual and group photos taken with Kalam uncle on the previous day through WhatsApp. At the time, Kalam was living at No. 10, Rajaji Marg, Delhi. He looked very happy.

This was a regular occurrence. My family members were frequent visitors to Kalam's residence. Even before Kalam became the President of India, we visited him. We became his "In House" guests when he became the President. My second grandson Ashwin celebrated his first birthday at the *Rashtrapati Bhavan*. He was more than twelve years old when he visited Kalam on July 24, 2015. After Kalam retired, we continued to maintain our friendship.

I travelled to Chennai on Sunday to take part in an event that was to happen on Monday. I thought to myself that I might have missed Kalam's phone call since I was on board.

On Monday, July 27, 2015, as soon as I got off my flight, I saw a message from my ISRO friend Dr. Jayaraman. "Kalam Critically ill," read the message. I was shocked and confused.

Rumours were normally spread about Kalam's health. Whenever concerned people asked me, I would talk to Kalam's personal secretary H. Sheridon or his private secretary R.K. Prasad to verify the news. When I informed Kalam of such rumours, he would say, "This is very bad! Tell me how to handle this."

However, this time it sounded serious. I contacted Sheridon to get the latest update. "It is true sir. This time it is serious! They have asked me to come to Delhi. I had to come to Tirunelveli for a family event. I will be going by car to Thiruvananthapuram to catch my flight to Delhi."

I did not know whom to approach. I received one more message from Mr. Jayaraman. "The Home Minister has announced the passing away of Dr. Kalam." It felt like lightning had struck me. Everything came to a sudden pause. I called my wife. "It is true. I am watching the news on TV now," she confirmed.

Even before I could reconcile myself, my phone started ringing. News channels and reporters were asking me questions one after another. They wanted to know if I could come for a live interview. I couldn't keep my phone down!

Some questions were well researched and were good. The reporters had studied Kalam's life thoroughly. They seemed to know of my friendship with Kalam and wanted to know of our work relations. However, some others were asking me foolish questions in an attempt to fill up their columns. I felt sad that social media could stoop down to such levels. On other days, I would have shouted at them. But now I didn't say a word. I was enveloped by darkness.

I felt a sudden lump in my throat and shooting pain in my left arm. It continued till 11 PM even after I reached home. Some TV reporters were waiting outside my house to get an interview.

Like me, my wife Koma too couldn't speak a word. We couldn't even contact Kalam's family in Rameswaram that day.

My son Vikram who was in Delhi at the time gathered all the news of Kalam's death. He assisted Sheridon and Kalam's grandsons there. I had to go to Delhi too. But before that, I had to speak with Kalam's brother Mohammed Muthu Meera Maraikayar (Chinna Maraikayar). I had written a poem 'Brother's Brother' about him earlier. Kalam's brother was fond of me.

Finally, I contacted Maraikayar's daughter Nazema. She said, "My father has informed people in Delhi. He has asked them to send Kalam's mortal remains to Rameswaram. He said that Kalam's last rites shall be performed in Rameswaram only. I will let you know when they release the dead body. You please come here directly to console my father."

On my family's behalf, my son Vikram was there in Delhi. "I never realised that I would have to see Kalam uncle like this! He was hale and hearty last Friday when we all visited him. In fact, I told Kalam uncle to stay this way," Vikram said. My son Vikram, who is a doctor, would advise Kalam uncle regularly to take care of his health and to avoid frequent travel.

Even when I saw the photos of Kalam with my family that were sent by my daughter-in-law recently, Kalam looked fine. In his phone conversation with me and my wife, Kalam sounded happy and well.

On July 27, 2015 when I heard the news, I couldn't convince myself that Kalam was no more. I was reminded of Thirukkural's 'Destiny'('ஊழ்'). As far as I am concerned, our relationship froze and had become eternal on July 25th when we spoke last.

Several days later, I realised that the number 25 had been an important one in Kalam's life. He became the Indian President on 25.7.2002. He retired from the post on 25.7.2007. His final call to me and Koma was on 25th July. The rest of my family were with him the previous day. Perhaps, he had some kind of a premonition that he would be leaving us forever.

Kalam rested in eternal peace. We were all grief-stricken at this unbearable loss. We were feeling disappointed and empty. Even after consoling Kalam's brother on July 30 (at about 2.30AM), my heart was burning. I was fighting internally with God and destiny.

Pointing to Kalam's mortal remains, his brother cried, "Look at your friend over there! He was planning to celebrate my hundredth birthday in all glory. Now this is all that remains of him!" He then sang a beautiful composition in Tamil lamenting his brother's death. He then gave instructions to fetch water in drums. After listing the places where jujuba leaves could be found to the youngsters, he asked them to put them in the drums.

How did he tolerate his brother's death? He asked us to come to the mosque the next day for last rites. We left so that he could get some time to rest. I was accompanied by Dr. Sivathanu Pillai and former Anna University Vice Chancellor, Dr. Kalanidhi.

When Nazema and her brother Jainulabdeen asked me to see Kalam's face one last time, I refused. "I can't see Kalam like this. I want to remember Kalam the way he was," I told them and left the place.

When we were going to our hotel in Rameswaram, we could see people flooding from all directions. Without stressing out the police force, people were marching silently to "House of Kalam" to get one last look at their beloved leader.

I couldn't rest in my hotel room. Overcome by grief, I couldn't go to the mosque on the 30th. It would have been difficult to go behind the military procession.

Kalam's brother gave us special honours. The Indian Prime Minister, Chief Ministers of various states, and other political leaders had come to pay their last respects to Kalam. Only a few people were therefore allowed to accompany Kalam's family members for his burial. Kalam's brother had made me a part of their family. He also asked me to be the first one to offer flowers to his dead brother.

Overcome with grief and anger, I wrote a poem when I was in my hotel room. I was angry with Kalam too for rushing with his life. *Could he not have lived longer, in case he had slowed down his pace a bit?* I wondered. This need not be true scientifically though. All his life, Kalam was running around. It had become a part of his lifestyle. I blamed destiny. I couldn't convince myself. I completed my poem in the burial ground. I had poured my heart out bringing out all my emotions such as anger, melancholy and despair. Most people who don't know me well could misinterpret it. So, I left the poem in the hotel room itself.

A year after Kalam's death on July 25, 2016, I read it out to Nazema over the phone. I am giving the English translation of my Tamil poem here...

30.7.2015 morning

You wanted to fly in the sky
And reach for the stars, but
You now lay buried under the ground
With people as witnesses
Can anyone achieve anything
By antagonising nature?
Can anyone become successful
By straining himself?

Blaming destiny won't
Bury the truth
The fault of over-speeding
Proved to be fatal indeed
If one works mechanically
Forgetting the food and sleep cycle
How can God surveil?
For Mother Nature's rules prevail!

(Completed at 7.00AM)

I had written the poem in the small pocket notebook in 'Daiwik' hotel in Rameswaram. When I went once again on November 4, 2016 for Kalam's brother's hundredth birthday celebrations, I was thrilled to see a similar notebook in the same hotel!

The anger and emotions which I felt on that day still remains intact. It was born out of my intimate bonding with Kalam. When Sirpi Balasubramaniam sir wanted me and Nazema Maraikayar to write a book on Kalam's biography, I decided to start from here.

Myself and Nazema decided to write about those incidents in Kalam's life which have not been brought to light in any of his earlier biographies. Many people have written about Kalam. Some are very good. Some mediocre. Some others are fictitious and totally unrealistic. However, we need to accept those too since they were written out of love and affection towards Kalam.

I am writing this biography of Kalam truthfully as per the request of Sirpi sir. I had requested a few other friends of Kalam to write about him as well. Their essays can also be found in this book.

I am hoping that when I complete this book, the anger and emotions which I felt that day in Rameswaram (which continued to exist for days on end) would mellow down. It is said that time is a great healer. However, the loss of a cherished friend can never heal over time. I hope to find my equilibrium reminiscing over the moments that we spent together by crying, laughing and teasing each other.

Let me start from the day we first met...

❑

First Meeting

I first met Kalam in 1965. I do not remember the date and the month now. After I finished my M.Sc. (Physics and Electronics) at Bombay *University*, I joined the *Physical Research Laboratory* (PRL) in Ahmedabad in 1964 to complete my Ph.D. The research using rocket payloads had just then begun in PRL. Before that time, they tested using ground equipment alone. They were designing a laboratory in Hyderabad to conduct tests using balloons. Space research using rockets had started at least ten years earlier in other countries.

Professor Dr. Vikram Sarabhai decided to spearhead a similar project in India as well. There were many stages in rocket launching. One of the most important stages is to identify a suitable location for launching the rocket. Rockets cannot be launched from densely populated zones. Ideally, the location should be close to the sea. Next, the location should be ideal to conduct space experiments as well. The Earth's magnetic poles running from north to south are not aligned exactly with the equator. It is slightly shifted from there. In India, some regions in Kerala are located closer to the magnetic equator. It was therefore decided to design a space to launch rockets in Thumba in Thiruvananthapuram. In 1962, *Thumba Equatorial Rocket Launching Station* (TERLS) was constructed. India did not have a rocket at the time. NASA agreed to give one to India after discussion. Complex calculations and equipment are needed to successfully launch a rocket. RADAR is used to identify the location of a rocket after it has been launched. The information gathered by equipment within the rocket has to be carefully recorded at the ground station. This is known as 'telemetry.'

The equipment within a rocket has to be designed to withstand the speed and vibration. This in itself is a special field of science. Scientists who were trained in the United States of America and Europe after completing their Ph.D under Sarabhai were designing suitable rocket equipment at the PRL.

Batteries must be installed to supply power to the equipment and then integrated with the telemetry devices. Post integration, the rocket should be tested to ascertain if it could withstand the vibration and heat. For this purpose, it is tested on a vibration table and a thermal chamber.

Equipment for these were supplied by the USA, France, and the Soviet Union. In 1963, Vikram Sarabhai sent Kalam, Aravamudan (Dan), and Eashwardas to get trained for 'Payload Integration', and 'tracking'. Besides these, they were also trained to operate and perform other tests related to rocket launching. Kalam has explained about all this in his *Wings of Fire*. He also mentioned these to me.

After returning to India, Kalam was assigned the post of a rocket engineer. Aravamudan was responsible for 'tracking' and related experiments wherein the trajectory of the rocket is identified. Eashwardas took charge of the TERLS workshop.

Kalam frequently visited the scientists in PRL, Ahmedabad. He would discuss the equipment needed in rocket launching. His job was to check whether these could be designed within the allotted time and also to ascertain the progress of the work. At times, the scientists would inform him that the equipment could not be designed according to the plan. This was because at the time of building, some equipment became more bulky, some would occupy more space, and some would require more power to operate. 'Nose Cone' is the portion on the top of the rocket where all equipment was placed and is so named since it is shaped like a cone.

It is not easy to change the nose cone. Even a small change could greatly impact the rocket trajectory. Kalam and his engineers were well trained to make all necessary changes without impacting the rocket flight. There is so much more to this. Rocket launching is not only about attaching equipment and making it fly. NASA has given special training to Indian engineers and scientists, who are all in great demand. It is important to know that rocket science is not only about research. It is an expertise that requires engineering as well as scientific skills. In order to explain the nature of our job, I have given a brief introduction here.

Kalam had to provide what was necessary to the engineers in Ahmedabad. In case of lack of availability, he discussed alternative options with them. Kalam usually visited with Aravamudan.

Even though it was not necessary for Kalam to know in detail about the space research equipment, he was always curious to learn more. Details of the make and purpose of space research equipment were a part of the space research initiative. Space research is an admixture of science and engineering and I had chosen that line for my Ph.D. Hence, it became necessary for me to learn in detail about the space equipment. Kalam was interested to learn about this and so would ask me several questions related to the topic. I would explain briefly to him. Kalam was not a man who would sit within the confines of his field of expertise. I admired and respected this attitude of Kalam. I too would enquire about a few skills related to operating rockets from him. It could be said that our friendship was born out of this mutual curiosity.

We both mostly interacted in Tamil, our mother tongue. We enjoyed discussing Tiruvalluvar and Bharati. In spite of the fact that he was older than me by twelve and a half years, we became good friends.

In 1966, when I took part in designing a rocket transponder, my intimacy with Kalam increased. Radar transponder is used to identify the location of a rocket in its trajectory. We developed it indigenously. My boss O. P. N. Calla and I visited Thumba frequently in order to conduct test experiments. Only after the results were successful, the transponder could be included in the rocket. Being a part of the 'transponder' team, totally transformed my life. At the time of joining, I did not know its importance. I turned my attention from space research and abruptly stopped my Ph.D. I got my domain expertise directly once I joined the 'Engineering Product Development' team.

Many describe Kalam as a scientist specialised in field research.

However, his work involved 'Product Development' and 'Research & Development' skills. This required engineering and technical expertise. Kalam was responsible for 'System Integration' that involves designing, assembling and integrating the equipment in a rocket to prepare for launch. This expertise made him the leader of the SLV-3 missile expedition later.

Moving away from science and cosmic ray research, I too shifted my line to product research and development. This helped me join NASA's *Applications Technology Satellite* (ATS) program later in 1970.

Changing my field of study not only took me to a new line of research but also increased my proximity to Kalam. Otherwise, our interactions would have stopped since we last met in PRL, Ahmedabad. Neither me nor Kalam knew the value of this bonding at the time.

Other than the 'transponder' program, which was assigned to me, we would discuss and debate over the engineering and technical skill sets needed for space research. Designing and developing indigenous products also became a part of our discussion.

Mahakavi Bharati had instilled patriotism and a deep devotion to the motherland in me. Kalam too wanted to empower India by making it one of the global leaders in space research like the USA and the Soviet Union (now Russia) back then. This attitude of Kalam brought me closer to him.

The *Indian Space Research Organisation* (ISRO) did not exist at the time. Only TERLS and *Space Science and Technology Centre* (SSTC) had been established. All space-related programmes and organisations were under *Indian National Committee for Space Research* (INCOSPAR) of PRL. Vikram Sarabhai who was the director of PRL and the chairman of Indian Space Research led all these teams. Sarabhai was a great mentor and a guide to people like myself, Kalam and other distinguished scientists of Indian Space Research (now ISRO). Sarabhai imbibed strength and determination in us. He would instil confidence that all of us were capable of performing various operations related to rocket launching. He would appreciate wholeheartedly even a small achievement. He would congratulate everyone in the team from a simple technician to the group head personally.

Whenever there was a failure, Sarabhai would discuss the upcoming prospects without demotivating the team.

Scientists and technicians at TERLS, SSTC and *Experimental Satellite Communication Earth Station* (ESCES) were not necessarily quick to handle the latest technology. However, most of them tried their best to keep up with the latest technical skills. There were others who would be very slow too. Some others tried to develop new skills with competence. Sarabhai knew that in order for India to become technically skilled, all these had to be encouraged. He therefore motivated everyone with enthusiasm. Whenever he came every month to visit us, he would approve such plans. His right hand and finance administrator S. R. Thakore would approve the finance request and release of the money to start the project.

Therefore, everything was happening at an extremely fast pace! Kalam was one of the few people who picked up with the pace.

The others were Dr. A. E. Muthunayagam, Dr. Vasant Gowariker, B. Ramakrishna Rao, and Y. J. Rao. Unlike Kalam, these people worked at SSTC. SSTC was the first organisation which was developed to support space research in India. After Sarabhai's death, SSTC was merged with other small organisations to become *Vikram Sarabhai Space Centre* (VSSC). I too joined SSTC in Ahmedabad to become a part of the 'Engineering Product Development' team after quitting my Ph.D. research abruptly.

Kalam knew that if he worked only in Thumba at TERLS, his R&D opportunities would be greatly diminished. He knew that if he worked only with technicians from PRL to integrate rocket components, his opportunity to work on the rockets that would launch satellites in outer space would reduce greatly.

Even though we did not make a great deal out of it, it was popularly considered that it would be better to work in SSTC rather than TERLS, *Rocket Propellant Plant* (RPP) or *Rocket Fabrication Facility* (RFF).

Moreover, in TERLS, RPP, and RFF, only those people who studied within India were there. No one with a Ph.D. worked in these places. Very few M.E.

and M.Tech. engineers worked. However, Indian space research evolved only from these persons. INCOSPAR (later ISRO) became our window to foreign countries. Space scientists and technologists from foreign countries arrived at TERLS in Thumba. Initially, foreign especially American rockets were launched from here to study weather. Shortly thereafter, in association with the French 'Sud Aviation', RPP and RFF started manufacturing rocket launch vehicles in India after getting the licence permit. The people who worked in RPP and RFF were instrumental in bringing this major breakthrough.

After this, Kalam started to design small indigenous rockets like Menaka and Rohini. These rockets helped in investigating the layers of earth's atmosphere. In order to help this investigation, initially the former Soviet Union supplied M-100 rockets weekly for free once to be launched from Thumba. The instrument made of thin copper wires was lifted up slowly into the layers of the atmosphere to conduct this experiment. This acted as the 'Chaffe Payload' of the rocket. The 'Cotal Radar' at the ground station would monitor these copper wires. Using this technique, the details of various components in the different layers of earth's atmosphere were collected and investigated.

Rohini and Menaka were rockets designed by Kalam and his team and were manufactured by RPP and RFF. *Rohini Sounding Rocket* (RSR) which was used to monitor weather was designed in this way.

Besides this, Kalam made his presence felt at the SSTC as well. Rockets mostly made use of stainless steel equipment. Advanced versions like *Polar Satellite Launch Vehicle* (PSLV) and *Geosynchronous Satellite Launch Vehicle* (GSLV) make use of a special aluminium alloy. In addition, an artificial non-metallic product is also used. Thin fibres of materials like glass and coal are compressed into cross-wires using a special glue. This is then subjected to excessive temperature and pressure in an autoclave. Nowadays, we see fibreglass chairs in India. However, in 1960, there were no manufacturing plants for these in India. In the 1960s, these materials were mostly used only in aeroplanes, missiles and rockets. This technology was prevalent in the US at the time and it was even integrated in their daily use materials back then.

Kalam submitted his project report to Vikram Sarabhai to manufacture such *Fibre Reinforced Plastics* (FRP). Through this, he set up a FRP-manufacturing plant in SSTC. This became Kalam's visiting card for his entry into the SSTC. Besides rocket launching and integrating component parts of a rocket, Kalam established his competency in the research and development sector as well through this initiative. One by one, he started taking up several roles within the space research organisation. In the SLV-3 mission, Kalam made use of a rocket motor manufactured using this FRP technology.

Besides INCOSPAR/ISRO, Kalam wanted to know whether his R&D products could be used for other purposes. He would talk about designing fishing boats for fishermen using FRP. However, at the time, owing to its complexity, FRP was used only for rockets. Making fishing boats out of them became a distant dream.

Several years later, when I became the director of *Technology Information Forecasting and Assessment Council* (TIFAC), we developed an 'Advanced Composite Mission' in 1991 under Kalam when he was leading the missile project in Hyderabad. I will discuss that later.

Since Kalam was competent in mechanical engineering, metallurgy and R&D, we were able to devise such techniques. However, since he was not that familiar with electronic engineering, he would approach his friend Dr. Aravamudan who worked with him in TERLS. Once, when I was with both of them, Kalam told Aravamudan, "Mr. Iyengar! We should manufacture the Cotal Radar which is used in the armed forces indigenously. I will design the 'Trailer' and the 'Antenna'. However, since I do not know electronics, you take care of that. Let us both design a radar together."

Kalam worked hard and fast to design products related to space technology indigenously. Therefore, when he actively pursued such interests, I became naturally attracted to him. Subramania Bharati's poems had already made a deep impact on me. In his poems, Bharati talked about mining and making instruments indigenously. It was due to this reason that I quit my Ph.D. which involved only writing essays on space research and joined the 'transponder' project which involved direct participation in product-making. I wanted to make many such products within India. When I noticed that Kalam too had a similar mindset, I became greatly drawn to him.

Let us stop here and talk about some of the great scientists and engineers of SSTC.

❑

Uniting Hands

Sarabhai knew that it wouldn't be possible to produce satellites and missiles using the infrastructure available in TERLS, RFF and RPP alone. He founded the SSTC in order to build a strong foundation for India's technological sector. TERLS, RFF and RPP had to supply materials for rockets or provide immediate assistance to tech requirements of the PRL engineers. On the other hand, SSTC people provided R&D support to manufacture missiles and satellites.

Some of the important sectors within SSTC are:

-Propellant

-Propulsion

-Structure

-Aerodynamics

-Electronics

-Computers & Applications

-Control & Guidance

Everything from individual machine workshops to canteens were there in all the sectors. There was a huge library. Their primary focus was in providing R&D to missiles and rockets. They did not have to prepare project reports. After research, they immediately manufactured the instrument which was installed inside a launch vehicle or a satellite.

All scientists and engineers of INCOSPAR/ISRO used to work only in this way. Since there weren't enough qualified R&D staff from within India, Sarabhai appointed a few people who had studied abroad to SSTC. Such people were given better stakes than those employed from within India. Such people who had worked in R&D, industries, or universities in the USA and the UK were less than forty years old. Their starting salary itself was high; Sarabhai made a new rule that for every $1000, they would be paid INR 1,000.

Dr. Vasant Gowariker (Propellant Division), Dr. A. E. Muthunayagam (Propulsion), Dr. S. C. Gupta (Control & Guidance) Dr. Y. J. Rao (Aerodynamics), Dr. Amba Rao (Structures), and Dr. M. K. Mukherjee (Materials) were these high profile people who had come from abroad to work in SSTC.

When the TERLS head H. G. S. Murthy tried to show his superiority as he was older than these people, they reported it to Sarabhai and SSTC became an independent group. Dr. Sarabhai became the head of the SSTC as well. When Sarabhai was not around, they managed SSTC by maintaining a group known as 'Technical Coordination and Finance Committee' (TCFC). We used to jokingly refer to it as 'Panchayat.' The members of the TCFC were the most powerful people of SSTC.

Kalam was not a part of the elite group. Since he and Aravamudan had come to work from within India, his salary was also not high and his job profile was lower than that of the elite group members. Naturally, his command was also low. In order for Kalam to rise up to the level of the SSTC elite, Aravamudan's group head Dr. H. G. S. Murthy helped a lot. He was always impressed looking at Kalam's active participation.

I am writing here about the SSTC elite members to show that in spite of being put down, Kalam never lowered his impetus. He was contributing to SSTC by creating many new projects.

Kalam never complained to me about his job. We have never discussed family matters. I never asked Kalam why he remained a bachelor even when he was 36-37 years old. I do not know how other people (especially the rocket club members of ISRO in Thiruvananthapuram) treated him. I have heard that in the club they played everything from cards to Tennis. I have not gone there. I used to visit there from Ahmedabad for several days together, but for office purposes only. I know that Kalam visited the club. However, when we both interacted our discussion would always be about 'What next should we do for India to grow?"

In a way, this could be treated as 'workaholism'. At that time, I used to advocate communism of Karl Marx, which was not similar to that advocated by the Indian communists or socialists. I believed in 'pure Marxism-Leninism'. My coworkers in PRL, Ahmedabad knew this; Kalam also knew it. But we never discussed all that when we were together. Sometimes, we both would quote from Bharati and Tiruvalluvar to energise our vision to empower India.

Even when Kalam was not holding a key position in INCOSPAR (which after 1969 became ISRO), and even though he did not have a Ph.D, Kalam did not lose heart. Instead, he focussed fully on developing indigenous products for space research. Noticing Kalam's absolute dedication, Vikram Sarabhai appointed Kalam on projects that would help the Indian armed forces. In his 'Wings of Fire', Kalam has written about RATO which stands for 'Rocket Assisted Take Off'.

'If you want quick production, then hand over the job to Kalam.' Kalam had made a mark for himself. However, he never stopped his pace. He was working non-stop without showing indications of fatigue or tiredness. Several years later, when Kalam was the Indian President, he used to frequently quote from Bharati's magnum-opus *The Oath of Draupadi* (பாஞ்சாலி சபதம்) where he prays to *Sarasvati*, the goddess of learning and wisdom:

"The physicists say that atoms whirl ceaselessly;
the astronomers opine that the orbs gyrate for ever and ever
If it be but natural for the things of globe to work ceaselessly,
O Mother of Arts!
Should not my heart, I pray, function ceaselessly, made one with thy Grace?"

-Compositions of Mahakavi Subramania Bharati
***The Oath of Draupadi* (பாஞ்சாலி சபதம்) Part 2;**
Section 3; Slave Sarga-அடிமை சருக்கம் (2)

When we were working together in Veli in Thumba or when I was the Scientific Secretary, ISRO, not even once had Kalam mentioned these verses. He must have constantly contemplated these verses all those years which probably energised him and made him the way he was!

Kalam never asked Sarabhai to promote him for working so hard. During those days, TERLS/SSTC/ISRO/PRL were all very small entities. Words spread like wildfire. News about anyone trying to approach the team head for promotion would reach others almost instantly, even though there were no phones at the time. Some people served as good broadcasters!

When I say that Kalam was working tirelessly, it does not mean that others were dull. In fact, many of them engaged in research and development and worked competently. This served to boost the Indian economy as well.

Dr. Vasant Gowariker's team were trying hard to indigenously produce rocket fuel. For test driving rockets, we were importing fuel and raw materials at the time. Owing to their team effort, it became possible to use indigenous fuel for the SLV-3 rocket.

Likewise, Dr. Muthunayagam's team selected propulsion techniques carefully and Dr. Y. J. Rao's team studied aerodynamics. These calculations are very important for uninterrupted functioning of the satellite/missile.

Therefore, everyone in SSTC was working hard to design and manufacture parts for missiles and rockets. Some were successful; some unsuccessful. However, all of us shared our success and failures wholeheartedly.

In 1966, 1967, and 1969 everyone in SSTC was obsessed about India launching her own satellite. Even before the satellite was born, it was given the name Rohini Satellite (RS). The electronics department of SSTC made all preparatory arrangements to serve this purpose. At first, it was led by P. P. Kale.

Kalam would learn about everything thoroughly.

In this way, by integrating several committees, Dr. Vikram Sarabhai established a central committee to design the satellite/missile. Everyone submitted their feasibility report after integrating component parts of the missile/satellite. However, since Y. J. Rao was a senior member, he was chosen to be the coordinator. Dr. Y. J. Rao founded other sub-committees to assist him. Kalam played a major role in assisting him. Dr. Madhavan Nayar and Dr. Sivathanu Pillai were the chief consultants.

Technological feasibility was discussed. Many participated in these heated debates to decide what was required and what wasn't for a successful launch of the missile/satellite. The important thing to note here is that most people who had joined as youngsters in SSTC, TERLS, RPP, and RFF were the ones that showed the most obsession towards building the rocket. Moreover, they were all a part of the R&D team as well. I would like to name a few of them here. Nambi Narayanan, R. M. Vasagam, Sridharan Das, N. Vedachalam, K. V. C. Rao, Y. V. Krishnamurthy, Shetty, Shastri, Mazumdar, V. P. Kulkarni, Dr. S. Srinivasan, B. K. Shankar, C. R. Satya, Rajaram Nagappa... I have given only a few names here. They later on became the roots, branches, aerial roots, and trees for ISRO. In order to decide upon the technicality to be used, model devices are built. These model devices were built by competent engineers and technicians. People who assisted by buying the necessary raw materials and machines, those who helped by bringing such workers from Thiruvananthapuram, those who helped by procuring food for employees, and those who assisted people who worked day and night. It is important to thank all of them. They supported and assisted the organisation in their own way.

Even a small clerk would function with the feeling that he was involved in a major project with utmost devotion and dedication.

This was all a result of Kalam's unassuming actions while at work. Treating everyone with respect, coordinating with co-workers, reaching out to achieve their common goal, patting each other's shoulders in case of success or failure—these were the backbone of ISRO's refined culture in those days. Even when Kalam pushed his coworkers to act fast, and even when he fought with a few, all of them knew that he was doing this for their collective success. Kalam symbolised victory. Youngsters who had joined recently noticed this distinct trait of Kalam.

❑

The Beginning of the Indian Space Era

Even to this day, many people from the laity to the adept believe that we achieved everything on our own. They think that Indian scientists and engineers were pioneers of space technology of the world.

It is important to learn the truth. The United States and the Soviet Union (Russia, Ukraine) started their research on rockets in 1920–30. It is a well-known fact that they were the pioneers of rocket missiles. They have submitted hundreds of research reports. In the 1960s, these became the study material and some were released as books.

Let us recall a few facts. The Soviet Union launched the world's first satellite on October 4, 1957. After this, Americans increased their pace in space research. The US government encouraged its industries to take part in space research programmes by supplying necessary technical equipment. It also motivated its R&D sector to actively participate in space research. The US government founded NASA and funded it with millions of dollars to enhance its aeronautics and space administration capabilities. They made space research their topmost priority and motivated it.

The then US President, John F. Kennedy stood before the Joint Session of Congress on May 25, 1961, and proposed that "the US should commit itself to achieving the goal, before the decade was out, of landing a man on the Moon and returning him safely to the Earth." We all know the famous statement made by Kennedy later on September 12, 1962. He announced to the world that 'A man, an American, would be the first person to set his foot on the moon and hoist the American flag there.' He informed the public about his plan to land a man on the moon before 1970. The gigantic Saturn rocket mission was commissioned for the purpose. It was led by Von Braun, a German, who had earlier served as the leader of Hitler's V2 missile project. A year earlier in 1961, the Soviet cosmonaut Yuri Gagarin became the first human to journey into outer space.

Not even in the early 1960s, did any of our Indian politicians, statesmen, and other intellectuals think that India should indulge in space research. To them, it was an 'esoteric field'.

At that time, Homi Bhabha led the nuclear research team in India. He had strong support from politicians and statesmen and he was a versatile administrator. Vikram Sarabhai, after investing several lakhs, approached him in order to get government's approval for his space research organisation.

As mentioned previously, Vikram Sarabhai got rockets (NASA, America) and gadgets required for ground control for free from other countries.

Thus, India's space mission began with a humble budget. Naturally, India's first satellite Rohini weighed only a tiny 50 kg. The rocket (SLV) to launch the satellite was also designed accordingly. SSTC employees carefully studied rocket fuels, propulsion techniques, and other details of space research from NASA's research documents. There were hundreds of them. Other than these, our scientists also studied various scientific journals to know about the success and failure of earlier space missions.

Kalam, Aravamudan and a few others received training for free by NASA. Here, they learnt about various stages of rocket launching.

America, France and the Soviet Union did not however help with the design and integration of our rockets. They did not even participate in the scheme discussion seminars. Hence, the due credit for rocket designing should go to the SSTC engineers, scientists and technicians.

Even the first SLV designed by India was to launch the Rohini satellite in low earth orbit close to earth. Nowadays we hear news about satellites being injected into precise orbit as planned. For example, PSLV is capable of injecting satellites even upto 35,000 km and operating within a few metres range efficiently. However, in those days, this was not the case. This was because India's first rocket did not have 'Closed Loop Guidance' that helps it to self-track and align with its exact orbit.

Therefore, back then India's first space mission was a humble one when compared to giants like the USA and USSR. But, hadn't we tried this back then, it would have become impossible for India to compete today in space science. Everyone, including Kalam, knew that our first mission was very simple. But none of us lost hope because we knew that we would secure more victories in future. Probably, none of us at the time felt that Americans and Russians have progressed very well in space research, are launching 40–50 space vehicles every year and are receiving huge finance from their governments. We weren't unsure whether India could even climb the first step of the ladder. We were all very confident.

After Vikram Sarabhai's death (December 30, 1971), ISRO was led by Professor Dr. Satish Dhawan from 1972. After several years, he described our state of mind with the following words: "I inherited an ISRO where there was a "suspension of disbelief" about their success and their capability to realise the vision bequeathed into the organisation by Dr. Vikram Sarabhai."

Kalam who had crossed 35 and approaching 40 years very well fit into that description 'suspension of disbelief'.

After quickly completing his project, he would invest his time to update himself about the latest techniques. He would then try to implement these in his new projects in order to reach his goal. He would encourage his coworkers to do the same thing.

The reason for comparing India with other world nations here is to bring to attention the confidence and resilience of the ISRO engineers/technicians/supervisors/scientists. Kalam was a role model. It was this attitude of Kalam that helped him successfully lead the '*Integrated Guided Missile Development Programme* (IGMDP)' when he worked in DRDO in 1982. More on that later.

❑

ISRO's Work Environment

Even though I have explained in detail about technology and science in this book, I will not be discussing all projects of Kalam in detail. I have already discussed the nature of his job and his first few years in space research. It is important to know the nature of the relationship he maintained with his coworkers. Those were the years that shaped him up to be a professional.

The way in which Kalam was born and brought up, as well as his personal charisma have been explained by Nazema earlier in the book.

Kalam has briefly explained some aspects of his work life starting from his thirty-fourth year in his *Wings of Fire*. In this book, I hope to disclose a few other aspects of him that were not brought to light in his book. When we look at all the achievements made by ISRO professionals today, it might look like a cake walk. However, during its initial years, ISRO faced several challenges. It is surprising to see how several professionals handled their work without compromising their ego, passion and individuality. Many small entities grew slowly on a daily basis.

In ISRO, the work would be broken down into smaller fragments and handed over to different groups. Just like the way water in a stream reaches a river, without giving way to their personal ego and expectations, all employees of ISRO worked together to attain their common goal. 'Teamwork' is ISRO's mantra. Everyone can't do everything. Each of them had to complete their work within the given time. In case of technical issues or sickness, the job would be handed over to other employees who willingly took it up.

Kalam would preach this mantra in his speech (in the 1990s and after he became the Indian President). He would motivate different groups to work hand-in-hand to make India a developed nation. 'Nation is bigger than individuals', he would say. Empowering India became the central theme of his speech.

Kalam derived his inspiration by reading several books as well as by learning from his practical experience while working in organisations like TERLS and SSTC. Throughout his life, he practised what he preached.

I have narrated about the foundation in much detail. Now let me pace up.

I was travelling back and forth from Ahmedabad to Thiruvananthapuram to complete my 'Transponder' project. I was recently married at the time. A few months earlier from December 1968 – May 1969, I was in Hyderabad. I would travel with my colleague C. J. Lewis to DRDL to test the transponder everyday. This was because this was the only place in India that had a proper 'vibrating chamber'. Protests over a separate 'Telangana' were at their peak at the time. Stones would be thrown at buses. Overcoming all difficulties, Lewis and I would go to DRDL in the Andhra Pradesh government buses.

One day, we got delayed having our breakfast. Our bus had already left. Protesters had set fire to the bus and the muslim driver died in the incident. We felt really sorry for him! I shudder to think what might have happened to the two of us had we gotten on the bus. All AP government buses were stopped. We both walked, then travelled in a private bus and after completing our tests we came to TERLS.

After completing all tests in TERLS, we handed over our transponder to Kalam and returned to Ahmedabad. (In 1969, INCOSPAR was renamed as ISRO. TERLS and all other such entities were integrated into ISRO).

I had not informed anyone, including Kalam, that I was getting married. We never discussed our personal life at the time.

During those six months in Hyderabad, I did not know that Kalam would head the DRDO and that he would be leading all the missile projects. Kalam himself might not have known at the time. At that time, Air Commodore Ganesan was heading the DRDL. In 1990, Kalam informed me that he had studied with Mr. Ganesan at MIT. He also shared a few funny experiences, which cannot be written here. Some of them have been conveyed as poems. But it would not be possible for others to identify those poems.

The Transponder project was a major project and my first important assignment. It is an important instrument attached to the rocket panel. The transponder not only showed the position of the rocket in orbit, but also the place where it landed in the sea.

It was our responsibility to hand over the transponder to Kalam's 'rocket integration' team. Then, they will take care of the rest. In case of any doubt, they would contact us.

After completing our job, Lewis and I came back to Ahmedabad. I got married on June 2, 1969. There were no big celebrations. My principle was more important to me than anything else. No dowry, no extravaganza, no gifts. I had not invited many people to my wedding. Only people from both our families were present. I don't remember giving an invitation to Vikram Sarabhai as well. He had several responsibilities at the time. Moreover, since Homi Bhabha died in 1966, Sarabhai had to handle the atomic plant as well. I did not feel like disturbing him. In a similar manner, I had imposed several restrictions on myself and had not invited many guests for my marriage.

I had not even invited my coworkers in Thiruvananthapuram. Now if I think about it, I feel that it was a mistake. In those days, I placed humanity over individual human relations. Initially, I was like that on account of my Marxist-Communist leanings, which slowly disappeared over time. Over time, my understanding of the world expanded as I got exposed to the myriad ways of human existence. Kalam too probably had a similar mindset. He was still a bachelor! Why would he talk about my marriage anyway?

There is another reason behind all this. We felt it our duty to empower India in space technology. Everything else became subordinate to this major goal. In the 1960s and 70s perhaps everyone else had a similar mindset.

After marriage, I came with my wife, my father's elder brother and his wife to Thiruvananthapuram. I was working in the electronics department of SSTC at the time. I was not directly associated with Kalam's line of work or TERLS. Even then, we both used to converse frequently. Kalam wouldn't discuss satellites and missiles because Dr. Y. J. Rao was heading the satellite/missile team at the time. Even though Kalam would give his opinions occasionally to make the design fully operational, he wasn't leading the team.

I lived in Thiruvananthapuram for a year. We both could have parted ways easily because the relationship was informal and we hardly discussed work.

❑

The SLV-3 Project

Sarabhai sent me to work at MIT in Massachusetts, USA. We see weather forecasts on TV news everyday. I was a member of the ISRO-MIT team which designed the INSAT (*Indian National Satellite*). Weather forecasts, early warning systems in case of floods and cyclones, and connecting remote areas of India through mobile networks—these were the primary goals of INSAT. R. M. Vasagam, who became the Vice Chancellor of Anna University was also a member. His thoughts were always about making indigenous rocket launch vehicles, missiles and satellites.

After completing our MIT assignment on behalf of ISRO, we were sent to NASA to take part in their *Applications Technology Satellite* (ATS) programme. ATS-F was a pioneer project which made use of advanced technological gadgets. It was developed to investigate and test a variety of satellite applications. It had a transponder and a remote sensor so that even the remotest areas of India could be connected under one network to receive telecommunication services (that is, without a TV tower, they were connected from a distance of 36,000 Km above earth). The signal received from the satellite would reach the 'Chicken Mesh Antenna' and programmes would be relayed on TV.

ATS-F satellite is the precursor to the modern day DTH (Tata, Sun TV etc). These satellite signals reach every home (including remote areas and hill stations) today.

Vikram Sarabhai wanted to bring this technological innovation to India and so he sent four ISRO engineers to NASA. After completing our assignment in ISRO-MIT, we were sent from Boston directly to *Goddard Space Flight Centre (GSFC)* near Washington D.C.

I worked intensely on the satellite project. I prepared documents for the NASA ATS-F project working alongside their scientists and engineers. In addition, I sent to Professor U. R. Rao many other NASA reports on their latest technical projects available in the GSFC library. He was heading the *Indian Scientific Satellite Project* (ISSP) in India and it was to help him in knowing more.

Besides learning about our satellite launch vehicle, R. M. Vasagam also focussed on NASA's other launch vehicles. We both conversed frequently. We would send NASA reports on satellite launch vehicles to SSTC.

During this time, I was not in touch with Kalam. We heard that some changes were being made to SSTC. We heard that Sriharikota was chosen as the site to launch Indian rockets. Efforts were in full swing in 1970-71.

In 1970, China launched a satellite made in China using its own launch vehicle. In a way, this became a big challenge to India.

India had planned to launch an indigenous satellite weighing 50 kg with the help of an indigenous rocket launch vehicle. Even though the satellite was being made quickly, we at ISRO knew that it could take another six or seven years to manufacture a rocket launch vehicle indigenously.

The Chinese satellite weighed 300 kg! In spite of confusion brought about by communism in China, the Chinese focussed on technological advancements that would help their military force.

China became one of the P-5 nations after testing its atomic bomb in the 1960s. Along with America, the Soviet Union, England and France, China had become a superpower. India could have become one back then. It is historically true that our national leaders and intellectuals gave minimal attention to equip our military force back then. It is because of this reason that even today our former and current Prime Ministers like Manmohan Singh and Narendra Modi have to beg for a place in the *Nuclear Suppliers Group* (NSG)!

The Chinese leaders knew that to carry the atomic bomb, a large-sized launch vehicle was needed. Accordingly, they planned their rocket launch mission with a 300 kg capacity.

India, on the other hand, planned to launch its 50 kg satellite in 1960, and decided to execute the same plan in 1968–69. Anything higher was beyond India's budget. The cost of setting up the necessary infrastructure for satellite and launch vehicle and other testing facilities would have become insurmountably high!

Vikram Sarabhai was not a part of the Indian government team responsible for making such decisions. People like Kalam had to take orders from Sarabhai. Sarabhai was heading the ISRO projects with whatever was made available to him at the time. There are no reports to suggest whether the Indian government at the time debated over this issue. Had we responded like China in 1960, India could have achieved more in space technology. ISRO executed its projects as per Sarabhai's instructions.

Ten years had elapsed in 1967 since the world saw *Sputnik*. The USA and USSR had already launched hundreds of satellites. France and the rest of Europe were getting ready to launch their own satellites. Those satellites weighed at least 400–500 kg and so their rocket launch vehicles were also massive. India, on the other hand, was still clinging on to the size of NASA's first satellite launch vehicle of 1960.

I had discussed this with R. M. Vasagam while working for INCOSPAR (later ISRO) in Thiruvananthapuram in 1965. He did not know much about the Chinese launch vehicles back then. He said that he could only make a guess based on his readings from American journals. In 1965, none of the world nations were aware of the Chinese space mission.

Years later, between 2008–18, I came to know of this from my retired ISRO friend S. Chandrasekar who worked as a professor in IIM, Bengaluru. He is an expert in analysing world space technological programmes and has studied in detail about the Chinese space mission. I will share a few details we discussed here.

After hearing news of the Soviet Union's *Sputnik* launch in 1957, the Chinese scientists and engineers approached Mao Tse Tung to receive his approval for their space mission.

"Among the spacecrafts launched first by other world nations, ours should be the biggest." This was Mao Tse Tung's instructions to them.

Hence, the Chinese satellite weighed 300 kg and its launch vehicle too was equally massive. After instructing them to create an atomic bomb, Mao Tse Tung's instructions for the launch vehicle were: "Create a launch vehicle that could attack Japan, Phillipines, and the US."

That was a massive launch vehicle as well.

In India, the situation was totally different. After running around the world, in consultation with scientists and engineers from the US, France, and the Soviet Union, Vikram Sarabhai established the rocket launching space in Thumba (TERLS) in 1962. In spite of all this and other financial constraints, Kalam worked hard with absolute dedication.

Here is a brief description of India's first satellite launch vehicle as given by R. M. Vasagam:

The aim of the team members who designed it was to somehow launch a satellite into space. Japan's Tokyo University had plans to launch a satellite that weighed 11 kg. After the world war, the Japanese reduced their participation in all missile and space research technologies in accordance with their constitution. The USA had imposed sanctions on Japan. They gave minimal finance to the Japanese military force.

India had no such restrictions. However, many of our leaders and intellectuals felt that since India was economically backward, we should not indulge in such extravaganza! In fact, some even argued against having Indian armed and paramilitary forces!

It was under these circumstances that Vikram Sarabhai tried to establish a space research organisation. In order to get the government approval, he tagged along with Homi Bhabha.

Sarabhai's master plan was that by proving that we could launch a small satellite weighing at least 10 kg, it would be possible to ask for more financial assistance from the government.

R. M. Vasagam continued further: Therefore, the technologists in ISRO designed the rocket by integrating other test rockets and America's first space launch vehicle. They finally arrived at six designs. They decided that the sixth design could carry at least a 40 kg satellite. In all other designs, only lesser weights could be allowed. Therefore, Vikram Sarabhai chose the sixth one known as the SLV-3. Everyone in SSTC including Kalam were engrossed in manufacturing the SLV-3. They were trying to increase the payload by 50 kg. However, none of them considered the possibility of carrying 100, 200, or 300 kg. They decided to keep higher payloads for future missions.

SLV-3 completely made use of solid fuel. By using liquid fuels, much bigger rockets could be built. However, they postponed that idea to a later date.

In 1972, when engineers from SSTC designed SLV-SYN which was bulkier, the project was postponed to a later date. Vikram Sarabhai died on December 30, 1971. The design that was approved by him towards the end became the model for SLV-3. Even when Sarabhai was alive, India's first satellite mission *Rohini (RS-1)* was integrated into the SLV-3 mission.

It was decided when Sarabhai was alive that India would launch her first satellite in the Soviet Union's '*Intercosmos*' launch vehicle. It was named as '*Indo-Soviet Satellite Project*' (ISSP). As the envoy from the Soviet Union announced that this should be bigger than the first Chinese satellite, the ISSP was designed to carry a satellite weighing 450 kg. Some parts were given by the Soviet Union while others were indigenously produced. In 1972, as per the instructions of the team head Dr. U. R. Rao, the project was transferred from Thiruvananthapuram to Bengaluru's Peenya workshop. Even Rohini's RS-1 (40 kg) was transferred to Bengaluru. But the work was progressing slowly. This was because the SLV-3 project had still not received its full approval. In 1971, Vikram Sarabhai initiated one more important project for ISRO. That was the establishment of SHAR (*Sriharikota Range*) in the east coast range of India. This was established in order to launch Indian satellites and missiles from the Sriharikota base. Industries to manufacture the solid fuels and to test the solid fuel motor system of SLV-3 were built here.

Since all these required constant monitoring and since this was an important project, the coordinator of SLV-3 project Dr. Y. J. Rao was shifted to the *Sriharikota Range*. A separate office was set up for him. All this happened after the demise of Dr. Vikram Sarabhai. This important decision was taken by Dr. Brahm Prakash and Professor Satish Dhawan. After Dr. Y. J. Rao left Thiruvananthapuram, they needed someone to take care of the SLV-3 project full time. They wanted the project to become fully functional. Senior members like Dr. Gowariker, Dr. Muthunayagam, and Dr. Gupta were already in charge of R&D. They were given the additional responsibility of making component parts for SLV-3.

They therefore wanted someone who had not taken up any major roles and at the same time had a thorough knowledge about rockets and satellite launch vehicles. Dr. Brahm Prakash and Prof. Satish Dhawan chose Kalam for the job.

This was God's gift to Kalam. It became the turning point of Kalam's life.

A. Sivathanu Pillai, who worked with Kalam in 1970, was also a part of Kalam's Agni Missile mission. When I was in the US between 1970 and 1973, Sivathanu Pillai had observed Kalam at close quarters. I had requested him to share his memories of Kalam. That is the subject of the following chapter.

❑

Scientist Dr. Sivathanu Pillai's Memories of Kalam

Dr. Sivathanu Pillai has worked closely with Kalam right from his SLV-3 project (1972). When Kalam worked at the DRDO, Hyderabad, Dr. Sivathanu Pillai assisted him in managing projects like the 'Agni missile mission'. When Kalam worked as the Scientific Adviser for the Defence Minister in Delhi, Dr. Pillai was with him. Dr. Sivathanu Pillai is the founder, and also served as the CEO and the Managing Director of BrahMos Aerospace Private Limited. BrahMos is a supersonic cruise missile which travels faster than the speed of sound and it can be used in submarines, ships, flights and on land. He also served as the primary superintendent of DRDO's R&D department.

It is important to understand Kalam from various perspectives. It is necessary to look at him from the lens of people who had worked closely with him from his middle age. In this book, I have gathered information from such people to reveal some of the lesser known qualities of Kalam. I have given it here without changing a word.

Dr. Sivathanu Pillai has played a major part in Kalam's life. After Kalam became the President, and even after his retirement from Presidency, Dr. Pillai has assisted him in several ways. He was a close friend of Kalam. He worked till his retirement in the DRDO and BrahMos. I have mentioned him in several places in this book. Now, he will be sharing his reminiscences of Kalam.

Dr. APJ Abdul Kalam

At VSSC during SLV-3 days

The SLV-3 team was formed with APJ Abdul Kalam as Project Manager in 1972 at Trivandrum to integrate all the design projects carried out during 1971. He chose his core team to evolve the management plan to progress the development activities for launch of SLV-3 in seven years. It was a tough task for him to get through the development process. Dr. Brahm Prakash (BP), Director of VSSC came to his rescue by restructuring the technology groups and unifying the effort for SLV-3. The nobility and stature of Dr. Brahm Prakash made everyone to contribute for SLV-3 in a focussed manner. The reorganized structure elevated the position of Project Director, equal to highly qualified Technology Directors. The *Space Centre Council* (SCC) which met every week started discussing and solving critical areas and things moved in the right direction.

I was already working in SSTC since December 1969 and I was chosen by Abdul Kalam during the formation of SLV-3 in 1972 as a core team member to support him in Project Management. When the project activities were progressing, Abdul Kalam thought of configuring a long range missile using SLV-3 stages. We prepared a detailed mission document for a long range missile in 1974. Kalam wanted to get permission from Prof. Satish Dhawan, Chairman, ISRO, to start the development in a secret way. He asked me to take the document in a sealed cover and hand it over to Prof. Satish Dhawan at Bangalore. Next day I was at Bangalore to meet Prof. Dhawan at the *Indian Institute of Science*, where he was serving as the Director. Opening the cover, Prof. Dhawan got very angry to see the title and said that ISRO missions are for peaceful purposes only and there is no intention to make missiles. Prof. Dhawan clearly thought of ISRO's future and to bring it to world level with co-operation of space faring countries. He called Kalam and advised him to concentrate on SLV-3.

Kalam thought that he must find a way to develop a long range missile and the re-entry technology so that the country will become strong in the nuclear delivery system. Thus the idea of the AGNI missile was born, the REX (*Re-entry EXperiment*) project, well before he left for DRDO.

On 10th August 1979, SLV 3E-01 was launched at Sriharikota. SLV-3 took off majestically but due to malfunction of the second stage control, the mission was a failure. It was a setback for Kalam. He soon came out with the next launch vehicle SLV-3 E-02 and the mission was successful on 18th July 1980. India became a member of the space club having its own launch capability. The vision of Vikram Sarabhai and the missionary zeal of Satish Dhawan with a structured organization created by Dr. Brahm Prakash gave a solid foundation for launch vehicles development in the country.

At DRDO

Abdul Kalam learnt a lot from these two leaders, when he migrated to DRDO in July 1982 as Director DRDL. It took nearly one year for him to evolve IGMDP (*Integrated Guided Missile Programme*). After the approval of the government, development of five missiles started in 1983 and he needed my assistance. I could support him while evolving the IGMDP project report from Bangalore at ISRO HQ. That was the time I was associated with defining future launch vehicle programs, especially the configuration of PSLV. Kalam's effort to take me to DRDL finally succeeded in 1986. When I joined him the designs were ready for review. The first task for me was to restructure the DRDL to suit program management culture and elevate the project activities. What we learnt as best practices at ISRO came to our hand to evolve suitable management structure, review system, problem solving method etc. It was a great time for all of us in the missile program to evolve methods to develop critical technologies overcoming the *Missile Technology Control Regime* (MTCR).

The innovative approach and strategy of Dr. Abdul Kalam was crucial in the development of indigenous missile technologies, with strong support from Dr. VS Arunachalam who was the then Scientific Advisor to the Defence Minister. Spotting the talents and partnership with multiple institutions and industries Kalam made the missile program as a national event and everyone associated was proud to work for the mission. Dr. Kalam was distinctly a leader of greatness to bring a high level of motivation in DRDO and other institutions and made IGMDP as the fore-runner among all projects of DRDO. Through the missile program he brought the culture of freedom in thinking, making everyone contribute to the best and in utilization of the young talents.

Dr. Kalam was so innovative to name the five missiles under the integrated programme. The name of '*Prithvi*' for short range surface to surface missile; '*Agni*' for the long range missile which goes to space and re-enter earth's atmosphere due to which the external temperature of the re-entry module is 3,000 degree C (Agni Pravesh); '*Akash*' for the multi-target engaging surface to air missile to destroy multiple aircraft leading war in Akash (sky); '*Nag*' for the 3rd generation anti tank missile which takes a cobra trajectory to hit at the top of the battle tank at the operator's man hole, being the weakest portion of the tank, and '*Trishul*' for the surface to air missile having three different roles in quick reaction. These names were reflections of the functions of the missiles in Sanskrit terminology linking Lord Shiva.

Dr. Kalam and his team spent long hours and evolved strategies continuously. He brought young blood in developing new infrastructure and technologies. *Research Centre Imarat* (RCI) at Hyderabad and Agni launch complex in Orissa were conceived by him as the most important infrastructure for the development of multiple missiles. IGMDP was the first to introduce a new procedure for accelerated development. One important component of IGMDP was the introduction of limited series production while the development was in progress. This enabled concurrent realisation of production facilities at Defence PSU's (*Public Sector Undertakings*) and exchange of teams enabling use of products made by industries to be used in development flights. Today *Prithvi*, *Agni* and *Akash* are in production on a large scale due to this approach.

Any new development will have its own problems and failures which are possible during testing and validating. Failures often give more knowledge and understanding technology details. Dr. Kalam was not afraid of failures. He often said **"We should have the courage to learn from failures and make them successful."**

This approach encouraged the project leaders to take bold decisions in technology options and try them out even in flights. One of the *Prithvi* flights launched from a seashore blasted off near the seashore itself after a few seconds of the flight. The analysis gave an understanding of a new phenomenon on control called Tail-Wag-Dog effect of the two engines of the *Prithvi* booster. This led to design changes. Similarly a failure of the second flight of the *Agni* brought in perfect understanding control-structure interaction and adaptive software. These types of failures at the initial stage of development led to continuous success in operational systems. The full support from Dr. V. S. Arunachalam and also the Defence Ministers helped IGMDP in a big way.

First SLV-3 was a failure, first PSLV was a failure, first two ASLV flights were failures. ISRO scientists learnt a lot from the data and today we see PSLV during its last 37 flights was successful, perfectly injecting the satellites with required velocity, making ISRO a very successful organisation. GSLV Mk-3 was a total success in the first attempt itself. So both ISRO and DRDO scientists have mastered the art of making missions successful, though they had initial failures.

Nuclear Test

While the missile projects were moving in the right direction showing significant progress, Dr. Kalam became the Scientific Advisor to the Defence Minister and DG of DRDO, which is a government position. He brought in DRDO to have a major role in the nuclear program and also in the development of light combat aircraft. Joining hands with the Department of Atomic Energy, DRDO enabled successful integration of switching circuits for the nuclear experiments with five different types, including thermo-nuclear experiments, were to be carried out in 1995. With the approval of Mr. Narasimha Rao's government, everything was arranged and Kalam was ready. But due to certain leakage of information and satellite pictures, the nuclear countries put pressure on Mr. Narasimha Rao to not perform the tests.

In the 1996 election, Mr. Narasimha Rao lost the elections and Mr. Atal Bihari Vajpayee was chosen as a leader of the coalition parties. Before leaving the chair of Prime Minister, Narasimha Rao promptly briefed the newly-elected Vajpayee about the preparedness of nuclear tests. As the government lost the vote of confidence in the Parliament, Vajpayee had to leave in a few days after he took the leadership.

Kalam's efforts with subsequent two Prime Ministers in 1996-97 could not succeed in conducting the nuclear test. During this time, Dr. Kalam was chairman of TIFAC. He and Dr. Y. S. Rajan brought the Vision 2020 document giving the road map for developed India. He was named for '*Bharat Ratna*' at the end of 1997 and conferred in 1998. Vajpayee came back as PM with a good majority for his alliance. He offered a cabinet post to Kalam. Realising it was time for a nuclear test, Kalam told Vajpayee that he would stay as scientific advisor to the defence minister instead of a cabinet minister to carry out the test. Five nuclear experiments were carried out on 11th and 13th, 1998 and made India a nuclear weapon state. Kalam initiated steps to produce minimum curable weapons and stored them in the right place and also delivered a missile body to quickly respond.

Concern for Society

Dr. Kalam also thought of contributing to society using missile technologies. The first opportunity came when the doctor from Nizam institute of medical sciences requested help for lightweight calipers for polio affected children. The composite group of DRDL developed a lightweight caliper, which was only one tenth of the weight of the conventional caliper (300 grams against 3 kg). The missile material became handy to achieve this device at a low cost with innovative design and development. It was possible for standardization of the calipers so that it can be fitted on the same day to the child. More than 50,000 children benefited with these calipers. Dr. Kalam used to say that more than his achievements in SLV-3, Agni, Nuclear test, he got bliss when he saw happy tears in the eyes of the parents when they saw that their child could walk normally with this missile caliper. Many other devices like Kalam-Raju stent, cardiac catheters, pace makers, 3D software for brain analysis etc came in a short time as offshoots of missile technologies.

BrahMos

One of the significant milestones of DRDO was the design, development and production of the supersonic cruise missile of BrahMos. It is a joint venture with Russia. We had collaboration with Russian institute NPOM from 1991 on underwater launch missile technology.

As Chief Controller R&D I had to coordinate with NPOM and Russian Institutes for R&D collaborations. In one such interaction in 1993 NPOM revealed the availability of a Ramjet engine, which could be used for supersonic cruise missiles. It happened just after the Gulf War in which the Tomahawk cruise missile played a crucial role in destroying the air defence radars. Realising the importance of cruise missiles, we thought of taking the Ramjet technology for the design. Dr. Kalam visited the Russian firm and established a good relationship with the directors of the Russian Institutes and invited them to visit DRDO. The idea was to forge a joint venture for the development of cruise missiles which could take India to the first position in the world. The idea clicked. Russian specialists who visited DRDO understood the capabilities and the agreement was finally approved and designed in February 1998. Thus the historical development started with the establishment of BrahMos Aerospace, an Indo-Russian company with me as CEO & MD. But for Kalam, BrahMos would not have seen the light of day. With a strong foundation the design and development of BrahMos started in 1999 when funds were made available from DRDO and Russia (diverted from the loan repayment to Russia).

Today, BrahMos is the frontline weapon for all the three services of the Armed Forces, and has no equivalent available with our adversaries or with the developed countries. In speed, precision and power BrahMos is superior and is a real threat for others. In President Putin's words, in 70 years of Indo-Russian cooperation, BrahMos is the best.

Dr. Sivathanu Pillai had closely worked with Kalam in the SLV-3 project, missile projects, atom bombs, and finally in the BrahMos mission. In the previous pages, he had shared his experiences with Kalam at a lightning fast pace. In the forthcoming pages, let us see about the various important stages of the SLV-3 project.

❑

SLV-3: Kalam Becomes Famous

In 1973, I returned to India with my family (wife Gomathy and son Vijay) after working in NASA. Since it was important to procure some of the component electronic parts for India's first satellite project from America, we renamed it as the 'Indian Scientific Satellite Project (ISSP)' after dropping 'Soviet' from the name. While I was in the US, I assisted the ISSP. Moreover, looking at my performance in the ATS-F project, the head of NASA had put in a good word to the head of ISRO, Professor Satish Dhawan about me. I therefore worked under Prof. Dhawan in Bangalore for the ISSP in 1974.

In 1974, ISRO had planned three major projects. One was the ISSP. The second was to bring NASA's satellite to Indian space and conduct television experiments using the satellite. This was known as SITE (Satellite Instructional Television Experiment). The third one was the SLV-3 mission. Other than these, the Sriharikota Range (SHAR) had to be prepared to launch SLV-3; R&D work for the project was also crucial. I was engrossed with my work in ISSP, work at ISRO's head office and other foreign travels.

Some of us at the ISRO head office were given the major job to consolidate all financial needs of ISRO. This was the method adopted by Prof. Dhawan. When Vikram Sarabhai was there, he used to take in requests from individual departments and sanction finance accordingly. However, since it would become difficult to secure finance from the government for all of ISRO's projects, we had to prioritise. While we were analysing this, we realised that three projects were crucial, of which SLV-3 was the most significant. However, it was still in its initial stages. Whereas the other two were almost nearing completion: 1975-Satellite launch; 1975-76-SITE testing.

We decided to invest everything in the SLV-3 project. We had to allot money for its R&D work, to prepare sites like SHAR for the launch and to buy other hightech gadgets.

Therefore, after taking in individual requests, we have to analyse and consolidate. R&D work not concerning the SLV-3 project was not given a high priority. Naturally, people working in those teams were infuriated. This would create more pressure on Kalam. His stand was that "I wouldn't say no to financing other R&D work!" Other than allocating money to the direct R&D of SLV-3, money should be allocated also for other R&D equipment related to the project. So, Kalam had to grant his approval for all these departments too. The expenses would become double of what was allocated in the government budget! We therefore had to reduce our expenses. "We became the bad men." We cannot do that blindly by allocating only half the finance to all the departments. We have to carefully gather data from the technology team and the R&D team, and look into the project timesheet and other long term requirements. We were popularly referred to as the ISRO HQ team and all members of our team must know the functioning methods of all of ISRO's departments. Sometimes, we had to discuss issues privately with Kalam. We told Kalam, "Let us know your important requirements. We won't report it to the other departments!" After consulting with him, we would cross-check to ascertain.

The stance taken by ISRO HQ further strengthened Kalam's role as the 'Project Director.' After Vikram Sarabhai's death, the SSTC, RFF, and RPP were consolidated into "*Vikram Sarabhai Space Centre* (VSSC)" in 1972. It was headed by Dr. Brahm Prakash. 70% of ISRO's budget was allocated to the VSSC. He too would carefully study and analyse all requirements for the SLV-3 project and give his wholehearted support to the ISRO HQ team which was responsible for deciding the finance allocation. Without his help, it wouldn't have been possible for us at ISRO to focus on the SLV-3 project without distraction.

Our aim was not to support Kalam and oppose others. Our primary concern was to enable the launch of SLV-3 as soon as possible. The department heads of all other departments were seniors of Kalam. The project manager cannot be put in charge of all those departments directly. Similar to NASA, only a small team was placed under the project manager. This team took care of the entire R&D work. The project management team members would review and instruct them. The 'review' team also had smaller units.

Therefore, the work of the project manager is burdensome. On top of this is the '*Project Management Board*' which consolidated the entire project work. The head of this department was Dr. Brahm Prakash who was the director of VSSC. Other department heads were made as the group members and the project manager served as the member secretary.

This further strengthened Kalam's position. Moreover, the repeated reviews helped in carefully inspecting the technical faults that arose out of ignorance or urgency. Otherwise, if these were caught in a later stage of the project, it would have resulted in financial loss, and loss of time. Furthermore, the entire project would have to be remodelled!

Therefore, in order to avoid such issues, each and every stage was reviewed thoroughly. For this, reports were prepared by carefully inspecting the measurements and by giving feedback of experiments conducted. The reports would be discussed and debated. These teams were given absolute independence. The review team would submit their reports without being partial to the technical or the managerial teams. Their findings would help strengthen the project further.

All this would look colourful on paper while describing. However, it would be difficult to endure practically. The ego, jealousy, and hatred of individuals would rise up like poison at crucial moments!

Teamwork is to work amidst all this and Kalam was an excellent team player. He tactfully handled everything by employing different tactics. Successfully completing the SLV-3 mission as planned, thereby making India and ISRO victorious was his only goal.

Kalam became famous in SLV-3 and VSSC circles within a year or two. Dr. Brahm Prakash and Professor Satish Dhawan aided him by providing administrative support and infrastructure support. They were his pillars of strength, which is why Kalam had applauded them in his '*Wings of Fire*'. He praised them both even after he became the Indian President. Vikram Sarabhai identified Kalam's dedication and devotion to work and assigned him the managerial and other smaller roles in TERLS. Sarabhai shaped Kalam to overcome failures and work tirelessly to achieve success.

Even though Kalam started his career from a low cadre, he took up hard assignments one after another and uplifted himself.

Kalam, who was thus shaped by Sarabhai, was given the role of the 'Project Manager' by Dr. Brahm Prakash and Professor Satish Dhawan. It was because of them that Kalam was able to improve his knowledge on research and development. This was how Kalam became the '*Missile man*' of India.

Even today, many regard Kalam to be a great scientist whose field of expertise is nuclear research. In general, we use the term 'Scientist' to denote people who create instruments to be used in practical applications and are well-versed in S&T. However, a few 'Basic researchers' regard scientists to be those who explore 'Nature's Laws' and write essays about their research findings. People like C. V. Raman, J. C. Bose, S. N. Bose, M. N. Saha, S. Chandrasekhar all come under this category. Nobel prizes are usually awarded to such scientists. Such scientists who prepare research essays are basic researchers.

Kalam has not written even a single research report like them. He was a good engineer. Engineers are those who create products for the benefit of the world.

They develop more new gadgets by doing further research. Only by employing such skilled engineers, it would be possible to make major breakthroughs. Such R&D technologists and engineers are employed in major applications like building aeroplanes, instruments, railways, electronic equipment, war equipment, medicine & bio-medicine, farming, satellites and telecommunications, and rockets.

R&D forms the backbone of a nation which was why Vikram Sarabhai established the SSTC. Many people like Kalam trained under him. Here, they learnt how to make equipment, put them to practical uses, and produce more such gadgets (Not by reading, writing exams and getting doctorates).

Kalam was an exceptional R&D engineer. It would not be wrong to say that Kalam was like America's Von Braun or Soviet Union's Korolev. The chief role of a project manager is to employ and integrate various people from different departments and successfully complete the assignment. Different people have different skill sets. Small entities are added together to become a part of a major project. Be it to build a mighty tower, a war craft, or an industry-everything requires workers skilled in building their component parts. The major role of the project manager is to guide all these employees along the right direction. The approach of various teams would be different. However, it is the job of the project manager to integrate them into his mission. Moreover, he should be supportive to all of them.

Kalam gained this 'experiential knowledge' while working in the SLV-3 project. This cannot be transferred from one person to another. It is not possible to express this through speech or words. This has to be experienced personally by witnessing and overcoming difficulties. A project manager must be able to identify the needs and wants of his employees. He has to rise over these without drowning in them in order to become victorious. He should then distribute his success equally among his team members. Kalam stood tall as a project manager.

These pearls of wisdom are mentioned by Kalam through his speech and writings after 1990:

-Focus on your goal/target

-Team Work

-Management of failures

He has also mentioned these in his '*Wings of Fire*'.

He never mentioned any of these while he was involved in the SLV-3 project. At that time, Kalam's complete focus was on the various stages of the project, timelines, and test results. He would not even smile much. At the time of the SLV-3 mission, he was not the cheerful leader that the world recognised him to be in his later years as the Indian President. Had he not been the way he was, it would have become impossible to accomplish the SLV-3 mission!

I have observed him at close quarters during different stages of his life. However, Kalam was at his best when he was the project manager of the SLV-3. I have told this to him many times as well. He led the first major mission for India, in spite of the fact that our industries were not so versatile at the time without showing the slightest trace of hesitancy or concern. In spite of the fact that our first experimental rocket launched on August 10, 1979 turned out to be a failure (more on that later), Kalam spearheaded the SLV-3 mission and successfully launched *Rohini* satellite on July 18, 1980. India became an empowered nation that day. That was the success of Kalam!

I wrote a poem that packed all my emotions. At that time, I was working non-stop day and night. I finished my poem within a month and handed it over to Kalam. It is there in my collection of poems. More on that later.

Kalam adopted a novel technique to handle the SLV-3 project. Instead of manufacturing all component parts within ISRO, he integrated various Indian industries to do the job. Professor U. R. Rao had earlier adopted a similar technique to make India's first ISSP satellite. But ISSP used its Peenya workshops alone. Kalam, on the other hand, used HAL (*Hindustan Aeronautics Limited*), BEL (*Bharat Electronics Limited*), Godrej, L&T, and Walchand to manufacture parts for SLV-3. This scheme adopted by ISRO in the 1970s became the precursor for the modern day cooperative schemes of factory-institute and factory-firms.

The SLV-3 project used these factories widely. This was because its first satellite weighed 450 kg and the weight of SLV-3 was about 13,000 kg. Therefore, the SLV-3 required massive machine parts and so it required bigger machines. Moreover, once SLV-3 became a success, if India manufactured component parts in its own industries, it would be helpful for all future space missions. ISRO could also focus on other rocket missions after SLV-3. All western countries and the Soviet Union adopted this technique only. However, Indian factories were not competent enough at that time and there weren't enough technical staff well versed in R&D and engineering employed by them. Therefore, many people working in VSSC argued that all rocket equipment be made in ISRO. Their argument was correct. There were no big factories anywhere near Thiruvananthapuram. HAL which helped in satellite-making was in Bengaluru. Other factories were in Hyderabad, Pune, Koraput (Orissa), and Lucknow. The Indian government prohibited the usage of telephones widely as it was considered to be an extravaganza in those days. Air transport was also minimal back then. Therefore, many people opposed the idea of working outside ISRO. Kalam too supported them. He needed the SLV-3 parts as quickly as possible. Also, it was important to inspect each and every stage of work. He therefore felt that it would be helpful if everything was done in Thiruvananthapuram itself.

In order to achieve all this, big factories must be installed in VSSC and more workers from ISRO must be recruited there. However, they will not be employed throughout the year. Expenses would mount. Moreover, machines will not be used all through the year. Unemployed workers, their supervisors and managers need to be paid unnecessarily. All these would create confusion within VSSC. Strikes by union workers were a frequent occurrence those days in India. Therefore, Professor Dhawan's vision to employ workers from different factories of India, created more job opportunities. This vision akin to "*Make in India*" of today was employed by Prof. Dhawan 45 years back in ISRO.

This decision was not taken by ISRO's executive committee alone. Several engineers from ISRO visited various Indian government and private organisations. After consulting with them, discussions and debates were conducted within ISRO to arrive at a final call. Funds from its SLV-3 project had to be allocated to these factories by ISRO. Kalam sent ISRO staff to the factories to procure necessary component parts and instruments for the SLV-3 project. Nearly 150 large, medium and small organisations benefited from this initiative of ISRO.

When Kalam worked at the DRDO after he left ISRO, these industries offered great help. Dr. Sivathanu Pillai has already explained this in detail. Kalam would have never expected that his work relations with the Indian factories would have continued even after the SLV-3 expedition! This happened because professor Satish Dhawan was a visionary.

❑

First Failure and Initiatives to Success

During 1973-74, there was much confusion within India. The organisation created by Jayaprakash Narayan spread across India. Many political parties instigated trade unions to perform strikes. The ISRO employees in Thiruvananthapuram too fell into this trap. Already in Thiruvananthapuram, due to the influence of the political left wing, workers refused to work properly. They revolted, frequently disrupting work. Dr. Brahm Prakash, who was leading ISRO then, handled the situation wisely. He would answer their queries, sometimes solved the disputes personally and employed all other tactics to curb the revolt. Many other group heads like Kalam too followed his approach. Due to this, Kalam got a good name from his employees and would persuade them to work as per the time schedule.

Kalam, therefore, sought help from everyone to accomplish his mission. This was an important reason behind his victory. This experience made him a trend-setter and improved his administrative capabilities.

ISSP's name was changed to '*Aryabhata*' after the '*Aryabhata*' satellite was successfully launched on 19 April, 1975. I was given additional responsibilities at the ISRO head office, significant among which was becoming a board member of the ISRO HQ, which handled the budget of SLV-3. Many financial conflicts were resolved by the board. It was at this time that my friendship with Kalam intensified, even though it had started several years earlier when Kalam was experimenting with his test rockets. Now, both of us played major roles within the organisation. We bonded well on account of our professional relationship.

Dr. Brahm Prakash did not support Kalam blindly. He would thoroughly analyse each and every stage. There were times when he argued with Kalam.

Kalam would become upset during these moments. All of this was for the success of Kalam's SLV-3 mission. Kalam has mentioned a few such moments in his '*Wings of Fire*'.

People like Madhavan Nair (he became ISRO's chairman and led the *Chandrayaan-1* mission) and Dr. Sivathanu Pillai (who manufactured BrahMos missile, a joint venture of India and Russia that is used by the Indian armed forces) joined at a young age and had worked alongside Kalam. Dr. Brahm Prakash appointed Dr. S. Srinivasan who was skilled in engineering and technology as Kalam's deputy project director. Kalam was not particularly impressed with this move. However, he took the cue that he should consult with Dr. S. Srinivasan for his SLV-3 project and acted accordingly.

T. N. Seshan offered great help to Kalam to complete the SLV-3 mission. ISRO directly came under the control of the Indian government in 1972. (Earlier, it was under PRL which was an organisation that sought government aid). Bulky government files too had to be handled now. None of the ISRO employees were familiar with this new system. They were afraid that like other government organisations, ISRO too would slow down. This transformation happened between 1972–75 and on April 1, 1975 ISRO became a complete government organisation.

Proper contracts had to be drawn with all the outside factories that supplied materials to ISRO. These were referred to as 'work centres'. Such work centres now became accountable to the Indian government and had to provide proper billing details. T. N. Seshan helped in smoothening this transformation. Earlier, when he was the Joint Secretary under the Indian government, while I was serving at the head office, I learnt a lot from him. Kalam approached T. N. Seshan to resolve administrative or financial crises and on matters related to contracts and purchase of products. The VSSC and Kalam's SLV-3 project operated smoothly since Dr. Brahm Prakash too had mastered these government administrative matters (I learnt a lot from him as well).

T. N. Seshan conveyed the rules to be followed by the *Space Commission*, which was created to take care of all government matters by a simple statement. He said that "Space Commission will exempt its units from needlessly inelastic rules."

This became the 'mantra' of ISRO. This helped in managing all R&D issues. Since this is a book about Kalam, I am not writing a great deal about Dr. Brahm Prakash and T. N. Seshan here. There are a few books on Sarabhai. However, there are no complete books about Satish Dhawan. Separate books could be written about the assistance offered by Dr. Brahm Prakash and T.N. Seshan to ISRO. Had they not assisted Dr. Satish Dhawan back then, ISRO wouldn't have risen up to the extent we see today. All three of them helped Abdul Kalam. At that time, Kalam was not a senior. However, since he was the project manager, he had to command his seniors to procure equipment for SLV-3. These three men helped Kalam accomplish this job without making the seniors realise it.

Kalam has written about the SLV-3 project in *Wings of Fire*. There is so much more to write about it. Since those are technical details, I do not want to mention it here. The technicalities of SLV-3 were thousand times more compared to previous projects in Thumba. ISRO's growth and Kalam's growth happened simultaneously.

Dr. Brahm Prakash, T. N. Seshan and I were members of the SLV-3 management board. Discussions and debates happened frequently. Kalam handled the board wisely in a way that would help his SLV-3 mission. This experience helped Kalam to successfully handle his job in DRDO that was ten thousand times bigger.

In 1978, after all these formalities were complete, component parts of SLV-3 were shipped to SHAR to be assembled. Workers employed in the SLV-3 mission started to stay in Sriharikota while their families lived in Thiruvananthapuram. Some changes happened within ISRO during this time. Since T. N. Seshan was an IAS officer, his job got transferred. He was replaced by Y. S. Das (IAAS). Das too was a good man like Seshan. His working style was different from that of T. N. Seshan. He was appointed in 1977. I learnt a lot about how the government handled finance from him. He liked and trusted me. He was older than me by twenty years.

Dr. Y. J. Rao, who helped prepare the SHAR base for launching SLV-3 got caught up in internal disputes within ISRO. He was transferred to ISRO's head office. I knew that he would leave ISRO since he had a high self-esteem. Dr. Brahm Prakash told me once: "I shouldn't have agreed to that 'gutter' committee in SHAR." Dr. Y. J. Rao was replaced by retired Colonel N. Pant who had worked in ISRO, Ahmedabad. Colonel N. Pant took charge of the SHAR base which would be used to launch the SLV-3.

Kalam was not impeded by these internal tensions. He focussed on his SLV-3 mission. He was forty-seven years old (in 1978). He maintained cordial relationships with Pant and Y. S. Das. Das offered personal assistance to Kalam. He wanted the SLV-3 mission to be a success.

It was decided to launch the satellite on August 10, 1979. It was named SLV-3E1 (SLV-3 Experimental flight-1). ISSP had sent the *Aryabhata* satellite in 1975 and was working to launch the *Bhaskara* satellite. After the SITE expedition, STEP experiments were underway. STEP was done using the French-German satellite '*Symphony*' in which the satellite was used to connect all mobile networks across India. Other experiments involving satellites were also underway. APPLE was India's first geosynchronous satellite. It was planned to launch APPLE using Europe's Ariane launch vehicle. APPLE stands for Ariane Passenger PayLoad Experiment. Therefore, SLV-3 was not the only project undertaken by ISRO at the time. ISRO was expanding its horizons in all directions. However, SLV-3 was given the topmost priority because it was now important to launch Indian satellites using an indigenous rocket launch vehicle, instead of using foreign launch vehicles. Even in 1980, 40 kg was the payload. However, we were all confident that after this first successful attempt, India would manufacture launch vehicles to support payloads as heavy as 500–1,000 kg.

Kalam had to operate under such heavy pressure. He had the immense responsibility of launching an Indian satellite from India's first launch vehicle. In spite of all concerns, he only showed his confidence to his coworkers.

On August 10, 1979, SLV-3E1 was launched from Sriharikota's SHAR base. After the first stage was complete, the rocket malfunctioned in the second stage and fell into the Bay of Bengal. It was such a disappointment to all of us! I was there too. Dr. Brahm Prakash and professor Satish Dhawan were also there. Kalam's disappointment could be seen in his face.

Even after *Aryabhata* was launched (April 1975), it had a few problems. Satish Dhawan got worried. However, the Soviet team and Professor U. R. Rao's Indian team together sorted out the issue. It was a big relief. After a few more days, the experimental gadgets within *Aryabhata* started to malfunction even though all other parts were functioning well. Some media men called it a failure! ISRO chairman Dr. Satish Dhawan had handled all these patiently. I was there with him at the time. In fact, my job was to work beside him in ISRO starting from 1974 onwards. However, it is impossible to make corrections to SLV-3 the way in which it was done to the *Aryabhata* satellite. This is because a satellite revolves around the earth. On the other hand, when there is any error in the orbit of a launch vehicle in any of its stages (totaling about 400 seconds only), the entire system would collapse. Kalam later used to say: "For Launch Vehicle fellows, the seven years of hard work is tested in 400 seconds!"

Yes! India's first mission was a failure! However, it worked well in the first stage. Few inputs were obtained from the second stage. From a S&T point of view, we gathered a lot of information. But others would not understand this. They would say that "Government is hiding things from them." We had arranged for a press meet. The technical team should analyse the reason for the failure. This is a part of our job. Even in case of success, all stages of the launch had to be analysed to check if our computations had worked correctly or if there were errors. So, whether it is a success or a failure, before and after launch, our work continued.

This is one thing. Since our department came under the Prime Minister of India directly, we have to submit our reports to him first. Only after this, the news of success or failure can be revealed to the press.

Y. S. Das and I prepared the report and after getting Prof. Dhawan's approval, sent it to the Prime Minister's Office via telex. In those days, fax machines too were not there. We informed the PMO through telephone of our submission. Only after getting news from the PMO, we could go to the press meet. At that time,

Chaudhary Charan Singh was the Indian Prime Minister. Even though the press usually mocked that he was an eighteenth century man, his telex reached Prof. Dhawan shortly. I handed it over to Dhawan. It had a beautiful message: "In such complicated scientific technological endeavours, it is not rare to encounter failures. I congratulate all ISRO members for your first attempt. Without losing heart, concentrate on future space missions. My congratulations for your future victories!"

The message directly reached Prof. Dhawan from the Prime Minister! It made us happy in spite of our grief. It was now time for our press meet. It had been decided that in case of success, Kalam would handle the press. The Q&A session would follow next. However, what to do now? Prof. Dhawan made Dr. Brahm Prakash and Kalam sit on the stage. He then started to explain the reasons for our failure to the press. It cannot be called a failure from a S&T point of view. After explaining everything, he said, "We faltered but did not fall flat." He was absolutely correct. The press wrote whatever came to their mind. They reported that crores of rupees got submerged in the Bay of Bengal.

After the press meet, Kalam went with Dr. Brahm Prakash and Prof. Dhawan to inspect reasons for the failure.

Kalam would always quote this experience. He said that this was an excellent example of statesmanship.

"If you are a leader, hand over the victory to someone else; however, take full responsibility in case of failure."

When a heated debate arose in the Parliament over who should be made responsible for the failure, we at the ISRO head office gave some long winding answers. Prof. Dhawan struck our reply and responded to the Prime Minister: "If responsibility is to be fixed, it is on Chairman ISRO, that is me."

We had the great opportunity to serve under such leaders! Without losing hope, Kalam dedicated his time and efforts completely to make his next mission a success. Technicians and engineers of ISRO analysed each and every stage carefully to identify the errors. "What was the reason for our failure? Was it because of a single reason or were there many reasons?" These were their line of enquiry. It could take several months to arrive at solutions. Some could be a wild guess too! It required acute technical expertise.

In order to ascertain a few errors, some modules had to be retested. Project management does not end there. Alternative options must be considered and acted upon. Our next mission was to launch a satellite using an indigenous SLV-3 E02 launch vehicle. Kalam took over this assignment. "What was needed? Which hardware could be reused? Which needs to be replaced?" He and his committee members contacted all 150 work centres (as mentioned previously, these work centres were distributed all over India).

❑

Smiling Face

Today, we hear terms like 'terrorism' and 'national security' frequently in news. ISRO, in 1978 was also subject to such encounters. Even though terrorism was not heard of at the time, it was prone to attack from enemies. All ISRO centres were in restricted zones. Sriharikota was even more isolated as it was an island. Shaped like the sixth day crescent moon, the southern end belonged to Tamil Nadu and the rest of it was lying in Andhra Pradesh. The Buckingham Canal separated this 36,000 acre island from the mainland. To the east lay the Bay of Bengal. It had several bushes, shrubs, a few cashew nut trees, and other forest trees like the Eucalyptus tree. ISRO built a thirteen kilometre road starting from Sullurupeta in Nellore. The security gate was built here. However, it was prone to attack from enemies who approached from the Bay of Bengal or the western frontier. Many local and foreign birds came to the sea. Professor Dhawan enjoyed watching these birds. After his retirement, he wrote a book on Aerodynamics titled *Birds in Flight*.

However, our concern at the time of launching the SLV-3E1 was something else. The launch vehicle must be placed in the launch pad for several days and the subsidiary equipment must be tested. This was an important procedure. The CISF (*Central Industrial Security Force*) alone was not enough to protect us. Prof. Satish Dhawan secretly visited the Indian government's Ministry of Home Affairs. I too had accompanied him. With a mouth filled with betel leaves, the Home Secretary T. C. A. Srinivasa Varadan welcomed us. Professor Dhawan explained to him about India's space mission and the SLV-3E1 project and its importance. He then informed him that it might take another month or two for us to prepare the base for launch. He asked the Home Secretary's help to protect the SHAR base from external attack since there were several explosives kept in the Sriharikota base. Even while Prof. Dhawan was explaining to him, the Home Secretary had to attend secret phone calls in his RAX. "Any firing? What is the death toll?" he asked and immediately gave instructions to resolve the issue. He was also listening simultaneously to Prof. Dhawan. Dhawan was never used to this kind of treatment!

The Home Secretary said: "Alright professor, I understood your problem. You need 24x7 security for the next two months in SHAR. In order to safeguard from external attacks, you need well trained security forces..." By then, he received another call and said: "Oh! Was Mohammed Younis arrested? Is he alright? Was he hurt? Please contact me after two hours."

He continued to us: "I am sorry about this, Professor. Throughout the day, I have to answer these phone calls since there are many disruptions all over the country. However, you need not fear. You continue with your work. We will supply military forces to safeguard your SHAR base."

Immediately Professor Dhawan intervened. "If you send military forces, that could create confusion. In ISRO, we perform peaceful operations only."

The Home Secretary replied: "Ok, I understand. Instead of sending military troops, we will send other trained security officers."

"But one thing, professor. You don't worry over all these issues. You concentrate on your S&T work. You leave this to us. You need not go to anyone else. Ask your joint secretary to contact ours. They will take care of everything."

He then pressed a button. His joint secretary entered. He gave instructions to him. "Do not send military troops. You be in touch with ISRO's jointsecretary. You can get his details from Professor Dhawan. Ensure that he is not concerned with anything. You and ISRO's joint secretary take full responsibility."

Professor Dhawan was not fully satisfied. This was because he was not used to handling things so quickly. He had to know each and every detail thoroughly. However, he did know that handling security issues within the country was a whole new world. He therefore gave the name of ISRO's joint secretary and thanked the Home Secretary for his assistance. We both left from there. I told what I had witnessed to the ISRO's joint secretary in Bangalore. This was an important episode in my life. I learnt that an important decision-maker of a country's security must be patient and swift. Had we discussed the same issue in ISRO, it would have taken several hours to resolve! This incident showed the significance of managerial experience. Security was handled so well that neither the SLV-3 crew nor Kalam felt any concern.

In this way, the Indian government protected everyone working at ISRO head office, and all other S&T and R&D technicians associated with space technology. Those at ISRO centres knew nothing about how we safeguarded them from external attacks. They knew only after they worked in other outside organisations. When Kalam headed the defence R&D department in 1992, he applauded the Indian government. More on that later.

When it was decided to launch the next SLV-3E2, a major change happened. Dr. Brahm Prakash retired from his post in the VSSC. He had recovered from his paralysis earlier. After retiring from the Indian Atomic Energy Centre when he reached 60 years, he was appointed by ISRO in 1972. Since it was important to take full time responsibility for the SLV-3 and related R&D operations, he decided to give his resignation.

Dr. Vasant Gowariker who was a senior in SSTC also set up the SPROB to manufacture fuel for SLV-3 after doing initial research was now appointed as the chairperson of VSSC. He too was an expert in his field. However, no one can even come near Dr. Brahm Prakash in handling administrative matters. Dr. Gowariker was posed with the delicate situation of also heading others who were his peers. He knew that if the SLV-3 mission were to succeed under him, he would earn a good name.

He therefore gave his complete cooperation for the SLV-3 mission. Even though Kalam had developed a good rapport with Dr. Brahm Prakash, he wasn't disheartened at this sudden change in leadership. Dr. Vasant Gowariker was not new to SSTC and ISRO. He had worked in SSTC for nearly 13 years. He too must be regarded as a pioneer. Since Prof. Dhawan was still heading ISRO, all seniors in VSSC accepted Dr. Vasant Gowariker's leadership and offered their full cooperation. This was very important because various subsidiary gadgets for SLV-3 had to be manufactured by different departments. ISRO underwent a smooth transformation under the new leadership. Most people at the VSSC were seniors who had similar qualifications. Even those belonging to the next lower cadre were over 40 years old like Kalam.

Work resumed as usual. After understanding the reasons for our first failure, a few changes were suggested to prepare for the second launch. A few spare parts had to be remade. All factory work centres worked in full swing.

One new problem had to be resolved now. We were nearing the finance allotted by the government for the project. We had to ask for some more financial assistance. Even after speeding up the process, it would take another 2-3 months to get government approval. Also, we were not sure whether we would be able to get approval in the first place. In case our request got rejected, it would complicate the SLV-3 operation because it would become impossible to receive our monthly salary, we would run short of resources, and we wouldn't be able to pay our work centres. Once the mission comes to a sudden pause, it would become difficult to speed up.

Kalam submitted his report about this to Prof. Dhawan. Dhawan consoled him saying that we would get our approval soon. It was necessary to get approval from the Space Commission. Kalam explained the situation to additional secretary Y. S. Das. Under normal circumstances, he would have said, "Alright, we would prepare a file and submit it to Delhi immediately." However, he knew the situation at the other end. Das was from Lucknow and he was very sophisticated. He would speak to me in fluent Hindi. Since Kalam did not know Hindi, he spoke to both of us in English.

"If I send a file now by explaining the facts that the budget has increased on account of the increase in foreign exchange rates, it would be in accordance with all rules and regulations. However, people would think only about SLV-3's first failure. Even though we know the reasons behind the failure, it could take several months to get approval. There is a slight possibility that it gets rejected!" Kalam was very worried. Kalam was not as close to Y. S. Das as he was with T. N. Seshan. This could probably be because they both used to interact in Tamil. Y. S. Das continued: "I have read the SLV-3 project report thoroughly. As per the report, the salaries of employees in the working stage have been mentioned. We then prepared for our first launch in 1978. We have also bought additional equipment for future launches. For example, fearing that the United States might restrict us, we bought the SAGEM launchpads from France in advance. These would not only help the SLV-3, but also all our future space missions...

"There are many such discrepancies. We have to compute everything correctly. After the first launch, prepare a table to show how many people are employed currently for this second mission. Leave all other expenses which are unrelated to this second launch mission to me... Submit a complete report. We will take care of the rest! You need not worry... Within one week's time, after you submit your report, you will get grants from the Space Commission."

Breathing a sigh of relief, Kalam left. He instructed people in Thiruvananthapuram to prepare a detailed report over the phone and went to board his flight. Y. S. Das asked me to stay back: If we deduct this salary and other unrelated expenses, the budget would go down by ₹ 2.5 crores. That would be more than enough for the second rocket launch. We will show the salaries of beginners under VSSC expenses. That would be the right approach too. We also have government allocation. We will take the rest from the VSSC and use it for future projects. The commission has the right to modify the profit-loss balance sheets and allocate funds accordingly.

"Sometimes, Prof. Dhawan would say why should we do all these, instead of submitting a report directly to the Space Commission. However, I know that it would become impossible to get grants if we did that. They would ask us why we have increased the budget in spite of our first failure. Many departments of the government function like this. There are certain discrepancies too. However, SLV-3 is not like that. We would make sure that we submitted the correct budget report after making suitable modifications. Let us first complete this second launch successfully. After that, we will explain in detail our budget planning to the Commission. We will show how our budget increased owing to the increase in foreign exchange rates. You too come along with me. Let us both approach Prof. Dhawan to get his consent. Even though I was several years younger to him, he always addressed me with respect. That is the Lucknowi style."

As expected by Das, Prof. Dhawan initially opposed his idea. "Why can't we follow a direct approach? Let us explain that our budget increased on account of increase in foreign exchange rates," he said. We made him comply after discussing the situation in detail. After Kalam submitted his report, we swiftly acted in compliance with all government rules and regulations and prepared the budget file. We sent the SLV-3 budget file to the director of VSSC for his approval. After this, Y. S. Das got approval from the space secretary and sent the government grant report.

A major complication disappeared like snow in front of the sun. Even now when I think about it, I find it hard to believe that someone like Das, who was always cautious and who was a member of the Indian government's audit team, handled the situation in this manner. Because many might fear that they could face repercussions from the CAG (*Comptroller and Auditor General of India*). He might have done so because he was an expert in his field and knew the nuances very well. Moreover, he knew that there were no black marks in the SLV-3 project.

After his tenure completion from the space department, he served as the cultural secretary. I visited him once in Lucknow at his house. He felt happy.

I think that since Kalam operated the SLV-3 mission without any expectations, help flowed from all directions. Moreover, everyone knew that SLV-3's victory was India's victory. In order for India to become a space power, it was not only necessary to make an indigenous satellite, but also it became important to make an indigenous launch vehicle. Mao Tse Tung said, "Government power flows through the nozzle of a gun." I replaced the statement and quite often said, "Space power flows through the nozzle of the launcher." If the nozzle was big, heavy satellites could be launched from the vehicle. Even though SLV-3 was a relatively small launch vehicle, we were all sure that India would design bigger launch vehicles in future.

All work related to SLV-3 was happening swiftly in Thiruvananthapuram, Sriharikota and other ISRO work centres. On account of internal conflicts within VSSC, CBI investigations and police investigations increased. These cannot be directly handled by the head office since many department heads were assigned major roles. Any action taken against them would impede the speed of the project. Even though there were internal conflicts within ISRO, there were no such CBI investigations and so the SLV-3 project went on smoothly. It was proved several years later, that all of these were false accusations that arose on account of internal conflicts. They were then removed from the CBI and police investigation. ISRO had to overcome all these shortcomings. I mentioned this because some people might like to think that Kalam lived in heaven while working at ISRO.

Such internal conflicts were there in ISRO even after Kalam left. The most recent unfortunate Nambi Narayanan episode was a similar one. After being prosecuted for several years, the Supreme Court finally released him recently. The Supreme court also criticised ISRO for such an act.

Crossing over all these thorns that came in their way, the ISRO employees worked diligently under the leadership of Kalam.

Finally, on July 18, 1980, SLV-3E2 successfully launched *Rohini-2* (RS2) satellite by placing it in its orbit. We all were thrilled. After completing all others in Sarabhai's ten-year plan (1970-80), we were yet to complete the rocket launch mission. However, now we have accomplished that as well.

There was a change in Indian politics. Indira Gandhi became the Prime Minister of India once again. Prof. Dhawan handed over the victory placard of the SLV-3E2 expedition to Kalam wholeheartedly. He made Kalam meet the press and the Indian Prime Minister. Kalam joined the Indian Space mission in 1962. After 18 years of hard work out of which he had worked exclusively for 7-8 years for the SLV-3 project, he finally enjoyed the fruit of his success.

ISRO never gave rewards for any achievements. That is the government rule. Like NASA, certificates would be distributed to participants.

However, the SLV-3 achievement was special. It was therefore decided that everyone who were not above the SF cadre would be awarded a HMT wrist watch to celebrate the accomplishment of Sarabhai's ten year dream plan. It was decided so because otherwise conflicts could arise if only the SLV-3 participants were rewarded. I assisted Prof. Dhawan to get the government approval. Since I was in SF cadre, I did not receive the wrist watch even though I was given the right to choose whether I wanted to receive it.

Therefore, everyone in VSSC, ISRO work centres, and those in ISRO (Bengaluru and Ahmedabad) celebrated Kalam's SLV-3 victory together. Now, Kalam has become a great hero to everyone.

From 1969 onwards, I had stopped writing poems due to my work pressure. Mahakavi Bharati was a great inspiration to me. I worked by dedicating my body, mind and soul to fulfil his dream of empowering India in science and technology. In spite of this, I wanted to write a poem on Kalam. Other than getting the aforementioned government approval, I had huge responsibilities in ISRO also at that time. After completing the poem within a month, I sent a copy of it to Kalam. On August 15, 1980, along with my other poems, that was also released in my first Tamil poem book "நெஞ்சக மலர்கள்" (*Blossoms of the Heart*). It was the first poem on Kalam worldwide. After he became the Indian President, many books were written about him.

I will reproduce that poem here. Each and every word in the poem came straight from my heart. It starts as "முகத்திலே முறுவல் கொண்டு..." When Kalam was engrossed in his SLV-3 project, there was hardly a smile on his face.

Earlier while working at TERLS and in Ahmedabad, I have seen him smile. His smiling face became his trademark that registered in the minds of people world over. I feel happy to have contributed the first poem on Kalam that too about his 'smiling face'. I thank God for this wonderful opportunity. I have given the English translation of the poem here...

THE VICTORY SONG OF S.L.V.

With a smile on his face
And effort as his creed
With strength rooted in mind
With intelligence as the escort
One can achieve the power
To jump over the universe
Prove did he by act
While propelling Bharath
To the skies;
Pave did he a practical path,
To convert Bharati's dreams
Expressed in honeyed Tamil
To good words of prescience;
'We will measure the skies,
And understand the moon;
Across the whole country
We will live so well'!
Let us say 'Long live
Abdul Kalam'
With our thundering voices,
All over the skies;
He who made a vehicle
To propel the satellite Rohini
To the outer space
And achieved victory with honour
And created a new speed of action!
If we work together,
Will we destroy the poverty cruel;
Will eradicate in days
The diseases and decline
All across our country;
To achieve all we desire;
Our own hands are our escorts;
If sixty crores get to act
Tell, will we ever
Suffer a short fall?

15-8-1980

I wrote it on the Independence Day of India. It was 33 years since India had attained her independence. I was 36 years old and Kalam was close to 49 at the time. He spent many more years of his life working on rockets and missiles. I left ISRO in 1988 and joined TIFAC (Technology Information & Forecasting Council) in Delhi. Kalam was in Hyderabad. In 1980, Kalam would have not even thought about leaving ISRO. However, thoughts of leaving ISRO were there on my mind already. I shared my feelings with Professor Dhawan. Professor Dhawan had safely kept all that along with some others and handed me his collection one day before he left ISRO, that is on September 29, 1984. I have used it as a reference material for this book.

❑

Question Mark Becomes an Exclamation Mark

As mentioned earlier, I had questions about my future in ISRO.

I could never believe that Kalam too would have to face a similar situation. Kalam was passionate about ISRO and missiles.

After the success of SLV-E2, questions about his future arose. Would he be launching more satellites in future? Each and every single launch would take at least an year to complete.

But it became sure now that he wouldn't be leading all SLV-3 projects. After Kalam, VSSC's V. P. Sandlas became the project manager. Now the letter 'E' which was used to mean '*Experimental*' was replaced by 'D' to mean '*Developmental*'. The project's name was SLV-3D1.

Using the same component parts of SLV-3, instead of the 40 kg payload, an Augmented Satellite Launch Vehicle (ASLV) was being made to carry a payload weighing 150 kg M. S. R. Dev, who worked with Kalam, was made in charge of the ASLV project.

Kalam also took part in the ASLV initiative. Besides all these, one more mega project to build a massive launch vehicle had been planned. It was still in its initial planning stages when Kalam was working under Dr. Brahm Prakash for the SLV-3E1. Usually, ISRO appointed the person in charge of the plan as its project manager. This is because he alone would be familiar with the most intricate parts of the design. Even if the project report covers everything in detail, some aspects would always remain intact within the human mind. This is popularly known as 'Person embodied tacit knowledge'. Experiential wisdom is also of a similar kind.

These rockets were designed to launch ISRO's remote-sensing satellites. These would circulate around the earth's north-south direction. That is, they would travel parallel to the two poles and so are termed as 'Polar Satellites'. It would take one and a half hours to travel from one pole to the other and back. This full circle is known as the 'orbit'. In a period of 24 hours, the satellite would cover 16 such orbits. (Likewise, the earth too revolves around the sun; it takes a year to complete its revolution). That is why Kalam normally said that he had "revolved around the sun for these many years" when asked about his age. This satellite orbits at a distance of 700–800 km above earth. ISRO had prepared reports about these remote sensing satellites at the time. As mentioned earlier, the main reason for the government to invest in space exploration is to benefit mankind. It is not done to simply please the ISRO scientists and engineers.

Remote sensing satellites are capable of sending data quickly about earth's resources (like water, forests, agricultural crops, land and so on). They also send data about weather conditions. More than all these, it can also be used to spy on enemy nations. Therefore, the PSLV satellite is very important for the nation. They designed a launch vehicle to launch a satellite weighing 1,000 kg at a distance of 700 km from the earth. This formed the 'study phase' of the PSLV. The PSLV project cannot be accomplished with the solid fuel that was used for the SLV-3 project alone. It requires liquid fuel as well. India had signed a contract with a French company in 1973 to manufacture liquid fuels. ISRO had named it the '*Vikas*' scheme. It was under Dr. A. E. Muthunayagam. The Indian team of engineers, technicians and administrators were sent to France for five years to receive training. The team was headed by Dr. Nambi Narayanan.

Vikas would supply fuel for the second stage of PSLV. For the first stage, it required much more solid fuel when compared to that required by SLV-3. Therefore, at that time, in 1980, PSLV required a new set of technological skills.

SLV-3's assistant project director Dr. S. Srinivasan was appointed as the '*Study Director*' for the PSLV project. Even though he reported to Kalam during the SLV-3 mission, he had to report to the chairpersons of ISRO and VSSC during the PSLV mission. Kalam may have wanted to take charge of the PSLV project. But, Dr. Brahm Prakash told me: "For the PSLV project planning and completion, it might take at least fifteen years. Kalam might want to take this up as a challenge. However, he is now already fifty years old, and he has to retire by 60 years. That is why, I chose a youngster Mr. Srinivasan to take charge of the PSLV project. It would be possible for him to launch the first PSLV before retirement."

His arguments cannot be countered. But what will happen to Kalam now? It is not the responsibility of ISRO to see everyone's cadre and assign jobs accordingly. They normally leave it to the individuals to take care of themselves. Kalam was disappointed! However, he was busy with his SLV-3E1 at the time.

In case the SLV-3E1 had been successful, Kalam could have replaced Dr. Brahm Prakash after he retired as VSSC's chairperson. However, even that wasn't sure since there were several seniors more experienced than Kalam eligible for the role. They had worked competently in SLV-3's R&D and component parts manufacturing wing. Kalam was only nearing his fifty at the time. However, SLV-3E1 was a failure. Therefore, after Dr. Brahm Prakash, Dr. Vasant Gowariker replaced him as the head of VSSC. He was then 50 years old (the age of retirement in ISRO is high. Kalam would have also reached his sixty by then!)

What harm could have come if Kalam led all the three projects viz. SLV-3D1, ASLV & PSLV? He could have become a senior project manager. Even if he had to submit all reports to the head of VSSC, he could have independently worked as a senior project manager. However, this is practically impossible. First of all, the chief role of the director of VSSC was to monitor these three key projects. Secondly, the project managers of these three projects have to submit their reports individually to the VSSC director. Therefore, an intermediary cannot be appointed.

Therefore, after SLV-3E2's successful launch, Kalam did not have a significant role. He led the 'Aerodynamics Group' at the time. Prof. Dhawan had great regard for Kalam. However, he couldn't get involved in work politics. After several years, Kalam had told me this: "Rajan, when I was in charge of the SLV-3 project, I met Von Braun. While we were talking, he told me: 'Kalam, in case the SLV-3 project becomes successful under your leadership, be prepared to retire from your job after that!' It happened exactly as he had told me."

After Von Braun's team successfully sent a man to the moon in the US, he also had to face a similar situation in NASA. He too was transferred to an insignificant role. Kalam too met with the same fate! Prof. Dhawan made Kalam as the director of 'special launch vehicle programme' in the head office. Kalam also was leading the 'Aerodynamics Group'. However, the VSSC, SHAR and all other satellite launch vehicle team members had to report only to Prof. Dhawan and not to Kalam. In this new job, Kalam could prepare reports and submit them to the head. No one in VSSC would be bothered even to look into it!

The funny thing is that when Dr. Y. J. Rao was about to leave SHAR, a new title 'Director Special Launch Services' was created and he worked for three months before leaving for the US. After he left, Prof. Dhawan gave the job to Kalam!

I knew that Kalam felt disappointed. But I couldn't do anything for him. He met the same fate as many others who had led successful missions earlier. It is the same situation in NASA too! However, in the USA, even as early as the 1960s, besides NASA there were several other private space research organisations. They got assignments from NASA and the US national security forces. Therefore, if anyone in NASA were not happy with their job position, they could easily switch over to any of these private entities. However, in India, the situation is totally different. ISRO is the only space research organisation, then and now. The R&D for space research had not collaborated well enough to set up private entities.

Dr. Sivathanu Pillai was working with Kalam. Those two years, 1980–82, were the hardest in Kalam's life. He had to run here and there in order to submit his reports. He never showed his pain outside. He never forgot those two years. When he became the Indian President, Kalam told me frequently: "Those two years were the most horrible, sir. I was sitting like a vegetable."

God had other plans for Kalam. In the 1960s and the 70s, the DRDO started working on a few missile programmes. However, there were no proper plans. Everyone in ISRO and the VSSC were against working with the DRDO, including Kalam. There was a heavy competition. Moreover, the DRDO did not have visionaries like Vikram Sarabhai and Satish Dhawan at the time.

It had stagnated on account of internal conflicts. There were conflicts between the head of the *Atomic Commision*, Dr. H. N. Sethna and the Director of the *Bhabha Atomic Research Centre* (BARC) Dr. Raja Ramanna. In order to solve their dispute, the then Prime Minister Smt. Indira Gandhi appointed Dr. Raja Ramanna as the head of the DRDO, as well as the Defence Research Secretary and the Science Adviser to the Defence Minister (three-in-one role). Raja Ramanna was a very good S&T visionary. When he was the director of the BARC, he helped by creating the Beryllium infrastructure for ISRO. He helped in many more ways. The administrative and work styles of Prof. Dhawan and Dr. Raja Ramanna varied greatly. Even though they weren't the best of friends, they helped each other on S&T matters.

Even though Raja Ramanna knew that he would work only for a short term at the DRDO (since PM Indira Gandhi had told him that he could head the atomic department after H. N. Sethna's retirement), he announced several new schemes for the DRDO so that it doesn't stagnate. He decided: 'My scientists cannot live in *barracks*' and built proper buildings for them. Moreover, he introduced the '*Merit Review Promotion*' similar to Atomic and Space Departments so that promotions did not happen like in other government departments where people were promoted based on availability of empty seats. But he could only complete it half way before leaving.

Besides these, he wanted the DRDO to engage in space research projects that helped the Indian Armed Forces in future. He knew that besides completing all other unrelated projects, it was also necessary to start space research projects immediately.

He said to Professor Dhawan, "Can I borrow Rajan for a few months?" Professor Dhawan knew that as Scientific Secretary, ISRO, I had a detailed knowledge about space research. He decided to offer assistance to Dr. Raja Ramanna because he knew that in order to protect India on all frontiers, space research was the key. Fearing that powerful world nations could impose sanctions on India, Prof. Dhawan said in his speeches that ISRO was meant for peaceful operations alone. Professor Dhawan told me: "You cannot work for days together at the DRDO because I need you here. However, you must offer full cooperation to Dr. Raja Ramanna. In case he needs you for more time, you can work with him for one or two days per week." He trusted me fully. It is because of the trust he had placed on all of us that we enthusiastically participated in our work.

I accompanied Dr. Raja Ramanna while he discussed the project with the representatives of the three wings of the Indian Armed Forces. He disclosed his lifelong dream: "Do not run behind one or two plans immediately. What is the situation worldwide? What do we need here in India? How are the different branches of the armed forces connected with each other? After investigating all these, let us decide on our priorities. You need not worry about finance now." In another 4–5 months, a clear comprehensive report was presented. He asked me to write it fully. I also gave a copy to Prof. Dhawan. I did not have a key role there since it was related to national security. Moreover, I had loads of work at ISRO.

A few important projects like '*Integrated Missile Project*', '*Spy Satellite Project*', and '*telecommunication infrastructure*' were listed in it. All these three are interconnected. It never occurred to me that Kalam would become a part of this assignment. I could not disclose these matters to anyone else either.

Meanwhile, a fantastic reward was awaiting Kalam. After Y. S. Das completed his tenure in DOS, T. N. Seshan once again became the additional secretary. He visited the Space Secretary to collect names for '*Padma*' awardees. The Ministry of Home Affairs of India wrote to all government departments to submit names for the '*Padma*' awards every year. T. N. Seshan told me: "I will definitely try to get a '*Padma Bhushan*' award for Kalam." He must have spoken to Prof. Dhawan as well. Prof. Dhawan might have felt that he couldn't assign major roles to Kalam at ISRO, he should at least recommend him for the '*Padma Bhushan*'. Indira Gandhi had great regard for Prof. Dhawan. Therefore, Kalam was awarded the '*Padma Bhushan*' directly when he was 50 years old. Normally, the '*Padma*' awards were given in order—'*Padma Shri*', '*Padma Bhushan*', '*Padma Vibhushan*' and finally the '*Bharat Ratna*'. Several years would elapse between these awards. Even Prof. Dhawan received only the '*Padma Shri*', '*Padma Bhushan*' and '*Padma Vibushan*' awards.

This was on one side. On the other hand, there was no improvement in his position in ISRO.

One day, suddenly the great scientist Dr. S. Ramaseshan called me. He was a close friend of Prof. Dhawan. They both were of the same age group. He liked me very much. I too had deep respect for him. He would speak openly about S&T in the country. He had the ability to mock even serious matters while speaking on stage or other places. His speech would be beautiful. He was an expert in the field of science. He asked me: "I need to ask you something. But you shouldn't disclose it to anyone. Especially if Prof. Dhawan knows about this, he will kill me!" He gave an intro like this before beginning to speak. Even when he was older than me by 25 years, he always addressed me politely, just like Kalam.

"You know I like Kalam very much. I think that ISRO is not making good use of him! Dr. Raja Ramanna has asked my advice about appointing a suitable man who could head a big missile programme. Would it be right to propose Kalam's name? After making all arrangements at the DRDO, Kalam won't refuse, right?"

I replied: "Sir, Kalam is an excellent choice! Even while working in the rocket programme, all his thoughts were about missiles only. His SLV-3 experience will be of great help too. He will readily accept the offer. He has no future in ISRO."

Dr. Ramaseshan said: "This is great news! Please do not inform anyone that I asked you, not even Kalam. Raja Ramanna had told me not to ask anyone. I wanted to confirm with you first before giving Kalam's name. I am going to submit only one name!"

Within a few weeks, Dr. Raja Ramanna's written request to Prof. Dhawan to send Kalam to work for the DRDO was received. (Kalam has written about what Dr. Ramaseshan spoke to him in *Wings of Fire*). I have seen the letter that Prof. Dhawan had received; T. N. Seshan talked about it. We both decided to send Kalam as quickly as possible to the DRDO.

Professor Dhawan was not ready to leave Kalam. T. N. Seshan and I tried to persuade him. Prof. Dhawan said, "We do not know how they are planning to use Kalam! Have they decided on his job profile?"

His concerns were not without reason. At that time, during the 1980s, DRDO had no proper vision. Professor Dhawan wanted to preserve Kalam's genius. He did not want him to end up in some gutter. He must have also felt that he could create some nice job profile within ISRO for Kalam.

He therefore sent a strong reply to Dr. Raja Ramanna: "What is the job that you have planned to assign Kalam?" Dr. Raja Ramanna might have been infuriated. However, he did not want to lose Kalam. He therefore sent Dr. V. S. Arunachalam who was the *Director of Metallurgical Research Laboratory* (DMRL) of DRDO to talk to Prof. Dhawan in order to explain Kalam's role in the '*Missiles*' programme. I have seen Dr. Arunachalam waiting patiently at Bengaluru ISRO headquarters. He visited several times. Whenever he came, I would sit and talk with him out of respect even though my workload was very heavy. Several months rolled by. Finally, Prof. Dhawan agreed. "I won't let Kalam permanently out of ISRO. He can work at the DRDO only temporarily," Prof. Dhawan was adamant. At last, T. N. Seshan and I managed to send the official letter on behalf of ISRO to the DRDO that they could appoint Kalam only on 'deputation' basis. Kalam left for Hyderabad to join as the director of the DRDL. Therefore, his government job profile became equivalent to that of seniors at the VSSC. He was no longer a junior! This helped him to rise up later to the role of *Minister's Scientific Adviser to Defence Minister/Secretary of Defence Research/ the director of the DRDO* simultaneously. Otherwise, citing job status, it would have been rejected. Kalam gladly accepted his new job. The question mark in his life now became an exclamation mark.

I do not know about the beginning of the DRDO or how Kalam fitted into his role in Hyderabad. I have asked a few youngsters who joined with him at the time and have added their inputs in this book. We were not in touch with each other because there were no telephones and also because of my workload in ISRO. Attempts to purchase INSAT-satellites from abroad had started in the 1980s. Other than that, we were doing research on manufacturing indigenous remote sensing satellites. From 1982 onwards, research on PSLV was speeded up.

SLV-3D1 was launched on May 31, 1981. That too was a failure! It went till the end and launched the *Rohini satellite* (RS-3) at a very low earth orbit that the satellite fell down towards the earth and burnt. At that time, Kalam was in ISRO. During its fourth attempt, while launching SLV-3D2, ISRO had invited the Indian Prime Minister. The Chief Minister Mr. N. T. Rama Rao insisted that he too shall come. An entire episode could be written about that! I was put in charge of security clearance. The first INSAT1 built by Ford Aerospace in America did not function properly and disappeared in space. T. N. Seshan had to leave for America to discuss insurance matters related to that. He told me: "Rajan, this is my job. However, you have to take care of it now. You know about our senior scientists! They could confuse everything! Therefore, you have to be very strict!" Also, NRSA (*National Remote Sensing Agency*) in Hyderabad came under the Department of Space and the work division between NRSA and ISRO had to be done . '*National Natural Resources Management System*(NNRMS)' was being formed within the Space department. All these were also assigned to me. I am not going to describe all that here.

On April 17, 1983 SLV-3D2 was successfully launched. I had the opportunity to watch alongside Smt. Indira Gandhi. She was a great leader. She felt very happy. V. P. Sandlas was the project manager. It was my birthday. I was 39 years old. I did not tell anyone.

Smt. Indira Gandhi gave a very good press meet. The preparatory arrangements we did for her and the way she handled the press, the order and decorum she maintained and N. T. Rama Rao's speech that day can be written as a whole new book!

In May, 1983, I had to run the workshop on NNRMS in Hyderabad. Since Kalam was not involved in that project, I couldn't meet him then.

Several years later Kalam told me: "No one in ISRO invited me to witness the launch of SLV-3D2, the one in which Prime Minister Smt. Indira Gandhi had presided! You were the Scientific Secretary, ISRO at that time, sir!"

Not just once, he had told this to me several times. I do not remember the exact reason. I did not remember the reason even when he asked me. The fact that Kalam repeatedly asked the same thing even though he had played several major roles over the years goes to show his attachment to ISRO. That was the final SLV-3 project. After that, we started focusing on ASLV and PSLV.

There could be many reasons for ISRO not to have invited Kalam. Firstly, it became a practice in ISRO to not invite people who had left the organisation (unless they held key positions). "Out of sight; out of mind!" seemed to be the norm. Besides, in those days, SHAR was a small place. Only a limited number of people can be seated there. That too when the PM and CM were chief guests, their own security guards would occupy most of the seats. There were many seniors in VSSC and SHAR who had to be invited too. Therefore the invitation list had to be kept down. Even then, people in ISRO's head office would have definitely seen the list of invitees. I do not know why Kalam's name was left out. Probably, some might have felt that if Kalam came, the importance given to the SLV-3D2 project manager, VSSC's director and the SHAR director would be reduced; they too have worked very hard to undo the failures of SLV-3D1.

On top of all that, since Kalam now worked for the missile programme of DRDO, world powers like the USA would misunderstand and impose sanctions on India. A few people in foreign media already criticised ISRO for secretly indulging in war weaponry when Kalam left ISRO to join DRDO.

Whatever be the reason, I never knew that Kalam was wounded by this issue. I did not know this even after several years had elapsed. Only when Kalam told me personally did I know about this. Otherwise while I was at the NNRMS workshop in 1983 in Hyderabad, I might have visited him!

Therefore, the era of SLV-3 in India finally came to an end. It gave a great reputation to India on the world stage. After April 17, 1983, SLV-3 became a memorable part of ISRO's history.

❑

Tipu and Kalam

Kalam had planned one very important project known as Integrated Guided Missile Development Programme (IGMDP) where the integrated missile system would act according to command. There were five missile projects under this:

1. *Agni,*
2. *Prithvi,*
3. *Trishul,*
4. *Aakash,*
5. *Nag*

Of these, Agni was the most significant; it could attack enemies by carrying nuclear weapons. Within a few months of Kalam joining the DRDO, Raja Ramanna became the chairperson of the atomic department; that was his lifeline! In order to complete the renovation works he had started at the DRDO, he appointed Dr. V. S. Arunachalam (47 years), who was younger, as the head of the DRDO. (50–55 years was the preferred age for the Secretary of State for India in those days). Arunachalam was younger than Kalam by four years. However, he was very experienced since he held a major post at the *Defence Metallurgical Research Laboratory* (DMRL) for several years.

Arunachalam left for Delhi. In a way, it was good that he was chosen as the head of the DRDO because he was the one who visited Prof. Dhawan to send Kalam to work at the DRDO. Arunachalam told me in Tamil: "Sir, remember how many times I came to Bangalore back and forth to Prof. Dhawan, lifting kaavadi, seeking his permission to send Kalam to work at the DRDO!" Arunachalam was not only active and energetic, but he also had a progressive mindset. IGMDP being a major project, if it becomes successful, he would also earn a good name. He therefore helped Kalam in multiple ways. DRDO administration and finance followed old protocols that were practised over several years now. In spite of this, Arunachalam made sure that Kalam was given complete independence to operate just like in ISRO. Kalam could therefore make independent decisions.

After one year of probation, DRDO sent a letter to Prof. Dhawan to permanently absorb into DRDO. Professor Dhawan was reluctant. He said: "No, Kalam cannot leave ISRO permanently; he can only go on deputation so that he can return back to ISRO whenever he wants." Professor Dhawan did not know the nuances of the government administration. Kalam also was not familiar with all that at the time. T. N. Seshan and I knew very well that only after getting formal consent from Dr. Dhawan and ISRO, DRDO could get government permission for Kalam to work there.

We both therefore explained the situation to Kalam lest he too should think like Prof. Dhawan and reject the DRDO absorption offer.

"Sir, now Professor Dhawan is there at ISRO. After a few years he will retire. Already, after turning sixty, he has worked for three more years here. Once he leaves, if the next chairperson of ISRO demands DRDO to send you back, they won't be able to object. Moreover, you could join ISRO from only where you left off. You won't even be able to hold a senior position then and your job profile would also be uncertain.

"Also, deputation can be given only for three years; special extension can be given for five more years. During that time, citing various reasons, the DRDO could send you back to ISRO!

"Therefore, this deputation is a dicey situation. Furthermore, you have been given a key role at the DRDO. We both recommend that you should take up a permanent job at the DRDO when both Prof. Dhawan and Dr. Arunachalam are there. You too can hold on to your senior job profile at the DRDO and benefit. We will persuade Prof. Dhawan. Whatever he says, you stay firm."

After several attempts, Seshan and I somehow managed to persuade Prof. Dhawan, who said, "But I want to keep the doors of ISRO open for him. I will record in the file that he is free to come back to ISRO any time, etc."

There is no point in writing anything in the file as there will be practical difficulties for Kalam to join ISRO after leaving. This is the situation in all government organisations. However, for Prof. Dhawan's personal satisfaction, we did not stop him from writing those lines. Professor Dhawan had a very good command over English. He was also an English post-graduate. He wrote wonderfully praising Kalam for his work and that the doors of ISRO would always be open for him. Finally, he wrote the lines we wanted : "ISRO grants permission to Kalam to join the DRDO."

Professor Dhawan was not familiar with the cruel horrors of government files. His letter would be submerged deep under hefty government files. Neither ISRO nor the DRDO would bother to look back into them.

'ISRO is willing to let go of Kalam; DRDO is willing to accept him.' This alone will be written in the file! At last, after the government's approval, Kalam joined DRDO permanently. His bonds with ISRO were all cut. His career records and other administrative files will now be sent to the DRDO. Everything related to Kalam is now a concern of the DRDO alone! I did not ask Kalam how he felt about this. I felt glad that Kalam has joined a senior cadre and his job is permanent in the DRDO. He therefore will now be able to focus fully on the missile programme without worrying over other repercussions.

I knew that Kalam had no future in ISRO even though Prof. Dhawan had great regards for him. This is the truth about government administration!

Kalam's new job was to successfully design the IGMDP programme. I got a writeup from one of Kalam's co-workers in Hyderabad to describe his work life at the DRDO between 1982–92 and am giving it in this book. In 1988 when I went to Delhi to join TIFAC, I discussed with Kalam frequently. Our discussion would not be related to any of the DRDO programmes as they involved security issues. I wrote to him about the use of technology in practical applications. Our bond became stronger now. I later indirectly helped Kalam to become the top head of the DRDO and government of India Secretary.. I will write about that as well. Kalam too knew about this.

The incidents narrated so far in Kalam's life were all important ones as they were about his life, his projects and his successes and failures.

There is an interesting episode totally unrelated to all these. After SLV-3, Kalam did not have any major assignments at the time. As a Scientific Secretary, ISRO, one of my jobs was to identify possibilities of cooperative projects between India and other foreign nations like France, Germany, other European nations, and Japan and initiate them. Of these, France and Germany were the major key players. We wanted to associate with Britain as well. For this, we took a few small steps. We then decided that after interacting with the members of the Royal Society, some of the senior ISRO scientists and technologists should identify areas in which both could work together. It was therefore decided that a few important senior officials should go to Britain (an important decision taken by Prof. Dhawan). Space science, weather and satellites were chosen as the possible fields for a joint venture. Kalam was not directly related to any of these fields. His expertise was rockets and launch vehicles. The *Royal Society* scientists never discussed those subjects. Moreover, Britain and ISRO did not have any joint cooperative programme on launch vehicle technology.

Even then, Prof. Dhawan decided to send Kalam with the team of ISRO scientists to Great Britain. He probably wanted Kalam to prepare for future prospects. Also, when Kalam was busy with the SLV-3 project, he hardly travelled to foreign nations. Dr. Dhawan must have felt that now that Kalam has some free time, he should be sent with the team.

As I was a Scientific Secretary, ISRO, I had a major role to play. Taking notes after visiting laboratories and capturing the minutes of the meeting were all part of my job. In case there was an overlap in both our programmes, I had to ask them to make necessary changes by making suitable adjustments. Kalam was free from all this burden and was like a free bird. Since we were travelling for 4-5 days together, he must have gotten bored. Moreover, Kalam did not go 'shopping' like others. I therefore would be talking with him whenever there was some intermission.

We both decided that we should go to Woolwich, which was outside London where models of Tipu Sultan's rockets that he fired against Britishers were kept inside the *Royal Artillery Museum* (Woolwich Arsenal, London). We cannot use government funds to go there and so we decided to go by bus.

One day, after our meeting got over, myself and Kalam went by bus to Woolwich. We both were wearing a coat as it was very cold. We were both running to get to the museum quickly as it was almost closing time. While we were running, I told Kalam: "Looking at your hair, my beard and our black skin...I hope that the military does not shoot us thinking that we both are some crazy Palestinians running around in the night!" At that time, Palestinian terrorism was a big threat to the world nations. Both of us got very worried! At last, we approached the entrance of the museum. The security told us that it had already closed. He asked us to come the next day. We told him that we had to see only one place inside the museum. The security said: "The Curator of the Museum has left already. Even if I allow you inside, the rooms will be closed now. Come tomorrow."

The next day, we arrived a few minutes early. (I couldn't leave the ISRO-Royal society meeting much earlier as I had many responsibilities!) The security took both of us to the museum curator. We both informed the curator:

"We both have come from India. We have to go back tomorrow. We have come to the meeting at the *Royal Society* here. We would like to see Tipu Sultan's rockets!"

Looking at our eagerness and honesty, he took us to the room. A small pipe was tied to the tip of a longsword. That pipe was the rocket. It was locked inside a glass cage. There were two such rockets there.

"Can I touch and see?" asked Kalam.

"We do not allow visitors to touch," replied the curator.

The room was filled with an uncomfortable silence.

I then introduced Kalam to the curator. I informed him that Kalam was the man who built India's first rocket launch vehicle to send satellites and that he is a great scientist and an engineer. I told the curator that we only needed a few minutes to see...

The curator brought a key and opened the glass cage. He then took Tipu Sultan's rocket and handed it over to Kalam. Kalam was thrilled. He touched each and every single part of the rocket. Only the sword was big. The rocket portion was just 6-9 inches only. It was tied closely to the sword.

At that time, neither I nor Kalam knew that he would go to work for the DRDO in future. Kalam, who became India's missile man later, felt a sense of excitement and exhilaration by touching Tipu Sultan's rocket that day. We returned Tipu's rocket and left.

On our way back, we both discussed that it should be brought back to India. It was then sent for the IAF (*International Astronautical Federation*) conference in India in 1988. England did not want to return it back to India. Abdul Kalam did not work for ISRO at the time.

Historically, Tipu's rocket is very special because this was the world's first rocket to be used as a war weapon. Britain's General Congreve inspected the rocket later. Since the rocket could not rotate, it couldn't hit the target like an arrow correctly. Even then, it caused a lot of panic and minimal destruction to the enemies. The Britishers removed this deficiency from the rocket and used it wisely to attack the French in the European war. The details of this can be obtained from a small book written by Sir Bertrand Joddrell titled *Economics of Space Exploration*. I still have the book with me. It can also be googled (in those days, we did not have the Google facility).

I consulted the book while writing this episode. Other than that, all my poems serve as important diary entries.

When I started writing this book, I had asked a few important people who have worked closely with Kalam to write about him. "Avoid singing praises of Kalam. Rather, write about Kalam as a human being, the way he lived, worked and uplifted himself...please write as much as you can remember correctly. There are a lot of fictitious stories nowadays. Please do not write like those. You had the great opportunity to work along with him. So, write about that," I told them. Starting from 1982—when Kalam joined the DRDO—until 1989—when he successfully launched the 'Agni' missile—is an important episode of Kalam's life. Since I did not work with Kalam at the time, I had asked a few of his coworkers to write about Kalam and his work culture. After six months of continuous reminders, Dr. Prahlada sent me seven pages of his hand-written copy on Kalam. Prahlada's essay will be the next chapter in this book. It registers an important episode of Kalam's life. Dr. Prahlada joined the DRDO as a young scientist in 1984.

❑

Dr. Prahlada's Narrative on Kalam

Kalam at the DRDO:

Kalam worked for long hours... His was the corner room on the first floor. He woke up very late, because he always had to work late into the night.

He used to meet all senior officials of the metallurgy department. Sometimes, he visited retired senior personnels in their respective houses to get their suggestions.

His office doors were always open to everyone. It was open to young scientists, employees, union members, and sports athletes at all times; until 9 PM.

Kalam had great faith and expectation from the young scientists and happily entrusted them with responsibilities.

At the same time, he maintained cordial relations with all senior professionals. Not only did he allocate them suitable workplaces, but also asked them for suggestions wherever required. For example, he employed Shri M. V. S. Suryakantha Rao and Shri P. V. R. Naidu in areas where they were skilled. Kalam employed them to be *Directors of Human Resources*, *Directors of Structural Designing*, and *Advanced Construction Managers*, which made them happy. Kalam appointed younger employees as project managers. He visited and inspected places that were way below his position.

Kalam introduced the young faculties of the DRDO to important senior officials who visited the DRDO labs in Hyderabad.

Kalam employed mid-cadre scientists (D&E Grades) to prepare his speeches and research reports, especially myself (Dr. Prahlada)!

Kalam had a keen interest in constructing advanced tech hubs such as the RCI (*Research Centre Imarat*), ITR (*Integrated Test Range* in Kalam wing), and PTR (*Pokhran Test Range*).

Kalam promoted competent employees and was generous in allocating funds.

Kalam enjoyed composing poems in Tamil and English. He learnt to play the Veena from the Defence Laboratory's music professor.

During his work tenure, Kalam brought all of the Indian Prime Ministers and defence ministers to the DRDO. He was talented in showcasing the importance of his work worldwide.

Kalam always thought of humongous projects. However, he also gave importance to minor factors.

He always quoted Prof. Satish Dhawan, Dr. Brahm Prakash, and Dr. Gowariker.

He did all the coordination with IIT and IISc professors and educationists. He liked working along with them.

Likewise, Kalam maintained cordial relations with senior industrialists as well as small, micro and medium industrialists.

In Delhi, he visited everyone from the junior to senior officials without any hesitation in order to accomplish his projects successfully.

He was never overcome by failures or mistakes. Since he remained a bachelor, he also attracted women, especially those in the financial sector.

He gave importance to manufacturing *Agni, Prithvi* and small fighter aircrafts and increased their production, since he knew their significance and utility very well.

Kalam in ITR (*Integrated Test Range*):

During the first launch of the *Agni* missile, he stayed in Balasore for about a month. There were a lot of problems, delays and technical difficulties which pulled it back. Two or three times the launch had to be halted. In spite of all this, Kalam stayed in the missile integration site, and missile launch site to cheer up the employees, even until midnight at times. There was so much disturbing news being spread. The Hyderabad media mocked the project. Launching the '*Agni*' missile itself became an '*Agni Pareeksha*' (trial by fire). Even Amul advertisement mocked the delay in the launch of the *Agni* missile. Kalam became tired of all this. He therefore handed over the responsibility to remove the technical hassles to the employees, and left for Hyderabad for a few days. He met the missile scientists in Hyderabad and boosted their confidence. He once again returned to

Balasore and engaged himself in the missile project. Finally came the day that made the nation proud. The missile was successfully launched and hit the target.

Kalam and politicians:

Kalam strangely maintained stable relations with all politicians and government administrators. All defence ministers have come to the DRDL labs and the missile complex. At the time of launch of the *Agni* and *Prithvi* missiles, they visited the ITR.

When large government funds were allocated for the IGMDP project, the then Prime Minister Smt. Indira Gandhi was invited to visit the DRDO to announce this big scheme and to meet all concerned staff members. 350 crore rupees were allotted for the scheme. There were no big rooms or auditoriums inside the defence laboratory complex to conduct the meeting.

There was a huge godown to store raw materials. We adjusted the place and created a temporary auditorium. The Prime Minister visited the place in order to learn all about the five IGMDP projects. She then inspected the campus. During the private session, she expressed her sharp views on the project.

Kalam's lectures:

Kalam came to the missile complex in 1982. No one knew him to be a great orator back then. However, he received invitations from all over India to deliver S&T lectures. He employed a panel consisting of his fellow scientists like myself Dr. Prahlada, Dr. Kapoor, and Dr. Sivathanu Pillai to prepare these lectures. They worked tirelessly to prepare his speeches by gathering relevant data for his audio visual sessions. Kalam would be busy till 10PM. Only after that did he have the time to assemble and reorganise all the data collected by them, and prepare for his speech.

Kalam gathered all supporting data and used them to answer questions put forth during the discussion. He gathered information about those conducting the meeting. He would make sure that he had a good collar mike and speaker. He kept a copy of his lecture in his hand and corrected it while he was on stage. Somehow in the end, he would convey his message by employing beautiful sentences and suitable words. He never read directly from his script. He always conveyed his message like a distinguished orator. His lectures would be in print in the news media the next day.

Kalam's relations with the DRDO directors:

Since Kalam was the program director of the IGMDP he was in charge of administration and handling the funds. He therefore was treated with great respect. At the same time, since he treated the faculty members humanely, all DRDO directors adored Kalam. The fact, that more than 30 DRDO directors worked under him for the IGMDP project is noteworthy.

(End of Dr. Prahlada's narrative)

❑

Technology for People

This could be rightly called as the second phase of Kalam's career. Kalam had been busy with his SLV-3 and IGMDP so far. After our regular meetings in Delhi, his inclination to use technology for social welfare became apparent. As an Adviser in the *Department of S&T (DST)* and the executive director of TIFAC, my major assignments revolved around application-oriented technology. Since Dr. V. S. Arunachalam who was a major leader in Indian science and technology was also the Scientific Adviser to the defence minister and the secretary for the department of defence research, he became a member of the TIFAC organisation. He assisted a great deal on such matters. At that time, Rajiv Gandhi was the Prime Minister of India. When people in the mainstream were discussing eradicating poverty, restrictions, high taxes, and other extravagances, Rajiv Gandhi introduced the term 'technology' to them. He made it clear to them that technological advancement was the key to nation's development, social welfare and for eradicating poverty. He was bold in his statement. When the rest of the world was advancing fast in technology, he wanted to get rid of the false propaganda that was being made in India that "Computers were an enemy of the people and they destroy job opportunities." He wanted to abolish the restrictions imposed on electronics and computers at the time. He therefore appointed Sam Pitroda as the technology adviser and helped him to establish the C-DOT (*Centre for Development of Telematics*) so that telecommunication networks could be provided to the rural areas. It was because of Rajiv Gandhi's motivation that the TIFAC and many such organisations were established in India. Drinking water mission and oil seeds mission were some such groups. Rajiv Gandhi motivated such groups to show that technology is not only used in nuclear bombs, missiles and space missions, but can also be used for day-to-day applications in order to speed up economic growth. Therefore, all S&T companies, many big industries, and even the banking sector used 'technology' as their mantra.

Even as early as the 1960s, NASA advertised spinoffs from materials/ instruments that were used in space technology when they had decided to set foot on the moon. For example, they advertised how materials like 'Teflon' used in space technology are also used in non-stick kitchen plates. Politicians need to cite such examples. Otherwise, they won't get enough support from the people for a 100-crore-dollar space project.

Even without such lofty advertisements, the DARPANET which was an exclusive software created for the US security forces (in which members within the US security forces could share secret information with each other without others knowing about it), has become today the 'world wide web'. Many such examples could be cited. Therefore, it became the norm of the DRDO too to create such spinoff materials and to advertise about them. Kalam tried to create such useful materials while he was working at the DRDO. Arunachalam supported him with his ideas even though not all were successful. However, Kalam engaged in producing such application-oriented materials only after completing his '*Agni*' missile programme successfully.

'*Prithvi*' missile had been tested several times earlier. However, '*Agni*' was the most important one. It was successfully tested in August 1989. The news spread like wildfire within India. Kalam became '*The Missile Man of India*'.

I too had contributed to the '*Agni*' project in my own way. The launch of '*Agni*' was getting delayed, even after it had reached Balasore. There is a connection between me and Balasore. When we were inspecting suitable locations to launch the '*Agni*' missile, I had come with Professor Dhawan and Dr. Raja Ramanna as I was a member of the committee. The three of us have flown up and down in the Avro jet plane. After that, I have also gone in the car with ISRO's Jayamani. It was a good site to launch ISRO's *Polar* satellite; it was better than SHAR. Finally, ISRO gave up the Balasore site to security forces for testing missiles.

As soon as news of '*Agni*' missile's success reached me, I wrote a poem instantly. It was similar to the one on the SLV-3 victory. I faxed a copy to Kalam and Dr. Arunachalam as he too was fluent in Tamil. This was the second poem that I sent to Kalam as this has become an important episode in Kalam's life. Even at that time, no one wrote a poem on Kalam.

The title of the poem is '*The Ascent of Agni*'. I wrote it on August 3, 1989. It is the second poem in "Blossoms of the Heart" (an English translation of my Tamil poem collection 'நெஞ்சக மலர்கள்') after "*The Victory Song of S.L.V.*" song. In Kalam's 'Foreword' to the Tamil book 'நெஞ்சகமலர்கள்' (June 17, 1999), he wrote:

"Rajan is my friend. This is for me a largesse bestowed on me by God. For more than twenty years we served together in ISRO. Close in joy and still closer in sorrow. The name Rajan has made sorrow feel sorry. It is my good fortune that I have found a place in his poems. His poetic temperament drew us together. Valluvar's 'Kurals' were the fonts for our thoughts. Bharathi's 'Panchali' and 'Kuil Geetham' were melodies..."

"What do we see in the fourteen poems composed about me? We see that scientific achievements can be described in poetry and sung. In the poem 'Ascent of Agni' the lines.

'Agni is a symbol of technology
If Indians join and hold on to ideals
With a resolve that work is worship,
Workers are heroes ....
————————————
They, the creators of the new Bharath!'

are a wonderful expression of thoughts. A joyful song evoking pleasure."

Kalam wrote this in 1999, ten years after '*The Ascent of Agni*' song and nineteen years after '*The Victory of the SLV-3*' song. He appreciated others written in 1990, 1991 and 1996 as well. I am not discussing those in detail here. I had composed one song on Kalam's father on 6.10.92 to which he said, "Beautiful composition, sir! No one has written about my father. Your composition melted my heart; it was simply superb." He has written about that also in his foreword to "*Blossoms of the Heart*."

In 1980, he was 49 years old. Yet he lived and worked hard for the SLV-3 project. It was the first of his never-ending goals. Even after he won the Padma Bhushan award, he kept on working to make bigger vehicles. Later on, after the successful completion of '*Agni*' in 1989, he probably curbed down his self-imposed goals. He started to focus now on application-oriented technology skills. I joined TIFAC only in 1988. However, since my days in ISRO, I have worked on a lot of social welfare application projects. Even though I was not directly involved in making satellites and launch vehicles, since I worked as the Scientific Secretary, ISRO, I had participated in technical and university-exchange programmes.

Kalam, on the other hand, had to directly participate in the SLV-3 and the IGMDP projects. His interaction with university members was also related to these projects. He focussed on spinoff equipment of the missile programme. The famous '*Kalam-Raju*' stent was an outcome of this vision of Kalam.

My work in TIFAC was to prepare '*Technology Market Survey Reports*', and '*Technical forecasting reports*'. Other than that, TIFAC engaged in several sectors to work for these application-oriented projects. Various technology missions for sugar, fly ash, leather and advanced composites were established by TIFAC for the purpose.

I knew that Kalam was the best choice to lead the '*Composites*' mission group. Not only did he successfully manufacture 'Fibreglass' in the 1960s and 1970s while working in ISRO, he also made use of this fibreglass in SLV-3's motor cover panel and other spare parts. He even wanted to produce fishing boats using the fibreglass technology to aid fishermen among others while he worked at ISRO. However, he did not get the time to make one.

I therefore asked him to lead the 'Composites' mission study group in TIFAC. He happily agreed. He agreed to lead the team composed of members from industrial, institutional and national laboratories. Even though there are several experts in the team, it is mandatory to analyse different reports and other innovations and hand it over to them for execution. The committee not only prepared reports, but also evolved several small and big schemes. For example, the 'Indian Environmental Department' had imposed restrictions on cutting trees for making the wooden beds of railway tracks and the wooden berths.

For the beds of railway tracks (called sleepers), plastics reinforced with fibreglass could be used. Using composite technology, natural fibres (such as jute fibres and coir wastes) could be used in train beds and berths. Other than these, carbon composites could be used for strings of a violin. There are many such practical applications for such technology. It comes in different prices, and could be used in multiple ways by various sectors. A catalogue of the detailed list of such products is beyond the scope of this book.

What products have a good market value, how quickly can they be made, who all can be involved in making it, which factories can be used for manufacturing, will they make enough profit? Will it be sold at a reasonable price to the consumer? Such questions have to be answered by the task force members. Otherwise, after making one or two such items, it would remain stagnant in the labs of the engineer/technician. That is why, even when the Indian government invests crores of tax money in S&T institutions, IITs and IISc., not much growth is seen in consumer-oriented products. For technological growth and exchange of technology, consumer satisfaction in product price and large-scale production are the two key factors. Such products should be made available within two to three years of inception. In a way, these technical jobs are much more difficult than making rockets and satellites.

After 1990, Kalam was satisfied that he had accomplished two major projects in his life. He was 59 years old. He had the experience of having worked with people from small, medium and large industries while he was engaged in projects like *'Agni'*. Besides these, the TIFAC reports submitted by us on market analysis and forecasting were very helpful. Kalam encouraged the team members to contribute more and more.

As in ISRO, we appointed youngsters to lead each team independently. I introduced Sunita Wadhwa who was a scientist/engineer to the TIFAC team. She had completed M.Tech. in IIT, Delhi. She was an expert in polymer science. She was a bit nervous about Kalam since he had worked on massive projects and was very famous. I encouraged her to work independently without any reservations.

Her nervousness reduced in the first meeting itself. Sunita submitted several competent reports to the team. Finally, a meeting was arranged in DRDO, Hyderabad. As soon as it started, many people were asking the same old questions even after repeatedly answering them. This is the practice of several scientists and educationists! We have experienced the same while in ISRO too; Kalam might have experienced it even more while working for the IGMDP projects. Many industrialists and politicians also do the same thing. Our team members listened patiently to all queries, doubts and other exciting project drafts. We then discussed and debated over them. Some were approved while others were rejected. Only by doing like this, would it be possible to slowly reach our goal. In the administration and education sector, people simply waste their time in such meaningless discussions! The training we had received while working for ISRO and the disciplines instilled by mentors like Dr. Brahm Prakash and Professor Dhawan enabled us to avoid such endless arguments and plan suitable methods to reach our goal. But we cannot do this just like that. We should know when to end the discussion. This sense won't come by merely reading reports and addressing committee members. It is an art in itself; Kalam was an expert at this.

After letting the team members speak for over an hour, Kalam finally said: "All of you could work for two or three days. You can split yourselves into smaller groups and then integrate. Rooms are available; typewriters are also available. Enough members are there. Rajan and Sunita are there from TIFAC. Prepare a detailed list of projects within two to three days. You all already know the committee requirements for various projects as we have discussed those several times already."

He then laughed and said: "Without a detailed list from all of you here, I won't let you leave these rooms!"

Everyone laughed. Kalam visited various groups and sub-groups once every three to four hours to check the status. "What is happening here?" he asked smilingly. Because of his enthusiasm and encouragement, the list was prepared within the next two days. Everyone in the group wholeheartedly submitted the final report to Kalam. After getting their reports, final approval had to be obtained from the integration committee. After this episode, Kalam always referred to Sunita Wadhwa as 'The Composites Lady'.

Besides these, Kalam established projects to synthesise products involved in medicine at the DRDL. Compared to the IGMDP projects, these were relatively smaller. The IGMDP programmes were not completed in the 1990s. Independent project managers were appointed for all of those five major missile projects. Since Kalam has explained in detail about it in his "Wings of Fire", I am not elaborating them here.

Preparations were being made to test those five missiles for use by the Indian army, navy and the air force. In order to manufacture equipment, companies like Bharat Dynamics Limited were expedited. Even when I had nothing to discuss about those projects with Kalam, I had to contact him for TIFAC projects frequently. Kalam frequently visited Delhi in order to explain the missiles to the Indian armed forces and also to help Arunachalam.

❑

Modifications Made by Scientist, Arunachalam

In 1991, when Kalam was about to turn sixty, scientist, Dr. Arunachalam gave him a letter starting with the words "My dear Abdul Kalam" in his beautiful handwriting. The rest of the letter was typed. The important news conveyed by the letter: The Indian government had agreed to extend Kalam's retirement age by three more years, and so Kalam need not retire in October 1991 after he turned sixty. Kalam was delighted. This was possible only because of Dr. Arunachalam's efforts. Dr. Arunachalam was the head of the DRDO as well as the secretary of defence research. Usually, the tenure was extended upto one or two years only. Usually, all government staff retire at the age of 58. One had to be very brave to ask for an extension till 63 years. However, Dr. Arunachalam knew that Kalam had a good reputation. This happened when Narasimha Rao was the Indian Prime Minister. Also, Kalam was now in the highest cadre of the DRDO. He was now a Secretary level scientist for the Indian government and held the post of '*Distinguished Scientist*'. It was Dr. Arunachalam who got this position for Kalam after the successful launch of *Agni*.

Kalam's continuance in the highest cadre was a major milestone for him. I handed him back the letter after congratulating him over and over again.

The uncertainty after he turned sixty was now over. Other than his missile programmes, now he could also focus on application-oriented technology for the socio-economic welfare of the people. He had several ideas which could be made operational, now that he held the highest grade in Government office.

Both Kalam and I did not know at the time that this job extension would enable him to reach the highest step of the ladder one day. Probably, Dr. Arunachalam might have done this to get a favourable job done for him. I could make a wild guess about it only in 1992.

It was the end of 1991 or sometime during the beginning of 1992. Dr. P. Rama Rao, the *Secretary of the Department of Science and Technology*,(DST) called me to his room to discuss a matter. His room was right next to mine and I went there.

He handed me a report of four or five pages (it was written by Professor Mahajan from *Carnegie Mellon University*). "Rajan, you have to convert this report into a good UNDP (*United Nations Development Programme*) report. No one should know about this. This is to help Dr. Arunachalam!" The last statement was meant perhaps to boost me up since I had great regards for Dr. Arunachalam. Even though he engaged in political scheming, he knew better on matters related to S&T than most others. It was very important to adjust to the needs of S&T intellectuals and the Delhi politicians and administrators in those days. I am therefore not willing to give Dr. Arunachalam a negative ranking for indulging in 'positive' politics.

"Ok, Sir! When do you need it?" I asked. "Immediately," replied Dr. Rama Rao. I understood the reason for the urgency only later. Apparently, Dr. Rama Rao had submitted a copy of the report to India's UNDP representative before handing it to me. This was wrong as per government rules! Even though he held a major post, only after getting permission from the Indian government's *Department of Economic Affairs* (DEA), can he hold discussions with members of the UNDP. Contracts with the UNDP can be made only by the DEA.

He called me within a few minutes of returning back to my room and said, "I will send two members from UNDP to your room now. Please talk to them about the project report."

As soon as the two members entered my room, they started bursting out with several questions. "Why are there no clear details in the report? What is the relation between this scheme and the development of India?"

The most important questions put to me were: "Finance from the UNDP should go to India's development. Then, why has *Carnegie Mellon University* (CMU) sent the project report? UNDP's investments are meant only for India, isn't that right? Only after knowing about this clearly, we could discuss any further!"

What they asked was right. Had Rama Rao told me before, I could have written a formal report that was in line with UNDP's rules and regulations. We could have put pressure on the UNDP's representative as well. Rama Rao's sudden urgency could have been avoided. Dr. Arunachalam and the UNDP Representative were friends. I persuaded the two UNDP members in my room somehow. When I informed Rama Rao of their questions, he stared blankly at me. Finally he said: "You solve this problem somehow."

The next day, the DEA joint secretary spoke with me over the phone. We were friends. He was an IAS with cadre from the state of Kerala. We mostly conversed in Tamil with a bit of English here and there.

"Rajan! How is there a discrepancy when you are there in the Science department? After the secretary of S&T had sent the scheme report to the UNDP representative only, we got the report! You must give advice to your secretary!" he said.

"Varadachari, can you inform the secretary of S&T yourself? Only yesterday, I got to know of the report," I told him. How could I inform Varadachari that this was for Dr. Arunachalam?

I felt that it would be better if Rama Rao conveyed the news directly. I then went to Dr. Rama Rao and told him: "You have to talk to Varadachari. If he does not permit it, then we cannot send the Indian government's formal request to the representative of UNDP. What you did was a procedural mistake."

Varadachari met Rama Rao. Rama Rao talked to him about the importance of the issue. He then came to me and said: "Rajan! Rama Rao told me that this was for Dr. Arunachalam and that the matter should be kept as a secret."

"He told the same thing to me one day before I received your phone call!" I said.

"This *Carnegie University* matter is quite complicated. We have to send Dr. Arunachalam over there somehow. Use your management ingenuity," he told me.

Arunachalam and Rama Rao must have felt that the finance from UNDP could be used like bank reserves probably. Since there were enough reserves at the DRDO, they did not know about all these practical rules and regulations thoroughly.

The burden ended up over my head now. However, I felt happy about two things; helping Arunachalam was one. Since he was working for the DRDO for several years now, people at the defence services and the defence ministry started talking behind his back. They could work only for 3-4 years and then they had to retire. However, he was their senior and so they couldn't oppose him directly. Arunachalam participated enthusiastically in many of the projects of the DRDO. The most important were the missile programmes; next was the '*Light Combat Aircraft* (LCA)' and designing the 'Kaveri' engine for it. He also had to complete the '*Main Battle Tank* (MBT)' which was started several generations earlier. Even though Arunachalam got permission to complete all these programmes, the 'Scientific and Engineering teams' at the DRDO couldn't finish these within stipulated time. ISRO was gifted because of the systematic approach of Professor Dhawan, whereas the DRDO did not have any such supervision.. Furthermore, Professor Dhawan entered ISRO where most people were at a reasonably young age and so he was able to mould them according to his needs. Even the postgraduate employees of ISRO were several years younger than him when he led the organisation. DRDO, on the other hand, suffered from a lack of good management. Several DRDO projects, including those of Dr. Arunachalam were therefore lagging behind.

In conclusion, the DRDO projects were not completed within stipulated time. They were not able to keep up their promises. Lack of time sense and not heeding to requests made by security forces became the attributes of the DRDO. This greatly impacted Dr. Arunachalam's plans (Dr. Arunachalam was the Head of the *Department of Defence Research*).

The initial successes of the missiles were mere test drives. In order to become fully operational, they must be fitted into the vehicles of the armed forces and tested again. At this stage, people in the Delhi administrative circles heard rumours that the defence forces and defence ministry preferred to have a change of head. This pressure started building up from 1989 itself. Had Rajiv Gandhi won in the elections, Arunachalam could have tackled the situation easily. But now, V. P. Singh became the Prime Minister in 1990. It was said that Arunachalam wanted to go to *Carnegie Mellon University* and so he made arrangements for Kalam to take up his role in the DRDO temporarily for 2–3 years. V. P. Singh agreed initially; he agreed that Kalam could take up the role. Kalam's '*Agni*' victory in 1989 made his entry all the more attractive to V. P. Singh. When cabinet secretary Vinod Pandey (who was V. P. Singh's school friend) saw the file, he approached V. P. Singh and told him apparently: "Honourable Prime Minister! It is ok for you to appoint Kalam in place of Dr. Arunachalam; but, how can you let someone like Arunachalam who held a major post in the defence ministry leave for *Carnegie Mellon University* in the USA, that too on deputation!" After hearing this, V.P.Singh slightly changed his decision—Kalam could replace Dr. Arunachalm; but Dr. Arunachalam cannot leave for CMU. Instead, he can hold a major post in IIM, Ahmedabad. Dr. Arunachalm was disappointed with this decision because he decided to let go of his job only to leave for Carnegie Mellon University! That was why he handed over his job willingly to Kalam... He then approached the Indian President R. Venkataraman who was his big supporter and managed to 'bury' those files. This was the rumour heard in the Delhi circles. Only at the time of preparing the UNDP report for Arunachalam, I heard of all this. I had not seen the files but heard of it from trustworthy people.

Likewise, Arunachalam initiated the UNDP project proposal when Narasimha Rao was the Indian Prime Minister. He knew that Carnegie Mellon University would not fund his research. (This was the case with most US universities. They had a capitalistic mindset. *If you want to do it for yourself, then you must bring your own funds!* was their mentality). He therefore decided to fund them through this UNDP project proposal. Anyhow, I was happy to help Arunachalam. The second reason was even more important; In another two years time, Kalam could become the Indian government's secretary that too from a powerful sector like the

DRDO. He would also become the *Scientific Adviser for the Defence Minister*. This was the highest possible position he could occupy. (At that time, me and Kalam could only think of so much.)

I never mentioned this to Kalam. Neither Arunachalam nor Rama Rao informed Kalam that he would become the secretary for the Indian government. My job was to get permission for the UNDP project proposal—so that using those funds Arunachalam would be able to stay in Carnegie Mellon University for two years.

Rama Rao could have desired to replace Arunachalam. I did not know how Arunachalam convinced him. "Only two years! His extension is only till 1994! He would be 63 years old by then! Therefore in 1994, I will get you the job back," he must have said. The reason I am writing this is because when these incidents happened, I was in the middle of all the discussions (More on that later).

Even though neither Rama Rao nor Arunachalam disclosed anything, it became clear to me that Kalam would be replacing Arunachalam through the above-mentioned incidents. Since Kalam was next only to Arunachalam at the DRDO, it would be easy to appoint him as the next head. Besides, he was also the renowned '*missile man*'.

I never breathed a word of all these to Kalam even though I felt sure since I had promised Rama Rao that I would maintain absolute secrecy. (Just like how I had promised Dr. Rama Seshan earlier and approved of his suggestion for Kalam to be in the missiles programme).

I do not know whether Arunachalam disclosed this to Kalam. Even later, I never discussed this with Kalam. The most important question asked by the UNDP members was "Why should an Indian be sent to *Carnegie Mellon University* to do this project?" Normally, UNDP funds would be directly invested in India and at times, foreign experts were invited to India. To resolve this became my biggest challenge! I made use of a historic truth to resolve this. In 1991, India announced 'Economic Liberalisation'; so far, initiatives were undertaken only as per existing plans. In order to function well, it became necessary to study the world economic powers. During that time, neither the Indian S&T technologists nor the industrialists were familiar with the world market scenarios.

I argued therefore that in order to carefully study and understand the world market situation, people from S&T should directly get trained in places like the USA that were far more experienced on such matters. They could stay there for two years and visit various S&T institutions, educational institutions and other industries to get hands-on experience. They must regularly keep in touch with experts in places like Japan and South Korea from there itself. We must send someone who is not just an expert in S&T, but also skilled in handling products from multiple sectors; he must therefore be someone with many years of experience holding the highest ranks in the S & T department.

The reasons mentioned above highlight why someone like Dr. Arunachalam must stay for training in CMU.

We cannot expect him however to lead the team in India only by instructing them. He could therefore function as the *Main Project Scientist* (MPS) from there. We need someone here in India to direct the team members as per his advice. That person could become the project manager. Other than this, a separate team in India will conduct research work on current S&T market trends. We will then compare and review them to know what all changes have to be made.

I submitted my 30–40 pages report formatted as per the UNDP norms to Rama Rao. I had mentioned the total project cost in my report and that 70% of it would be transferred to Carnegie Mellon University in various stages of project completion. This was necessary for the project financial supervisors to know about the structure of the funds being disbursed.

As was expected by me, Rama Rao handed the report to Arunachalam. Arunachalam was not pleased to know that he will be functioning only as the '*Main Project Scientist* (MPS)' and that he must now work under Rama Rao who would be the complete project manager! Even Rama Rao opposed the idea at the time. I told him: "But sir, the project proposal would be rejected then! Do you remember the questions posed by the members of the UNDP a few days ago? They will agree only if we make the S&T secretary as the project manager. Furthermore, they will be satisfied only when finance sent from India to CMU is being used for India's own developments. They will be delighted to know that the UNDP funds will be used only for India. MPS will be like a subcontractor who receives a salary like a foreign consultant." I did not allow them to change any key points in my report. They wanted to replace the word '*Main Project Scientist*' with '*Dr. V. S. Arunachalam*'. I told them stubbornly: "It is impossible for the S & T department to write the name of someone like V. S. Arunachalam who is holding a sensitive post. In the project proposal, we can only mention as '*Main Project Scientist*'. After it gets proper approvals, the project management committee has the ultimate authority to decide the name of the MPS. You have to wait till then."

To cut a long story short, finally, Varadachari saw my report and got consent from the DEA. It was then sent to the UNDP for approval. Since the project proposal was in accordance with their norms and also because their representative wanted to help Dr. Arunachalam, the UNDP approved. Since Arunachalam wanted 50% funds to be disbursed immediately to CMU, I strongly emphasised that point in my project proposal report justifying his request.

It was then sent to CMU for approval.

"Rajan, can we now mention Arunachalam's name. He has already spoken with the Prime Minister and is sure to get his approval!"

"It is not enough, sir. Arunachalam is in a key post. Therefore, he has to send his request only through the cabinet secretary."

Earlier I mentioned the way in which Arunachalam got his approval from V. P. Singh. I knew that if it goes through the cabinet secretary, then it would be in accordance with government rules and regulations.

Rama Rao and Arunachalam were upset with me. Arunachalam complained to Rama Rao that I was a strict bureaucrat. Rama Rao felt that I was too adamant. He was angry with me for a few months.

Finally, when they got approval from the cabinet secretary, Rama Rao showed it to me. I told him: "Please lock it up safely and use the xerox copies for all other formalities." A big burden was removed from my head. I completed all other pending work related to CMU.

The most important incident. It was announced that Dr. Arunachalam would leave on probation for two years and that A. P. J. Abdul Kalam would now take over his role. In June 1992, Kalam reached the highest possible post for a scientist in a government office. It was bigger than his role in ISRO. He was now the Scientific advisor for the defence minister. Big role. His office was in the 'South Block', which was the administrative headquarters in Delhi. The *Prime Minister's Office (PMO)* is in the South Block. All defence chiefs and the ministry of foreign affairs are located there. In front of it is the North Block-inside where the Finance Ministry is located. If an office is located within the south block, it was regarded as a huge honour. People would say, "Oh! In the South Block!" Now, Kalam occupied Arunachalam's big room and office. Initially, the orders were for him to continue for two years till Arunachalam returns back from his probation. By then, Kalam too would have reached his retirement age and would have to retire.

Even though I felt excited, I did not write a separate poem to celebrate this. I wrote '*The Ascent of Agni*' on 3.8.89. On 23.3.90, in '*India's Missile Hero*', I wrote:

To compete with the mother who
Gave birth to you in this earth,
There are three women!
The biggest Mother Bharath;
Giver of a taste
Sweeter than honey, the Mother Tamil!
And the bestower of boons to all humankind
The Mother Technology!

After that I wrote '*Tamil Mother's Gift*' on 23.3.90. I wrote '*Abdul Kalam*' on 21, 22.3.1990, and '*Kalam is sixty*' and one more '*Abdul Kalam*' on 15.10.91. All these are in the "*Blossoms of the Heart*" poem collection.[2]

---

[2]*Notes: All English/Tamil poem collections of Dr. Y.S. Rajan can be found on his website www.ysrajan.com under the Google Link section.*

As he now held a key position, we had more opportunities to discuss progressive matters. "What can I accomplish in my new role?" was Kalam's question to me.

My TIFAC projects were going on smoothly. (When V. P. Singh was the Prime Minister, M. G. K. Menon was the S&T minister, and C. N. R. Rao was the chairman of the Scientific Advisory Committee to the PM SACto PM (1986–90).) When Rama Rao became the secretary for S&T in April 1990, doubts on TIFAC raised by these two big-wigs were also erased. He now realised that he could earn a good name by supporting TIFAC. He particularly helped with Dr. V. Krishnamoorthi's *Home Grown Technology* (HGT) project. Dr. V. Krishnamoorthi was the TIFAC Chairman at the time. Besides that, with the assistance of the joint secretaries of S&T, and Minister of State for S&T Rangarajan Kumaramangalam, TIFAC was focussing on other key technology missions (Sugar, fly ash, leather, and composites). I have already mentioned Kalam's participation in the creation of the composite technology mission. I am reiterating it here because Rama Rao's involvement with the TIFAC opened up a new chapter in Kalam's life. More about that later.

❑

Responsibilities and Failures in the Defence Ministry

In 1992, when Kalam took responsibility as the Secretary and Head of the *Department of Defence Research* and as the Defence Minister's Scientific Adviser, everyone trusted him. On account of his successful completion of the *Agni* missile programme in 1989 and also due to his successful launch of SLV-3 despite its first failure, he earned name and fame everywhere. His unique hair style and his name were added attractions. The Chiefs of the Defence Forces too must have felt this way. Even though Narasimha Rao, who was the Indian Prime Minister at that time, did not speak much in the public arena, he made a quick decision in replacing Arunachalam with Kalam. The media was compassionate towards Kalam. Since Kalam worked extremely hard and reached this position all by himself without lobbying with big-wigs, he was treated with respect in the Delhi circles.

Kalam must have realised his specialty too. Within a few days of joining the defence ministry, he called me one day and said: "Rajan, I will be going to Hyderabad. I will be staying in the RCI (*Research Centre Imarat*). You too must come; after completing reviews, we shall eat together. There is so much to discuss with you."

Since my work schedule was also not disturbed, I met him at the RCI, which was Kalam's favourite spot. In my *Blossoms of the Heart* poem anthology, he has mentioned RCI as 'nature's cradle'. When he was the Director, DRDL, while building the RCI, he initiated the planting of multi-coloured floral trees. As we were walking down the path after dinner, Kalam was pointing at them during the course of our discussion.

Kalam told me: "Sir, now that I have become the head of the department of defence research and the defence minister's scientific adviser, tell me what I should do to empower India?"

Even though our conversation began there, we would go around in circles discussing several unrelated topics in between. He would then point out to me, "Sir, where are you taking me? Let's discuss the central topic now."

I replied: "Sir, you were asking me many questions and I was merely replying to them." Then we would discuss our central issue.

However, on that day, we were focussed. A brief summary of what I told him: "Sir, it is true that the ministry of defence is a big department. However, they have not supplied any proper equipment to our armed forces so far. All important equipment is being imported. The statement made by the defence research scientists that 'people in the armed forces and the defence ministry patronise imports' is not wholly true. At the same time, the department of defence research has not made a single usable equipment for our armed forces. 'Use whatever we have made' has been their approach and this is not correct. You know that ISRO doesn't operate that way; ISRO never agrees to manufacture everything. They agree to make a product only if they are sure to hand it over within the given time.

Look at the history of the DRDO. Only after you joined, for the past 7-8 years, were they able to show some missile launches. Look at the status of '*Light Combat Aircraft* (LCA)' which started in 1983...what is the progress now? Where is MBT (*Main Battle Tank*)? It has been more than 25 years now. Poor Arunachalam! He employed all tactics to make all these. But nothing seems to have happened.

"Besides, there are more than 50 work centres within the DRDO... half the lifetime will go by running from one centre to another..."

During those days, Kalam used to talk a lot about core competence. I made use of this and said: "You think deeply about the core competences and possible goals of the DRDO. You have been working for the past ten years in DRDO."

We spoke about that for sometime. "Furthermore, you must plan to manufacture those equipment which would be very important in the future. The missiles are significant not only because you made them first, but also because it is like a shield which protects our nation...target precision and confidence are the key. For this, they must be tested at large and so, you must build a big production unit...you already know all this...but production needs speeding up...since the DRDO has been manufacturing the same old big and small equipment, things have slowed down."

"You know how Professor Dhawan introduced the Zero Base Budget (ZBB) plan in ISRO... you also know how he split it between SLV-3, research and development projects, and the rest for future R&D work. If you do not adopt a similar procedure at the DRDO, then none of the projects will bear fruit. Adopting the same old path will not benefit anyone in the long run!

"You could distribute other work to other departments, enclosing the financial allotment. The DRDO does not suffer from financial shortcomings... only there are administrative shortcomings. Is it really required for all those fifty work centres to be located within the DRDO? For example, consider the 'Defence Food Research Lab'. Now it is possible to buy those production equipment from various industries... it would be great if out of those 50, at least 10 work centres are relocated elsewhere. It could improve administrative efficiency!"

Will it be possible for him to do all this? This is a big question. In India, I know that there is always a big value associated with 'gigantic buildings'. Moreover, those technicians, engineers and scientists who are sent out could feel that they have fallen down from heaven! Media would have a field day! They could publish all sorts of things like "loss of precious manpower," "The DRDO has lost valuable technology," "Defence research and development is not all about missiles alone!" and so on. I know all this is likely to happen. However, it is up to you to change the current status of the DRDO. In order to focus on the future, the defence minister's scientific adviser should be able to make independent decisions!" In between our conversation, I repeated these words over and over again.

"Ok, Rajan! You have given me some good advice! What do you think of the LCA? It started in 1983. You were a part of the review team recently."

I said, "Yes, sir! I do have a strong opinion about it. For the past eight or nine years, there has been no progress. Besides, since several years have elapsed, is it still viable for use by the *Indian Air Force*? It is very difficult to arrive at a conclusion. Even though you are a space scientist, if you stop that LCA project now, rumours will be spread that you did so because you are the 'missile man'. You could do one thing though. Professor Dhawan has great regard for you. You might approach him and ask him to do an independent review of the LCA project similar to the way he did the 'Avro Review'. He could investigate along the following lines:

1. *Is the project still underway? Will it help the Indian Air Force?*
2. *If there are any marginal errors, can we rectify those ourselves?*
3. *Should we stop the project if it is no longer needed? How best can we make use of the LCA experience?*

"Tell him that you need his guidance within the next six months. He will initially object. But you know how to convince him."

"No one can object to his views (that too, in aeronautics). All government officers respect him. He could arrive at a conclusion after getting inputs from people working in the ministry, IAF and *Hindustan Aeronautics Limited*... At this rate, the LCA project is never going to get done... Probably, they might end up creating something flyable. But, I do not know if it could be used by our air force. If not, then there could be further complications!"

Even in 2016, LCA was not a part of the *Indian Air Force*. India is importing new fighter aircrafts from Russia and America!

"Good idea, let's see!" Kalam said.

After that day, we did not indulge in any other discussion related to the DRDO. Nothing that I said that day took shape. He must have felt that it was impossible. Moreover, he had to retire in two years. *Once Arunachalam returns in 1994, he will take over as the defence minister's scientific adviser, etc.*. Such thoughts could have probably crossed Kalam's mind. He must have felt that he should earn a good name within these two years before retiring and it would be unwise to indulge in anything serious for the time being.

I noticed that after the SLV-3 success, Kalam's intensity had reduced. After he joined the DRDO (1982), he got his job done by patting other people's shoulders. When he left for Hyderabad, he was 51 years old. Most people were of his age or his seniors. There were many youngsters like Dr. Prahlada Rama Rao (called Prahlada in DRDO) whose writeup has been given in an earlier chapter in this book. (Prahlada later became the director of the DRDL; he became the Vice-Chancellor of *Defence Institute of Advanced Technology* (DIAT) in Pune).

As Dr. Prahlada rightly pointed out in his writeup on Kalam:

"Kalam used to meet all senior officials of the metallurgy department. Sometimes, he visited retired senior personnels in their respective houses to get their suggestions. His office doors were always open to everyone. It was open to young scientists, employees, union members, and sports athletes at all times; until 9 PM."

"Kalam had great faith and expectation from the young scientists and happily entrusted them with responsibilities. At the same time, he maintained cordial relations with all senior professionals. Not only did he allocate them suitable workplaces, but also asked them for suggestions wherever required. For example, he employed Shri M. V. S. Suryakantha Rao and Shri P. V. R. Naidu in areas where they were skilled. Kalam employed them to be *Directors of Human Resources*, *Directors of Structural designing*, and *Advanced Construction Managers*, which made them happy."

This last section is very important. It was possible for Kalam to successfully launch *Agni* in 1989 since he maintained cordial relations with all his staff ever since he joined in 1982 at the DRDO.

It was difficult for Kalam to change this attitude in 1992 when he was already 61 years old. Moreover, Kalam was holding a sensitive and an extremely responsible job as the defence minister's scientific adviser, with headquarters in Delhi and centres all over India including the northeast. Had he shown his anger at anyone, it could have triggered some unwanted consequences.

Kalam must have felt that it would be enough at the current pace at the DRDO; youngsters who joined in 1982 in the IGMDP missiles programme could contribute to development and production of such missiles. Arunachalam had already given his approval to the IGMDP. Following the footsteps of Professor Dhawan in ISRO, Kalam established a similar framework at the DRDO since his presence for nearly ten years. These were put to practice and one or two missiles were launched during his tenure at the DRDO. So, he must have felt that all other projects could happen at their own pace without rushing them. He was correct in his approach. At that time, PM Narasimha Rao was running a minority government. He was trying to resolve the big financial crisis that had fallen over India (1990-91). He introduced 'economic liberalisation' silently without any opposition from other parties. Dr. Manmohan Singh took care of other technicalities. As A. N. Verma, the principal secretary to the Prime Minister, took care of all administrative activities, and the government was running smoothly.

Therefore, all that the Indian PM wanted at that time was for Kalam to run the DRDO without any issues. Besides, V. S. Arunachalam visited the DRDO once every 3-4 months in order to establish his supremacy; his travel expenses were borne by the DRDO. Nothing about his travel had been specified in the UNDP proposal. During his visits, he would contact all senior members of the DRDO. Kalam, being the DRDO secretary, had to grant him permission without objection. These were the work pressures Kalam faced during his tenure. In spite of everything, Kalam maintained his own work style, without unnecessarily blowing minor issues out of proportion.

In order to avoid such unnecessary internal conflicts and controversies, Kalam invited various centre directors (around 50 people) for weekly conference sessions. This was his method. They discussed every issue, big and small, and identified possible solutions. Many would become tired at the end of the session.

This was against good managerial practice because the directors would forego their responsibilities. Instead of taking decisions independently, they brought everything to the conference. Kalam told me about this method.

I said: "But sir, if you do this, everyone would become irresponsible. They would bring all their concerns to the conference table!"

Kalam replied: "Rajan, it is better that it happens once every week. Otherwise, I would be grounded every single day!" Neither did he stop any slow moving long term projects nor did he say 'no' to new ones.

Eighteen months went by like this. He earned a good name as the head of the DRDO and as the secretary for the department of defence research. Also, the DRDO gave financial assistance to various Indian universities, the IIT, and the IISc. Kalam increased this financial aid. Hence, they too supported Kalam. Many in their 40s and 50s who had trained under him, executed the IGMDP projects successfully.

In 1992, Narasimha Rao's government arrested many within the Congress and other opposing parties under corruption cases. Dr. V. Krishnamoorthi who was like a right hand to Sonia Gandhi and the executive trustee of the *Rajiv Gandhi Foundation* was also arrested and sent to the Tihar jail as per court orders. He was a member of the government's planning commission and took care of various industries at the policy level. He was the Chairman of TIFAC as well.

Dr. P. Rama Rao (Secretary of S&T) asked me, "What do we do now? Should we appoint a new Chairman?" to which I replied: "Only the PMO can decide about the Chairman of TIFAC, sir! Let them decide and come back to us. We have to wait till then. We cannot change the Chairman of TIFAC everyday!"

TIFAC was functioning the way it was. The Governing Council Meeting (which happened once in every 3-4 months) was chaired by the senior member Dr. P. K. Iyengar who was the secretary of the nuclear department at that time. (As provided in the rules). Since TIFAC had earned a good name and since I was regularly in touch with all staff members for nearly four years, the meeting happened peacefully.

Dr. V. Krishnamoorthi (VK) was out on bail. However, the court proceedings happened very slowly. I visited him once or twice at his place. On one such occasion, Dr. P. Rama Rao asked me:

"Can we ask the PMO to appoint Prof. Dhawan as the Chairman of TIFAC? Can you find out from him?"

I was still in touch with Professor Dhawan. I visited him personally at least 4-5 times every year and consulted him on many matters. However, given his age, I knew that he would not accept any new job offers. Moreover, he wouldn't want to enter into Delhi politics that was already under confusion.

"Sir, Professor Dhawan is a good choice. But you must ask him yourself. You must visit him 2–3 times personally," I said.

After a few moments, he once again asked, "How about Dr. Abdul Kalam? He already knows about TIFAC. He is also a member here now!"

I was very happy to hear this. Without letting out my emotions, I replied: "That is great! Please ask him!" So, Kalam became the C*hairman of TIFAC* in September 1993. This was a part-time job. We both could therefore focus more on bigger opportunities for India. The government had already given its approval to three of TIFAC's missions (Sugar technology, Advanced Composites and Fly AshUtilisation). Other than these, HGT started by V. K. became fully functional. Also, TIFAC's project reports were readily accepted and purchased by Indian factories and institutes. Kalam knew all these because he was already a member of TIFAC.

After Kalam became the Chairman of TIFAC, he posed a question to all the Council members after completion of the scheduled agenda during his first meeting as Chairman:

"So far TIFAC has planned and executed several short term and medium term projects. There is no doubt that all these would be executed successfully. My question now to you all is whether we can do some long term projects that could help in India's overall development. How long can India remain a developing nation? When will we become a developed nation?"

There was a good discussion after that. It was decided that TIFAC should prepare a 25-year visionary long term projections for India by including all major sectors and competent technologies. They wanted to complete the project reports within six months. I knew that even to decide what all sectors have to be included will take upto six months. I requested the TIFAC members: "We are thankful that you have placed your trust in TIFAC and handed out a major initiative. We won't be able to complete this within a few months. It could take at least a year or a year and a half. We will try to speed up the process. Under the leadership of the secretary of S&T, we shall invite experts from laboratories, and industries for a discussion. We shall decide what all sectors need to be chosen, what are the 'terms of reference' and who should be the Chair/co-Chair of these sectoral committees. We must first prepare time schedules too. We will update the Council members of TIFAC regularly regarding our scale of development, our ideas and our estimates. Only then, can TIFAC give us proper goals to accomplish..." Everyone agreed to my idea. After the meeting, Kalam, Rama Rao, and I discussed a few sectors. I had the job of compiling everything together.

I would update Kalam regularly about TIFAC reports. We realised that it would be possible to submit the final report only by the end of 1995. We therefore kept our deadline as 1995+25=2020. Earlier Kalam was popularly known as the 'missile man'. Now he has become renowned for his *'India Vision 2020'*. This was possible only because of the plans we made that day. Neither Kalam nor I knew that it would gain so much popularity.

While the DRDO and TIFAC were functioning smoothly, trouble came from elsewhere. Initially, Arunachalam got a job extension for Kalam for three years starting from 1991. Then, Kalam replaced Arunachalam while he was on deputation in 1992 as the head of the DRDO. After that time, Arunachalam had to come back and work for DRDO as its head. Arunachalam would not have reached 60 in June 1994, whereas Kalam could continue only till October

1994; Kalam would be 63 years. Back then, government staff could work till 58! (exceptions were the nuclear, space departments and DRDO). Oh, is he 63 would be the surprise that was shown those days.

All these thoughts might have crossed Arunachalam's friend Rama Rao's mind. Rama Rao was about to turn 58 in July 1995. His job as the Secretary of S&T would become a big question mark. The same thing happened to Gowariker as well. Even though he was meant to retire at 60 in ISRO, he retired at the age of 58 itself because of DST! Rama Rao replaced him. Now, would Rama Rao too meet with a similar fate? Only the head of the DRDO was allowed to work till 60.

Therefore, Arunachalam pressured Kalam to retire early. "Kalam! You must retire in October 1994 as per your original orders. However, since you have to step out as the Secretary in June 1994 itself, you should submit your voluntary retirement then. The Secretary of S&T Rama Rao is also an employee of the DRDO. Therefore, while you resign, please inform the Prime Minister that Rama Rao should be appointed as the new head of the DRDO."

He further asked Kalam to tell the PM: "I am already 63 years old, whereas Rama Rao is only 57. Since he is younger to me, it would be better if he becomes the DRDO head." I do not know for how long Kalam was pressured this way.

One night, Kalam called me over the phone. (During those days, there were no cell phones. We only had the black phone supplied by the telephone department). I stayed in a government colony in Kidwai Nagar. He was in DRDO guest house (Asian Games Village). Both were located nearby. Even though he knew that I normally sleep around 9.30–10.00 PM, he asked me to come to his place.

"Rajan, good that you are not outside Delhi. I need to consult you on something urgently. Please come to my guest house. I will send a car," Kalam said.

I had to travel a lot in those days. Most of them were within India. Even though we conversed a lot over the phone, he hardly invited me to his office or house. He knew that I had a lot of work pressure in TIFAC and also my sleeping routine. Sensing urgency, I immediately wore my shirt and trousers and got into the car to go to his guest house.

He handed out a single sheet of typed paper. "Tomorrow, Arunachalam, Rama Rao, and I will be going to meet our Prime Minister. Arunachalam has asked me to sign this sheet of paper and hand it over to the Prime Minister. Please see this..." Kalam said to me.

I read it carefully and then asked, "What happened, sir?"

He said: "Arunachalam might not return from the US, and so he wants me to resign and hand over the job to Rama Rao!"

"Who arranged for the meeting with the PM? Did you?" I asked.

"No, he did. But he wants me to sign this paper addressed to the PM before starting my conversation. He wants me to say that I have become old and he has asked me to appreciate Rama Rao in front of the PM. I am being pressured. What do you say?"

"If Arunachalam is not returning to India in June 1994, then it is good news since you could continue!" I said.

"But my extension ends in October 1994. What do I do after that?" he asked. Having trained under T. N. Seshan starting from 1974, and several other IAS officers after him, I had become an expert in these administrative matters.

"Sir, I don't think that the Prime Minister would be bothered with replacing you. He won't interfere with your job as the head of the DRDO. These are all small matters to him. Moreover, he seems to be happy with the way you have performed in the DRDO. There have been no complaints from the head of the defence forces or the defence secretary about your performance there...besides, you are the missile man!

"In case Arunachalam had plans of returning, then the PM should take a decision. Now that he does not want to be back, you can easily continue your role!" I said.

Something else crossed my mind, which I did not tell Kalam. Many people within the Congress condemned the Ayodhya issue of 1992 citing the religion of Narasimha Rao to be one of the reasons. Now, how can he take an opposing stand on Kalam? Moreover, the Parliamentary elections were about to happen a year later, in 1995!

"Sir, you don't do anything. Do not sign the piece of paper. Don't even keep it in your hand at the time of meeting the PM. If you want, you could keep it inside the coat pocket of your favourite blue-coloured coat. Arunachalam would ask you to start the conversation. Since you did not arrange for the meeting, you simply keep quiet and sit still!" I advised Kalam.

I continued. "He will be forced to start the conversation next. You merely watch the proceedings..."

"Before meeting the PM, Arunachalam will give you enough training. Do not fall into his trap..."

It was past midnight. I came back to my house. Kalam called me the next evening: "What sir! How did you read the PM's mind beforehand! They wanted me to start the conversation! Arunachalam was furious; Rama Rao felt deceived, and scared too."

Later on, when I visited him personally, he told me everything that had transpired there. All three of them (Kalam, Arunachalam, and Rama Rao) sat in front of the PM. The Prime Minister started the conversation: "What is the matter, Mr. Arunachalam?... Why did you want to meet me?... please tell me..."

Without replying, Arunachalam pressed Kalam's hand and said "Tell him, sir!" A few minutes went this way.

PM Narasimha Rao: "What is the matter, Arunachalam? Please tell me."

Arunachalam slowly started to say: "Sir! Kalam and I were having a discussion. Since his tenure is about to get over, he wanted to resign and hand over the responsibility to Rama Rao..."

The PM did not allow him to continue. He asked, "Arunachalam, are you coming back?"

Hesitantly, Arunachalam replied: "Sir, there is some more unfinished work left at *Carnegie Mellon University*..."

PM: "Ok, alright! So, you have no plans to come back here. Sitting across the other side of the Atlantic, you have come here to give me suggestions, haven't you?"

Rama Rao was shell-shocked! He was afraid that the PM might think that he only instigated Arunachalam to speak this way.

The PM continued: "Kalam, you are younger and more energetic than I am. You continue your job! Please come and meet me later!"

Kalam said: "The meeting ended, sir...the PM asked us to leave. Both of them were very angry with me. They did not speak a word after that!"

"Hearty Congratulations, sir! We will discuss what to do after October 1994. You should get an extension beyond that!" I told Kalam.

Some news reporters in Delhi reported that Arunachalam and Rama Rao were trying to remove Kalam from his job. They wrote several things about Arunachalam. "Somehow, the *Department of Science and Technology of the government of India (DST)* managed to erase its footprints wisely" they reported. Similar to the ones in 1992-93, a few questions were raised in the Parliament. Rama Rao, who did not talk to me for several months because of Arunachalam's UNDP issue, told the joint Secretary of S&T, S. B. Krishnan while I was there: "I was upset with Rajan while discussing the UNDP issue. Arunachalam kept pointing out to me that Rajan functioned with a bureaucratic mentality while he wanted to keep it simple. Thankfully, because of Rajan, the DST and I escaped the *Parliamentary Committee Inquiry*."

In the same manner, this time too, there was no mistake on the part of the DST. But questions were being raised about Rama Rao trying to replace Kalam from his job.

"Everyone is thinking and saying that I want to replace Kalam. But, I swear in my mother's name that I had no intentions of heading the DRDO," Rama Rao told me.

He probably thought that I knew nothing about the meeting with the PM. I showed no emotions when he said this to me. Later, when I told Kalam about this, he laughed.

Whatever be the case, owing to that meeting with the PM, Kalam was able to continue with his job. But none of us ever imagined that he would reach greater heights one day!

Kalam might have waited for his job to stabilise. None of his missile programmes could be completed without him. The Indian government did not speak a word about it. They even mentioned '*Agni*' as a test missile only because many spare equipment and instruments had to be imported for the missile. This was because the *Missile Technology Control Regime* (MTCR) nations prohibited selling of some of these equipment to India.. After the *Agni* missile's successful launch, when a few media personnel guessed the situation and asked him, Kalam replied: "The *Agni* missile is not meant for sending flowers." Nuclear bomb must be installed inside the *Agni* missile. Smt. Indira Gandhi had described in her 1974 speech that an atomic bomb was exploded for peaceful applications (*Peaceful Nuclear Explosion*). Only after the atom bomb was inserted in the *Agni* missile and tested will the missile programme get completed. Therefore, the *Agni* missile programme was still incomplete as far as Kalam was concerned. We never spoke about this either personally or over the phone.

Kalam sought PM Narasimha Rao's permission to complete this *Agni* missile mission. After Kalam got his approval from the PM, Kalam started planning it with the nuclear department. Since elections were announced in 1995, the PM spoke with Kalam from Tirupati and said: "Kalam! Do not do anything now! Let us decide after the election." Only after Vajpayee became the Prime Minister, Kalam was able to complete the project entirely. Therefore, Kalam was carrying the burden of this enormous task in his mind. He could not talk about this to anyone either. (He did not tell me about this then. He told me much later.) He was waiting for someone to say, "Please continue the task!" After Congress under Narasimha Rao was defeated, Kalam could have sought permission from the two next prime ministers. However, even their position was not stable.

I was very busy with TIFAC operations. Moreover, *India Vision 2020* added on to my work pressure. Kalam attended all the Governing council meetings well. It happened once every 3-4 months (which was a rarity in Delhi). Kalam also encouraged the Vision 2020 meetings. Agricultural scientist, (Late) S. K. Sinha chairman agriculture and food task force and industrialist Smt. Lila Poonawalla of agrofood processing task force became close friends of Kalam. The names of the chairpersons of various sectoral task forces can be found in the India 2020 book. Kalam's participation in all the task force committee and subcommittee meetings boosted their confidence. He was not a '*Bharat Ratna*' at the time. He was the *head of the DRDO*, *defence minister's scientific adviser* as well as *the Chairman of TIFAC Governing Council* at the time. However, I noticed he had a personal charisma that strongly attracted others towards him.

Professor V. S. Ramamurthy, who was appointed as the secretary of S&T after Rama Rao, told me once, "Rajan! Kalam is the Amitabh Bachchan of Indian Science." Some of the big wigs in India's science departments and the later S&T minister Dr. Murli Manohar Joshi were jealous of Kalam's leadership skills. I will narrate some of those incidents later! (Between 2000 and 2002, Kalam's life was an admixture of joy and misery, with fame on one side and jealousy of such people on the other!)

I gave a piece of advice to Kalam in September 1994: "Sir, your three-year job extension is about to be completed this October. Also, you must secure your job as the defence minister's scientific adviser. You can't wait for the defence ministry to do this for you. Before someone else comes with a file, you submit yours to the Prime Minister!"

Earlier, when Chandrasekhar was the Prime Minister, he had promised Dr. Gowariker that he would continue his job. However, the S&T big wigs organised a selection committee for the post of S&T secretary and Gowariker had to be replaced! Kalam knew about this. As I did not want Kalam to undergo the same thing, I advised him so.

We were sure that Kalam would continue until Narasimha Rao was the Prime Minister. 'Continue until further orders.' This was the instruction for Kalam. Even though it could be precarious to his position, we knew that since Kalam's name and fame had spread far and wide, no one could discharge him of his duties. Since in the file the word 'continue' was mentioned rather than 'one or two years extension', all later Prime Ministers also allowed Kalam to continue as the head of the DRDO. It continued when Deve Gowda became the Indian PM in 1996, later when I. K. Gujral was the PM and even later when Vajpayee became the Indian Prime Minister, Kalam received the same orders: "Continue until further orders!"

❑

My Voluntary Retirement

TIFAC was functioning successfully. Meanwhile, Rama Rao was about to retire. He was close to 58 in June 1995. However, since he worked at the DRDO, his age of retirement was 60 years. Probably, he might be allowed to continue just like Kalam. Shri Rangarajan Kumaramangalam who performed effectively as the S&T Deputy Minister under Prime Minister, Narasimha Rao resigned in 1993. He forgot to turn off his microphone while making a casual remark about the Prime Minister, and so he resigned on his own. Personally, it was a big setback to me; just like the sudden deaths of former Indian Prime ministers, Smt. Indira Gandhi and Shri Rajiv Gandhi. They knew me well and respected me. Like them, Shri Rangarajan Kumaramangalam, who was younger than me, also respected me. He was a good friend of mine. After he left, PM Narasimha Rao appointed Shri Bhuvanesh Chaturvedi as the minister of state for S&T departments as well. When Rangarajan was the minister, Kalam was the defence minister's scientific adviser and he became the chairman of TIFAC (September 93). Rangarajan left in November 93.

All other operations within TIFAC were happening smoothly. Rama Rao's situation was still uncertain. Instead of shifting him to DRDO, he might have been asked to continue with DST. Or else after sending him to DRDO, I could have been made as the DST secretary; I have been the additional secretary level for seven years and had contributed to many achievements at the ISRO and TIFAC. Besides, as per government files my age was only 53 years.

I had mentioned this to Kalam once or twice. I told him, "Can you recommend my name for the job of Secretary DST to the Prime Minister? Or else, can you talk to the PM's Secretary or the Cabinet Secretary?" I don't think he did anything about it. Rama Rao was sent to the DRDO in July, 1995. Till he turned 60, Kalam would be heading the department!

All my work and seniority had gone to waste! I decided to resign from my government and S&T jobs in July1995 itself. Later, Kalam told me: "I had asked Rama Rao to help you." There is no point to that since Rama Rao was already approaching several people for his DST job continuation. How will he ask them to appoint me who was next in line to the post?

Kalam was always scared of the big shots of the DST. 'Kalam is no scientist as he has not written any research papers' is what they said behind Kalam's back! Kalam knew about this. He was scared that they might join together and destroy his reputation. He, therefore, was reluctant to help me. I have helped both Kalam and Rama Rao in many ways. In September 1995, I wrote in my letter addressed to both of them separately: "This Karna's biggest mistake was asking you to help me; kindly excuse my mistake."

I was delaying my voluntary retirement because the work on *Vision 2020* by the task forces was at its peak. It could take another 6-7 months for proper reports to be formulated. Besides, I had several responsibilities in the DST such as formulating the five-year plan, Pay Commision S&T personnel related subcommittee chairman and so on. I was working speedily and efficiently. Neither Kalam nor the newly appointed V. S. Ramamurthy would have anticipated my voluntary retirement. Besides, to improve the work life of all TIFAC employees, I had introduced a promotion policy after a lot of work to get government approvals.

Kalam participated in many of the *Vision 2020* conferences; V. S. Ramamurthy also attended a few of them. Two or three times, the summary of different reports were submitted by the respective task force Chair persons. Everyone, including Kalam, was very happy. Other projects that were in the pipe- line in TIFAC as well as technology mission projects which promoted indigenous technology capabilities and technical skills were in full swing. We were sending reports about all these projects also to the TIFAC Council members. Therefore, Kalam's wish that besides rockets and missiles, India should prosper through development of small and medium enterprises (SME) , modernised agricultural techniques and other social-welfare schemes were also getting fulfilled due to TIFAC initiatives. Kalam had established one or two small initiatives in DRDO. He asked me about their performance. However, those heading them were involved in crucial DRDO activities and so were not able to focus fully on these small industries.

DRDO was functioning as before. Kalam visited all their laboratories. He also visited the launch location in Orissa (Near Balasore) to get it prepared for the important missile launch.

Even on Saturdays and Sundays, Kalam worked tirelessly. Family people sometimes found it difficult to adjust to his routine. However, Kalam's smile and his leadership skills helped them overcome all difficulties. His work routine in SLV-3, IGMDP, DRDL (recollect Dr. Prahlada's essay), and in Delhi were almost similar. Only after he became the Indian President, he was compelled to make a few adjustments while he lived in the big Presidential house instead of a small guest house. More on that later.

Rama Rao, who was the S&T secretary was now transferred to the DRDO as a distinguished scientist. Even though his pay was good, he had no major powers. Besides, he cannot function as the laboratory director. Kalam arranged a 1,000-crore-rupee self-reliant scheme for him so that he can function independently. He had the freedom to invest it in projects that he felt worthy. However, he needed to recruit team members from various labs. In a country like India, employees respected only senior officials in power. So, Rama Rao couldn't perform greatly in his new role. Kalam couldn't have bothered much either. Rama Rao couldn't have focussed fully on the project. Through his contacts, he approached the secretary of the atomic energy department, Dr. R. Chidambaram and after completing his two years at the DRDO, he became the chairman of Atomic Energy Regulatory Board under department of atomic energy.

Arunachalam stayed in the USA and tried to bring several new projects to India. He had several good contacts in India with persons in powerful positions.

A major turning point happened in my life. Some twenty-five reports were being prepared by 17 task forces under TIFAC Vision 2020. After approval from all concerned task forces, it got its approval from the Governing Council members as well. All these reports were ready to be released in the Governing Council meeting.

The TIFAC Governing Council meeting was arranged on April 17, 1996. (I completed my 52 years on that day. As per the official files, my birthday was on April 10, 1943). Kalam was not in the habit of remembering birthdays of others.

I submitted my letter of resignation to the DST on 16th April itself. I requested Dr Ramamurthy's principal private secretary not to give it to Dr. V. S. Ramamurthy till the TIFAC Governing Council meeting was over on 17th. I never informed Kalam on this matter. It was a decision taken in consultation with my family members.

Everyone assembled to the meeting before time on April 17th. I happily conversed with everyone. Kalam, as usual, came late to the meeting. All were delighted to see him. Releasing Vision 2020 projects were a part of the programme schedule. It was not just a formality. Chairpersons and Co-Chairs of all the task forces had gathered there. After a few minutes of briefing by each of them, the Governing Council approved Vision 2020 projects wholeheartedly as they had been briefed about elaborate in earlier meetings. It was then decided that a higher authority, preferably the Prime Minister should officially release it.

These cannot rest simply as reports. They have to be implemented in order to become fully functional. TIFAC had to assist with this. All the existing and planned government schemes should be dovetailed to the recommendations of the TIFAC Vision 2020 reports. This is a major job. The Indian government must use all its force fully to incorporate the TIFAC projects for Vision 2020. Most importantly, the Indian government has to ensure that the members of all other government departments must fully cooperate with TIFAC. The Council members desired these and spoke about these. Their intentions were sincere. Their request had to be acknowledged. However, this cannot be done by merely giving scientific and technical explanations as it required steering of the huge government machinery and to make it move forward. In order to run the programme effectively, all government departments must be suitably interlinked. 'Government rules' for various departments are very strictly laid out and are like fortresses. That is why, even to get a government job done, it is very difficult to get permission from four or five departments in a row. TIFAC 2020 needed participation from not only the government employees, but also from private sectors, public sector factories, agro-sector among others.

TIFAC had no control over this. However, the department secretaries can approach the government departments. I was able to get approval for various TIFAC projects from the government so far, as I served as the Adviser DST at a high position (Indian government) and used my personal experience in handling government work. To get approval for each and every single project proposal and project was a cumbersome task.

Kalam did not know all this as he was in a secretary post. Besides TIFAC, the DST secretary also had to stay in touch with other scientific organisations and S&T bigwigs.

I was therefore not willing to continue my arduous journey in TIFAC in spite of having prepared an extensive Vision 2020 project report (totally 25 reports each covering 300 A4 size pages). I did not want to hang on to them and do bodily circumambulation (angapradakshinam) to get approvals for each project, at that stage in my life. Neither the secretary DST (Ramamurthy) nor Chairman TIFAC (Kalam) did anything to empower TIFAC and me with the government powers to deal effectively with other government departments. It was because of this that I decided to quit DST and TIFAC and had already submitted my resignation.

On that day, the TIFAC meeting went well. I spoke cheerfully with everyone (that is my nature). After having his lunch, Kalam went back to his office.

I too went back to my desk in the DST. At around 4PM, the department secretary Ramamurthy called me to his room.

"What is this sudden bomb, sir?" he asked me.

"What is it sir?" I asked him.

"What do you mean? I am talking about your voluntary retirement. Now only, we finished the Vision 2020 council meeting. Do you know how much more work is pending?" he said to me.

"............"

He kept on speaking. But I did not speak a single word.

"What happened suddenly? Have you written this out of some emotion? Tell me what is the matter?" he asked. (Myself, Kalam and Ramamurthy usually spoke in Tamil with each other)

I replied patiently: "Sir, everyone knows about me from my days in PRL that I never take decisions emotionally. If you recall all incidents ever since I joined the DST, you will understand the reason for my resignation!"

He realised that I was not going to take back my letter of resignation.

"Did you inform Kalam about your decision?" he asked me.

"Sir, my appointment is only as Adviser DST; I have been given additional responsibilities of TIFAC. I don't get paid by TIFAC; in order to resign from my government job, I only need your permission. There is no link to TIFAC whatsoever. Therefore, I have not informed Kalam about this," I replied.

"Whatever be the case, I can take a final call only after consulting with Kalam," he said.

"Of course, you can do that. If you are going to speak with him, then I won't inform him now. Once you have consulted him, do let me know. I will then talk to him," I said.

Kalam spoke that night with me. But he never mentioned my resignation. He spoke cheerfully about the TIFAC meeting, Vision 2020 and so on. I understood that Ramamurthy had not yet conveyed the matter to him. A week went by. Kalam spoke with me every day, however, he never mentioned my resignation. I told Ramamurthy: "Sir, you said that you would inform Kalam about my resignation. Since that is the proper procedure, I have been maintaining silence. Kalam is regularly in touch with me. I am finding it very difficult to hide the matter from him."

Ramamurthy said, "Actually, I wanted to visit him personally and inform him. I feel that talking over the phone will not be a good idea." I replied: "Ok, then. Please inform him at the earliest and take suitable action over my letter of resignation."

Ramamurthy spoke with me a day or two later: "Myself and Kalam are planning to have lunch at the *India International Centre* (IIC). He asked you to join us!"

Kalam loved the food in IIC and Lodhi hotel. Lodhi hotel's 'tamarind rice' is one of his favourite dishes.

Soup was served before lunch. Kalam and Ramamurthy were seated on one side while I sat across.

Kalam started the conversation: "Rajan, why did you do this!"

"Sir, you know me very well. You will understand why I did this..."

Ramamurthy said: "Please let us know your request. We will try our best to fulfil it..."

It continued like this. I did not reply to many of their questions.

Kalam said: "Rajan, can we make you as the TIFAC's Director General? Now you are the executive director!"

I replied: "What is the point of changing the job title when I have no government powers?" Kalam could have advised Ramamurthy earlier to make me as Indian government's special secretary. I have told this to Kalam when Rama Rao was there itself. I was getting frustrated.

As I had written to him earlier, this Karna made the mistake of asking a favour once, and he is no longer ready to ask for more favours!

Our conversation continued in this manner. They were trying to persuade me to take back my resignation. I said: "When I worked for ISRO, if I requested one thing, I got things ten times more! It helped me to do more work. In such a huge organisation, I had such a position and powers!

"I knew that DST would not be similar to that. However, I willingly accepted the challenges posed by TIFAC. If I worked hard for five items, only one could fructify; that was the situation for TIFAC! Now, eight years after I joined here, only one out of ten are getting done!

"You have to think about this sincerely. As far as I am concerned I have to leave the organisation now!"

We spoke on other unrelated matters in between our lunch. "Rajan, have you looked up a suitable place to work?" Kalam asked me. He was probably worried about my family. "Not yet! I have to look for one soon. I was held up with the Vision 2020 project," I replied. Amidst all this, after two days of the TIFAC Governing Council meeting, that is, on 19-4-96, I sent a poem to Kalam titled 'பொறியியல் தொலைநோக்கு' (*Futuristic Vision of Technology*). Kalam's life and India 2020 are intertwined in the poem. I wrote it in order to realise the dreams of many people who worked in the India 2020 project. He appreciated my poem!...I have attached it here as I feel it would be relevant.

He must have wondered how I could have possibly sent my resignation letter three days prior to writing the poem.

Futuristic Vision of Technology
Dreamt he when he was twelve
Looking at a picture of a fighter plane
That he'll also build one like that!
When he joined work

Rockets and missiles
Entwined his life
In a thirty year vision.
Offered he to the country
Satellite launchers and missiles
That frighten the foes;
Distant dreams all blossomed into reality!
Now did he something greater
Offered he a futuristic vision of technology
To make country prosper
And to raise the quality of the life of people
very high
To make India· grow great by 2020
He got together many persons
Who researched many papers,
To analyse which technologies
Are to be grown;
A nectar like long term vision
Was given
With the mix of knowledge and dreams
Of five thousand people!
When sixty four will he
In a renewed youth
Realize this great dream
Did you see Rameswaram
Lifting in pride
For giving the beacon of the future?

19-4-1996

Blossoms of the heart

I wrote பிறந்தநாள் பாட்டுக்கள் (*birthday songs*) on 17-4-96 (*my birthday*). In the '*Blossoms of the Heart*' Tamil version (நெஞ்சக மலர்கள்) it appears on page 94. The song is a projection of my 'Existential reality'. I also wrote புதுச்சீதை (*New Sita*) on 17-4-96 (நெஞ்சக மலர்கள், page 95). I wrote a poem on '*Culture*' (page 29). During those days, debates over revealing female body parts were a topic of discussion in the media, as a topic of civilisational culture.

Finally, Ramamurthy started taking action over my letter of resignation. The announcement of elections made it even more difficult. I am not describing all that here. Only after, Congress under Narasimha Rao lost and Deve Gowda became the Prime Minister, was my resignation accepted. I was willing to resign from the government Adviser, DST as well as Executive Director, TIFAC even though the resignation letter was meant only for my job as Adviser DST which needed government approval.

I wrote a letter to all TIFAC Governing Council members and others who had contributed to the TIFAC/DST in my works. I received heart-melting replies from them. Kalam too sent a beautiful reply. Everyone should read it; it is a depiction of his good character.

SCIENTIFIC ADVISER TO DEFENCE MINISTER
AND
SECRETARY
DEPTT OF DEFENCE RESEARCH AND DEVELOPMENT
MINISTRY OF DEFENCE
SOUTH BLOCK
NEW DELHI-110 011

19th July,1996

My Dear Rajan,

It is my great fortune that I got the opportunity to work with you in TIFAC and evolve the Technology Vision document with industrial and academic partnerships apart from the many achievements of yours as the TIFAC Executive Director. Very rarely I have come across one single individual with his band of few who have contributed in building the organisation. Always it is a pleasure for me to receive your call any time in the day or night, which is a source of inspiration for me. My friendship and work with you remind me, our common source of inspiration, Thiruvalluvar and his famous verse:

எண்ணிய எண்ணியாங்(கு) எய்துப எண்ணியார்
திண்ணியர் ஆகப் பெறின்

Wher-ever you are you will subjugate the mission and tasks however tough and you will succeed. May God Bless you.

With regards,

Yours sincerely,

APJ Abdul Kalam

Shri Y S Rajan,
Executive Director, TIFAC
Department of Science and Technology,
Technology Bhavan,
New Delhi - 110 016.

Even though I had resigned from my job, Kalam did not cut out our relations. We continued to have our conversation everyday.

Ramamurthy asked me for one favour. He said: "Rajan, you have resigned only as Adviser DST; however, you can continue to work for TIFAC till 60. You have said that you won't receive any salary for your TIFAC job. It is alright. Even if you work elsewhere, please continue to work for TIFAC." It was a heartfelt request. I agreed. Kalam was happy to hear this. We continued to work together for TIFAC. Gossipping about Delhi and S&T matters also became a part of our conversation.

We couldn't release *TIFAC Vision 2020* at the national level because of upcoming elections. The PMO informed that as they were busy with election arrangements, they did not have the time for all these activities. I have noticed that many such welfare activities had to be suspended on account of elections; then and now! There is no way out! Parliamentary elections, state elections and even the local body elections stunt developmental programmes. Two out of five years are wasted in this manner! Citing democracy, how long are we going to inhibit these welfare schemes meant for the Indian people?

Ramamurthy made one more request. "Even though your resignation was accepted, you should not leave the DST till the *India Vision 2020* is officially released at the national level. Even though you are the executive director of TIFAC, you have to be seated on the dais as Adviser DST!"

I agreed.

❑

I Joined the CII

I started looking for a salaried job to run my family. I asked the head of the '*Confederation of Indian Industries* (CII)' Tarun Das for some suitable suggestions. He requested me to give my biodata.

In reply to my letter, Ratan Tata stated that I could work for the Tata group. After seeing my letter, Tarun Das told me: "Rajan, you could be well placed in a private organisation and their pay scale would also be high. However, your vast experience and extensive knowledge will go for waste. You will be forced to work within their narrow group boundaries. CII, on the other hand, is not affiliated to the government. We operate at the national level. You know about us well. You could join the CII and exhibit your S&T skills with absolute independence. We cannot afford to pay the salary of private entities. However, your quality of life here would be better when compared to working in the government sector."

After consulting with my wife Gomati, I decided to join the CII. This was a major milestone not only to me, but also to Kalam. I was able to get in touch with many of the leading industrialists of India and explain the use of S&T in the industrial sector and how they could contribute productively to our Indian economy. I informed Tarun Das that I was willing to join the CII. As per the government rules, an individual exiting out of the government sector should get prior permission from the government before joining in a non-governmental organisation. Nowadays, it has been reduced to one year. I submitted my appointment letter from the CII to the DST to get formal government approval. I informed Kalam also.

"Sir, as soon as you go to your new office, I would like to meet you there! Please call me without fail!" Kalam said.

Meanwhile, I also had an important task of contacting the PMO (PM Office) to invite the Prime Minister to introduce and dedicate the *India Vision 2020 documents* to the Indian people. I knew the S&T minister, Prof. Y. K. Alagh well. He told me: "Rajan! You don't worry. I will take care of it." On August 2, 1996, the programme was conducted extremely well in the parliamentary annexe. Prime Minister, Kalam, Ramamurthy, Y. K. Alagh, and I were on stage. Kalam introduced the projects of Vision 2020 and submitted the reports to PM, Shri Deve Gowda. He also spoke for a while.

The programme received good press coverage. Kalam, who was so far known only as the 'missile man of India', earned a reputation as the 'path-maker to empower India'. Since Kalam was the scientific adviser to the defence minister, he was invited to several programmes. In all those programmes, empowering India through the *India Vision 2020* projects became his subject of speech. Computers and powerpoint presentations were used sparingly in those days. Therefore, TIFAC drew graphs and submitted them to Kalam for all his speeches.

Finally, on September 1, 1996, I joined CII. Even though I resigned my job as Adviser DST, I continued to work for TIFAC as its CEO. Since the CII was not affiliated to the government, it was run from funds received from its members and funds received through various programmes conducted by the organisation. Even senior CII secretariat staff were given rooms with small or no doors. Moreover, its offices were located in two or three places in Delhi. I was allotted the *India Habitat Centre* (IHC) office. I informed Kalam about this. As mentioned earlier, he said: "I will come there this afternoon!" How could I object!

Tarun Das was not there in Delhi. His next in line authority N. Srinivasan told me: "Rajan, I too must be there to receive Kalam on behalf of CII. When such a big representative from the Indian government is arriving here, we need to take care of all formalities properly!"

Kalam, who was a senior member of the Indian government, was usually seen in huge stage programmes. However, he was going to come to such a small organisation as the CII. I was about to become a senior adviser there!

I informed Kalam. He said, "There is no need for the presence of senior CII officials. I will be coming there only to see you personally. I will be there at around 2PM; I could also get delayed!"

When Kalam became the 'missile man', T. N. Seshan was the cabinet secretary and Rajiv Gandhi was the Indian Prime Minister. Even back then, in 1989, T. N. Seshan gave the 'Z-security' for Kalam. Now, Kalam was the scientific adviser of the defence minister. He therefore came to CII followed by several security personnel. He got delayed. Everyone in CII, including N. Srinivasan, was waiting near the elevator to receive him. There were several offices within the IHC. CII was on the fourth floor occupying a small portion. It was fully air-conditioned.

As soon as Kalam entered, N. Srinivasan completed all formalities. Kalam said, "Rajan, I would like to meet you in your room personally!" He asked the others to leave. We were both seated in my room. It had huge glass windows. Beautiful green parrots were perched outside the IHC building. They always came there.

Kalam said: "Look over here, sir! Such beautiful parrots! Wherever there are parrots, the place will be cheerful! You have a beautiful office, sir!"

He then asked me about my role at the CII. I explained: "We cannot do massive projects like those of the DST or TIFAC here due to shortage of funds. However, I can contact industrialists and create awareness by talking about the scope of S&T in industries. I can outline possible developmental opportunities. We will conduct workshops and conferences. Other than that, we will help train workers on various S&T technical skills related to their job."

"TIFAC and CII can join hands together to successfully complete the Vision 2020 projects," he said.

Then he asked how many people worked with me. "Mr. Anbu and Ms. Rachna; two people," I told him.

"Can I meet those two now?" he asked.

I called them to my room. Both of them were engineers who had finished college three years ago. Kalam spoke with them. Since CII took part in *Vision 2020* task forces, Anbu and Rachna knew about *Vision 2020*.

Kalam explained in detail and asked them to integrate their work with the *Vision 2020* project.

After explaining everything, he pointed at me and said, "Rajan is an excellent man! Simply fantastic!"

He was indirectly asking them to cooperate with me.

We all came out of the room cheerfully. We had spent almost an hour together.

Kalam rushed outside. Srinivasan (who was waiting outside) and I took him to the elevator. Kalam spoke cheerfully with Srinivasan and left. Srinivasan told me: "Such a great man! He respects your friendship. This is a big booster to the CII employees!"

The news of Kalam's visit spread within CII like wildfire (even in those days when there were no cell phones). This incident further strengthened me in many ways.

❑

The Backdrop of the 'Vision 2020' Book

Now that I have joined the CII, I had to leave the government quarters in Kidwai Nagar that had been allotted to me while I was employed in the DST. My house hunt began. CII would sign the rental agreement with my new house owner. CII asked me to look for a suitable house. My wife Goma took care of that.

My first son Vijay had completed his engineering course and was working in Bengaluru in 1996. My second son Vikram had completed one year of MBBS course and stayed with us.

I had enormous work pressure since I had to work for both TIFAC and CII now. Since I was new to CII, I had to prove my competence there.

I spoke with Kalam everyday. CII gave me a dedicated Maruti 800 car with a driver. I was therefore able to roam around freely to go to CII, to visit meetings and to take care of a few TIFAC initiatives in between my work.

Meanwhile, we found a suitable bride for my son Vijay. Her name is Mahalakshmi and she was doing her final year post graduation in Delhi. They met during October. Vijay was getting several job opportunities in the USA and so had to probably go there soon after marriage.

Therefore, everything happened in a hurry. My father selected an auspicious day for the engagement ceremony. It happened in our Kidwai nagar house. T. N. Seshan attended. Kalam cheerfully attended and was there throughout the function. The wedding day was fixed in December 1996 before the onset of the Tamil 'Margazhi' month. The wedding happened in Ambassador Hotel. Many ministers and eminent persons from Delhi attended the event. Shri K. R.

Narayanan was the Vice President. He was the minister of our department while I served at ISRO and DST. We both maintained cordial relations. For Vijay's wedding, he sent a bouquet and a complimentary letter to Vijay and a bouquet and a cheque to my daughter-in-law Mahalakshmi.

Kalam was very happy to attend Vijay's wedding. Both my sons and Mahalakshmi addressed him as 'Kalam uncle'. Four months after resigning from my government job, at the end of December, we hurriedly shifted from the Kidwai Nagar house to an apartment in Safdarjung campus on the top floor. It was less spacious, but the rent was still exorbitant!

Vijay too got a good job in Delhi itself. The newlyweds stayed with us. Vijay postponed his trip to the US.

Amidst all these changes, the Kalam-Rajan conversation continued to happen everyday. TIFAC meetings happened regularly.

The CII director general Tarun Das gave me enough freedom to strengthen the technology division I headed. Besides Anbu and Rachna, I now added five more engineers/scientists. Kalam was very happy to know this.

It was 1997. Six years had elapsed since 'economic liberalisation' and 'globalisation' had been introduced in India. This being the case, it became necessary for the Indian industrialists to introduce S&T skills to their field. Since they were used to the licence-permit-quota-inspection-Raj, they hardly knew anything about the modern technical skill sets. Therefore, Tarun Das decided to refresh them about S&T skills. That was the reason for him letting me operate freely and allowing me to appoint more qualified youngsters to CII's technology department. CII was facing a financial crunch. In spite of this, he said to me: "Rajan, please do your duty without any inhibitions."

He felt that this was not enough. He therefore decided to bring in a great man to address these people. He knew the impulse of the industrialists and traders.

One day, he asked me: "Rajan, do you know about various national committees within CII? Many big industrialists and traders desire to become its members and chair the committees. Such people traditionally are chosen from within the CII. I want to break that tradition. I want to make Kalam as the head of the CII National Council for Technology. What do you think? Will he accept?"

"I also feel that it would be great if he accepts the responsibility. Let me speak with him and come back to you," I said.

I explained in detail over the phone conversation that night to Kalam: "Sir, will you please agree?" I asked. Kalam replied immediately; heading the *CII National Council on Technology* will be a whole new experience for him. Likewise, it would be a whole new experience for different industrial organisations which were members within the CII. Even though the achievements were less, the awareness was more. Kalam adopted a new technique to handle this. He assured them that the technical knowhow of the DRDO would be put to use for industries. CII's Anbu helped in a great way to accomplish this. Nearly thirty technology transfers were effected successfully.

In 1997, TIFAC started engaging in *Vision 2020* followup activities. Also, media people interested in S&T matters approached Kalam. We got an opportunity to write about several S&T matters. Secretary DST V S Ramamurthy gave the title 'The Amitabh Bachchan of Indian Science' to Kalam. Wherever TIFAC meetings were arranged, people would crowd around Kalam. Many big wigs of S&T in India were even jealous of him. More on that later! Some of the reporters asked Kalam: "Can we look at all the twenty five reports of *Vision 2020* and write a book about that." Kalam sent them to me. I decided not to give away these report documents for free, lest it should lose its value. TIFAC had to invest a lot to prepare them including travel and stay expenses of experts.

Some tried to get these for free. I therefore made a strict rule that they could read all documents only by staying inside the TIFAC campus. I explained the key points of several *Vision 2020* projects to many of them. All this was time consuming. Six months went by. Several precious hours of my work life were expended.

Finally, I told Kalam: "Sir, the people you are sending are wasting my time. They are not doing anything productive. Please do not send anyone to me anymore. It is true that we need to write a 300 page book on *TIFAC Vision 2020*, but no one would be interested in reading an exhaustive 250-300 page book containing some 25 research reports. There is no use if we submit our brief report comprising some 5-10 pages. They will make a big issue out of it in the ministries...just think about it."

After a few days, Kalam told me: "Rajan, we can do one thing. We both can write a book on Vision 2020." I was hesitant to do it amidst all my work pressure. My CII job was picking up great speed; TIFAC was taking steps to implement a 100-crore rupees project. There were no buildings for TIFAC. I had to handle several difficult administrative issues.

One day, we both sat together and drew a rough draft. I wrote it by hand. I used to write from 5AM to 7AM. After this, I had to work for CII and TIFAC. Since activities at the CII had begun recently, I worked mostly on that. As I had several colleagues in TIFAC who had worked with me for a few years, I called them over the phone in order to complete TIFAC activities.

It was decided that Kalam should correct my rough draft and hand it over to his personal secretary Sheridon. I sent three chapters; but Kalam hardly spoke about them. "Sir, I am going to stop writing," I said. Fortunately, I came to know that a team of scientists were going to write a book based on these reports. One of them was the Government of India's S&T secretary of a department under the Ministry of Science and Technology!

I immediately informed Kalam about this: "Sir, did you know that this was happening?"

"Oh! Is that so! This is so bad! All this is happening because we released the *Vision 2020* project in front of everyone. Alright, I will speed up my work," Kalam said.

After this, we speeded up. I asked those in TIFAC to give me a brief report of their projects. I sat with them and showed them how to do this. I created the economic part of the book using the material available with CII's economic expert T. K. Bhaumik (who was younger than me). We have thanked each and everyone for their help and have mentioned their names in the respective sections of the Vision 2020 book.

Even now, I am astonished to think about how we were able to accomplish this arduous task.

After Shri Deve Gowda resigned as the PM, I. K. Gujral became the new PM. Kalam sought permission to continue with his work. Like he did with all Indian PMs earlier, Kalam took his file to the PM. (Told to me by Kalam much later.)

Since there wasn't enough support, I. K. Gujral had to resign. Before resigning, he had decided to give the '*Bharat Ratna*' award to Kalam and did so. Soon after, he had to resign. Shri. K. R. Narayanan became the Indian President in July 1997.

But only after Vajpayee became the Indian Prime Minister, Kalam was formally awarded the '*Bharat Ratna*' in 1998.

Our book '*India 2020 A Vision for a New Millenium*' was getting ready fast. It was the beginning of 1998. The last three chapters were pending. I had written as per Kalam's suggestions.

"Sir, I am going to Chandigarh; after completing my DRDO activities, let us finalise the last few chapters. I am going to extend my stay there by one or two days," Kalam said to me.

I went too. We sat down and did the job for a few minutes. He fell asleep as he was very tired. I left him there to get some good sleep. He called me after a few hours. Finally, we finished working on it.

"I have too much work! I couldn't sleep properly for the past few days. That is why I came here. I also felt that we should complete our book. Even after this, I have too much work to complete...," Kalam said.

After everything was complete, he said: "Sir! The book is complete! I will take leave now!" He left quickly.

Penguin publishers had approached Kalam earlier to get permission to publish our book. Kishan Chopra spoke with me. I gave him the title and a brief introduction about the book. He wanted to discuss more. However, I had to leave due to lack of time. Once, Penguin Publishers invited us to a writers' party. Kalam did not go to such places. He said: "Everyone would be drinking there. I can't come...you can go if you want." I too did not attend such celebrations due to lack of time. One time, a foreign representative head of Penguin Publishers had come. I went there since Kishan Chopra had specially requested me. The head told me: "We are strictly time-bound. We are totally professional in approach." He told me this because we were first-time writers for Penguin publications. He did not know anything about me or Kalam. Neither did these big publishers know anything about S&T books nor about the S&T profession.

I can't tolerate people who make such generalised statements and so I replied, "It is true that we both are first-time writers for your publishing firm. I do not know what you think of our book. We both are trained space scientists. Abiding by time is one of the most important requirements of our profession there!"

The conversation ended.

He shook my hands and left. I joked about this incident to Kalam. Several years later, we came to know of the delay caused by some of *Penguin Publishing* firm's writers. It seems that even after getting advance payment from Penguin, some of their favourite writers would delay their submission by many years!

Neither me nor Kalam got any advance payment. No one spoke to us about all that either!

When Kalam said "We have finished!," he actually meant that we had completed the book by July 1998 which was the decided date of submission.

I completed my writing work for the book. After Sheridon submitted the last three typed chapters of the book to Kishan Chopra, I got this news!

That is...

Within a few weeks of the release of the India 2020 book (1998), Kalam's autobiography '*Wings of Fire*' hit the stands. It was translated to multiple languages quickly. I knew that Kalam had started working on it several years earlier (even before Kalam became the scientific adviser to the defence minister) because he asked Arun Tiwari to show me a copy of his first draft. I read it while I was in my Kidwai Nagar government. allotted house in Delhi. Even though it was a good compilation, there were many gaps. I pointed them out. Arun Tiwari wanted to bring it out as soon as possible. Since he got the opportunity to write with Kalam, he was hurrying it up.

I had one more concern; why was Kalam writing his autobiography so urgently? He had earned a great reputation within India and overseas after the successful launch of the *'Agni'* missile in 1989. He was 60 years old. His achievements were not yet over. When Tiwari showed me the first draft, Kalam was not the Chairman of TIFAC; he had not yet become the defence minister's scientific adviser yet. Even though I did not know what he would become in his 60s or even after 62, I knew for sure that Kalam would not waste his time doing nothing. My poems to him in the '*Blossoms of the Heart*' collection are proof of this!

After sending back Arun Tiwari, I spoke with Kalam over the phone:

"Sir, I saw your first draft of your autobiography brought to me by Arun Tiwari. I have suggested a lot of corrections. He was a bit upset! But those are all significant corrections," I told Kalam.

"One more thought also crossed my mind. What is the urgency to write your autobiography? Only those people who think that life is over and that they have to convey everything to the world before leaving, usually write their autobiographies. But your job is not yet over! You have not yet reached your peak point in life. You have only become the missile man and have earned the 'Padma Bhushan' award. That's all! I personally feel that if you write your autobiography now itself, then you are not doing justice to the future that is ahead of you. Many people will understand you differently and could possibly misinterpret you.

Your life is going on successfully now. Please delay your autobiography by another 5-6 years at least!," I advised Kalam.

"Why are you talking like this, sir?" Kalam said.

"Sir! I have thought this over and over again. This book will certainly not be your life's biggest achievement. However, this should not become a hurdle to your future accomplishments. The decision is yours!" I told him decisively.

Either because of my firm stand or because of other reasons, Kalam never spoke about the book to me. But I think he definitely agreed with me.

It was published only after another 6-7 years probably with a lot of modifications. He did not show me the final rough draft. But, when 'India 2020' was being sent to the publishing firm, Kalam told me that he was also sending his 'Wings of Fire' book to be published. He was 67 years old at the time. He received his '*Bharat ratna*' award and had become the scientific adviser to the defence minister within these six years. He also became famous as the Chairman of TIFAC who wrote the India 2020 book. All Indians got attracted to Kalam after this book. Even though a few popular books portrayed Kalam in a wrong sense (for example, that he was born in a fisherman's family and so on), overall the book was a major milestone in Kalam's life. It became a motivational epic.

He gave me a copy of his book. I was thrilled to see his comments about me.

After 1998 (after *Bharat Ratna*, *Nuclear bomb*, and *India Vision 2020*), Kalam's life attained stellar magnificence. It must be mentioned here that '*Wings of Fire*' was one of the major reasons behind this.

❑

Nuclear Bomb and Sai Baba

May 11, 1998 – India conducted the nuclear bomb test explosions. I was very happy to hear the news. I immediately composed three poems in English. Kalam had already become a *Bharat Ratna*. All my family members viz. My father, myself, Goma, Vijay, Vikram, Mahalakshmi (Anu) attended the ceremony. Kalam had invited all of us. For the first time, my father met Kalam's elder brother. They both instantly hugged each other. They were roughly the same age. Kalam was very happy. Unfortunately, there was sadness that we did not have a picture of them hugging. Recently on Facebook, I saw a picture of all of us with Kalam at that time.

During the occasion, I had the opportunity to interact closely with Kalam's elder brother, Muthu Meera Maraikayar. I will write about that later when I describe Kalam's swearing in ceremony as the Rashtrapati (Indian President).

May 11, 1998 was celebrated as the '*Technology Day*'. It was Buddha Purnima too. The English poems that I wrote that day have been published in my first English poem collection '*Agony and Harmony*'. It was published by *NCBH publications*. The book was translated into Tamil by Shri Sirpi Balasubramaniam; it was a big honour for me. He named the Tamil translation as 'துன்ப வீணையும் ஆனந்த பைரவியும்'. Here are my English poems:

THE THREE BOMBS

The three Bombs nuclear;
Make it all clear,
That India is no longer unclear
About the politics of power.

Restraint is good,
Not when being kicked around
In a global playground
Without any end!

It is a proud feeling
That Indians can master
Any knowledge on the earth
To meet their goals!

Let the three bombs
Be symbols for us,
To have Feeling, Faith and Firmness
For our people's well being!

Let the strengths grow more in us
To serve the people
To remove poverty
And for a newer Vision of
Developed India
Om Shanti! Shanti! Shanti!

May 12, 1998

NEW LIFE

The unleashed Energy
Of technology
Can destroy or defend
Or create and find
New ways of life

Benefits for all
Good lives for all
Are things that missed
Many generations

The new knowledge
And the newer life
That technology
Does offer to us
Gives us hope
That we can achieve

Richer lives
For all and each
And healthy
Bodies and minds as well
Right away
On this lovely Earth.

May 12, 1998

After those nuclear explosions, Kalam became widely popular. Everyone spoke about him and all news was about him. I did not want to disturb him at that time.

He was so tired when we were there in Chandigarh, probably because the arrangements for the explosion were at its peak. That was the reason behind his tiredness and fatigue. That also explains why he left in a hurry. Later on, Kalam told me about it.

The Indian government named May 11th as the '*Technology Day*'. In between all this (I think sometime in June 1998), Kalam called me: "Rajan, please come to Bengaluru immediately. I have to attend a meeting. After that, we both have to visit a place urgently. Please postpone all your activities" , he said. He never asked me to postpone my work. So, I booked my flight ticket and left.

After his meeting got over, he said: "We will be leaving tomorrow morning to Puttaparthi. Only the two of us. Please don't tell anyone yet. I will explain everything in detail tomorrow."

I had never heard him speak of Puttaparthi Sai Baba before this. When I worked in ISRO, Bengaluru (1974–88), we used to get requests from the central government foreign ministry. After visiting ISRO, we had to make arrangements to take those visitors to Puttaparthi Sai Baba. The S&T minister at the time, Shri Shivraj Patil was a frequent visitor to the place. ISRO's deputy secretary T. S. Venkataraman used to take him there. I had never gone there at those times. Later, the director of IIT Professor Sampath became the Vice-Chancellor of *Satya Sai University*. He was chairing a committee to consider avenues for promotion of the employees committee in IMD (around 1990). I too was a member since I was Adviser DST. Many meetings took place in Delhi. Some participants wanted to get the darshan of Sai Baba. Therefore, professor Sampath organised a few meetings in Puttaparthi. We have to go there at 5AM. There was a huge crowd, however, they were well-organised. Baba would walk in between them and give his blessings. His bodyguards would follow him so that no untoward incident happens. He would place his hand over the head of a few children in between out of love and fondly pull their hairs.

Finally, he will be seated in a room. The door was intricately decorated as in temples. There is a long corridor, but not everyone is allowed to be seated there. It is meant for VIPs. Baba used to invite a few people from there to his room. When we visited with professor Sampath, all of us had the opportunity to sit in that VIP corridor. It was very close to Baba's room. Therefore, we all had a very close darshan of Sai Baba. However, not once any of us was called to his room. None of us received special blessings with a smile from him either.

I did not take any effort either. I did not approach T. S. Venkataraman for assistance. (He had a lot of influence there.) That is my nature. It is good if it happens ; otherwise, there is no loss.

This is the backdrop. Now, I will be going there with Kalam who was not only a '*Bharat Ratna*' but also the scientific adviser of the defence minister. I felt that VIPs would get special treatment from Baba's secretariat. I was waiting to go with Kalam this time.

We got into our car. Other than the driver, only the two of us were there. No security guards followed us. Kalam had avoided using the car provided by the DRDO and had hired a cab at his own personal expense. As soon as we sat in the car, Kalam started explaining the reason for this trip:

"Rajan! For the past few days, I have been feeling extremely confused. After the 'Funny Happening', I am now confused. (I knew about what he was referring to; he had spent most of his life on missiles and atom bombs. From one prime minister to the next, he was running around, carrying his file with him like a kavadi, seeking their permission for the nuclear explosion and doing his tapas. Finally, he was crowned with victory. He mentioned this biggest achievement of his, jokingly in this manner. Moreover, he might have felt uncomfortable to mention it in front of the driver). Many people are commenting in different ways! Some say, 'Kalam, you have made a big mistake!' Others talk about future complications. ``Technology denials for India will increase!" they say. Besides all these, as an individual I have a huge doubt. I decided to visit a few punya atmas (blessed souls) and seek their advice. I felt that when I speak with Baba, you too must be present with me. This is the reason behind this trip."

On other occasions, I would have argued with him. I would have analysed the situation in many ways. I knew how much Kalam had struggled to bring this nuclear explosion test project to fruition. He first got approval from Narasimha Rao which later stopped abruptly. Then he approached Vajpayee, who in spite of knowing his precarious position as the PM, granted consent. At that time, also, Kalam's mission did not bear any fruits. Next, he waited patiently for two years when Deve Gowda and I. K. Gujral were the Prime Ministers. Finally, his dream was fulfilled on May 11, 1998 under the leadership of PM Vajpayee, on Buddha Purnima. Moreover, as Kalam himself had pointed out to one of the reporters, 'The *Agni missile* was not meant to carry flower bouquets'. Normally, I would have argued all this with Kalam.

As far as I am concerned, it is mandatory for India to make indigenous missiles and nuclear bombs. To run a nation, its security forces must be strengthened. There can be no room for compassion when it comes to running a government. That is why Tiruvalluvar created different segments like virtue, wealth and kama (desire).

Kalam also thought like me only. He wanted to deter enemy nations from attacking India which was why he felt that India should make indigenous modern weapons. Even though a few intellectuals, and politicians talked ill about missiles, nuclear weapons and security, Kalam did not have any confusion in his mind.

I do not know what happened after that! I also maintained silence as I did not want to hurt his feelings. 'Let's see what Baba has to say', I told myself.

We finally arrived at Puttaparthi. It was already night. We received a special welcome from the ashram people. We were served dinner and each of us were allotted separate AC rooms. I noticed that many devotees were lying down on the floor as they had no rooms to stay.

We were going to meet Baba the next morning. We were both taken to the 'privileged corridor'. Kalam was made to sit in front of everyone. They made me sit behind him. It took some 40-50 minutes for Baba to arrive. Everyone was quiet. Many Indian nationals and some foreigners were there. Bhajans were being played through loudspeakers. Some people shouted out Baba's name out of devotion. There were more than 10,000 people. There was a huge race to be seated in the privileged corridor. Two people came between me and Kalam (I noticed that both of them were very famous). Kalam kept looking back and said softly: "Sir, please stay behind me. As soon as Baba enters, you also should join me!"

He noticed that those two VIPs had managed to sneak in between myself and Kalam. Meanwhile, Baba had already joined the crowd. He pointed to a few people in the crowd signalling them to join him. They were very happy. Others might have become jealous. However, they maintained absolute discipline. When Baba approached his room door, some four or five people tried to go with him. Baba shouted at them in Telugu condemning their action. Only those he called were allowed to enter his room with him.

Once Baba neared his room, he called out with a big smile "Kalam!" Kalam approached Baba. Meanwhile, a few other VIPs seated in the privileged corridor and other devotees from the crowd got up along with Kalam. (The rule over there was that all others must be seated until Baba calls their name).

I did not want to compete with them. Baba had already condemned a few such people in front of my eyes. Moreover, I valued discipline and self-respect. I did not want to get shouted at like the others. Everyone whom Baba had called, including Kalam, were about to enter inside Baba's room. We could only see their backs! "What was going to happen to me? Most importantly, what is Kalam going to say?" These were my concerns. Once Baba enters the room, the door would be shut and they wouldn't open it after that.

Suddenly, I heard Baba's loud voice "Rajan!" I stood up. He signalled me to approach him. After I joined them, all of us entered the room. The door was closed behind us. It was a small, compact room. Baba sat down on his throne. Everyone sat down. Kalam sat on the floor. I sat next to him. Baba looked compassionately at Kalam and myself. He blessed each one present there. He spoke one or two words with each of them. Baba said to one of them: "Nepal is going down and down..." He gestured with his hand by bringing it from higher up and slowly lowering it down. We realised that Baba was talking to one of the former prime ministers of Nepal. Baba then started to distribute his prasad to everyone.

Baba looked at me with a naughty smile and said: "Scientist see...see" and handed out 'Vibhuti' and other small prize items to everyone in the room. He smiled mischievously some 2-3 times as if to say that 'he had identified the suspecting scientist lurking inside me'.

Kalam might have been truly filled with deep devotion. I was looking at things without showing any emotion. Baba sent away everyone else. Only Baba, Kalam, and I were there. "Please come," he said and took us to another room inside. It was a tiny room with a throne. There were two other ordinary chairs next to it. He asked Kalam to sit in one of the chairs. Kalam sat down. Baba asked me to sit in the other one. I sat down on the floor. Kalam also sat down. We were able to sit very close to Baba. I was seated behind Kalam.

In order to see us clearly, Baba adjusted his seat. Even before Kalam started to speak, Baba said:

"Kalam, you did a great thing!...please do not worry..the country should be secure..." Kalam must have been surprised. I could see the relief in his face.

Baba gave him his answer. There is no point in talking about it any longer. The main point of Kalam's Puttaparthi visit was fulfilled.

Kalam spoke with vigour. "Baba! We have prepared reports on how various sectors within India should develop and could develop..." Kalam then explained the role of TIFAC and its various initiatives. Kalam then said:

"Baba! Both of us are writing a book." Before he could finish his sentence, Baba said:

"Yes, I know. You and Rajan are like brothers and are working together." While he was saying this, Baba interlocked his fingers from both hands.

"It is a very good thing! Please proceed!" Baba said.

He then talked about life. He said that life is not always the same. It keeps changing with time. He made some hand gestures and said: "Life is pleasure.. pain..pleasure...pain." He repeated this a few times.

I also spoke with Baba and he replied. Thirty minutes went by. Then, Baba said to Kalam: “Kalam, please keep this!” and handed out a wrist watch to him. Kalam received it with great regards. Both of us stood up to leave. Baba got up to send us out of the tiny room. I stood behind Kalam and was about to leave.

Baba did not give me anything, not even ‘Vibhuthi!’ When I was near the outside door, Baba held my right hand and said: “Scientist, the ring in your hand has gotten old...”

Before I could say that the ring was given to me by my wife at the time of our wedding, Baba said holding my right hand:

“Look here! I am going to give you a bigger ring!” He inserted a ring with several valuable gemstones in my hand. I came to know only later that it was a ‘Navaratna ring’.

Baba sent us out compassionately. We both went back to our rooms. Kalam later asked me to come to his room. He said: “Rajan! We had a good darshan! I got rid of a big burden after meeting him. He told us that the two of us are like brothers and has blessed us! He blessed our book as well..”

He then said: “Show me your hand!” I showed him. “Please wear this permanently in your hand, sir! Don’t keep it inside” Later (I think the next day), seeing that the ring was not in my hand, Kalam asked: “I told you to wear it permanently. Where is it now?” I said: “Sir, it fell down while I was sleeping. I have kept it safely inside.” No! No! Please wear it on a finger in which it fits well,” Kalam told me. I therefore started to wear it on my middle finger.

Many people who saw me with this ‘special’ Navratna ring asked me if there were any special prayers or if I had a separate ‘Guru’. I never replied clearly to any of them. “I am wearing this upon the request of a great man!” is all I would say. I am not bothered about what they think of me. I was more concerned that people should not misrepresent the Kalam-Baba meeting.

At that time, Kalam served as the scientific adviser for the defence minister for six years and had also received the ‘*Bharat Ratna*’ award. However, I felt strongly that he would accomplish more.

When he received his ‘*Bharat Ratna*’, I had composed a Tamil poem கனிந்த மனம். Here is the English translation from the “*Blossoms of the Heart*” collection:

A Kind Heart

Where is the Bharath of Bharathi’s dream?
Where is valour? Where is capable action?
Where is the motherland? Where is self
respect?
Did we think that it’s all an illusion!

There are still a few who live like him
Dreaming that Bharath will grow in this world
Toiling hard!
Increasing his resolve!

(Ending lines)

Such a treasure house is he,
Born and grew in the country's southern corner
Every day does he in every corner of the country
Gives a strong faith that we'll succeed!
Dedicate did he to God's feet and in the
Midst of men, his kind heart
Good that he is called the Indian Rathna
Better still is to fulfil his dreams.!

(27-11-1997)

❑

Kalam's Efforts to Empower India

In order to bring about many economic changes in India, Kalam must occupy a senior post in the government. *TIFAC's Vision 2020* reports have shown very good paths for India's progress. I had a firm desire that with the help of Kalam, these initiatives could be brought into every walks of life. The CII National Council can change the mindsets of some. With this in mind, I fully supported Tarun Das' proposal to request Kalam to chair it. I informed Kalam accordingly. Since Kalam also aimed to 'Empower India', he readily agreed.

We wrote India 2020, thinking that it would be read widely by several Indians. We felt that if it reaches those in power and authority, they could bring about suitable changes to empower India. Baba also blessed our book now! Kalam became busy after he got back to Delhi. I too became busy with my CII and TIFAC activities!

Kalam continued his usual work at the DRDO. He felt relieved that the nuclear tests were successful. Some criticisms were made about it. A few science magazines continued to make critical comments about the power of the bombs that were tested. Kalam had to attend to all that too! Later on, such remarks continued when Kalam openly supported the nuclear treaty made by India with America under the leadership of Prime Minister Dr. Manmohan Singh. More on that later.

Kalam always appreciated hard work and efforts. This happened when George Fernandes was the defence minister in June 1998. Fernandes did not favour the fact that India had to import many of her defence weapons. Other than missiles and a few other weapons, not much was made indigenously. He wanted India to design, develop and manufacture such war weapons. *Hindustan Aeronautics*

Limited, *Bharat Electronics Limited*, and *Ordnance Factories* manufactured weapons by buying foreign technology. They had to execute purchase agreements to manufacture these. The design and development happened abroad. India therefore did not have the capability to develop such weapons; even if we had the capability, we were prohibited from using such skills on account of the strict conditions of the purchase agreements.

Fernandes wanted to manufacture weapons indigenously. The third route of getting military equipment (first is totally indigenous, second purchase of foreign technology and manufacturing in India) is to have everything manufactured abroad and India had to import by paying a suitable price. Nearly 70% was imported (that is the third route). Not only did this affect the foreign exchange rates, but also it was possible for those countries to ban such imports due to prevailing political situations! Moreover, many Indians would be missing suitable job opportunities when manufactured abroad. Many small and medium sectors of our nation would stagnate if they don't have the opportunity to manufacture such products. It is not enough to create talents only within DRDO. For our nation to prosper, many of the small, medium and other private sector factories must manufacture such products on a large scale. Developed nations have progressed and are progressing considerably because business strengths, technological and engineering progresses are spread to all their industries.

One cannot say that higher authorities of India did not know about this. Most of the prime ministers and defence ministers talked about 'self-reliance', 'self-sufficiency' only on the public platforms and left it at that. Some others think that it is the responsibility of DRDO to realise it and so they allot more funds to DRDO. The defence forces do not care much about this. As far as they are concerned, they require modern weapons, aircraft, and other war equipment. Their important job is defending our nation from enemies and being war-ready. The government has to seek their assistance and devise plans for the manufacturing sector. However, many leaders felt that this was only possible for public sector organisations and therefore established companies like HAL, BEL, Midhani and Ordnance Factories. The manufacturing capability, labour skills, design, development skills and skills for innovative products in these organisations were fairly poor. One main reason for this was because the DDP (*Department of Defence Production*) of the defence ministry was under the IAS (*Indian Administrative Service*) officers.

If we look at the sad history of India's defence sector, one thing becomes clear. The defence sector had always been a public sector organisation serving the Delhi administrators. One of the main reasons for this was because the import of defence products was prone to corruption! The cost of defence products would be around many thousand crores! It is easy to deposit bribes in foreign banks.

These were beyond Kalam's reach. The defence forces and the DRDO hardly maintained cordial relations. The scientists in DRDO did not know how to maintain a smooth rapport with the defence force authorities. Even though Kalam had a special radiance around him, he couldn't do anything about the long standing hiatus between the two groups.

Changes were possible only if the defence minister took the first step. Most importantly, the higher authorities of the defence ministry should transform themselves to suit the requirements of the defence forces and the DRDO.

George Fernandes was an impatient man. In 1957, when I was a small boy in Bombay (now Mumbai), everyone knew about him. He led several trade unions. When he announced a 'bandh', all activities in Mumbai would come to a sudden halt. He was a powerful socialist devoted to his country and people.

He brought that spirit to the defence ministry. He consulted his officials, the chiefs of the armed forces, their next in line personnel, and other workers from industrial organisations like the CII. He gave special privileges to Kalam in the meeting. He made Kalam sit next to him, not only because Kalam was a *'Bharat Ratna'* but also because Fernandes saw him to be a symbol of 'India's empowerment'.

My friend S. Sen was the CII representative who stayed in touch with the defence ministry. I was also invited because they felt that this required skilled S&T knowledge. I went there. The President of CII Sekhar Datta and many big industrialists attended the meeting. On behalf of the government, public sector officers and higher officials from the defence manufacturing units were present.

George Fernandes listed out the defence equipment being imported from abroad at that time (1998). He explained what is given so far in this chapter in the earlier paragraphs.

"For how long are we going to be dependent on other nations? Whatever secretive clause you might write in your contract agreement, when their government asks them to provide details of export, the foreign companies have to give it to them. Our Indian factories must unite and change this situation. In all those developed nations, their government, private and defence sector industries are manufacturing more and more products by making use of newer defence equipment. They are exporting products which are at least two generations old to other countries. Therefore, besides the government companies and ordnance factories unit of India, other private industries also need to get involved. We should now think seriously about changing the rules of the defence ministry accordingly. We should identify the changes that need to be made in consultation with the Indian industries.."

The heads of industries, personnel from armed forces, and the public sector chiefs suggested many possibilities. A person from the defence force intervened: "If we involve private sector organisations in this, how can we keep our schemes and instruments secretive?" George replied immediately: "It is not necessary that security be granted only to government personnel or men in uniforms; even men like me, who are wearing a pyjama and a kurta, are also being trusted, isn't it? As I told you before, we cannot be completely sure whether all defence products being imported from abroad are kept secretive. In other countries, there are good security protocols that provide for work by the private sector and educational entities for defence works. We may not do all that here. But it is insane to think that only those in the government are devoted to the nation whereas others are not." At the end of the meeting, Kalam briefed them about his conceptual idea. "Ten years from now, can we change the current status of 70% import and 30% indigenous production to 70% indigenous production and 30% import?" Kalam asked.

After several discussions, it was considered to be a possible scenario. Finally, George Fernandes announced his key points:

"The current 70%-30% should change to 30%-70% in another ten years. In order to achieve that, modifications should be made in import of defence products. It should be done in steps to our advantage. We should manufacture more products indigenously (by DRDO and other industries).

"In order to speed up the process efficiently, let us set up a task force with seven committees. The function of the task force will be to identify possibilities for indigenous manufacture and to suggest suitable modifications to existing rules. Personnel from the government sector, defence sector, public sector, private sector, and the finance sector will be a part of the task force. The reports should get ready within 45 days. CII should support by providing secretarial assistance.

Other than this, without waiting for those 45 days, the industries can submit a report to the DRDO about what all they could do and how ready they are at present!"

Kalam announced then and there: "Industrial personnel who wish to see me, can come to my office after 7 PM on any day; kindly fix up an appointment before coming." Recall what Dr. Prahlada wrote about how Kalam started the IGMDP initiative in Hyderabad in 1989. Kalam had not reduced his pace even after all these years! (In 1989, Kalam was 58 years old. His pace hadn't reduced in 1998 when he was 67).

The seven-committee task force functioned efficiently and swiftly. I participated on behalf of CII in many of their proceedings. I was loaded with work at the time of releasing those reports. They were prepared within 2-3 months.

Meanwhile, for the first time since independence, the Indian Parliament wanted the DST to produce a video on India's S&T achievements. The S&T minister at the time was Dr. Murli Manohar Joshi. This was his idea. The department secretary V S Ramamurthy handed over the responsibility to me. It was to be finalised by June 1998 and to be released in August 1998! It was for the golden jubilee celebrations of Indian independence; he saw the last segment.

It was getting created well in spite of many challenges. This brought me closer to Dr. Murli Manohar Joshi. This friendship also helped Kalam later. More on that later.

A quick recap of 1998.

In spite of the excessive workload, overall 1998 was a fruitful year. The '*Bharat Ratna*' award which was announced for Kalam in 1997, was handed to Smt. M. S. Subbulakshmi, Shri C. Subramaniam and Kalam in 1998.

On May 11, 1998, nuclear explosion test and *Agni missile* test was conducted. All these had a good impact on Kalam's later life.

Then our visit to Puttaparthi Saibaba. The final work on our India 2020 book got over in June '98. The book was released before August 15 golden jubilee celebrations in 1998. People all over India talked about it. Kalam was invited to live shows. An important message was conveyed by the RSS weekly magazine "*Panchajanya*" in its December 13, 1998 issue which had Kalam's picture on the front page. The heading was *"Abdul Kalam Ka Bharat" ('Abdul Kalam's Bharat')* with the statement: "A big reply to domination of world powers like America: development of self-reliant technology!"

The fifth page of the magazine was entirely dedicated to the '*India 2020*' book. They had translated several portions of the book and compiled it into a big Hindi essay. In between the essay, there was a big picture of Kalam. Beneath that there was a title which read: "Warfare these days is not done with weapons, instead by competing in global markets for economic prosperity." There is a note which says 'To be continued...'

This was a major milestone in Kalam's life. It was clear that R.S.S. saw Kalam to be a modern-day symbol for economic and technical growth. The essay states very clearly that beside being the 'missile man of India', Kalam also strengthened its other sectors like S&T and economics. The outcome of R.S.S. visualising Kalam like this certainly helped in securing his Presidential candidature. (Kalam became the Rashtrapati in another four years).

❑

Some Sorrows and Kalam's Self-Confidence

1996, 1997, 1998, 1999 were the fastest years in Kalam's life and my life. Many changes, many big happenings and some sorrows too happened during these four years. Overall, even though these four years contributed to exponential growth in Kalam's life, he was upset because of problems created by a few senior members of the DRDO and was tormented by other jealous S&T bigwigs from outside. Many of them tried to underestimate his May 1998 nuclear test explosions. Many said that the credit belongs only to those in the nuclear department. A few other big shots felt that they had achieved more than Kalam and that they truly deserved the '*Bharat Ratna*' award and not Kalam; they even spoke ill of Kalam in their close circles. All these accusations also reached Kalam's ears. The fact that he was the top secretary of the Indian government (DDRD & SA to RM) at the age of 65 in 1996 was in itself a great achievement. (Prof. Dhawan was only there till his age of 64). Kalam continued to hold the position till he was 68 years old in 1999. No one has broken that record yet. In 2010, three people held the post till they were 66.

Even in 1996, there were indications of the aforementioned facts. Many S&T big shots became jealous of Kalam since he wasn't sent out of the department in 1994. In the years 1995 and 1996, Kalam's fame and glory spread far and wide. In spite of this, around June 1996, Kalam told me with deep regret during our regular conversation:

"Rajan! We have been doing our work diligently. But a few people are giving me a lot of trouble...sometimes I wonder if I should leave all this and go away..."

Not just for one or two days, Kalam was in this mindset for several days on end. He was deeply hurt. He was not troubled by the Prime Minister or the Defence Minister. In June 1996, we had finished all work related to Vision 2020 reports. We waited for the Prime Minister to release it. One or two years had passed since Kalam's nuclear mission test plans, which was initiated with Narasimha Rao's 'Start' signal, then halted with his 'Not now, stop' signal. Even though Vajpayee reinitiated the plans with his 'Start' signal, he served as the PM only for 13 days. Kalam was really concerned over this setback.

Some of the senior DRDO officials detested Kalam since he continued to work there and therefore hindered their promotion. They started complaining. Kalam helped many of them in special ways by getting an extension for 2, 3, or 4 years for those who were more than 60 years old. The Indian government had never done this before. Other than this, he increased the number of employees in the second and third levels within the defence minister's scientific consultant's office, and appointed many of these senior officials there.

Whatever be the case, Kalam gave full freedom of speech to everyone in the DRDO office during the regular weekly meetings of the directors. I got to know through a few DRDO officials that a few senior officials targeted Kalam during those sessions. Kalam never mentioned their names even once to me. In fact, he got them promotion and other benefits. He was heartbroken that in spite of all his efforts to appease them, they were talking behind his back. During our conversation, Kalam only said that he was being hassled without mentioning any names.

In order to console him and to alleviate his pain, I wrote a poem instantly and sent it to him.

It is there in the '*Blossoms of the Heart*' collection. It begins with the following lines:

The Soft Music of Toil

Noises heard outside,
The garrulous gossips,
The deeds of rogues
Who do not share the joys,
With their lives' goal of
Speaking about dividing people,
With separate directions for each of them
And forgetting the Mother,
My friend! Forget the barbs
Released by them!

————————————

————————————

You became a symbol of strength in
everybody's mind

Construct a mental fort of stone and bury
your wounds!

Flowers will bloom!
New music will be heard!
People's sorrow
Will vanish quickly!
The country will grow
Meanness will reduce!
True freedom,
Will spread everywhere
Divisions will vanish!
Love will be on rise!
To achieve this state
There are people who are itching to work
With trust in you!
Listen to their call!
Let music inside you
Live forever!

11-6-1996
10:45AM

As soon as he read my poem, Kalam called me and said: "What sir? You have turned into a fortune teller (kudu kudu paandi in Tamil as the poem in Tamil had that rhythm)!" There was a change in his tone. He sounded excited. This was not just because of my poem, but also because he was inspired to work tirelessly for the nation. I knew that India could progress only because of people like Kalam and so I always liked to encourage him. I felt that he will become a famous symbol of India. This I had depicted in my very first SLV poem that was meant for Kalam (1980). With every passing year, the feeling further strengthened. In 1996 after he became the scientific adviser to the defence minister, when he prepared the twenty five reports successfully for the TIFAC Vision 2020 initiative as its head Chairman, I was completely confident that Kalam would become an epitome of success one day. In the meeting with the defence minister in June 1998, Kalam suggested transforming 70%–30% to 30%–70%. This initiative was in full swing. Even after retiring voluntarily from my government service, as mentioned earlier, my proximity with Kalam never ceased to exist.

It became important for me to soothe Kalam with my words so that his pain would be relieved. I tried my level best to do this and Kalam too would applaud me for this.

As described earlier, on August 2, 1996, TIFAC's India Vision 2020 was dedicated to the nation by the then Indian Prime Minister Shri Deve Gowda. It was a big inspiration to Kalam. He was satisfied that he had placed goals for progress with a vision in front of the nation. Meanwhile, he also focussed on his DRDO activities. At the end of 1997, *'Bharat Ratna'* award was announced. In 1998, he successfully completed the nuclear tests and tested the *'Agni'* missile's performance. In 1999, the Kargil war happened! That was the time when India's telephone department grew alongside broadcasting agencies like news channels. The foundation for cell phones was being made at the time.

On October 8, 1999, '*Bharat Ratna*' Kalam delivered his first P N Haksar memorial lecture. The topic was '*Developed Nation – A Vision*'. It was a joint programme organised by *Science and Technology Agenda for National Development* (STAND) and IIT, Delhi. It received good coverage from Delhi magazines and newspapers. I still have the copies from *Times of India*, *The Hindu*, and *Hindustan Times* dated October 9, 1999 with me.

Kalam's preparations to welcome the new millenia were portrayed in those articles. The article in *Hindustan Times* began with the following lines:

"While ancient Rome, Greece and Egypt were lost to history, having overcome foreign invasions and the test of time, India is about to witness the beginning of the next millennium in another 83 days. With its growing population of over 100 crore people, it would suit India well to evolve into a developed nation in the next twenty years."

Bharat Ratna Kalam delivered his first P N Haksar memorial speech to a full house at the IIT Delhi auditorium. This was his vision for Bharat.

Here are a few excerpts from the October 9, 1999 edition of '*The Hindu*':

"Besides creating newer equipment and manufacturing products, technology will lead to national development by promoting economic growth. The western world has designed its own plans for technological growth and development. In today's world, it is true that strength will respect only strength. Therefore, for India to grow economically, self-reliant technological growth is the key. There is no doubt about this.

In the minds of the Indian youth, who are the key and strong resource for change, the idea of a developed India is causing a revolutionary expectation."

The article continued further: Dr. Kalam mentioned five sectors that could contribute to Indian growth and development as recommended by the *TIFAC's Vision 2020* report. These are: Agriculture & Food processing, uninterrupted electric supply throughout India, Education & Health, News technology, and Defence & Security. All these are interrelated. These are very important for the country's security, food security, and economic security.

Kalam did not stop with this. He emphasised that modifications must be made in government systems and methods of working.

"Many bureaucratic government departments must be shut down. A tough competition between departments striving to achieve this goal must prevail.

For this to happen, the rules and regulations must be liberalised along with the participation of the private sectors." He was getting ready to enter into the most important phase of his life. Even though missiles and launch vehicles formed the lifeline of the DRDO, Kalam insisted on focussing on these five sectors as these were key to India's economic and technical growth. Empowering India became Kalam's important agenda.

In 1993, when Kalam became the Secretary, DDRD, he put forth several new initiatives. In spite of many ups and downs, after getting government approval, some of them were successful. The most important among those was the *BrahMos Supersonic Cruise Missile*. Even though Kalam was the father of Indian missiles, he realised a few gaps in them when he examined defence requirements. BrahMos missile offered the solution to fill the gaps. Not only does it travel unnoticed by the enemy radar, it also flies very close to earth. It could easily destroy a target that was even 500 km away. The BrahMos missile could be launched from land, flight, ship or a submarine.

Indians had gained expertise to design and develop all other missiles. Right from the SLV-3 initiative, they were trained in fuel technology, ballistics, equipment and other infrastructure. In 1993, they had gained some 25 years of experience. Industries were trained to manufacture indigenous spare parts and other component parts. There were hundreds of well-trained engineers, technicians and other experts. We had enough manpower to design and manufacture all other missiles. However, this alone is not sufficient to make a supersonic cruise missile.

Kalam knew the difficulties involved in making such a missile. Therefore, without being adamant that it should be designed and produced indigenously, he analysed the possibility of manufacturing it with the assistance of a friendly foreign industry/organisation. He realised that it could be made with Russia's assistance (the Soviet Union had broken down at the time into smaller countries). I believe that he must have consulted the Prime Minister and the Defence Minister. I was not sure of this at the time. I came to know of this from Kalam and Dr. Sivathanu Pillai only at the start of the BrahMos Missile project. Dr. Sivathanu Pillai has explained this in detail in his segment of the present work. Dr. Sivathanu Pillai assisted Kalam right from his SLV-3 days. He worked with Kalam in the IGMDP project as well.

Kalam boldly analysed this BrahMos project in 1993 and in 1995, he signed a memorandum of understanding with Prof. Yefremov. The BrahMos organisation was formed on February 12, 1998 after overcoming several setbacks caused due to the political turmoil in Russia. The name '*BrahMos*' was derived by joining the first few letters of the Indian '*Brahmaputra*' river and the Russian '*Moskva*' river. This was one of the biggest achievements of the DRDO. All branches of the Indian Defence Force viz. Army, Navy and Air Force readily included BrahMos in their operations. Due to the land boundaries established in those days (due to MTCR restrictions), the boundary for the BrahMos missile was set to be 290 km. We are finding this limit to be useful even today. Many foreign nations were willing to buy this missile.

This joint initiative that was undertaken by the Indian government was the precursor to several other future technical projects. Kalam was extremely pleased with his BrahMos mission. It becomes important to mention here that several big shots of the DRDO initially made fun of this initiative and opposed it. They said that this was not entirely designed by India. They forgot the fact that many DRDO projects got delayed on account of this self-sufficiency accusation; and their attempts for self-sufficiency caused serious delays. On account of such delays, they couldn't be put to immediate use by our armed forces. Chief examples of this were the *Main Combat Tank* (MCT) and *Light Combat Aircraft* (LCA). I am mentioning this here to convey the message that even though Kalam was a senior official at the DRDO, he understood the requirements of the Indian Armed forces and took initiatives to manufacture such products and took pragmatic steps without obsession with complete self sufficiency.

Likewise, Kalam also tried to conduct joint initiatives with Israel that had the state-of-the art technology that could be used in India. Today, we realise that all his initiatives have been very helpful indeed. When Kalam talked about his Israel trip later, he also talked about his prayers at the Al Aqsa Mosque there.

Meanwhile, the readers might be wondering about the Abdul Kalam-George Fernandes 70%-30% initiative. Fernandes and Kalam tried their best. However, to execute such plans in a democracy is a big challenge (even now this is the case). As per the request made by George Fernandes, the seven reports were prepared by the end of 1998. He also received them. The NDA government with Vajpayee as the PM was ruling at the time. BJP did not have the full majority. Rajiv Gandhi resigned as the PM in 1989 (as he did not have a clear majority in the elections, he left it to V. P. Singh's coalition to rule). None of the parties at the centre got a clear majority. The major supporters of the NDA were Telugu Desam of Chandrababu Naidu, ADMK of Jayalalitha, Trinamul Congress of Mamta Banerjee, JD(U) of George Fernandes and a few other small parties. Fernandes had the responsibility to manage this coalition; he was the alliance convenor. Jayalalitha was pressuring the central government according to her needs. One of her major requests was to dismiss the ruling DMK party in Tamil Nadu and to conduct fresh state elections there. Vajpayee did not oblige to her request since that would be a gross disrespect to Indian democracy. On April 17, 1999, Jayalalitha pulled out of the NDA alliance by passing a no-confidence motion. The Vajpayee government lost its leadership by a single vote. Therefore, Vajpayee who came to power on March 18, 1998 had to resign on April 18, 1999. The Indian President Shri K. R. Narayanan announced general elections. He asked Vajpayee to remain as PM till results were announced. The elections were held between September 5 to October 3, 1999.

This being the situation, no big tasks could be undertaken. Besides, Pakistan attacked India at the Kargil border. The Kargil war lasted from May to July, 1999. It was a major event in Indian history. Earlier, Vajpayee had visited Pakistan to maintain friendly relations. For the first time, an Indian Prime Minister visited Pakistan! In spite of several oppositions, he took bold steps to strengthen peace and harmony and to maintain friendly relationships. In spite of this, Pakistan attacked India. Many people were frustrated by this.

India emerged victorious in the Kargil war. In the September-October, 1999 elections, the NDA alliance won. Vajpayee continued as the Prime minister. The Kargil war brought to light the weaknesses of the border security forces. Therefore, India decided to strengthen this through a joint initiative with Israel. Being the *Scientific Adviser to the Defence Minister*, Kalam had to focus on that. Naturally, Fernandes's scheme with the seven-committee task force was pushed down to the bottom of the list. Their goal to transform Indian import from 70% to 30% and Indian export from 30% to 70% became less significant.

Neither the ruling nor the opposition parties in India have any interest in schemes that run for some ten or twenty years. They prefer short-term plans instead. To strengthen the foundation of our nation, it is important for all schemes to run consecutively for at least twenty years. However, our politicians are not worried about that. It is surprising that the *Indian Space Department* managed to establish itself somehow. In order to achieve further, changes must be made by the government administration. We need to wait for something like that to happen!

Likewise, for successful missile launches, a change in the pattern of our administrative system is a must. However, even these are happening at a slow pace.

A few schemes like national highways, modernising Indian airports etc have achieved some success.

If that 70%-30% to 30%-70% had started as planned in 1998, then today India would have been in a better position. Indian security and military operations could have been strengthened. Also, many defence/military factories could have been established (through government and private sectors). It could have increased the employment opportunities to many people; they could have remained permanently employed.

A few 'mature' politicians from Delhi have mentioned this to me: "Rajan! These changes are not brought about by technical or industrial skills. More imports mean more corruption. It could be easily hidden abroad. Therefore, we need to wait patiently for everything to become clean!"

This is a 'foolish approach' according to me. There is some truth to this. I know this from my personal experiences since 1990. Even then, we must try to do our best. We must continue to do our best. We must work with the spirit that it will dawn soon!

The slogan '*Make in India*' is the latest morale booster to many Indians today. We will have to wait and see whether the productivity in India will increase due to this. Let us hope for the best. The first shoots of these efforts can be seen only in 2020. It might take another 5-10 years to grow into a big tree. Had he been alive, Kalam would have been thrilled. Let us keep our fingers crossed!

❑

Kalam Becomes the Principal Scientific Adviser to the Indian Government

1999 was an important year in Kalam's life. He was getting close to 68. He had completed seven successful years as the *Scientific Adviser of the Defence Minister Secretary DDRD* and was entering into his eighth.

The most important job for successfully launching a missile with a nuclear bomb was completed. After one year of its completion, the Kargil War happened. Even though India emerged victorious, the deficiencies of our defence sector in some areas became apparent. Therefore, the DRDO was unable to proceed any further.

But most importantly, our armed forces needed several war equipment.The projects undertaken by the DRDO were taking longer than expected, especially the LCA.

Kalam alone cannot change everything. He needed political support. He also had to answer those with opposing viewpoints (as mentioned earlier)!

The senior officials of DRDO were only eyeing for his post.

Therefore, the thought of leaving his job was foremost in Kalam's mind. On the one hand, he was happy that he had achieved his important goals. On the other hand, he wanted to know about the unaccomplished ones and possibly newer ones. But he could not continue in the same post. Already he had created a record in crossing the official age limit!

He also spoke to me about changing his job. After Vajpayee returned with a strong majority, Kalam decided that it would be the right time to approach him.

Kalam was not someone who would retire entirely from his activities. Even as an individual, he liked to work non-stop. The time he spent with his family occupied only a small portion of his life.

All his life, he had never remained jobless. He worked 365 days in ordinary years and 366 days in a leap year. He was now 68 years old. How could he change his habit now? Besides, he would meet at least 500 people per day. He was alone only while sleeping at night; someone or the other will be there with him till then.

How could he cut away from all this? From his point of view, all that remained in front of him was absolute darkness (soonya).

Also, one big problem faced by most senior officials is the lack of crowd gathering around them soon after retirement.

Therefore, the biggest challenge in front of him was what to do after resigning from his post as the defence minister's scientific adviser.

One thing became clear though! He must occupy a major post within the government. Many should come and visit him. Other than that, it would be even better if the new job involved creating many more visionary projects.

But, it should not be within the DRDO where he currently worked!

But he wasn't sure about his future once he retires from the DRDO. The cost of all projects of the DRDO usually amounted to some few 100 crores. Whereas, in smaller organisations like the TIFAC which was meant to devise technical schemes for the Indian citizens, even 10, 20 or 30 crores will be more than enough.

Kalam who had worked with ISRO and DRDO was only familiar with high-budget projects.

He told me one day:

"Rajan, there is a 10,000-crore initiative. If I accept the challenge, it could take some 10 or 15 years to get completed..there is a chance for me to get the job...what do you say?" Kalam asked.

I immediately asked: "Is it within the DRDO?"

Kalam said: "Yes! It could also be within the defence ministry. Why do you ask?"

I replied: "Sir! You have been an emperor there. It may not suit you to become a king, or a tiny chieftain over there. In India, 'authority' is the topmost priority. With power comes authority!"

Kalam said, "Alright...could this project be attempted as a separate initiative with powers directly given to the project manager?"

I replied, "Sir, even if it is written in the document that you will directly report to the *Defence Minister*, as per the rules of the government of India, it should come only under a department. The minister cannot help you in any way directly. Only a department can send a finance request report to the government. The fund requests for your SLV-3 and IGMDP initiatives were sent only through the respective departments. For SLV-3, it was the Space department and for IGMDP it was the DDRD. The powers that you have at present are those of the secretary of the DDRD department. The official powers of the head of the DRDO and the *Defence Minister's Scientific Adviser* are also obtained from the DDRD department. Now that you are holding all the three posts, you wouldn't realise it. Besides in ISRO, the secretary of the department of space (DOS) has the rightful government power and authority. The powers of the Chairman ISRO and the Chairman*Space Commission* are obtained from the *Secretary* DOS alone."

"That is the reason why those three posts in ISRO are held by the same person. Even though you had complete independence while undertaking your SLV-3 and IGMDP initiatives, recall how many hurdles you had to cross. Dr. Brahm Prakash and Prof. Dhawan protected you at ISRO. Likewise, Dr. V. S. Arunachalam protected you during the IGMDP initiative."

"But now you have become the emperor. Don't you think that you would require some such department for yourself? However, it is unsure if a separate department would be established to fulfil your visionary goals. It would only come under the DDRD or DRDO; moreover, the DRDO engineers and technicians have to make use of available resources there! They will only approach the DDRD secretary. They would probably salute you when they see you. However, they know that their future lies only in the hands of the DDRD secretary and DG DRDO. This is the world!"

"An emperor cannot become the king of his own land. He could get out of it and stay under a peepal or a banyan tree! He could even establish a new country over there! However, when a new emperor arrives to take his place, he must leave his country!"

Kalam said, "What sir! Why are you giving me such a big lecture!"

I said, "To cut it short, once you leave your post at the DRDO, you must no longer stay there. You should not sign up for any big projects over there. Likewise, in ISRO as well. You must therefore ask the Indian government to create a new big post for yourself. Besides your personal charisma, the current Indian Prime minister has great respect and regards for you."

"Therefore, let them create a new '*Cabinet Rank*' position for you. Let them make you in charge of all S&T activities and grant you the power to govern their applications. Now that you have become a '*Bharat Ratna*', no one including the higher officials would object to you becoming a cabinet minister!"

"It would be better for you to leave your current DRDO post. If you stay there any longer, those in your lower ranks would create more trouble. It is best to leave. You should immediately take up a higher role. Please take steps for that!"

Kalam said, "Ok, I understand your point now!"

It was a tough call for him. He has never served in a big post involving only policy and supervision without accomplishing any major projects. Plans, reviews, timesheets, travel, launching in space, more plans, accomplishments, failures, research reviews, then further accomplishments, new schemes–he was used to this routine in his professional life. In 1982, when he joined the DRDO, he was involved in many big projects with several crores as their budget. He could have easily accepted the 10,000-crore project with a 10–15 years timeline; however, it will all be under the DRDO.

I did not pour cold water over that opportunity. He has accomplished many things in his life. Is it necessary for him to run here and there seeking permission and becoming an easy target for others to hit on him like before? Those who had gained enough experience from him could take care of such jobs. I did not want him to exert himself since he was already 68 years old.

Moreover, his charisma and charm would help accomplish many of the *TIFAC Vision 2020* projects. At the time, he was chairmanTIFAC for nearly five years. He knew several industrialists and trade experts through CII. If he gets the post of a cabinet minister, then he could easily convince them to take up many of the *Vision 2020* initiatives. As he was already close to the Prime minister, I felt that at least a few major projects could be accomplished. It is not possible to accomplish them merely through TIFAC or DST.

Therefore, I felt that Kalam could serve our nation in a big way. He too understood me. However, he had a fond hope to do a big budget project for the DRDO. Moreover, for the Vision 2020 projects to materialise he had to enter into a whole new sphere! He probably hesitated because of that too.

Finally, he was cleared of his confusion. Now his only ambition was to empower India and he got ready to accept this challenge. *Vision 2020* had already paved the pathway to achieve this. He knew the reach of our book and how all Indians appreciated its ideas. It was translated to many Indian languages within a year. Kalam was getting prepared to take up a whole new *avatar*.

He called me urgently one day in December 1999. At that time, I was in TIFAC. "Rajan! Please come immediately! I spoke with the PM, right? Now, Brijesh Mishra is asking me to prepare a brief summary of my job profile. Dr. Sivathanu Pillai is already here in my office with me. Please come here urgently..."

Usually, his conversation started with "Have you eaten? What was your breakfast today?..." Only after speaking for a few minutes like this, will he come to the central point of discussion. I therefore realised that he was in an urgency today. I understood that Brijesh Mishra was going to place his request in the cabinet on the same day.

The three of us consulted with each other. There was no confusion. It is not enough if he was appointed only as the Principal Scientific Adviser to the PM. I already discussed the case of Prof. M. G. K. Menon and Dr. Vasant Gowariker. Therefore, we wrote his profile as '*The Principal Scientific Adviser to the Government of India*'. We also included the supervision of scientific, technical skills in socio-economic sectors and authority to decide relevant applications as a part of his job profile. Besides being an adviser, he can now start and complete several socio-economic projects.

For the first time in the history of government administration, Kalam became a *Cabinet Minister* and was appointed as 'The Principal Scientific Adviser (PSA) to the Government of India'. He was asked to appoint a '*Scientific Advisory Committee to the Cabinet* (SACC)'. Even though there was a committee like this earlier, it did not have enough authority.

He was also made a member in the selection committee to decide a suitable candidate for his earlier post; usually, this was never done. Kalam's age and experience could have been the reason for this. DRDO's experienced senior official Dr. Vasudev K. Aatre was appointed by the selection committee. He had crossed his 60 then (on August 28, 1999). He was allowed to work for five years.

Kalam's new office was not yet ready! This happened frequently in government circles. They were yet to decide a suitable place for the office of the *Indian government's Principal Scientific Adviser*! For a few days, Kalam worked from his old office. Since he had to give way to Dr. Aatre, Kalam vacated his office room and relocated to the room next to it. Kalam felt that this would be a big hindrance to Aatre and so decided to prepare a suitable office space.

Major General Swaminathan (who worked as a Chief Controller of R&D (CCRD) at the DRDO) assisted him. Kalam also wanted me to go with him. We selected a room for Kalam in *Vigyan Bhawan Annexe* building. Everything (even toilet) should be optimised according to the needs of Kalam's Z-security! We installed phones and a RAX (which was a secret phone). In this way, the *Office of the Principal Scientific Adviser* was linked with the Cabinet *Secretariat*. All jobs must go through them. Moreover, in Delhi, offices were frequently relocated as per the needs of the VIPs and the VVIPs. Therefore, those who allotted the rooms and those who had to change rooms would be running here and there.

Kalam's office room and his private secretary's room were finalised at last! Kalam sat down in his new office room. I was getting a salary from the CII; I was with TIFAC to heed to the request of the DST secretary, V S Ramamurthy who told me: "Please do not leave us. You should work for us till you are 60 (as per the government gazette, I would turn 60 in April 2003!)" Moreover, Kalam was the Chairman of TIFAC.

Now my workload increased with Kalam's new role. I had to ensure that he had a suitable work space in the *Vigyan Bhawan* annexe building. I also wanted to make sure that his office space was different from those of others. I did not want him to have an office space with the usual senior official, a few secretaries and drivers. It must be a work space that conveyed power. This in itself was a big challenge. Because many big shots worked in huge offices, lived in the government Lutyens bungalows, and earned salaries for years together without doing anything. Those in power never respected such people. They used to say that they worked for 'time pass' only.

Many offices in that *Vigyan Bhawan* link building were like that. Most of them were retired judges heading some enquiry commission or another. I mentioned this as a joke to Kalam: "Sir, for the first time, you have brought a Science Office (Office of the *Principal Scientific Adviser* to the Indian government) to the *Vigyan Bhawan* Annexe Building. All others over here are either enquiry commissions or councils that resolve interstate conflicts."

"Is that so?" said Kalam and laughed.

To assist him with office matters, H. Sheridon was sent from the DRDO. Dr. Aatre is a good man. He felt that Kalam would be comfortable with a familiar face and so sent H. Sheridon for assistance.

Even though I visited him frequently, he had not selected me to work with him. For that to happen, he had to create a fresh post. As he was the cabinet minister, they gave him a few assistants. Those were the government rules. But the office of S&T must be created anew. Even to employ people from all other departments, it was mandatory to take this first step. Kalam was not used to this. While he worked at the ISRO and the DRDO, the respective organisations took care of such matters for him.

Next, Kalam had to appoint members for the SACC. He had to get approvals for them from the government.

One day when I was in Goa for a TIFAC matter, Kalam called me urgently.

"Rajan! You have to come back here soon and accept a job in my office. I have to appoint a member secretary to the SACC. I have to send a proposal to the PM." I never stayed for days on end in any place. Right from my ISRO days, I got used to travelling. Now, I was travelling more than ever! Since Kalam had called me, I urgently left Goa.

As soon as I returned, I met Kalam. "Rajan, we have to start this office as soon as possible. The cabinet secretariat officials are asking about the SACC members. The post of SACC's member secretary is equivalent to that of the secretary of the Indian government. I need an expert scientist to fill the post. Everyone is recommending only your name. What is the formality in CII to announce your resignation? Kalam asked me.

I gave my reply.

"Three months is the official advance notice in CII to send resignation! However, several tasks that I undertook last year are still incomplete..."

Kalam asked, "Can you ask Tarun Das?"

I said, "Ok, let me see! But one important thing. It wouldn't be nice if I was simply assigned the role of member secretary to SACC. My job should be equivalent to that of the secretaries of other departments. Only then will I get the authority to accomplish my job."

Kalam said, "Ok, I will try!"

Moreover, if I join here, I would incur a loss; the salary I get here will be deducted from my pension. If my job isn't equivalent to that of an Indian government secretary, then I won't be able to push those in power to complete our job. Since Kalam headed the department as Minister, he cannot directly be in touch with other officials. All department jobs must be done only by the respective officials!

I met Tarun Das and informed him. He knew that the CII technology division was established by me. But since there were no suitable candidates in Kalam's new office, Tarun Das told me, "Rajan! I feel sorry that we will be losing you. Please write a job description of your new job. Ask for immediate resignation. I will sign it. That's all! After this, the Indian government will grant you your new job!"

Tarun Das is an admirable person.

I did as he told and got the letter accepting my resignation from CII.

Before I left the place, Tarun Das told me, "Rajan, the government people are very funny. You or your family should not get affected. Until they allot you a government quarters, you can stay in the house given to you by the CII. You could use our car too. They could possibly delay your quarters allotment!"

What he foretold happened. In spite of being a high level official, I found it difficult to get government quarters. I would have been happy had they even given me a house even in the quarters of lower officials. It took me three months to get a government quarters. The cabinet secretariat refused to pay to CII the rent they paid for me for those three months! I felt really sad that Kalam did not take any initiative to return this money to the CII. I was given the government car only after a few more weeks!

The name given to my new job was also meaningless! There was no reason to consider it equivalent to the Indian government's secretary. I asked Kalam specifically for a role as the Secretary to the Government of India in the Principal Scientific Adviser's office. Nothing happened. This was a big setback not only to me but also to the activities undertaken by the office of the Principal Scientific

The eleventh President of India Dr. A. P. J. Abdul Kalam

Young Abdul Kalam

Kalam in deep thought

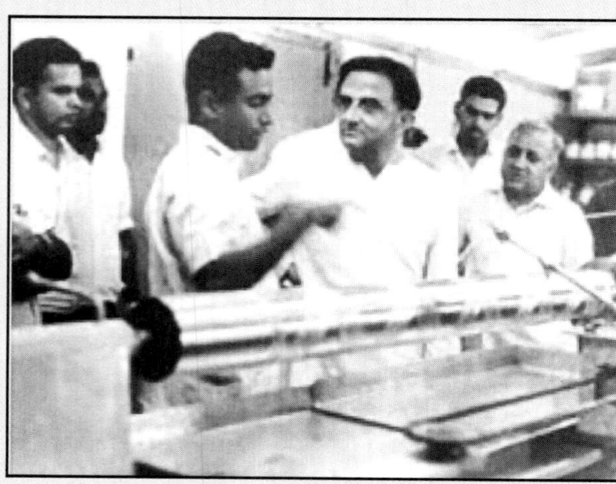

Young Abdul Kalam with Dr. Vikram Sarabhai; standing on the left is Madhavan Nair

People who studied with Kalam (from left) Iyyappan Nair, H. S. R. Iyengar. (Seated) T. R. Dhanaseelan, S. Krishnasamy, A. P. J. Kalam, V. G. Uppin

After SLV's victory in 1980, Kalam with Prime Minister Indira Gandhi and Professor Satish Dhawan

Scientist Kalam with Prime Minister Indira Gandhi

Kalam with Prime Minister Narasimha Rao. Standing on the extreme right is A. Sivathanu Pillai

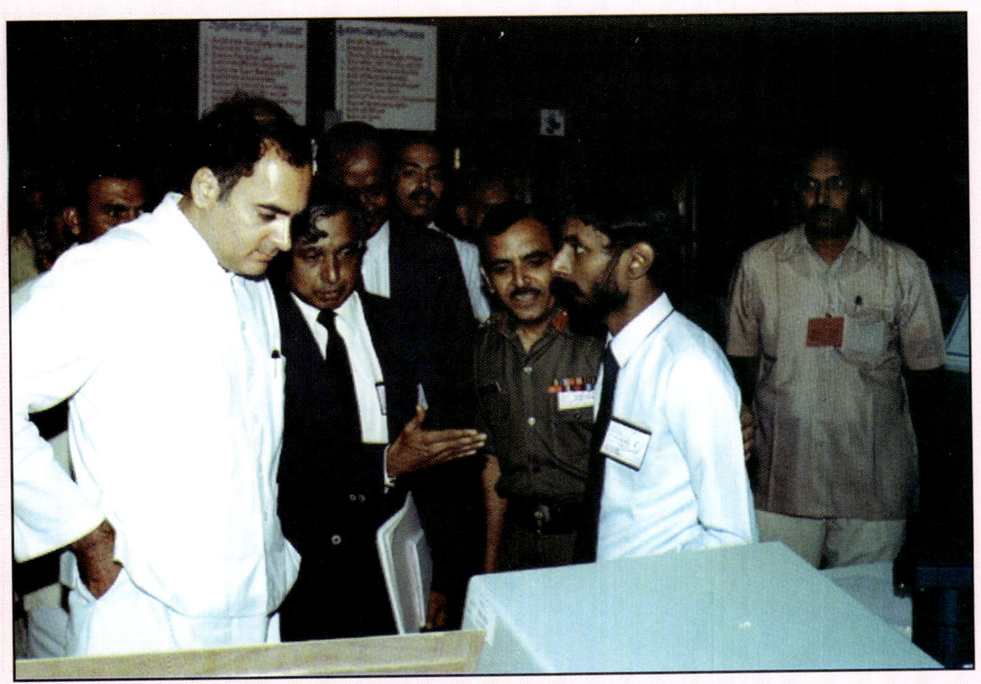

Kalam briefs Prime Minister Rajiv Gandhi of the technical details

Kalam with Prime Minister I. K. Gujral in a Science Exhibition

Kalam in blissful conversation with his mentor (Professor Satish Dhawan, Dr. Kalam)

Kalam with nuclear scientist Raja Ramanna

Kalam receives the 'Padma Bhushan' award from President Sanjeeva Reddy

Kalam receives the 'Padma Vibhushan' award from President R. Venkataraman

Kalam receives the 'Bharat Ratna' award from President K. R. Narayanan

Kalam delivering his Presidential address (27 July 2002)

Kalam while delivering his Presidential address

Kalam with Murli Manohar Joshi in the international conference held for Technology Vision operations (10-11 February 2008)

Kalam with his brother and Rajan's father at Rashtrapati Bhawan

Back left Gomati, Shahul Hamid and family, Nazema.
Front: Kalam's brother, Kalam, Saleem

On the Oath taking function of Kalam as President Kalam's brother and Rajan's father in front seat as desired by Kalam

Dr. Mahalingam honouring President Kalam Dr. Manikkam behind

Dr. Mahalingam and Kalam

Dr. Mahalingam presenting a special art work to Kalam

Dr. Manikkam and Kalam

Kalam delivering his address

At Kuthodaw Pagoda, Mandalay , Myanmar near 250 years old The Star Flower Tree during State visit of President Kalam

President Kalam with Indian Members of Parliament in his team during the State Visit to Myanmar

Kalam and Dr. Murli Manohar Joshi discussing with V S Ramamurthy Secretary DST Rajan at two ends

President Kalam at the first convocation of Punjab Technical University March 2003 with the Governor and Chief Minister on either side

State visit to Greece

At 10 Rajaji Marg lawns From left Rajan, his second son Vikram, Kalam and Vijay the elder son

Kalam, Anu (Rajan's daughter-in- law) with her son Ashwin near Kalam when celebrating the first anniversary of Ashwin at the Rashtrapati Bhawan

Release of the Technology Vision for India 2020-25 documents. Along with the then Prime Minister Shri Deve Gowda are the Minister of Science Y. K. Alagh, Kalam, Dr. Y. S. Rajan, and the Secretary DST Ramamurthy

In a programme organised by the National Agro Foundation in 2002. (The organisation was founded by C. Subramaniam)

Kalam welcoming American President George Bush upon his arrival to India (March, 2006)

Prayers and wishes by the Rameswaram Hindu, Christian and Muslim religious leaders when Kalam became the Indian President (Kalam's brother and Dr. Y. S. Rajan's father are standing next to each other)

First Graduation ceremony held in Punjab Technical University (21 March 2003). An Indian President is visiting Punjab after twenty years. Here, Vice Chancellor Dr. Y. S. Rajan is delivering his commemoration address

Unexpected visit by the Indian President Kalam to Dr. Y. S. Rajan's Chandigarh house- Gomati (left), Geetha Raghuraman (right). (The President who voluntarily offered to eat whatever was there in Kuchela's house)

National Science Conference, Ukraine June 3, 2005 (Chairperson of ISRO Madhavan Nair, is seated next to Kalam)

During the President's Myanmar trip in Kuthodaw Pagoda Buddhist stupa (10 March 2006)

Kalam with Singapore President (February 1, 2006)

Kalam with General Than Shwe, Chairman of the State Peace and Development Council, Myanmar (Myanmar trip, March 8-10, 2006)

Kalam with his elder brother Mohammed Muthu Meera Maraikayar

What's so strange! Kalam with his niece Dr. Nazema Maraikayar in the newly built House of Kalam

The President cuddling his brother

Kalam with children

Walking exercise in the Rashtrapati Bhavan Mughal Garden

President undertakes an adventurous flight journey

Kalam in the Rashtrapati Bhavan Mughal garden

Kalam lighting lamp at TIFAC function with Sunita Wadhwa "the Composites Lady" and Dr. Y.S. Rajan

Kalam playing his Veena

Kalam honours Arutchelvar N. Mahalingam. Standing nearby are M. Manikkam and secretary C. Ramasamy

Kalam during the diamond jubilee celebration of Kavignar Sirpi Balasubramaniam

President Kalam with Gomati in kitchen at Rajan's Chandigarh house

Kalam is cutting the birthday cake of Dr. Y. S. Rajan's grandson Ashwin. Standing near him are Vijay, Mahalakshmi, Ashwin, Koma, Vikram, Aditya and Dr. Y. S. Rajan

Kalam with his personal secretary Sheridon

Kalam with his relatives in Rameswaram while discussing his brother's centennial celebration

Kalam with Acharya Mahapragya

Acharya Mahapragya at the left end when Kalam visited his place

Aerial view of Kalam Memorial

Prime Minister Shri Narendra Modi pays homage at the Kalam Memorial

President Of India Kovind in another function paying floral tributes to Kalam in the memorial

Prime Minister Shri Narendra Modi pays homage to the mortal remains of Kalam

Kalam with Prime Minister Atal Bihari Vajpayee

The things used by Kalam are displayed in Kalam Memorial in Rameswaram

Kalam Memorial, Rameswaram

Prime Minister Shri Narendra Modi inaugurates Dr. A. P. J. Abdul Kalam National Memorial in Rameswaram

Prime Minister with Kalam's brother and Nazema at the Kalam memorial on the inaugural day

PM with part of Kalam family at the Kalam memorial

The house where Kalam was born (House of Kalam) in Rameswaram

On the 100 year completion of Kalam's brother at Rameswaram first cake piece given by his grandson Sheikh

(After Kalam's death) During the Centennial celebration of Kalam's brother Muthu Meera Maraikayar. Near him are Dr. Nazema Maraikayar and Dr. Y. S. Rajan

Adviser. Kalam's weakness was that he was not familiar with the formalities of the government departments. He never understood the difficulties of those who worked under him. He already knew why I left the DST.

I kept all my anxieties within myself. I trusted that by being a part of the Indian government's Principal Scientific Adviser team, I could reach out to the needs of the Indian people. I realised that this was possible only through Kalam's charisma and charm. He is the *Bharat Ratna*, the missile man of India, and a visionary who could accomplish the *India 2020* initiatives. His '*Wings of Fire*' was translated to many Indian languages that greatly attracted the politicians and people of various states. It was very important to reach out to the people and leaders of various states. Already S. K. Sinha's TIFAC agriculture projects had been tested successfully in Bihar, and Kanchipuram of Tamil Nadu.

❑

Conflicts between Science and Engineering

Kalam was appreciated by people worldover. However, some of the Indian S&T big shots opposed him.

These big shots controlled Indian S&T from outside. They got hold of some big politicians (mainly the ministers and the Prime Minister) and established *Science Advisory Committees.* They would then head the committee and make their 'cronies' as the committee members. In this way, they laid down a strong foundation for their own rule over S&T. This practice started as early as the 1970s. Slowly, they started to appoint the *Directors of the National Laboratories*, and other S&T government secretaries (DST, Biotechnology Department, Ocean Department, and Department of Scientific and Industrial Research and directors of its labs), and headed those selection committees too. In this manner, they selected those people who were responsible for handling government funds. Therefore, it became easy for them to keep them under their control (as their puppets).

Satish Dhawan ensured that ISRO and the Space department did not fall into the hands of such people (1972–84).He was the secretary of the Space department. Without a doubt, he was the senior amongst all of S&T officials. But he avoided unnecessary politics in Science. He made sure that neither himself nor ISRO were affected by such a culture of politicking. That is the main reason for all of ISRO's achievements.

It was because of the impenetrable fort that Professor Dhawan built that ISRO was able to achieve more and more. His successors like Professor U. R. Rao continued his legacy and carefully protected ISRO.

Likewise, an impenetrable fort was built by Dr. Raja Ramanna at the DDRD and DRDO. He ensured the appointment of Dr. Arunachalam at a young age as the secretary of the DDRD and DG DRDO and SA to RM and strengthened it. Dr. Arunachalam was very efficient in handling these matters. He ensured that these S&T big shots did not interfere in the activities of the DRDO. Besides, since the DRDO received massive government funding, he ensured that the experts in the S & T field received good financial aid to their projects.

It was because of this that Dr. Arunachalam's post was handed over to Kalam without the interference of these big shots. Arunachalam himself became one of the Indian S&T big shots. Since he left to America, he lost his influence.

These big shots did not accept Kalam as a scientist. This was unfortunate to India's S&T policy and administration. Like scientific skills, engineering skills too are important. One is not superior to the other. Science analyses and identifies the basic laws of nature. But, engineering/technical skills are the source of supply of products and services needed by the people, for the economy, and the country's security. Satellites, rockets, cars, agricultural machinery, fertilisers, medicines, X-Ray and blood pressure measuring instruments, computers, guns, mobile phones, air conditioners and many such products are born out of engineering/ technical skills. Science knowledge alone will not suffice.

This is what differentiates people in DRDO and ISRO, especially Kalam, from others. He was action oriented. His engineering and technical capabilities were amazing, and he was a capable *Project Manager* as well.

Take for example the mobile phones we all use everyday. It is made up of more than 100 components, all of which should function properly and then integrate well for the mobile phone to work efficiently. Hundreds of technical skills are incorporated into this. The term '*Electronic manufacture*' alone does not explain mobile. Research takes place in a very narrow boundary. For efficient production (of product and services), this research alone won't be enough.

Individual researchers are needed. But we also need innovators and technicians who make products for the country and its people. Without doing it, just reciting 'Science' 'Science' in their own corners, these big shots in India have made the Indian S&T field stagnant.

In order to show their supremacy, they held onto the *Indian National Science Academy* (INSA). They prevented people like Kalam from entering it. They did the same thing with Prof. Dhawan earlier; however, Dhawan was not a man to beg for a place. Finally, when Raja Ramanna took over as the President INSA, he asked: " INSA without Professor Dhawan who heads a large S&T organisation? How is that even possible?" Raja Ramanna was not a great friend of Prof. Dhawan. But he did not want the country to forget the service rendered by Prof. Dhawan. He got phlegmatic replies: "Sir, he did not apply!"

Raja Ramanna asked back: “Then how come Jawaharlal Nehru is an INSA Fellow? He was not even a Science Graduate?”

“Sir, that was done by the INSA President back then!”

“Then I will also do the same,” said Raja Ramanna and made Prof. Dhawan as an INSA Fellow.

Kalam’s achievements were ignored by the later INSA Presidents and officials. They looked upon science with a narrow lens. Kalam was already the President of the *Indian National Academy of Engineering* (INAE). INAE got separated because of this narrow-mindedness of INSA. Sir C. V. Raman came out of INSA and established the Indian Academy of Science (IAS). Kalam was an elected member of IAS too.

Those INSA big shots did not allow Kalam to get recognition as a researcher. They also started talking behind his back: “Kalam is not a scientist. How can he be made the Principal Scientific Adviser?”

I have written a poem about how these big shots in India have spoiled the name of science and technology in India. It was written on 1.12.96 and I gave a copy to Kalam. It appears in the ‘*Blossoms of the Heart*’ poetry collection. It was written after the 25 reports of *TIFAC’s Vision 2020* were dedicated to the nation (2.8.96).

A few lines from ‘The New Saffron Robes’ poem:

Science did he wear as a
New saffron robe;
Everywhere did he raise on his name
His flag;
With a motley crowd near him
Does he rule,
Only with the aim
Of perpetuating it;

No use to country,
No help to the people;
The Government has no time
To question and correct!
In the hunt of jackals
Did the good get hurt;
In technology and science
Does Bharath hang its head!

The way how these people portrayed Kalam behind his back must have reached Kalam’s ears. All the cheerfulness he had while he was appointed as the *Principal Scientific Adviser* turned into bitterness because of such people. (The way these same people came to Kalam and genuflecting before him, when he became the Indian President, is yet another matter! More about that later!)

On the one hand, Kalam had to hear such talks even when he was seated on the chair of PSA office; on the other hand, he felt a shock over the fact that he left such a big organisation as the DRDO having over 25,000 employees where per day transactions was more than ten crores on several big projects, and is now sitting alone as PSA! It took several weeks for him to heal.

As soon as I joined him, I attempted to create more posts to bring in more employees. H. Sheridon took care of typing and other activities in his office room.

The important part is to identify the SACC members and get it approved by the government. Kalam was given absolute authority to decide upon the proposal. Earlier, in SACC (which was at the time non-existent for several years in a row!), a few big shots, heads of various Science departments (DST, Biotechnology department, *Department of Scientific and Industrial Research* DSIR), a few senior professors, and research scientists were made as members. The big shots would speak to secretaries of science departments and the meeting would end soon thereafter. The bigwigs used this as a mode of getting cleared their pet projects. Therefore (unlike before) in order to have a broad base of S&T representation , we carefully selected the members of SACC. In order to avoid big shots into the SACC, we created a separate *Consultative Group of Eminent Scientists* (CGES) meant to obtain guidance and advice from eminent scientists and prepared a detailed list of such members. Those who did not indulge in science politics but were high achievers in the S&T field were made as members. Examples: Dr. S. Z. Qasim who was the first Indian to go to Antarctica; former Secretary, Department of Ocean Professor U. R. Rao; Space Secretary, responsible for the launch of India's first satellite Aryabhata satellite and so on... We also enlisted a few big shots who engaged more in politics.

We therefore chose active persons engaged in various S&T activities from various national labs and academic institutions in the country. We looked at their work profile while selecting and not so much the positions they held. We also ensured that S&T people from all over India including women were selected as SACC members. Many were researchers elected as fellows of INSA, INAE, IAS, and *National Academy of Scientists* (NAS). There were also senior persons from the corporate sector.

Besides these two, in order for other socio-economic ministries to support our S&T projects (so that it would help our Indian people and Indian Economy), we enlisted secretaries of various departments (mostly IAS officers) involved in implementation of S&T intensive socio-economic projects. I think that something like this was being done for the first time in the Indian government. This third group was called the *Consultative Group for Departments Applying Science and Technology* referred to as *'CGDAST'*.

Kalam being the *Principal Scientific Adviser* was the chairman of all the three groups/ committees viz. SACC, CGES, and CGDAST. I was the *Member Secretary*. After the PM's approval, all these were notified in the Government Gazette. We gave the addresses of all members to the Cabinet Secretariat. There were no changes to what we had sent. We had submitted the details of work and responsibilities of all the three groups.

People in SACC and CGDAST were very happy. They immediately sent a response note to Kalam thanking him for selecting them. The same with most of CGES members too; only a few big shots and their close friends did not send a letter. In the cabinet secretariat, the gazettes are usually signed by the deputy secretary. A few big shots rejected the offer citing that they were tied up in other jobs; someone asked us to appoint another man in his place! Yet another was silent. All others (who were seniors to Kalam) cheerfully accepted Kalam as the leader and wrote that they were eagerly looking forward to work in the respective committees; they directly wrote this to Kalam. Those who rejected the offer only wrote to the deputy secretary without informing Kalam. Their letters were sent from the office of the deputy secretary to the PSA office!

Kalam was disappointed to note that a few big shots had rejected his offer. It was very important to conduct the committee meetings for the office to run smoothly. Even if there weren't enough people from the office of the Principal Scientific Adviser, I decided to seek assistance from the TIFAC employees since I was the Executive Director of TIFAC. These meetings will help promote TIFAC activities too.

Kalam was a bit hesitant because of the way in which some of these big shots handled the situation. Kalam also came to know that a few of these big shots went along with their friends to the Prime Minister to complain about Kalam. They probably told the PM: "Kalam is good for nothing; we are only big scientists. How could we work under him?" There was no news from the PMO.

I told Kalam: "There is no confusion about the other two groups (SACC and CGDAST). Let us hand over their list of initiatives to them."

Even in this high-profile CGES group, 75% of people have responded positively to you. You need not worry about the remaining 25%. You need not call them back or write to them. I will request the deputy secretary to whom they responded to advise on the course of action. We will do as he says!

He was still upset. Hesitantly, he nodded his head. I wrote about the CGES to the deputy secretary: "Such and such persons have responded to you. We need to invite the rest to attend the CGES meeting. Please advise."

In two days, we got our reply: "Leave them out of it and conduct the CGES meeting." Kalam was relieved after he saw the response. I invited everyone to the meeting. I even invited the big shot who hadn't responded. He did not even reply!

All meetings went very well. Everyone greatly respected Kalam. The secretaries of CGDAST said that they will give their full support to the *Vision 2020* initiatives and use all their powers to accomplish them. They decided to form 2 or 3 subcommittees to execute the tasks. A few core committees were formed to integrate the work of the subcommittees and to create large projects. Each sub-committee consisted of a secretary, a head, and a few members. It is very rare for such high level people to willingly offer their assistance.

Likewise, there were good debates held by the SACC. Discussions about improving our national laboratories, universities, and institutions happened. They pointed out the sections of the government rules and regulations that need to be changed in order to make progress. They also suggested ways in which scientists in various national laboratories and professors of universities and institutions could contribute to the ongoing *Vision 2020* projects.

In order to put this to practise, proper reports need to be prepared. Therefore, subcommittees were formed here too.

Overall, Kalam was very happy. He forgot all about the backbiting of a few big shots. A person who had gone with one of these big shots (who was a senior scientist who didn't indulge in politics), personally met Kalam and asked Kalam to forgive him: "I shouldn't have gone with them," he said. He is older than me but a good friend.

A few days later, the CGES meeting also happened. Those who attended it encouraged Kalam. They knew about the other big shots who refused to become a part of the CGES. They mocked those big shots without mentioning their names. A few important members helped to take specific action in their respective sectors (Example, *Energy*) by forming subcommittees.

In order for these three main groups to not become watertight compartments, I distributed the minutes of activities of one group to the other. I also prepared reports briefing them of the initiatives undertaken by other committee members, and asked them their feedback. A few people replied back. Everyone appreciated this technique.

They were therefore preparing reports on key initiatives for India's welfare. A few of them pointed to the shortcomings in the existing government policies and procedures. They also suggested suitable ways to rectify them. There were many constraints and hurdles to design, develop and manufacture on a large scale within India. (I feel sad that this is the case even today). Even if our industries are ready, due to faulty government policies and procedures as well as other difficulties in securing government industries purchase orders, India cannot manufacture on scale. As a consequence, India has to import!

❑

The Relationship between Murli Manohar Joshi and Kalam

Once the project proposals have been finalised in the PSA office, they have to be sent to the government for approval. Kalam, being a minister, cannot directly send it to the cabinet. I have already discussed all these in detail earlier. The office of the Principal Scientific Adviser is not a department. Had I been an Indian government secretary, I could have sent the files directly to other departments. If the files of *PM's Principal Scientific Adviser* are first sent to the DSTs, there would be no meaning to the existence of an office for the PSA. Moreover, if the files are sent to the DST directly, they will be making several rounds internally and I would have had to run from one department to the next. At most, Kalam could ask the secretary of the DST to take action swiftly, but for him PSA office work is not the priority. I therefore decided to solve this problem in another way by making use of the existing government rules and regulations. Since Kalam was a *Cabinet Minister*, he could approve sending it directly to a group of ministers. We then wouldn't have to rotate the files between various departments. Due to Kalam's stature, I felt that they would approve his request to create a '*Group Of Ministers*'(GOM). A senior *Cabinet Minister* can then head the GOM.

I consulted with Kalam who readily agreed to this arrangement. Since the *Office of the Principal Scientific Adviser's* primary assignments were related to the DST, it became clear that the GOM should be headed only by the S&T minister. Otherwise, the S&T minister could possibly raise objections during discussions at the GOM meetings! But there was a problem! The relationship with Kalam and Dr. Murli Manohar Joshi (MMJ) was not always smooth. It was not because

Joshi was close to R.S.S.; in fact, R.S.S. had great regard for Kalam. This was actually a personal conflict. Moreover, Kalam did not know Hindi, whereas even though Joshi spoke good English, he would be pleased if we interspersed our dialogue with Hindi while conversing with him. Besides, Joshi was a bit jealous of Kalam. I have seen Joshi and Kalam together in several TIFAC and other S&T meetings and workshops. Even though Joshi and Kalam were friendly towards each other, Joshi would be surprised to see a bigger crowd gathering near Kalam than himself. As mentioned earlier, 'Kalam was the Amitabh Bhachchan of S&T' and the media people flocked around him. Naturally, this caused bitterness and jealousy in Joshi's mind towards Kalam.

Other than this, a few people tried to create dissensions between Kalam and Joshi. I have seen this happen in Delhi circles. They had their own personal opinion about me. Even though Kalam and I were friends for a long time, it was the first time for me to work under him at the office in the office of PSA. So they labelled me as 'Kalam's Man'. I got introduced to Joshi during the leadership of Vajpayee (NDA) in 1998. I was working for CII and was also the executive director of TIFAC. I received my monthly salary from CII. Kalam and Joshi participated in TIFAC events. One day, Joshi asked me to prepare his speech. Joshi was very particular about his speeches. He used to correct copies of speech materials sent by other members of various departments under him. As he was doing it on his own, he lost a lot of time. I was not sure of the model in which I was supposed to prepare his speech material. (Earlier, I had prepared a few for PM Smt. Indira Gandhi). I understood while going through his earlier speeches that he liked to quote from the Vedas, Upanishads and other ancient texts. I made sure that the material I provided for his speech fit him well. Since he liked my first draft, he called me personally and said: "Rajan, I like your draft. For the first time, without making any changes, I am going to read from it." I too was pleased to hear this.

I therefore got several such opportunities. Moreover, a BJP leader M. L. Sondhi (an intellectual genius who served as a M.P. with Vajpayee) took me to visit Joshi frequently. Sondhi, popularly known as MLS, was a visionary who felt that India could be transformed by making use of science and technology. He therefore would insist on Murli Manohar Joshi to participate in many big S&T activities. He did not believe in symbolic efforts. He greatly enjoyed our India 2020 book. He therefore forced me to get in touch with Joshi (MMJ) directly. Since Joshi was the S&T minister, TIFAC was also under him.

Once, MLS took me to Jayalalitha to talk about the *Vision 2020* initiatives (for TN). It was an excellent meeting.

Sondhi was extremely pleased when Kalam became the scientific adviser. He requested Kalam to empower India with the aid of S&T.

My relationship with Joshi had always been cordial. He sought my help for some of his committee activities. He asked me to sketch plans for his Allahabad constituency, and asked me to implement *Vision 2020* initiatives in Uttarakhand, Uttar Pradesh, and Goa.

To Kalam, Joshi was 'My Friend'.

I served as a bridge between two of the greatest leaders of the S&T in the country.

I strongly felt that the GOM would unite everyone involved in S&T before the documents from the *Office of the Principal Scientific Adviser* were sent to the cabinet for approval. If this works according to plan, Murli Manohar Joshi will also earn a special status as he would be able to make an impact on other socio-economic ministers. This is why (that is the fact of not having such integrative link) in India where we have separate departments like S&T, trade, infrastructure, industries, chemical, fertiliser, and electricity they function as watertight compartments.

Due to the skillful management and integration techniques employed by Professor Dhawan, ISRO was able to get in touch with the ministries of the Indian socio-economic sectors and helped them by providing satellites. Whereas, the nuclear department couldn't even get in touch with the electricity department since they had not employed Dhawan's technique.

Gladdened by Kalam's smiling face and his stature, many of the IAS secretaries of the socio-economic sectors would gladly consent to the project proposals from PSA office. Once they approve through CGDAST, and after the group of ministers have seen it, then there will be no problems in the Cabinet. This is because the different secretaries would have informed their respective department ministers about the project earlier itself.

At that time, Murli Manohar Joshi was a powerful man within the BJP. The three-man team Vajpayee-Advani-Joshi was very popular. Even though he was not as powerful as the other two, Joshi was acting as the bridge between them. Even though Joshi was leading the *Human Resources Development Department* as well as the *Science and Technology Department*, he invested his time mostly in political activities.

How can I directly inform him: "Doctor sir! If you join hands with Kalam and engage in many S&T activities, it will also benefit your political front!"

I told Kalam: "The GOM is the best way to get approval for the projects proposed by the *Office of the Principal Scientific Adviser*. If Murli Manohar Joshi is not made as the head of the GOM, then the files would be trapped within the offices of various ministries and the Cabinet. Besides Vajpayee and Advani, he is the senior leader. He therefore should head the GOM. You have to cooperate with him. I will also assist you. Otherwise, we would get caught up with the DST files permanently. You will have to discuss them frequently with the DST secretary to get them sent out of DST.

Looking at the justification, Kalam agreed. George Fernandes was also a minister. He was next only to Joshi. Therefore, Kalam was more confident. Kalam and Fernandes were friendly with each other.

We therefore identified a good solution to get government approval for the projects of the office of the Principal *Scientific Adviser*. A government order was issued forming GOM. Meanwhile, I also got the permission to appoint staff members to the office of the *PSA*. It was a tough job since the finance ministry had banned the employment of new staff. Satisfied with our proposal, they readily approved. The additional secretary A. P. Venkateswaran, who was incharge of approving such projects, became good friends with me due to our common interest in Tamil *bhakti* poems! He and the joint secretary Usha Mathur asked me a lot of questions before granting approval. I answered them well. I explained: "I am not exactly sure about the structure of this office of the *PSA*. However, we have a clear picture on how to develop it. There are several departments and other S&T fields involved in this. Myself and Kalam alone are not enough. We need several scientists and engineers/technicians in various cadres. Also, we want to put several initiatives into practice. However, besides the government, other participants could also fund our projects. We did the same thing in TIFAC and successfully implemented..."

After explaining everything, we were able to get some 20 members of staff (for science and administration). Therefore, within four months since I joined, the office of PSA started functioning well. Sheridon was brought from another department to this office as a full-time employee.

From June 2000, we started working in full swing. A few high-level government offices wouldn't even have started their job. Yet another reason for the office to run smoothly was because I was the executive director of TIFAC and Kalam was its Chairman. TIFAC (which had been running for nearly twelve years smoothly) and the *Office of the PSA* (that had more responsibilities) were well-integrated. Together, they performed their operations effectively.

❑

Projects for the people

The initiatives undertaken by the office of the PSA were effectively done through SACC, CGDAST, and CGES. Forgetting all about his former big budget jobs at the defence ministry, Kalam now fully focussed on his new job as the PSA to government of India and other TIFAC initiatives. I have not listed them out in order here. Let me give a few examples. Kalam delivered lectures in several places. He was honoured with the doctorate degrees in many places. Everywhere he spoke about the *Vision 2020* projects, empowerment of India and integrating technology.

Dairy and agriculture were Kalam's favourite sectors. He was greatly impressed by the initiatives undertaken by Prof. S. K. Sinha through TIFAC in the field of agriculture. Me and a few others from TIFAC accompanied Kalam and Prof. S. K. Sinha to villages in and around Patna. This project started in 1998. The fruits of the TIFAC projects were duly received by the villagers (that is, by increasing the yield in their own land, their profit margins increased considerably). The scientists in S. K. Sinha's team employed various techniques like collecting data, soil testing, seed selection, and micronutrients for improving the yield. The sowing period was decided based on the market needs. Since the farmers were extremely happy with the results, they wanted to meet Kalam. We told them: "Kalam will come. But he cannot come in an ordinary ambassador car or a jeep to your fields. Since he has to be given Z-security, he can only come in his upgraded ambassador car. It is too heavy and so might get trapped in the sludge here."

The state government did not bother much. They didn't even show any interest in our projects for their farmers! Why would they put concrete roads for

Kalam's visit? "We will give you protection and you can go wherever you like." This seemed to be their mentality.

Using stones, bricks, and other hard materials, the farmers themselves built a proper road for Kalam's car to travel. They even did a 'test run' on the road. Kalam happily visited them. The Bihari farmers became his friends for a lifetime. He frequently visited them; even after he became the Indian President, Kalam went there. Even today, the farmers over there celebrate Kalam's birthday. Valmiki Sharma functioned as the group organiser. He calls me over the phone once every year even now.

Kalam became their friend even though he did not know how to speak Hindi. Those farmers only knew Hindi, just like how the farmers in Tamil Nadu spoke only Tamil. This later helped him in his meeting with C. Subramaniam. TIFAC was able to help him in a project close to his heart. This is how the *National Agro Foundation* (NAF) evolved.

Kalam visited Kanchipuram once or twice for the TIFAC agro projects. More importantly, *Jagadguru Kanchi Kamakoti Peetam*'s Swami Jayendra Saraswathi helped a lot with the PURA (*Provision of Urban Amenities in Rural Areas*) projects which were very close to Kalam's heart. They both became very close after that. Several such series of chains and interlinks were made possible through the TIFAC initiatives.

Let us discuss PURA now. It is one of the 17 sectors within *TIFAC-Vision 2020* initiatives. It is all about 'Driving Forces and Impedances'. Impedances were those which hindered growth. Prof. P. V. Indiresan led this team. He and Kalam became good friends. Both of them were the President of INAE earlier.

Indiresan was not only a great professor and a S&T expert but was also a practical man. He has written a lot of essays on India's growth and development. Through this TIFAC project, he conducted surveys on reasons behind the backlog of rural India, and also identified possible solutions. He showed the way to developing rural India. It appears in my Tamil poem collection *'Vattratha Uttrukkal' ('Perennial Springs')* under the heading *'Nagaramum Gramamum' ('City and village')*.

Prof. Indiresan met several officers of the state governments as a followup of the Vision 2020 for implementation. Finally, it was given the impressive name 'PURA'. Kalam also liked it very much. He spoke about it in many of his lectures. The key was to interconnect at least 50 villages through good roads. Also, they were to be connected externally to a city and through electricity and other scientific and communication infrastructure. With the support of the office of the PSA, funds were allocated to undertake this initiative in 25 places in India.

After Kalam left his job as the *PSA*, those projects remained stagnant. After he became the Indian President, PURA became Kalam's pet project. He spoke about it in many places, even abroad. He even spoke about it to important leaders. (Kalam told me that he made a presentation to the US President Bush on his laptop).

Kalam's fame and glory spread far and wide. This was because since he was now PSA, he did not have the burden of handling the excessive responsibilities of his earlier job as secretary DDRD/ SA to RM. Likewise, this new job did not involve DRDO's tough routine like handling time schedules, missiles, instruments, testing, reviews, endless meetings with people and the defence minister and so on. He need not handle defence ministry officials, senior officials of the armed forces, and industrialists seeking permission to approve their projects at the DRDO anymore. Now he was a free man. He could now fully devote his time to socio-economic welfare schemes of the *TIFAC Vision 2020* initiatives. Various organisations across India invited him to deliver opening speeches and graduation speeches because he was the PSA and also a *Bharat Ratna* awardee. He too enjoyed those lectures. He had not yet started meeting school children. That was a later episode in his life. We will discuss that later.

M. L. Sondhi saw him to be a symbol of rising India. I have introduced him in an earlier segment of this book. He was appointed as the Chairman of ICSSR (*Indian Council of Social Science Research*) that undertook various social science research activities. He had a broad vision about India. He felt that India should get its due recognition in the world arena. He was a man seeking very fast actions. When NDA came to power, his dreams were getting fulfilled. He visited Kalam. One of his dreams was to set up a magnificent S&T garden in Jammu & Kashmir in order to resolve the conflicts in the region. He wanted Kalam to head the project. As per his desire, the Chairman of ICSSR also became a member of CGDAST. He proposed his dream project over there as well. He also personally met Kalam. Kalam happily conversed with him. Kalam wasn't prepared to handle projects that involved major political consequences.

I wonder how this project would have turned out today had it been made a part of the millennium schemes. In case Kalam had spoken directly to Vajpayee, he most probably might have readily agreed. Had Kalam, who made missiles to combat enemy forces like Pakistan, taken initiatives to build this magnificent S&T garden in J&K, he would have won the hearts of several Indian youths and could have changed the mindset of common men over there.

Later, when he became the Indian President, I had the opportunity to travel with Kalam. Mufti Mohammed Sayeed was the Chief Minister then. Everywhere he went, people flocked around Kalam. The Indian National Anthem was played wherever he went. He received a grand welcome in the HazratBal Mosque there. He also conducted special prayers. I composed a few songs based on incidents that happened there. They have been published in my Tamil poem collection *'Marakaatha Thedalkal' ('Unforgettable Quests')* as four short poems. All four were written on June 28, 2003 under the headings:

1) *Shikara trip*

2) *Voice of Unity*

3) *Kashmir Sinar tree*

4) *Brave heroes*

(See www.ysrajan.com ; link for poems Google Link there)

One segment of the ***'Voice of Unity'***:

By churning the Dal lake
He fed the divine nectarine
By his sweet smile
He scorched the 'Halahala' poison;
He called upon them
To nurture India
By working vigorously
Every morning, noon, evening and night!

(June 28, 2003)

I wrote this poem after I directly witnessed several young entrepreneurs getting inspired by Kalam. Looking at their body language, I got inspired to write this poem.

Back then, I wondered how the magnificent S&T garden would have evolved under Kalam during the NDA leadership in 2000; even now I feel the same way.

Had Kalam himself decided not to speak to PM Vajpayee about this? Or had a few powerful people around the PM, especially Brajesh Mishra, built a strong fortress around the PM, that it became impossible for Kalam to approach him? That is a big riddle.

I feel that the second one must be true. It was the reason behind why many good projects undertaken by the office of the *PSA* were never realised even though they were shaped well in their initial stages. Many people would blame Murli Manohar Joshi for this. However, it need not be entirely true. Had Kalam directly approached Vajpayee personally and spoken his mind out, he could have successfully accomplished many projects.

We shall discuss more about this later while talking about the final stages of activities undertaken by the office of PSA.

A few others in the government used Kalam's name and fame for their personal agenda. One such person was Dr. Venkata Subramaniam. He was a member of education in the Planning Commission. Using his status as a Tamil person, he frequently visited Kalam. He wanted to prepare a report to create an Indian intellectual community as a part of the *Vision 2020* initiatives. Such reports are meant for paper and they serve no practical purpose. I felt that Kalam was wasting his energy unnecessarily on this. By attaching Kalam's name to his project, Prof. Venkata Subramaniam elevated his own status. After he became the Indian President, Kalam unnecessarily wasted his time on such matters more frequently. I felt sad that many were using his name for their own personal benefits. At times, without mentioning any names, I spoke to Kalam about this.

"Sir, why are you letting other people use your name, fame and glory! Do you realise what they could do with that?!" Kalam would simply smile and forget about the matter.

V. Raghuraman from the Energy Division of CII who had contributed immensely to Vision 2020 initiatives and worked as Secretary General of the *Associated Chambers of Commerce and Industry of India* (ASSOCHAM) is one of my very good friends. He worked with me in the CII. He also commented about this:

"Rajan, I feel that like many other leaders, Kalam too is in a broadcast mode. There are people who talk to him about tasks they wish to perform, and he too nods without thinking decisively about the possibility of future goals. He probably might have not bothered much thinking that if such seeds are sowed in fertile land, they could bloom into healthy trees in the future..."

Perhaps, he was correct. Since Kalam had gained the status of a prominent leader of the nation, all he could do was to broadcast. But it is also true that many have made ill-use of Kalam's good nature of referring to people as 'my friend' and planted thorny and poisonous trees instead!

Dr. D. N. Tiwari (who was Member Science in the Planning Commision) helped a lot in converting Kalam's PSA office into a big S&T integration centre. All departments were busy preparing for the five-year plan. As per the usual procedures, each Department dealing with some part of S&T would form a big Committee to produce the final report for that department. After this, the proposals would be sent to the planning commission. Under the leadership of the planning commission's Member Science representative, a few of these proposals would be accepted, a few rejected and a few others altered. Later on, it would be reviewed by all members of the planning commission. Dr. D. N. Tiwari made all the departments dealing with S&T to be reviewed by a single high profile committee. This committee was chaired by the government's *Principal Scientific Adviser* (Kalam) and Tiwari was co-chair.

This was an added burden on the secretaries of various departments dealing with S&T. Normally, the government's scientific adviser office would propose a few proposals through the SACC and these secretaries would register such proposals. They had no other relations with the Office of the Scientific Adviser. It is logical for the secretaries therefore to think that the introduction of a new high profile executive committee to review their proposals was an unnecessary extra step. However, since several departments dealing with S&T were functioning independently (with little coordination between them), it was becoming impossible to achieve anything productive from them. In spite of allocating several crores of rupees to various S&T initiatives in the budget plan, none of the industries seemed to be producing anything new. Therefore, Dr. T. N. Tiwari must have felt that in order to improve productivity of funds allotted to S&T by the government, the various departments dealing with S&T need to be integrated towards a common goal. He felt that Kalam being the *Vision 2020* man would be the best person to head such a committee. It is very rare for people to hand over their authority and power to others. Tiwari handed over this responsibility to Kalam out of his deep respect towards him.

Not only that, Tiwari's joint adviser P. K. Biswas also willingly gave up his position. He made me as the member secretary to the high profile executive committee to assist Kalam. It was very rare for people to give up their role, that too in Delhi!

The committee functioned well even though it was an added burden to my workload. As per the advice given by the secretary DST, V. S. Ramamurthy, we tried to create a special fund as assistance to be given to market indigenous products within India. As per the existing plan, it received support only till a new product was made by TIFAC or TDB (*Technology Development Board*), or until 2 or 3 prototypes were made. After this stage, none of the banks offered financial support to any of our Indian industries to manufacture in bulk. They only helped foreign technology based products as they weren't sure of the demand for indigenous goods! This is the case with independent India! Ever since the days of Nehru, this trend of S&T import, payments to foreign consultants, and buying foreign equipment had been the norm.

After a few more years, once again some more foreign technologies were bought. In Japan and Korea, they manufacture equipment using their own newer innovations, after acquiring technologies. This did not happen, even in the Indian public sector! The banks were afraid to invest in indigenous products! If the foreign goods failed, no one would blame the banks; be it the Central Auditor General (CAG) Office or the Parliament.

They never considered the huge victory achieved by ISRO. ISRO launched one or two rockets every year and it was a steady field. ISRO wasn't their competitor. Hundreds of thousands of Indian industries only imported goods. There were a few successes like those achieved by Amul and Nirma soap. Even these companies imported equipment for manufacturing their products. Many big factories in India like HMT, *National Dairy Development Corporation*, and car manufacturers buy everything from foreign factories and function as instructed by their foreign bosses. Even the famous IT sector functions like this! They buy all their primary software from abroad by paying an enormous royalty or licence fees and then use it here.

In order to come out of this vicious circle which works against indigenisation, it was not only enough to fund our R&D projects, but also important to fund our manufacturing sector to produce in bulk. All relevant steps have to be encouraged (including advertising these indigenous products). The DST felt that they did not have the authority to do this. The only way to change their attitude is to prepare a project proposal to raise funds. I wrote one for ₹ 100 crores. V. S. Ramamurthy told me: "Rajan! Our most revered Dr. Kalam is leading the high level committee. Instead of writing for just 100 crore rupees, please write a proposal for 1,000 crores! That is the way to execute the indigenous mission successfully." I wrote as suggested. After it was approved by the committee of DST, it had to go through several other stages. Finally, the project proposal was approved by the high level committee headed by Dr. Kalam. It served as the precursor to the venture capital investments of today. We did not discover this for the first time in India. It was already in practice in other countries like Japan, Korea, Israel, Singapore and so on. We tailor-made the proposal as per our Indian needs.

Had the financing scheme started from 2001 itself as proposed, India could have achieved major successes in at least a few of the S&T segments today. Unfortunately, Kalam resigned from the post of the *Government's Principal Scientific Adviser*. I too left after him. There was no one left to support Prof. V. S. Ramamurthy. He too was about to retire at the age of 60 in 2002. Even if he got a job extension, he wouldn't be able to support all these project proposals! Many big shots in the field of science need to be satisfied!

The *Office of the Government's Principal Scientific Adviser* took yet another progressive step. Since TIFAC was a trustworthy organisation that performed well, Kalam made a recommendation to the *Finance Minister* Shri. Yashwant Sinha. Since there were many talented individuals in institutes other than the IITs and the IISc. The *Department of Science and Technology* (DST) and other government departments gave (gives) funds mostly to the IITs and the IISc. We therefore made a proposal to give substantial funds to other institutions where there are talented individuals. Kalam proposed that such institutions should tie-up with some industry and receive at least 30% of their investment from the industry and arrive upon a good project proposal. If the proposal turned out to be a good one, TIFAC would fund the remaining 70% of the cost. The finance minister approved Kalam's recommendation. In order to select good project proposals received from various institutions across India, competitions were held at the pan Indian level with strict rules and regulations. Three people were in the selection committee.

Prof. V. S. R., secretary DST; Prof. P. V. Indiresan, former director of IIT; and Prof. N. C. Nigam, Chairman of AICTE (*All India Council for Technical Education*) and former director of IIT Delhi. These were the three members of the selection committee. All of them were great, truthful scholars. Initially, many people doubted the scheme. They thought: "The institutes and universities weren't competent enough to take part in S&T activities. Likewise, the industries too were reluctant in spending their money on these institutes. Their only concern is tax benefits."

To put it briefly the performance was well above expectations. Some 20 TIFAC centres were established within a short span of time. Soon after the institutes received their funding, they were eager to meet Kalam. He visited many such universities even though they were not regarded on par with IITs and the IISc (that received major government funding) in order to receive their feedback. They took up many small activities that were centred around socio-economic welfare of India. Many of them have become leading universities today.

There was a new confusion now. Many people felt that the TIFAC centres were located in southern India. They shared their concern with Kalam, who called me and a senior official of the PSA who assisted in these schemes (was a co-worker of Kalam in the DRDO) Dr. Vijayaraghavan, and told us—"All TIFAC centres are located in southern India. Since all three of us are from the south, we need to be more careful!" From the way he spoke, it became clear that he wanted a few TIFAC centres in the north.

Dr. Vijayaraghavan explained in detail about the number of universities that had applied, those that got selected, and others that got rejected. He brought a detailed list from his office.

"I know all this! But what will they say outside?" asked Kalam.

When Kalam was involved in the SLV-3 project, he wasn't like this. Now that he had earned great fame and glory, he was very careful about others' opinions. He tried to satisfy the press and the IAS officers mostly. He tried to please a few vocal scientists (even though what they said were incorrect!). He gave extra value to their opinions!

From one point of view, this could look like a good leadership attribute. However, in some cases, this could lead to confusion.

The TIFAC centre was established with a fixed goal in which 'relevance' became the key factor. The socio-welfare schemes were very important for the organisation. Only the industry or the consumer can provide funds to help the projects. It wasn't a free service. 'Excellence' was another key factor. We had therefore explained that the exams would be of a very high grade. (*TIFAC Centres of Relevance and Excellence*—TIFAC CORE explains this point clearly).

There were many institutes and universities in south India. At that time (2000-1), out of some 1,400 engineering colleges affiliated to the AICTE, 884 were located to the south of the Vindhya mountain. The South Indian states and Maharashtra established many private engineering colleges starting from the 1970s. The northern states were far behind. (Now, since 2017, the situation has changed. Currently, more than 4,000 private engineering colleges are there all over India. Earlier, North Indian students went to the southern states to study. UP's former Chief Minister Shri Akilesh Yadav did his B.Tech. in Karnataka. Now, there is a good balance between the northern and southern states which is why many south Indian colleges that did not perform well had to be closed!)

But back then in 2000-1, many successful engineering colleges were there in the south. Since they were well-established, industries were willing to fund their projects. There were only a few north Indian colleges at that time. Therefore, only a few such colleges could be funded.

Therefore, on account of such rumours, if the funds were given to incompetent colleges, it would be a great loss to TIFAC! There were other S&T schemes which could allocate government funds to such institutions without a competition. Therefore, the initiatives undertaken by TIFAC CORE centres would raise the standard of the Indian education system.

After summarising all these points, "Sir! If we do as suggested by you, it would shake the very foundation of the TIFAC CORE's! Why are you worrying unnecessarily, sir! Only the secretary of S&T has the authority over these projects. All administrative duties are also handled only by the DST. All you did was to get permission from the finance minister. This is an entirely new scheme. None of the institutes/universities whose project proposals got qualified serve under you. Neither did you recommend them to the selection committee.

"If an issue was raised in the Parliament about this, we will take care of it," we consoled Kalam. He also saw our point. This scheme was not meant for individual states. It was a pan India scheme that was highly competitive. One good attitude of Kalam was that if he was convinced of the truth, he stopped being adamant.

After a few days, Kalam said: "You both managed to convince me. Now, the finance minister Yashwant Sinha is asking me, 'Kalam, I approved your recommendation in a single day. Now I am hearing that the college within my constituency was not granted an approval! Can you take care of that?' He wants to know the reason for this. What is the matter?"

There were neither any industries nor a government entity that could make use of the project proposed by the college!

"Sir, their project is related to space. We told them several times to try their best to get 30% of funding at least from ISRO. They did not even try, probably because they wanted to put pressure through the finance minister himself! Please explain this to the finance minister. Please ask him to send a few representatives from that college to ISRO." Kalam agreed.

Yashwant Sinha understood the situation and so did not pressurise us any further. The college also did not bother about this.

Besides these, a question was raised in the Parliament to the DST regarding this north-south divide. It was a star question too which means that after answering that, many more relevant questions could be raised in the Parliament. To encounter such questions, the respective department minister would prepare well in advance. The officials of the department would assist the minister. In 1980, I had prepared many notes for the *Prime Minister* and his deputy, while working for ISRO.

After I came to the DST, I did not get many such opportunities. Since the DST had to answer several questions, they had a big section to answer these questions. They consulted me on a few complex queries.

Since I left my government job in 1996, I was not an official of the DST in 2000. Even though Kalam's post was equivalent to that of a cabinet minister, questions raised in the Parliament did not come under his jurisdiction. Only the ministers in the Parliament can answer them. Therefore, Kalam did not get this question. It went to the Minister of S&T. The S&T officials asked me to assist them. Such questions would be raised to the then S&T minister Shri Murli Manohar Joshi and it would be answered by his deputy minister Shri Bachi Singh Rawat. We both were good friends. He was from Uttarakhand. He knew English, but his strength was Hindi.

I explained everything in detail to him in Hindi. I told him that TIFAC centres were not government organisations. I explained why its status cannot be degraded at any cost. I also explained how Indian universities were spread out in the north and south (the points I had mentioned earlier in this segment). He is a good man totally free from corruption.

Finally, he laughed and said: "*Abhi Poora Samajh Gaya*, that is, 'Now I understand fully'. I now understand that this question was raised to create confusion in the Parliament. Next time, if that Parliament member asks about this, I will teach him a good lesson...Thanks."

Therefore, everything was explained clearly even in the Parliament. Some 20 TIFAC centres were established quickly. Kalam was extremely happy. Wherever he went, he also spoke about this Mission REACH TIFAC CORE. He announced that 100 such TIFAC centres need to be established soon.

When Kalam was the government's *Principal Scientific Adviser*, he made one more announcement. It started soon after the Gujarat earthquake. TIFAC built safe and secure houses (*Habitat*) in Kutch and Bhuj regions of Gujarat. The earthquake happened at the end of January 2001. Summer in Gujarat began in April. It would become extremely hot. Therefore, instead of building thatched huts, we built houses with composite technology using fibres, ropes, and jute wastes. Since the sunlight did not fall in directly, these houses would not become hot. With the help of the parliamentary members from that constituency and the state government's co-operation, we built some 1000 houses there. We also built toilets using this composite technology. I have explained earlier in detail about the development of this composite technology under Kalam (even before he became the chairman of TIFAC). India's small and medium enterprises did these projects. This technology was the one used in railway berths and seats earlier under TIFAC projects. TIFAC allotted funds for this. Kalam inspected the houses at the time of construction. Soumitra Biswas and Srikanth from the TIFAC supervised the work.

The first hundred houses built by TIFAC were handed over by Shri Murli Manohar Joshi since he was the S&T Cabinet Minister. Later, Kalam handed over a few. The houses built by TIFAC were not temporary ones. They were used for many more years. Soon after Kalam became the Indian President, his first trip was to Gujarat. I accompanied him. Besides Ahmedabad, Kalam also visited this colony built by TIFAC. I saw how the people cheerfully welcomed Kalam. More on that later. Likewise, in Tamil Nadu, after the Tsunami such houses were built. I was not with TIFAC at the time. Kalam was the President.

Kalam wanted to help the victims of such natural disasters and therefore set up a disaster management committee in his office. This committee would not only address earthquakes, but also cyclones, Tsunamis, landslides and floods. The activities to be covered included:

1. Forewarning as far as possible.
2. Keeping ready resources to alleviate the pain of the people. This must be done soon after the disaster strikes them.
3. Finding out possible technical/administrative solutions to minimise the impact of the disaster.

Example: Building quake-resistant buildings. At the same time, in order to make provisions for already existing buildings to withstand the earthquake, not only the officials, scientists, and engineers, but also industrialists and business leaders were well prepared all through the year. CII's director general Tarun Das was extremely helpful in this. Even after we submitted a good report to the the government, it appointed a minister to implement disaster management. That would be their only response to disaster management!

There is no need to elaborate as to how well India is prepared towards disaster management. However, crisis management actions by running here and there after the disaster has struck have improved.

There was one other important report centred around women scientists/technologists of those days. Women who completed M.Sc., Ph.D., B.Tech., M.Tech. and so on would start to work in S&T related fields. However, soon after they get children, their progress would be hindered. This was because they weren't allowed to take one or two-year breaks and so they had to resign from their government jobs. After they become 35, they will not be allowed to apply for any government (laboratories/universities) jobs. In order to prevent this, the SACC came up with a good scheme for qualified women scientists/technologists (based on the Britain model). Three women members of SACC consulted many others and wrote a detailed proposal which was later on debated at the SACC. We were shocked to see the opposition by some of the male members of the committee to the scheme! Kalam supported the scheme. Finally, we reached a consensus. We felt that the government could implement it at the earliest. We therefore had mentioned it as a plan to be tested for five years. Kalam sent it to the Prime Minister. The PM acknowledged that he received it. Nothing much happened after that. I asked Kalam to insist on the scheme to the PM. I do not know what he did after that. Nothing happened!

Other than this, yet another project proposal was prepared for the electric power sector. It was prepared by CGES, the purpose of which was to use pure coal to generate electricity using the '*Coal Gasification Method*'. The proposal was sent to the PM. It was recommended as a joint venture between India and America. Kalam was asked to send a representative from his office. I was sent. Besides this, Kalam wanted me to discuss his project which involved 'Generating electric power from space satellites'. He arranged for a meeting with Mr. Glazer who was a lifelong supporter of the project. I was not convinced with the project. Kalam also knew this. It is not enough to see only space, satellites and solar panels. The financial feasibility of the project must also be kept in mind. Moreover, the impact of energy released on the environment, and other radio devices was unknown. I spoke with Glazer. He himself was not sure of the project. However, Kalam supported it till the end.

A major incident happened in my life. I had the opportunity to meet the Nobel Laureate and Physicist Murray Gell Mann and converse with him. Earlier I had reviewed his book "*Quark and the Jaguar*" for the '*Business Standard*' magazine. He became my guru. I felt delighted to meet him in person. He gave me his address in a hand-written note. However, since his health deteriorated, we lost touch.

The decision taken by the PM to send someone from the *Office of the Principal Scientific Adviser* was an indication that he valued this office very much.

Likewise, when the American President Bill Clinton visited India, Kalam was invited to dinner. Kalam took CDs and other discs to talk to Clinton. Kalam couldn't show it on his laptop as planned. However, after speaking with Clinton he handed over the CDs and the discs to him.

Clinton mentioned a few points to Kalam about his presidency. Kalam later shared this with me. A few points were: "Since the rate of unemployment in the US was on the rise, soon after Clinton became the President, he engaged in projects involving revampment of old roads and highways. He speeded up these projects so that American people in low economic status could get suitable jobs. This improved employment opportunities in the US!"

Kalam said one other thing: “Even though the American President had many powers, he had to convince the members of the Congress, the Senate members as well as his own democratic party members while undertaking any project. It seems Clinton used a trick to convince them. Even though a project proposal contained several projects inside, he did not talk about all of them in one go. He did it one-at-a-time! That was the reason for his success! Let us also do likewise!”

❑

Cyber Security

The '*Society for Electronic Transactions* (SETS)' was one of the pioneer projects of the *Office of the PM's Principal Scientific Adviser*. Several foreign S&T companies and other public/private sectors abroad engaged in cyber security activities from the 2000s. They created hardware and software related to cyber security and used them. As was the case with several major projects, Indian labs, institutes, industries and the public sector lagged behind in cyber security. This was because at the time, many Indians were not using online services widely. Even though the technical ICT sector grew from 1995 onwards, around 95% of them worked for foreign companies which took care of cyber security for them.

Only a few people in India knew about cyber security and engaged in R&D and research. Through the findings of the Vision 2020 reports of TIFAC and other such organisations, it became very clear that development in the ICT sector was the key to the development of all other sectors, viz. agriculture, manufacturing,, small industries, banks, government works with files, police department, other service departments, defence, education, medicine, cinema and other production centres. It became clear that besides the respective field-knowledge, ICT knowledge was very important to all sectors. This contributed to the economic growth, and rise in per capita income. Besides, all jobs could be finished rapidly. (We are witnessing this from 2016 onwards in India). Railway tickets were issued online from 2000 onwards. However, the other sectors were lagging behind in ICT. It even picked up slowly in the production sector, though not to the level expected by the TIFAC Vision 2020. Many tools and equipment in the industrial sector are now controlled using *Computer Numerical Control* (CNC) from 2016 onwards.

ICT resources cannot be shared or done in partnership with others because of threats from our enemies. Using various software and hardware resources, our people have to be protected from enemy attacks. If ICT is not secure enough, it could cause large scale destruction and huge economic losses. Therefore, based on the recommendation given by the SACC, a special committee was created under the leadership of Dr. M. Vidyasagar who was an expert in the field of IT, Robotics and AI. The aim of this committee was to understand the cyber security requirements of India and take necessary action.

He established the AI and Robotics wing of the DRDO named *Centre for Artificial Intelligence and Robotics* (CAIR) in Bengaluru. The DST had funded the establishment. When Kalam left his job as the defence minister's science secretary and was succeeded by Dr. Aatre, Dr. Vidyasagar resigned from the DRDO. It was a huge loss. In order to do this job well, his experience and expertise were required. Within a few months, an excellent project was proposed. It would take many years to manufacture cyber security instruments within India. Moreover, it would be impossible to check the status of the project since even ordinary people in India perform millions of transactions per day. We therefore needed potent computers. The Indian consumers and good businessmen should install such computers and get trained on cyber security. Even ordinary users need to know a few basics of cyber security.

Ideally, India's electronics department should have handled this. Had various departments within India performed their jobs thoroughly, by now India could have become a developed nation. The electronics department would receive the project proposed by the office of the *PM's Principal Scientific Adviser* through the CGDAST office.

Since the authority of the *Office of the Principal Scientific Adviser* extended far and wide, we decided to implement a low-cost plan. The idea was to introduce the concept of cyber security to important consumers (banks, industries, and traders) and ask them to implement this in their respective offices. Therefore, our first agenda was to establish an organisation which could train such people.

If it were to be a part of the *Office of the PM's Principal Scientific Adviser*, then it wouldn't be able to function fully. Therefore, it must be an establishment that received funds to run initially and later on function independently on its own. If it performed inefficiently, then the end user won't be satisfied and the organisation will be permanently shut down. We therefore decided to make this an independent organisation. The government will most probably not grant an approval for this (to create an independent establishment like TIFAC). This was because the government would then have to allocate funds for this organisation every year. Hundreds of such organisations that received government funds were not functioning effectively. They were simply receiving government funds and were showing accounts statements every year.

We therefore thought of a novel plan. The organisation would receive government funds only for the first time. After that, it should earn its own income. Since consumer satisfaction was the primary goal, we decided that the organisation should earn its income from them.

We developed the SETS for this purpose. The government's electronics company *'Electronics Corporation of India Limited (ECIL)'* was willing to give some money as initial funds. One of India's leading association of IT companies, *NASSCOM*, was ready to work closely with SETS. Therefore, NASSCOM's members automatically became the consumers of SETS. The Governing Council members of SETS were CMD, ECIL, *NASSCOM*'s head Kiran Karnik, and other experts from industries and IITs. I felt that the head of a big bank or someone like Ratan Tata who was a distinguished industrialist must lead this panel.

However, implementing the DRDO style, Dr. Vijayaraghavan recommended that this Council must be headed by the *Principal Scientific Adviser* (Dr. Kalam). If Kalam sustained for another ten more years, the SETS could perform effectively. But his post as the *Principal Scientific Adviser* was subject to change. When the ruling central government changes, Kalam's post could become uncertain! When I recommended Kalam to the post of chairman of TIFAC (when P. Rama Rao was the DST secretary), we had specified in the file that Kalam by name as an individual who was currently the *DDRO Secretary*, *Defence Minister's Scientific Adviser*. Therefore, it was possible for him to continue as the chairman of TIFAC even after he retired from those posts. After Kalam, Dr. Aatre who succeeded him as the *Defence Minister's SA* became a member of TIFAC. I felt that someone who used computers frequently in their job (e.g. bank) should head this special cyber security division.

Since we were the only two members from the PSA office with S&T background to assist Kalam, I did not convey my suggestion. Moreover, Kalam might have wanted to head the *Council of SETS*. I left it at that.

The first two meetings went well. As per their decision (I wasn't a member of the Council), under my leadership, they created a selection committee to select the CEO of SETS. Shri Kiran Karnik of NASSCOM, CMD of ECIL who were also members of the Governing Council of SETS were other two members, in addition to Dr Vijayaraghavan of PSA office.

After carefully laying down the rules and advertising for the post nationwide, we selected a person from the list of applicants. Several months earlier, Kalam resigned from his post as the *Principal Scientific Adviser*. (More on that later). Therefore, when the government selected Dr. R. Chidambaram to succeed Kalam as the *Principal Scientific Adviser* he automatically became the chairman of SETS governing council. It happened as I feared. It was not the primary job for him. Besides, Dr. R. Chidambaram did not like our candidate Dr. A. Kalanidhi (who was the former Vice-Chancellor of *Anna University*) for some unknown reasons. He did not even inform me. He only sent a message through Dr. Vijayaraghavan to me. It was a huge loss for Vijaraghavan too! Therefore, Kiran Karnik and I lost interest in the matter. I too left my job in the *Office of Principal Scientific Adviser* due to various other reasons.

Therefore, the SETS organisation did not make much of an impact in India. This was a major setback. Today in India, there are organisations like the NTRO (*National Technical Research Organisation*) for electronic cyber security. However, SETS could have developed as an independent organisation and functioned well.

Therefore, an important progressive effort which was undertaken by Kalam lost its glory. There were other major setbacks too. Kalam and Joshi couldn't unite together to carry on projects proposed by the *Office of Principal Scientific Adviser* (SACC, CGDAST, CGES). Probably Joshi regarded Kalam as his competitor. Even though I served as a bridge between the two of them, all I could do was to walk from one end to the other! But Kalam visited Joshi twice at his residence seeking permission to conduct the GOM meeting. Joshi spoke politely and treated Kalam with great respect. But then he was under extreme work pressure as he headed two ministries viz. *Human Resources* and *S&T*. Besides, he also had to travel abroad frequently. He told Kalam that he would look at his schedule and allot suitable dates. Several weeks went by. We also reminded Joshi's private secretary Shri Gupta who always said: "Doctor saab has not given his dates yet. I keep reminding him." On account of Joshi's poor time management skills, not only Kalam but many others were also affected. People in Delhi circles said that everything that was sent to Joshi got delayed. This even appeared in newspapers at times. He wasn't able to maintain a good balance between his official responsibilities and other major assignments. He also invested his time in R.S.S. activities.

Eventually, Kalam became depressed. He felt that Joshi was purposefully avoiding him. Kalam did not want to report this to the *Prime Minister* as he felt that it would look bad. So far, the *Office of the Principal Scientific Adviser* performed effectively within a year. The SACC, CGDAST, and CGES members were impressed that all project proposals had been finalised within a short span of time. They too might have felt that there was no use for all that effort since everything had come to a sudden pause. They might have imagined Kalam to make use of his post that was equivalent to that of a *Cabinet Minister* and get permission from the PM directly to undertake their initiatives. Kalam too could have felt the same way at first.

When Kalam worked at the *Ministry of Defence*, he was able to directly meet the Defence Minister and the Indian Prime Minister and get permission for various initiatives. However, socio-economic welfare schemes are not like that. Most of the activities undertaken to benefit people , industries and agriculture, go around in vicious, endless loops. In order to get out of them, several tricks need to be performed. That is why, the Indian PM does not directly get involved in these schemes (excepting those he feels relevant!) Only those who have worked at the senior level in government offices know about this situation! Therefore, many think that the problem could be solved by directly reporting to the PM! Since Kalam served at a senior level, he never resorted to any mean tricks.

Kalam was concerned that even major initiatives were not getting permission at the right time. One day, I told Kalam while we were discussing this topic: "Sir! George Fernandes is one of your close friends. Why don't you explain our situation to him."

Kalam agreed. After he spoke to George Fernandes, he said: "George told me, 'Ask Joshi one more time. If he keeps buying more time, just inform him about the importance of these initiatives and tell him that you would conduct the meeting within two more weeks. Ask him to make any changes after that! Then you can consult me regarding the meeting date. In case Joshi cannot make it to the meeting, I will preside over it as I am next in line to him.' I feel confused. However, Fernandes is a great man. He has helped me several times earlier. Even now he is ready to help me!" Kalam told this to me.

I was happy that at last a door was opening.

"Sir! Let us do as suggested. We need to get rid of this obstacle. If at all Joshi wants to come, then let him come. You have asked him several times. It wouldn't make any difference if the meeting was presided over by Fernandes. The PMO won't object to it since they need Fernandes's support to strengthen their coalition. Moreover, Joshi is not younger than the PM. There would be a tug of war. But there is no other way to proceed!"

Kalam did not say anything further.

❑

Kalam Under Pressure

I don't think that Kalam reported the matter to the Prime Minister. He seemed to be under extreme pressure. While joining the *Office of the Principal Scientific Adviser*, during the initial days, Kalam was totally free from exhaustion. In fact, he thoroughly enjoyed his new job. During that time, Kalam spoke with the coordinator of our *Vision 2020* book from *Penguin Publications* Shri Kishan Chopra and launched yet another book of ours titled '*Ignited Minds*.' Kalam had mentioned about me in his *Wings of Fire*. In this book, he also has mentioned about my grandfather and great grandfather. Incidentally, the book was a huge success.

He also gave lectures in various places. He visited all branches of TIFAC where either the projects were successfully undertaken or were happening currently. I had mentioned about his Bihar trip earlier. Kalam participated in several TIFAC meetings and other anniversaries.

Even though he had some pressure, overall he wasn't unhappy. During this time, Prof. V. S. Ramamurthy (Secretary of S&T) called me. "Rajan, can you please come to my office?" I went.

He showed me a file. It was from the PMO. I read it. Dr. Abdul Kalam's job extended twice (1993–96, 1996–99). However, due to the slow movement of the files, his job extension from 2000 onwards was getting slightly delayed. He had therefore served as the head of TIFAC for eight years.

Ramamurthy said: "Murli Manohar Joshi asked me about the TIFAC chairman's tenure. I think he wanted to terminate Kalam as its head. He spoke about you also and said, 'I like Rajan. However, he must not be there in the *Office of the Principal Scientific Adviser*. Instead, why can't he be there either in the *DST* or *TIFAC* permanently?' I would change the topic somehow. Now we sent the files related to the chairman of TIFAC without any special recommendation. We felt that whatever Joshi wrote, the PM would still want Kalam to continue in the role. Did you look into the files? Joshi has recommended Dr. R. Chidambaram's name and the reply from the PMO states, 'The Prime Minister has approved.' Soon, the S&T officials would confirm this in their executive appointment order."

"I wanted to show this to you before they write the order letter," Dr. Ramamurthy said.

Now, nothing could be done. The DST Secretary could not override the desires of his minister and get to the PM. What could have happened? Murli Manohar Joshi must have felt that R. Chidambaram (who was a senior to Dr. V. S. Ramamurthy in the *Nuclear Department*) deserved to lead TIFAC since he has now retired from his old job as the head of the atomic energy commission. Since he had also headed the Pokhran nuclear tests, Joshi might have wanted to give him this special gift. It would be difficult to create a separate organisation for R. Chidambaram the way the office of the principal scientific adviser was created for Kalam. Since Kalam had already completed eight years in TIFAC (3 years twice + 2 more years), it was quite reasonable to hand over the job of the head of TIFAC to Chidambaram, who too was a deserving candidate.

"Sir, have you already informed *Periyavar* about this?" I asked. (Usually, in our conversation we referred to Kalam as '*Periyavar*' which means 'respectable old man').

"No," he said.

"Sir, Kalam has a special affinity towards TIFAC. Moreover, TIFAC served as a pillar to the *Office of the Principal Scientific Adviser*. Even if we cannot do anything further now, at least speak to him!"

I continued, "Otherwise, if he comes to know about this news from the S&T deputy secretary/Joint secretary or anyone else, he would become upset!"

"You are correct! Thank you! I should have done that!" Dr. V. S. Ramamurthy said and immediately contacted Kalam's office. Since Kalam had gone outside, the meeting was fixed for the following day. Ramamurthy said to me: "Rajan, please don't go anywhere else. I want you with me when I meet Kalam!"

I did not inform Kalam since it would be right for only Ramamurthy to do that.

V. S. Ramamurthy came to Kalam's office the next day. Since it was a sensitive matter, I told Ramamurthy: "Sir! You first go and talk to him. Later, either you or Kalam call me! I won't go anywhere. I will be in my office only!"

"No! No! Let both of us go together," said Ramamurthy and dragged me with him.

Kalam invited him with a smile on his face. “Hello, Ramamurthy sir! You attend all SACC, CGDAST meetings held here without fail. But, you never come to visit me! You, being the Secretary of the DST, must be a very busy man!”

V. S. Ramamurthy replied, “No, sir! It is not like that. I too have to travel a lot like you.”

Kalam got up from his chair and took Ramamurthy to the sofa that was meant for special visitors. I was still standing. Since Kalam knew that I had many jobs to complete, he did not force me to sit down. Sensing that I might escape the scene, Ramamurthy said, “Rajan, you too sit with me.” I sat down.

After sharing their initial greetings, Ramamurthy was forced to disclose the reason for his arrival. Hesitantly, he began... “Sir! You became the head of TIFAC in September 1993. Now, TIFAC has grown into a big organisation. We renewed your extension once in the middle of your term. You have been here for another four more years after that. Usually, the position is extended upto three years. We managed to extend it further in your case...”

Kalam intervened: “If my term has ended, please send the files for extension.” He was calm and composed.

Ramamurthy was in a fix! He realised that Kalam was expecting an extension of chairmanship. He wasn’t expecting any hindrance in the way. Ramamurthy said: “That is why...we sent your file for extension to the PMO...we received their reply yesterday...they have mentioned that Dr. R.Chidambaram will be appointed as the new TIFAC chairman...that is why...”

Kalam’s face darkened. It revealed anger and frustration. I have never seen Kalam get this angry before. Kalam said, “Alright, sir!” He then looked at me and said, “Rajan, you too must resign from your position as the Executive Director of TIFAC!” I was silent. Since I knew about this on the previous day itself, I wasn’t shocked.

I wanted to do something good for the nation through the initiatives undertaken by TIFAC and the *Office of the Principal Scientific Adviser*. I was keen on bringing about economic development through modern technological innovations. However, my earnestness received a deathblow from the hands of selfish leaders and higher authorities. The important culprits responsible for this were the senior S&T officials who worked in national laboratories and educational institutions! On account of their selfish governance, India faced major setbacks. However, impressed with Kalam’s eagerness and charm, I felt that we could contribute productively to the nation through TIFAC. That was why I continued to work there. When I took voluntary retirement from my post as the *Adviser DST (government)* in 1996, I was able to offer assistance to the TIFAC initiatives by working in the CII. In January 2000, when Kalam became the *Principal Scientific Adviser*, I became even more confident. However, besides generating a number of good reports, and a couple of new projects by the PSA office, and by continuing several other successful TIFAC initiatives which were being implemented by TIFAC much earlier (without any special help from PSA office), it was becoming impossible in the PSA office to bring into fruition the *Vision 2020* projects in terms of policies, procedures, necessary orientation of the national R&D institutions etc.

When V. S. Ramamurthy came to inform Kalam, Kalam already had worked for eighteen months at the *Office of the Principal Scientific Adviser*. I left CII in March 2000 and so, I too had completed 15 months. We tried our level best to change existing government policies to make them more amenable to productive end results. I tried my best to serve as a bridge between Kalam and Joshi. I knew that the implementation of the policy and procedural changes proposed in the reports by the office of the principal scientific adviser would not be liked by the technologists and the big shots and their sidekicks who were enjoying cosy power-positions in the academic institutions. Still I had a fond hope that Kalam's new role as the *Principal Scientific Adviser* (which had authority mainly in its name) could make some impact.

Kalam too must have felt the same way. Now he alone had the responsibility in his hand for some transformation. Most of those in the SACC, CGDAST, and CGES, who had worked with their full hearts for the PSA office, expected this from him.

I had a total vision and therefore most of my hopes were getting shattered! Many poems in my second poem compilation "Vattratha Uttrukkal" published by NCBH talk about my loss of confidence. I had sent copies of them to Kalam too. Most of them were written in 1999, till the beginning of 2001. They all conveyed my mindset of how I was losing all hope but was still keen on 'trying harder'. (Examples: 'வெற்றி காண்', 'பாரதமாதா', 'புதிய ஒளி', 'ஏமாற்றுக் கணக்கு', 'நகரமும் கிராமமும்-மக்கள் வாழ்விடம்', 'முதிர்ந்த அக்கினி', 'மனிதரின் சிலுவை', 'செம்மறி ஆடுகள்').

One of them conveys Kalam's mindset. The title is 'தலைவன் பிரிவு' ('*Separation of the Leader*'). Here are a few verses from page 77 onwards...

A Voice:

With a firm mind
You reigned as an icon!
Your friends surrounded
To do your deeds for you

Leader's Voice:

I have heard enough
For I want to be independent,
My body and mind
Demand a change now!
Your great mighty warrior

Opened up his mind and spoke;
Though a mighty mountain
He fell due to exploitation;
Though having a caring mind
Like a cow for its calf
He got depressed
By the behaviour of the elites.
I have had enough
For there are many more saints
Who will do their duties
In spite of many disappointments;
To bring out their true potential
Therefore will I today
Quit from it all
For I need bondage no more!
With folded hands
He spoke thus
Those surrounding him
Acknowledged him
With downcast eyes
And disquietude ness.

Many Voices:

We know your mind
For you devoted your body, mind and soul;
With selfless attitude
You bestowed strength upon us;
Still there are many immoral men
In this beloved country!
Savagely they'll ruin
All that we did before!

You need not do anything
To protect us
You act now
To protect what you did for the nation!
This is all
we ask of you
Wherever you shall be
You'll fill up our hearts!

After speaking thus
When sadness spread all around!
Those pure men knew
Precisely in their hearts!

Like a cow rushing to its calf
He too will
Rush to his people
He shall live amidst them!

———————————

(This poem was written between 3-8-1999 to 12-8-99, when he was going to leave DRDO due to the barbs he was getting daily. We have described them in the earlier chapters. His situation was similar to this since early half of 2001)

This poem is not about vision, foresight etc. I had worked with Kalam in *TIFAC* and at the *Office of the Principal Scientific Adviser with a hope of doing many wonderful things for India*; many beneficial works; some good persons were willing to cooperate with us to successfully implement the socio-economic welfare schemes. However, most of them were stagnating without action... due to the indifferent attitude of high level power that be; we see daily the mean selfish persons in S&T. Such poems were written by me out of frustration.

Kalam had also shared a few of his disappointments while he worked at the *Office of the Principal Scientific Adviser*. Such poems were also a result of such interaction.

Kalam would go through my poems as I used to send him a handwritten copy the next day.

One day, he called me from his DRDO guest house and said: "Rajan, do you have a pen and a paper with you now? Please write this down."

It appears in my "*Vattratha Uttrukkal*" collection under the title "ராஜனுக்கு திரு. கலாம் சொன்ன கவிதை" meaning '*A poem conveyed by Shri Kalam to Rajan.*'

"Dear God! Bless my friend Rajan
To recite verses like the poet Kamban
Like Valluvar let his heart
That values good conduct
Rise up like a mountain!
Let Rajan be seated
Within people's mind
And let harmony bloom!"

Kalam lost all his hope and confidence. He no longer felt that it would be possible to implement the *TIFAC Vision 2020 initiatives* by working as the *Principal Scientific Adviser*. He got frustrated.

I never expected Kalam to get this angry. He could have kept one last hope that something could be achieved through his job as the *Principal Scientific Adviser*! However, he had to be chairman of TIFAC for that. Even though I was the Executive Director of TIFAC, we weren't sure to what extent the newly appointed TIFAC chairman Dr. R. Chidambaram would welcome our initiatives!

Ramamurthy begged Kalam to reconsider: "Sir! Your TIFAC position is dependent on the extension given by the *Prime Minister*. However, Rajan was appointed by the TIFAC governing council.He can continue to work there till he is 60! Please give me at least two to three months' time. What will I do in TIFAC if both you and Rajan leave simultaneously? Please consider my situation!"

Kalam did not reply. However, his anger had gone down now.

Coffee and biscuits were served.

After drinking his coffee, Ramamurthy got up to leave. Normally, when a senior official like Ramamurthy visits our office, it is customary to accompany them till the elevator. I therefore told Kalam: "Sir! I will go and drop Prof. Ramamurthy downstairs." Kalam did not reply. He did not stop me either.

I went with Ramamurthy in the elevator and accompanied him to his car. Ramamurthy said: "I think that Kalam sir is totally upset. But what can I do? But one thing sir! Please do not leave TIFAC in a hurry. If Murli Manohar Joshi comes to know about it, he would agree instantly. He is a bit frustrated since you have been assisting Kalam in various initiatives. He might want to appoint you under him permanently. He would ask you to resign from the *Office of the Principal Scientific Adviser*!"

I became totally confused now. What would Kalam say when I get back to him? I was also getting worried about shifting my house. We had shifted only a year ago to a government quarters. I had earlier mentioned the difficulties I faced while shifting to a new house. My younger son Vikram was studying MBBS. We had shifted twice already while he was still in medical college!

I did not go to Kalam's office room. I went to my cabin instead. Kalam could call me in case he felt like talking to me. Moreover, it would be impossible to convince him. The government officials could have at least informed Kalam before taking an action. Joshi could have informed Kalam about this over the phone. Kalam wouldn't have stopped him in any way. He wouldn't have leaked it to the press! They could have also asked him to suggest a suitable successor!

When administrators handle their job elegantly, administration becomes an art. This must be taught to the people. Administration is not all about rules and regulations alone. It is important for the concerned officials to handle this elegant art wisely.

❑

A Few Funny Episodes

Before proceeding further, I would like to share a few funny episodes while Kalam worked as the *Principal Scientific Adviser*.

When Kalam was working as the *Defence Minister's Science Secretary*, he had to travel a lot within India. However, he was not compelled to travel much while he was the *Principal Scientific Adviser*. But he got used to travelling frequently. He was approaching 70. In 2000, he received several invitations to deliver lectures and attend meetings. We also suggested that he should visit the TIFAC- CORE centres.

Therefore, at times he wouldn't come to the office during weekdays. He said that he would complete his work during weekends. Being a small office, all other employees worked tirelessly during the weekdays. They wanted to stay with their family during weekends. In Kalam's own office room, there were some four or five people. However, Kalam always preferred for Sheridon to stay.

At times, Sheridon would have a few guests during weekends. Sheridon preferred to have his lunch with them and then take them out for shopping in the evening. It took one hour to reach Sheridon's house from the office.

Sheridon came every weekend to the office (except while Kalam was not in Delhi). He also had to come during weekdays since Kalam would call him and ask for copies of his lectures or other such matters. Besides, since Kalam instructed Sheridon only orally, and since there would not be any written drafts, only Sheridon would be able to handle phone calls in Kalam's office.

In spite of all this, Sheridon enjoyed the company of his special guests. When he told this to Kalam during Saturdays, Kalam replied: "Sheridon! I will come to the office at 10AM. Let us finish working on a few letters. At noon, you can go home for lunch!"

What to say! I told Sheridon: "Sheridon, you inform your wife to make arrangements without you since it is uncertain to know when Kalam would relieve you!"

This was because it was impossible for Kalam to come at 10AM unless there was an important meeting with a special guest. He mostly had his dinner after midnight and then slept. Whenever I describe sunrise and morning birds, Kalam said: "I have not seen all that! It has been many years. I am not a sun man. I am rather a moon man. I see the moon at night."

However, Sheridon had to come around 9.30AM in order to keep everything ready for Kalam in case he came to the office at 10AM. One or two assistants of Sheridon also came to help him. I told Kalam that it was unnecessary for other office staff members to come during weekends since they need to spend time with their family. When Kalam asked me, I said: "Sir, they are all family men. That too only junior staff. They might have thousands of commitments during weekends...I will come. Vijayaraghavan will be there. Sheridon and his assistants would also be there." All his life, Kalam was surrounded by many people while working in big offices!

Mostly (almost 100%), Kalam would not be there at 10 AM. He would come only around 12.30 PM. Sheridon would be giving a live commentary to people in his house. Kalam then said, "Sheridon! Just one or two tasks only!" The work would go on endlessly! Sheridon would then order lunch at around 1.30 PM. It would be the usual menu—a masala dosa, oily vada and occasionally idlis. By the time Sheridon left, it would already be 3 PM!

After lunch (around 2.30 PM), Sheridon would inform us that everything that Kalam required was ready. Then Vijayaraghavan said: "Show us the files after lunch; myself and Rajan would be here."

Vijayaraghavan prepared four or five reports. Back then (2000-1), there weren't any powerpoint presentations like today. He prepared everything on CDs. Most of them were for Kalam's lectures. A few were for new project proposals, and some others were briefs that summarised reports of the *Office of the Principal Scientific Adviser*. These would be very useful for future presentations. Vijayaraghavan would begin by explaining the background clearly. All three of us would be seated around the table. The screen would be in front of Kalam. In the beginning, Kalam would raise one or two questions or offer a few suggestions. Vijayaraghavan would cheerfully offer his reply and then become engrossed in his presentation. Within a few moments, when Vijayaraghavan turned to look at Kalam, Kalam would have dozed off! Vijayaraghavan would stop for a while, but to no avail! He then would finish explaining the slides quickly. Suddenly in the middle, Kalam would wake up and ask a few questions to which Vijayaraghavan would have already answered during his slide presentation. He therefore told Kalam: "I have already answered all that, sir! Shall we proceed to the next one now?" Vijayaraghavan would then start his next presentation.

Vijayaraghavan was the only man in the office who prepared these reports and slides for Kalam. He had an assistant. Sometimes, Vijayaraghavan told me: "Throughout last week, my assistant and I worked day and night to prepare slides for the presentation. I told Kalam that I will show on Monday since they weren't urgent ones. However, Kalam said that they must be presented to him on Saturday at 10 AM without fail. We therefore spent Thursday and Friday night at the studio. We literally had to beg the man at the studio to help us. I also had to help my wife during the weekend. I couldn't do that either.

"Look at him! He is sleeping during my presentation. Later on, when it was time for him to show this to his audience, he would ask me, 'What is this and what is that?' He would then suggest a few changes too!" Vijayaraghavan would become upset. This trend became a habit!

In spite of all this, Sheridon and Vijayaraghavan always loved Kalam! They weren't paid anything extra for all their special efforts! Kalam was lucky to get such good assistants. Kalam taxed his body unnecessarily like this all the time.

Even after he became the President, his food and sleep cycle did not change. More on that later.

Yet another practice of Kalam that made life difficult for those around him was scheduling meetings without keeping any track of time. Instead of scheduling six, he would schedule ten! Sheridon had to handle all this clumsiness! One more difficulty was boarding flights! "Sir! It is getting late. Even if your policemen try or even if we arrange for pre-boarding, you need to get into your flight before the door closes," we had to tell this repeatedly to Kalam. During those days, when the media presence was lower than what it is today, Sheridon (earlier, when Kalam was the *Defence Minister's Scientific Adviser*, it used to be Sheridon and R. K. Prasad) would talk to the airline's people and ensure that the flight did not leave without Kalam!

Once, I too got struck! It was when Kalam was the *Principal Scientific Adviser*, M. M. K. Sardana, joint secretary in DST (my dear friend), wanted to prepare a comprehensive document on *Technologies for Rural Development* under Kalam. The government would often ask DST to prepare. It then became the duty of the DST to prepare an attractive draft. (Even today, this trend continues!)

Due to Kalam's personal charisma, his interest towards rural development, and his special status at the *Principal Scientific Adviser Office*, Sardana wanted to prepare a special report under Kalam's leadership covering all sectors (S&T and those related to rural development). He also issued a government order constituting such a group. A few meetings took place in the DST. Reports with suggestions from many persons, some earlier reports describing the achievements of various people etc. were received. There was also a desire to include the achievements of some non-governmental organisations (NGOs). They decided to look at Bunker Roy's project near Jodhpur. I knew about it. It was a limited work but mostly hyped very much. It was one of the non-governmental entities supported by Rajiv Gandhi when he was the *Prime Minister*. The government invested crores of rupees in the project. There are many such NGOs in India. There were only a few NGOs which functioned efficiently and truthfully. They are limited in number. The biggest drawback in India is that there were only a few good people working in rural villages and that too, they helped only a few hundred villages. But what will happen to the remaining Indian 60,000 villages? Where were the 100–200 model villages which were talked about? Bunker Roy made Kalam come to his place in the village Tilonia.. After seeing a few more such places, when Kalam visited Tilonia a second time, some more people were there. They were showing us around the place, but we were getting really late. As Kalam had to board his flight, I was hurrying things up. Bunker Roy started showing us the solar power plant.

Dr. Ram Gopal, *Director of Jodhpur Water Resources Laboratory* which was a unit of DRDO was also present. I requested Kalam to raise a question: "Mr. Roy, you have done well. How can we scale this up to some 100–1,000 villages?"

Kalam finally asked my question. Bunker Roy avoided giving a direct reply. I told Kalam: "Sir, your project should reach a wider audience. A single village won't be enough!"

When Kalam repeated his question, Bunker Roy said: "If you want this for 100–1,000 villages, then you will need 100–1,000 Bunker Roys!" I had to drag Kalam out after lunch to get to our flight on time. Without understanding our situation, the Jodhpur Director said, "It is alright! I know someone in the Jodhpur airport." When we enquired how long it would take to reach the airport, we got several different answers.

Finally, we decided to go straight to the airport. While we were going correctly, Ram Gopal said: "Kalam sir! There is a fantastic tea shop on the way. Let us all get down to drink!"

I was furious. Kalam did not have the habit of drinking tea soon after lunch. But he agreed because Ram Gopal persisted. I refused to get down and said: "Sir, we cannot finish drinking tea within 5–10 minutes! You can all drink tea at the airport instead!"

Without listening to me, Kalam said, "We do have time," and got down to drink tea. We lost some thirty minutes there. We literally raced to the airport. Ram Gopal's calculations were wrong. Kalam was the special guest in Delhi that night where an official dinner had been arranged for the French President.

The blood pressure of one Colonel (DRDO officer) waiting at the airport to check in and assist Kalam shot up! Finally, when there was just 20 minutes to take off, we reached there. Ram Gopal mumbled something like: "Colonel...hurry up!" Thankfully, Kalam did not have any check in baggage. Another person and I were supposed to travel with Kalam on that flight.

I held Kalam's ticket in my hand and ran towards the counter. It was a *Jet Airways* flight.

The officer at the counter was about to go to the aircraft after checking in everyone and closing the flight passenger list. I told him "Sir, this is an urgent matter! We have a meeting with the French President. There are three of us. But you can leave the two of us here. Please permit only Dr. Kalam to board the flight." Many people did not know Kalam back then in 2000-1. He was widely known only after he became the Indian President.

The *Jet Airways* officer replied: "Sir we have closed the list!"

"I know that! Kindly excuse us. It is important that he leaves. Please announce in your walkie-talkie that a VIP passenger is about to board the flight. Please include him in your passenger list and allow him to go..."

All this happened within some two to three minutes. They allowed Kalam to go. The other person and I were stuck. Finally, we left on another flight.

Kalam's meeting with the French President went well. Kalam told me about this the next day in Delhi: "Rajan, do you know that I have never missed an aeroplane before?" He said this with a victorious smile on his face! "Yes, I know sir! Actually, what I did yesterday was against the law. Sheridon or Prasad have to hold the flight for you just like I did yesterday by citing various reasons every time. Otherwise, you would have missed at least 50% of your flights. Maybe then, you would have learnt your lesson."

When he became the President, it was compulsory to take off the helicopter before sunset. The military official in charge had to struggle with Kalam's time sense. Kalam would simply say, "It is ok!" More on that later.

Even before he left his job as the head of TIFAC, we arranged for the soil testing equipment of C. Subramaniam. (now Late) Prof. S. K. Sinha who led the *TIFAC Agro Vision 2020 team*, helped a lot in this. Kalam met C. Subramaniam. Besides, he was also the chairman of the Governing Council of the *National Agro Federation (NAF)*. NAF operated well. After C. Subramaniam, his son Shri. Rajasekar carried on his father's legacy. The *Soil Health Card Mission* announced by the current Central Government in 2016 was introduced by NAF. Nearly after fifteen years! Neither the centre nor the state governments show a keen interest in such good projects that could benefit a majority of the people (in this case, farmers' productivity and therefore economic growth).

Kalam met a few Chief Ministers while he served as the *Principal Scientific Adviser*. The Punjab CM, Prakash Singh Badal visited a few times seeking Kalam's advice to resolve a few problems. I went to assist. One of the programmes was a

Science Exhibition in Punjab.. We were able to do a few of them well and before starting others, elections intervened. I have seen many ordinary schemes getting stopped on account of elections.

Kalam also met Kalaignar Karunanidhi who was the CM of Tamil Nadu at the time to introduce the *Vision 2020* projects. I was also there. A few ministers from his cabinet and a few high officials were there. The picture came in the '*Malai Murasu*' newspaper. Nothing much happened after that.

The Madhya Pradesh Chief Minister, Digvijay Singh came to visit along with his principal secretary. They were in a hurry to implement value-addition to agro products. I tried my best to help but to no avail!

Many such incidents!

Ministers and higher officials were keen only to handle a few pressing matters. No one thought of doing something with foresight and to implement some good initiatives. Since they take care of only urgent matters, they gain special status in the media. Moreover, when technology and products are bought from abroad they also reap benefits from such transactions in "many ways"! They do not understand or care that this reduces the employment opportunities within India! This wasn't a result of economic liberalisation; in fact, this was the case even in the 1970s.

All TIFAC's *Vision 2020* projects, some of which were meant to happen after 2020, got new life when Kalam was appointed as its chairperson. Now, judging by the way in which Kalam was expelled from his post, all hopes faded!

The *Nalanda University* project which George Fernandes undertook with Kalam was a very good initiative. Fernandes was the Parliament member from Bihar's Gaya constituency. He therefore tried to bring several good schemes to his constituency. He already brought quite a few with the help of the DRDO.

He had a lot of friends in Japan. A big company sought help from Fernandes to renovate the old *Nalanda University* building and construct a new one in its place. Since it was related to higher studies, he handed over their proposal to Murli Manohar Joshi. Joshi added a few points to their project proposal and sent it for review to them. Japanese government policy was such that they could only offer assistance for other countries on matters related to philosophy and not religion. They therefore asked Fernandes to reconsider.

As Kalam was the *Principal Scientific Adviser*, he could undertake such initiatives. Fernandes therefore explained everything to Kalam (Kalam told me later that he learnt of all this only from Fernandes) and asked whether he could develop a suitable project proposal. Kalam knew that I was fond of Nalanda and Buddha. (The name of my Bengaluru house that was built in 1993-94 is *Nalanda*). Kalam handed over the Japanese files that were given to him by Fernandes and said: "Rajan, your favourite Nalanda! We must do something to help Fernandes."

I was happy to oblige. It would be a good break from my TIFAC and PSA Office routine. Besides, there were many setbacks in those projects as I had explained earlier. I therefore saw a new ray of hope! I even considered taking this as a full-time job in case everything fell in place. I knew by heart all rules and regulations related to India's higher education system. Earlier in 1997, while working for CII, I had helped the higher education committee formed by Murli Manohar Joshi. Dr. Manmohan Jha was the joint secretary for the department of Human Resource Development at the time. He belonged to the Bihar cadre IAS. Back then in 1997, I never imagined that I would work along with him for Nalanda. But I have studied all the rules and regulations of higher education through him.

It helped a lot in the job now given by George Fernandes. He felt that it would be good to start off with something small which would later evolve into a bigger one. A lot of initial work is involved when constructing a new university complex. Besides, other than government universities no other universities will be granted permission. Even to get that permission it would take several years.

Therefore, it would be wise to start it initially as *Nalanda Institute for Higher Studies*. Initially, productive work could be done by setting up a few faculties, and undertaking India-Japan collaborative projects. After a few years, it could slowly evolve into *Nalanda University* comprising all branches of higher education.

In consultation with Kalam, I developed this proposal. Kalam explained in detail to Fernandes who welcomed this project happily. It took care of all concerns raised by the Japanese. He wanted to start it immediately. Kalam asked me to talk to Fernandes.

I spoke with him. Fernandes asked me whether it would be possible to develop a plan that reveals the historicity of Nalanda to everyone within the budget of a few crore rupees.

I replied: "Sir, let us save ancient Indian manuscripts on computers. We can also trace Nalanda related historical facts through that. The Japanese have innovative technologies. We will discuss that later. We can also start classes on how to save these old scriptures and manuscripts on computers. Let this be the basis for education."

We discussed it two or three times. Earlier in TIFAC, we had proposed projects to digitalise such ancient works. Vijaya Bhargava, an expert in the field, is a good friend of mine. As requested by Fernandes, I gathered information about instruments related to the project. It could be started at two crores. I even selected places to start this.

Fernandes was under extreme work pressure at the time. It was getting difficult to fix an appointment. In spite of this, we met one day.

Fernandes said: "It would be difficult to get an appointment through my office. You therefore contact Ashok in my office and he will take care of it."

I felt confident! However, Fernandes fell into the evil trap of his enemies. He had to face corruption charges. He also had to take care of coalition with the ruling party. What was started by him stopped abruptly! However, the project initialisation stage helped a lot.

Later on, when Kalam became the President, it was re-initiated through Nitish Kumar. During that time, Dr. M. M. Jha served as the Principal Secretary of the education department in Bihar.

M. M. Jha, Nitish Kumar, Kalam, and I laid the foundation for today's *Nalanda University* building campus.

We had to encounter a few perversions later. I will discuss that while talking about Kalam's life as the Indian President and other episodes.

One or two days after Ramamurthy left, Kalam came back to work in the office. He started to do his routine office work. Meanwhile, many people in Delhi heard about the change in TIFAC leadership.

The former director of IIT, and an expert in socio-economic, S&T, and computer fields, Prof. Indiresan was a member of TIFAC. He came to see Kalam. He was extremely upset that Kalam was expelled from his post. He was older than Kalam by a few years. No law would be broken had Kalam received an extension for a few more years to continue as the chairperson of TIFAC. Moreover, it was apparent that the TIFAC job and the job as the *Principal Scientific Adviser* were intertwined. Indiresan openly said to Kalam: "Sir! Joshi knew that TIFAC was your right hand. He knew that TIFAC was very important to you both at the individual level and at the professional level as the *Principal Scientific Adviser*. He chopped off your right hand!" Indiresan was a renowned IIT professor. Like any good teacher, he always spoke his mind without hesitation!

Both of them had no idea how to proceed any further with their TIFAC initiative. They were well past the age of complaining about this matter to PM Vajpayee. Already Vajpayee had to handle BJP and its coalition at the time. Most leaders weren't sure of their survival with daily crises! We should have to think about how these democratic processes could possibly work for a developing nation like India. In order to strengthen its industries (small, medium, and large), and also to improve agricultural productivity using modern mechanised systems for the farmers to gain economically, many new S&T initiatives need to be undertaken. PURA was one such scheme for the rural villages. While Indiresan took steps to implement the PURA projects, Kalam supported PURA in his lectures. Now both of them were stuck. It was the time when all Panchayats in Kanchipuram district of Tamil Nadu agreed formally in writing to the PURA initiatives. How can we help them now?

Taiwan, South Korea and Singapore were famous for developing their industries to rise upto international standards. These lagged behind India during 1960–70. They all became major world business centres in 2000. Their agro sector was also doing well. Yet another example is China. It could be said that in 1980, India was slightly ahead of China. Look at the situation at present! We need to think about all these matters. It cannot be said that the poor people living there are suffering. However, we need to think about how people at the lower substratum are suffering in India. What good has democracy served here? How efficient are our government policies and administrative skills?

Kalam worked as per his routine schedule in June 2001. Dr. R. Chidambaram was an expert in the field of crystallography. He was renowned worldwide. He was also an expert in the field of atomic physics. Given the nature of his job and time, it was not even necessary for him to think about TIFAC operations that would help common people. He spent his entire life working in the nuclear department. He contributed immensely in the nuclear bomb projects. Even before the success of the nuclear tests, Kalam was selected as the '*Bharat Ratna*' candidate (at the end of 1997 when I.K.Gujral was the PM). Before the nuclear tests were performed (May 11, 1998), it was decided to hand over the '*Bharat Ratna*' award to Kalam (March 1998), and yet many people to this day think that Kalam received this award only for the nuclear tests. A few people raised doubts as to why Dr. R. Chidambaram did not receive the award with Kalam. Dr. Chidambaram must also have felt the same way.

When Dr. R. Chidambaram succeeded as the TIFAC Chairperson after Kalam, he wanted to undertake an initiative that revealed his stamp. Without understanding the details of the PURA project and without consulting either Kalam, Dr. Indiresan, or me, he told me over the phone: "Please stop the PURA project in Kanchipuram. I want to check its feasibility in and around the Kalpakkam nuclear plant." One of the fundamental factors for PURA was to interconnect villages that weren't surrounded by any big cities or factories and promote the growth and development of such villages. I lost interest in arguing with him. I informed Indiresan. He became very upset because we were trying to prepare a business plan for those villages near Kanchipuram. The government of Tamil Nadu agreed to finance it.

"What to do, Indiresan sir? You are proposing a project centred around villages. Only fields and forests lie in between them. However, Dr. Chidambaram is a nuclear scientist. How can there be an atom without a nucleus in the centre, isn't it? He therefore wishes to propose a project centred around the Kalpakkam nuclear plant surrounded by villages!" Indiresan laughed out loud; a sad, unhappy laugh!

Otherwise, Dr. Chidambaram was a good man. He spoke well. He had a good sense of humour too. He was a great physicist. In case the government had given him a job related to his field of expertise, he could have contributed productively after retirement. TIFAC jobs would be confusing to pure scientists. An entirely different mindset is needed to think about land, waste management, new fuel technology, manufacturing modern instruments, robotics, micro-small-medium-large industries and so on.

I did not inform Kalam. Why unnecessarily trouble him?

On July 4, 2001, he called me: "Rajan! I have decided to resign from my post as the *Principal Scientific Adviser*. I need a small draft of the letter!" I did not stop him since it was naturally the wisest choice at the time. (Recall my song about '*Separation of Leader*').

I prepared a draft with just 4–5 lines. Normally, while quitting from a job, people mentioned various reasons. I did not mention any. I felt that in case the PM asked Kalam, he could answer it on his own. Kalam too agreed. Sheridon typed it and sent it to the PMO. Only the three of us knew about this July 4, 2001 letter.

I later told Kalam: "Let's see what happens! Anyhow, July 4th is the day of American Independence!"

Kalam laughed heartily. He felt relieved that he got rid of a big burden.

He did not tell me what he planned to do after retirement. However, I think I knew his plan.

Immediately after Kalam had joined as the PSA (*Principal Scientific Adviser*) in January 2000, the then ISRO chief offered him a job. Kalam showed me a letter from his table drawer. The Space joint-Secretary, *Department of Space (DOS)* had offered him the post of Dr Brahm Prakash Distinguished Professor. "I tried to get this post earlier. I wanted to take it up once I left my job as the *Defence Minister's Scientific Adviser*. There was no reply from ISRO at the time. However, I was offered the job as the *Principal Scientific Adviser by the Central government*. Now ISRO has also accepted my request. I think I will inform the PM about this."

I had not yet joined him in the *Office of the Principal Scientific Adviser* then. I worked for CII. I said: "Sir, are you planning to quit your post as *the Principal Scientific Adviser*?"

Kalam: "No, let me also accept this offer! I do not need the salary quoted here!"

I said, "Sir! Even the ink of your appointment order from the PM's office wouldn't have dried yet! What will the PM think about you? He would wonder whether you constantly looked out for other jobs!

"What would you think of me if within a few days of joining you, I asked you permission to accept the post of a distinguished professor?"

Kalam said nothing.

I continued, "Please read carefully the appointment order from ISRO/DOS. They have not mentioned the date of joining. Therefore, it won't get nullified. You could join there anytime you want to. There is no urgency. Wait for another six months. If you still feel the same way, you can join there." I stressed my point.

He left it for the time being. Kalam had a special liking towards the post of a professor in colleges and universities. There was no teaching involved in this ISRO's 'distinguished professor' job!

Kalam had told me once earlier. I think it was in 1994. At the time, his job as the Secretary DDRD /DG DRDO/SA to RM was shaky. (We had described in an earlier chapter about what Arunachalam did.) At the time, Tamil Nadu CM, Jayalalitha wanted to offer Kalam the post of Vice-Chancellor of *Madras University*. Kalam said: "It is a great opportunity, sir. I showed it to the PM (Narasimha Rao), who told me, 'Kalam! Keep that aside! In case you have lost hope in everything, then do all this!' He insisted on what he said. I asked, 'Sir! I got your approval before applying. Now what should I do?' and the PM replied, 'I will take care of it. Leave it to me. Now go do your work.'"

In case Narasimha Rao had not stopped Kalam, what course would Kalam have taken? Besides, Kalam had a deep 'romantic' interpretation of posts like Vice-Chancellor and Professor. He did not know the truth!

I was correct. Without telling me, he had the post of distinguished professor of ISRO in his mind after he retired. (I was not keen on his decision to take up this ISRO post. As I said before while mentioning about the DRDO offer, an emperor cannot become a king in his own land!)

As a response to his July 4 letter, the *PM's Principal Secretary,* Brajesh Mishra who held high authority back then, spoke with Kalam.

Kalam told me about this. He said: "Sir, Nandi sir (this is how he referred to Brajesh Mishra) called me and said, 'Kalam, right now the PM is under so much pressure. He said he wanted to speak exclusively with you. He will call you soon. Please continue as the *Principal Scientific Adviser* till then!' This is what he said."

I told Kalam: "Sir! Maybe there is a reason for him to delay! He probably thinks that time is the best healer. You can continue. Let us wait and see!"

There was no signal from the PMO.

Kalam participated in all meetings he had accepted earlier. He travelled a lot and delivered lectures. Since I had to handle TIFAC and the *Principal Scientific Adviser Office,* he travelled sometimes alone. Otherwise, Vijayaraghavan accompanied him.

On one such occasion, while Kalam travelled out, I was at home. (I think it was a holiday). I received several phone calls in the evening. It was September 30, 2001. Mobile phones weren't used widely in those days.

Many of my friends called me over the land line phone and asked: "Rajan, are you safe?" I asked them why they were concerned about me. They said: "Didn't you travel with Kalam? His helicopter has crashed. See on TV!" I immediately turned on the TV. Flash news: "Helicopter carrying Kalam fell!" They did not explain clearly about what happened to Kalam.

After trying several times to reach Sheridon, he finally came on line. "Sir! Kalam sir is safe. Not even a single scratch in his body. They will continue their journey in the car now!" I shared the happy news with all those who asked me earlier. A few minutes later, Kalam himself spoke: "Rajan! I am safe. Thankfully, we didn't fall from a height of 100 feet; the engine stopped working at 50 feet itself. Otherwise, everything would have been over by now. I have informed my people in Rameswaram. Please speak to my brother. He will get convinced that I am safe only if you inform him. They are talking rubbish on TV channels. I won't be able to talk over the phone as I am travelling. Please tell my brother."

My phone was ringing non-stop. In an intermediary gap, I called Rameswaram. I asked Nazema to hand over the phone to Kalam's brother (i.e. Nazema's father).

I informed him that Kalam was alright and narrated my phone conversation with Kalam.

He had a sharp mind. He asked, "Did you speak with him personally...how is he doing?"

"Yes, I spoke with him personally. He was not in shock. He was acting normal. Therefore, I think that he must be safe. He asked me to personally inform you of this!"

He got convinced.

"Please advise him to be more careful in future!" he said.

"Ok!" I said.

I had to attend to several phone calls even at night. I got no break. However, a poem echoed in my mind. It is there in my third poem collection "அழியாத உயிர்கள்" ("*Indestructible lives*") under the title 'நண்பனின் கேள்விகள்' ('*Questions of a Friend*'). I gave a copy of my poem to Kalam after he returned...

Why did Allah bestow upon you
    One more life?
Is it to launch yet another missile?
    Is it to get rid of poverty?
Is it to praise
    The glories of the past?
Or is it for giving prosperity
    To crores of impoverished people?

Many useless men will call you
    In the name of Science
And pile up hundreds
    Of files and reports!
For changinging the state of people,

Withering without opportunities,
Through practical actions
They won't participate!

These elite men
Have filled up our land!
Do you derive pleasure
In the praises they tell you?
Our Creator who rules the world
Bestowed you with a matchless life!
Have you ever researched
How to make good use of it?

In our big country
Where all religions are accepted
Fanatic hatred many spread
Widely uncontrolled!
Will you have the courage
To be a symbol for uniting our men?
Will you strive to build with love
Bridges that link hearts?

Will you go on
The Holy Haj Pilgrimage?
With a defile free mind
Will you get rid of the people's miseries?
With the blessings of God Almighty
May you live beyond seventy!
Pray and seek His blessings
To act further with distinctness!

(1-10-2001)

That accident became a turning point in his life. He would complete his 70 on 15-10-2001. He continued his government job! "How many tortures one undergoes between 20 to 70" – these famous lines of Kannadasan fit him well!

One day, Kalam called me and said, "Rajan, neither the PM nor Nandi sir called me. I don't want to send a reminder letter. I would like to hand over my resignation letter mentioning my date of retirement. Please send me a rough draft at the earliest!"

I prepared one. As per government rules, it ended with the statement: "I will demit office on... (14 Nov 2001, I think so). The letter was sent to the PMO."

"Rajan, they might ask me who to appoint as my successor. What should I say?" Kalam asked me.

He mentioned a few names. I immediately told him: "Sir, if these are your recommendations, then I too have to quit office immediately." Finally, he came to the conclusion that it would be better if Dr. Chidambaram became his successor. Since Dr. Chidambaram was already heading TIFAC and since TIFAC worked hand-in-hand with the *Office of the Principal Scientific Adviser*, Kalam felt that he was the right person. He felt that it would benefit both the organisations."

Govt, PM Office agreed to the resignation of Kalam and to replace Kalam with Dr. Chidambaram at PSA.

Kalam was courageous throughout all this. But how was he going to answer questions posed by others? He wasn't ready to put the blame on anyone. He did not want to create any unnecessary difficulties for the PM.

"I will go away silently, sir!" Kalam said to me many times.

I said: "Never! You are no rat to hide in a hole. We shall arrange for a press meet and inform formally."

While Kalam was in the midst of all this controversy, his application to the post of distinguished professor for ISRO had already reached its final stages. Kalam never mentioned this to me. IISc's Dr. R. Balakrishnan took care of the processing of it. He had a small room inside his computer centre. Poor Balki (as Balakrishnan was popularly called) did not know about our country's administrative system. 'I am letting Kalam inside my own office room only. Such a great man! A '*Bharat Ratna*' awardee who sanctioned several crore rupees to the S&T researchers while working at the DRDO!' Such thoughts must have crossed Balki's mind.

Many rumours spread when Kalam left his job as the *Principal Scientific Adviser*. Many S&T big shots felt happy inside.

In order to teach Kalam a lesson, the then director of the *Indian Institute of Science,* Dr. Govardhan Mehta told Kalam that he could no longer stay inside the IISc building. They did not have to pay anything for Kalam's stay there. Whereas ISRO allotted funds even to staff, professional and administrative. On top of that, Dr. Mehta along with a few others started citing reasons for not permitting Kalam to be inside their building. They informed newspapers and the press that Kalam did not have a PhD; he had not written any research papers. He was 70 years old. Kalam must have been heartbroken.

Since Kalam was to serve as a distinguished professor of ISRO, he met Kasturirangan (ISRO chief who offered Kalam for the job). But it was of no use.

Kalam mentioned this incident (after he became the Indian President and several times after that) to me frequently: "Sir! You know what the chief of ISRO did to me? While I served as the defence minister's Scientific Adviser and even during my term at the office of principal scientific adviser, whenever I visited the ISRO head office, he would come downstairs to receive me. He would take me with him from the security gate. However, after I resigned, when I went to discuss the ISRO distinguished professor job to explain the way I was troubled by the IISc people... (He would repeat that once again)...when I went to talk after fixing up an appointment, sir...I went there...he wasn't waiting for me down... no one was there to receive me...A policeman took me to the room of the head of ISRO.

Then, the lady who worked with you while you were the *Scientific Secretary*, told me: 'Sir, the chairman is currently busy in a meeting. It will take another 10–15 minutes. Please sit down here.' She then served me some coffee and biscuits...

After fifteen minutes, she sent me inside. He didn't even come out to receive me. No one came out of the room either!

He was sitting down in his seat. I sat in front of him. I explained my situation to him. He replied: 'Okay; I will have it examined by my additional secretary.'

He sent me out immediately, sir. I can never forget it!"

Kalam would also frequently recall those two years in ISRO after the successful launch of SLV-3!

"I was sitting like a vegetable for those two years, sir," he said.

This incident about the way he was treated by the ISRO chief which he narrated frequently till the last days of his life, goes to show how much Kalam was hurt by the incident.

One good quality of Kalam was that even when such people crowded around him at the time of his Presidency, he spoke with them pleasantly with a smile. If they were on a stage, he would appreciate them without any bias. I would get furious. I have openly disclosed this to him. After Kalam became the Indian President, one such S&T big shot who had condemned him earlier, invited him to his office and started applauding Kalam.

The Indian President Kalam spoke well about the S&T big shot in the meeting. They earned a good name since the Indian President himself had come there. I was also there. I wrote a small poem on that in my fourth poem collection under the title 'மறக்காத தேடல்கள்'('*Unforgettable Quests*'):

Excused

I forgive you, you fool!
You hit me on my cheek, you rogue!
I will not hurt myself for God is there !
Try to correct yourself, you may get mukti!

(July 07, 2003)

I gave my poem to Kalam after his speech was over. I said: "Sir, you will worship these fellows with flowers in an open dais! At least when you are alone you could have said what I wrote! How badly these fellows have spoken about you. They pushed you out of the IISc campus!"

Kalam enjoyed my poem. He had a hearty laugh. He said: "I will keep it with me!" He kept it inside his pocket. Amidst all this, I had to attend my TIFAC meetings too. We all went to Kanchipuram to explain our TIFAC initiatives to the people (as per the advice of Shri Sankaracharya Swamigal). Kalam showed great interest in the Kanchipuram project. He and Swami Jayendra Saraswathi became close friends. After Kalam applied for the post of the Indian President, he visited a few places; he paid a visit also to Kanchipuram Sankaracharya at the time.

I have written a poem titled 'காஞ்சி மாவட்ட மக்களுக்கு' (*'To the people of Kanchi district'*) in my "அழியாத உயிர்கள்" (*"Indestructible Lives"*) poem collection. While we were there, I asked Sankaracharya about '*Bhairava*'. He arranged a visit to the '*Swarna Kaala Bhairava darshan*' for me. After completing our TIFAC work, I went to have the darshan. It was a unique experience. I wrote it as a poem. It appears in my "அழியாத உயிர்கள்"(*"Indestructible Lives"*) poem collection as 'பைரவர்'*('Bhairava')*.

A key (ancient key) from the inside sanctum of Bhairava fell on the little finger of my left foot and I started to bleed. The archaka tied it up with a band-aid. Others would have taken it to be a curse or a sin. However, I felt something else.

"...He destroyed
All my sins and Karma
To bring me
Closer to him!"

Kalam has read that poem. I have told of it before to him (written on 26, 27-10-2001)

Both of us did not know at the time that this would be related to the most important day of Kalam's life. It happened a month and a week later. More about that later!

Kalam was desperately looking for a job soon after he resigned from the *Office of the Principal Scientific Adviser*. Looking at all the comments made by some big scientists (mostly against Kalam) in the media, a man immediately arranged for Kalam's job. He wrote a simple letter containing 4–5 lines. It was written by the Vice-Chancellor of *Anna University*, Dr. Kalanidhi. I did not know about him at the time. I had gone to *Anna University* as a Visiting Professor when Shri V. C. Kuzhandaisami was the Vice Chancellor in order to promote the '*Remote Sensing Applications*' on behalf of ISRO.

I did not know about Kalanidhi. Kalam showed me the letter. He had arranged for Kalam to take the role of a special professor.

"What do you say?" Kalam asked me.

"Sir! I do not know who he is. But it looks like he has great regard and respect for you. Please accept the appointment order," I said.

He asked me to go and see. The incident with IISc. earlier must have given him some fears. Vice-Chancellor Kalanidhi had arranged a good room with assistants for Kalam. He had planned to allocate a separate guest house for Kalam's stay.

Kalam felt happy. He wrote a letter of acceptance. He also did not know about Kalanidhi. Several rumours spread in the media about rejecting Kalam from IISc. campus and why he had to forgo the role of a distinguished professor for ISRO. (If not the IISc. campus, they could have at least asked Kalam to stay in any of the ISRO centres or the ISRO head office). The pressure was also building up inside Delhi circles. Kalam wanted to get out of Delhi as quickly as possible. "Sir! Your dates are approaching soon! Please arrange for a press meet to make a formal announcement!" I said.

"No! Let us leave it at that!" Kalam replied. He was afraid to answer any unwanted questions that could be asked by the press people. The last thing that Kalam wanted now was a fresh controversy.

I said, "If you leave without answering, then it would lead to more confusion. They will blow up the matter by interviewing the 'big shots' or they could spread some more rumours. If you remained silent now, then you could end up getting into trouble. Even if you go to Chennai, you can't escape from it!"

"Moreover, it would be easy for me to arrange a press meet for you while you are still working in the *Office of the Principal Scientific Adviser* in Delhi. After you resign from your job, none of the important press people would come to your press meeting. All of them would only go behind the newly employed *Principal Scientific Adviser*."

My persistence yielded a good result. He finally asked, "What is the notice time you will require?"

"It would be better to arrange it immediately. Press people are very busy. Our Sadhana Sharma could arrange for a good press meet!" I said. Sadhana Sharma was in charge of handling TIFAC's media interface. (Magazines, TV and people). She maintained a cordial relationship with all press reporters. If she asks, they will definitely come.

Kalam also knew about her. Sadhana had helped him several times by arranging for good press meets.

"Please ask Sadhana madam. Do not pressurise her. Instead, ask her about how long she can wait to arrange for the press meeting!" This happened in the beginning of November 2001.

I conveyed Sadhana's reply to him: "Sir, Sadhana said that since it is Diwali on November 14th, everyone would go on vacation. November 9 is the deadline; otherwise November 10th morning is also fine. She will send the letter to all press people. She has to arrange for a room for the press meeting and she has to send personal invitations to all of them."

I knew that Sadhana was extremely busy. I also knew about Kalam's poor time management skills (recall the airport incident I had mentioned earlier). He will be postponing till the very last minute! Everyday, Sadhana called me at least 4 or 5 times to confirm. I will then ask Kalam each and every time.

On Friday (November 10) evening, Kalam called me over the phone and said: "Sir, is the deadline over? Can you check with Sadhana madam if I could say by tomorrow (Saturday) morning."

"Sir, it is going to get delayed further and further. In fact, I wanted to erase any memories of this by tonight," I said.

"No, sir! I will certainly confirm tomorrow morning. Please check with Sadhana madam..." Kalam said.

I spoke with Sadhana. She is a very kind lady; a very strong woman. She wanted to arrange a big press meeting for Kalam. (Since Kalam was highly appreciated by many people in TIFAC).

Sadhana told me: "Alright, sir. This is going to be very tough though. But I can manage if he confirms it within Saturday afternoon!"

I told her: "Sadhana, I will talk to him. 'There is a limit for everything. If he did not wish to listen to my advice, then I will tell him that he can erase everything from his mind and continue doing his other work!"

I informed my conversation with Sadhana to Kalam.

"Sir, I will certainly decide about this by tomorrow, Saturday before 12 noon. After that time, I will completely erase this from my memory. Not only that, I will also erase all wounds caused by this incident from my memory!"

"Certainly by tomorrow noon, sir... please do not cancel anything before that time," Kalam said.

"Ok...," I said. I was there in my house that Saturday. I actually forgot all about the press meet arrangement.

Afternoon passed...evening passed...no news from Kalam yet. I also did not ask him further.

He called me over the phone on Sunday morning at 10 AM. He never got ready this early, that too when he was in Delhi!

"Why have you called so early in the morning, sir!" I asked.

"About that only...," he said.

"About what?" I asked.

"Why are you talking like this, sir? How long have you been pestering me to do it!," he said.

"Which one, sir?" I tried to conceal my frustration and anger. So, I pretended as if I had forgotten everything.

"About that press meeting, sir!" Kalam said.

"Oh! About that! I erased it from my memory yesterday itself, sir!" I said.

"Sir...I couldn't do it yesterday, sir...Please check with Sadhana madam again... Please do not erase it from your memory yet!" he said.

"Ok...I will try! I feel sorry for her. She is newly married and she must be having a lot of responsibilities at home during weekends. Let me try...," I said.

I called Sadhana.

"Tell me, sir. This is Sadhana speaking," she said.

"Sadhana, our Kalam sir has finally agreed for the press meet. He asked me to check with you whether it would be possible to arrange one for tomorrow, that is, Monday afternoon? Ok, what are you doing now? There is so much noise in the background?"

"Sir, from the morning I have been cleaning my house. Right now, I am cleaning the floor..."

"Oh my God! Please try, but you don't have to trouble yourself to make the press meet arrangements..."

"Ok, sir! Since today is a Sunday, most of the press people would be asleep at this time! I will try to wake them up. I will try. Now, this has become my topmost priority for the day."

As expected, Sadhana had done her job well. She contacted many big people in the Press Information Bureau and had arranged for a very good auditorium for Kalam's press meet. She contacted me on Sunday evening.

"Sir, you can confirm tomorrow's meeting with Kalam sir!"

Something good happened. Kalam wanted to bid farewell to Delhi, most of it was accomplished by Sadhana's efforts.

I informed Kalam. "Your Sadhana madam is fantastic, sir...Now, we have to prepare my speech...after arranging for such a huge press meet, it won't look nice if I go there unprepared!" Kalam said.

We spoke about that. I said: "Yes, you are right. It shouldn't sound like a report card manual from the *Office of the Principal Scientific Adviser*. There is no use in talking about *Vision 2020* here. You have been talking only about that for the past five years..."

I continued: "In their interview, they will ask you why you decided to quit. They will ask whether you and Murli Manohar Joshi have any hostility or competition..."

We need to plan a different course of action. You turned 70 last month. So, it would sound better if you said you wanted to open a fresh chapter in your life. What should that be? You think about that. I too will think it over. We need to finalise that for sure by tomorrow morning. Then, you have to get prepared for the *Q&A* session. Think of ways to avoid controversies... think of an entirely new goal. If it is different from your existing work routine, then no one will ask about your past and the present. Let us see, sir!," I said.

The next day, I visited Kalam in his office. I need not worry about the press meet arrangements since Sadhana was an expert in that. In case she needed anything, she would approach me. Me and Kalam finalised the speech. After thanking everyone for their presence, Kalam would briefly explain his professional journey. He would talk about TIFAC's space, defence, socio-economic schemes...then he would talk about his next major plan. He would also have to inform about his teaching job in *Anna University*. Nothing much.

Now, his next major plan: "I want to speak with all our Indian children. Within the next five years, I would like to interact with at least a million Indian children!"

Kalam came to the press meet. I was also there. The auditorium was full. Some 100–150 people from magazines, TV channels, and even foreign media like NHK were present.

Kalam began with his trademark charming smile. After explaining briefly his professional journey... "Next, I have a new major initiative to undertake. I want to meet a million young children and interact with them." He explained his plan briefly.

Then the Q&A session. Most of the questions were about this new initiative of Kalam.

The whole auditorium reverberated with questions on this new initiative. None of them asked about Kalam's past or about Murli Manohar Joshi. Everyone was eager to know about this new initiative.

The press meet came to an end. Kalam breathed a sigh of relief.

After thanking Sadhana, he left. I too left with him.

"You did a fabulous job, sir!" Kalam told me.

"Please do not meet anyone from the press privately till you go to Chennai. Just tell them that you are busy packing your things..."

Now let us give importance to your new job and accomodation.

Since Kalam was eligible for Z-security (at the time of the launch of the first Agni missile in 1989, as per the order issued by the then cabinet secretary T. N. Seshan), he had to be given special protection. Wherever he lived, he had to be safeguarded. Now that his destination had been confirmed, I wrote a letter to the Home secretary since I was the chief at the office of PSA. I had to remind them again and again since they were very busy. Since Kalam was leaving Delhi, the protection protocol will change. The Central home ministry should grant approval for this.

Then, I informed Dr. Kalanidhi: "Sir, you have covered everything well.. this security issue is very important. Please inform them orally and then write a formal letter..I will send a copy of all my letters to the home ministry to you. Keeping that as your proof, you can then write to the Tamil Nadu police. Let us not make any recommendations. Let them handle everything on their own."

I knew about all these protocols while working for ISRO when I had to make arrangements for Smt. Indira Gandhi's visit. I also learnt while discussing terrorism and security issues with senior defence officials like K. B. S. Gill in Delhi. Terrorism became a major threat in Tamil Nadu around 2001. Besides, many see Kalam as 'the missile man' and 'the atom bomb man'! (While discussing incidents that happened in Chennai later, the reason for my caution will be understood clearly).

One of the joint secretaries of the Home Ministry spoke with me: "Rajan, you need not worry. We will take care," he said. There was no written response. So, I wrote a letter thanking him for what he conveyed over the phone and made it official. I also wrote that I would send a copy to Kalanidhi, the Vice Chancellor of Anna University.

So, the Tamil Nadu policemen met Kalanidhi. I too had gone there once. I carefully examined Kalam's accommodation. After inspecting his office, guest house, nearby buildings, trees..., I told the Superintendent of Police: "Sir, you can listen to Kalam sir and the Vice Chancellor. However, the final authority rests with you. Please do whatever it takes to give Kalam maximum protection. Kindly inspect the place regularly. This is not just because Kalam is a good man and a very great person."

The Superintendent of Police was happy. They took good care.

It was finalised that Kalam would occupy his seat on December 5, 2001 in Anna University, Chennai.

Kalam's press meet made a huge impact all over India. Many wrote to him that they were willing to assist him. One Mr. Shankar from Mumbai wrote to Kalam that he would take care of all his travel expenses within India. Kalam became a sensation and a role model.

Looking at all this, people in the PMO felt that if Kalam was not given a formal farewell, they would lose their image.

Amidst all this, Dr. R. Chidambaram who became the newly employed *Principal Scientific Adviser* after Kalam wanted me to arrange a press meet for him. Sadhana arranged for that as well. I also wrote to the home ministry to give him special protection similar to that given for Kalam. My work overload increased. Besides, I had to travel too...

After Kalam left his job in the PSA office, he stayed in the DRDO guest house for three weeks. Sheridon took care of the arrangements. Kalam travelled extensively. He delivered many S&T lectures.

One day, Prof. V. S. Ramamurthy desperately tried to reach me. He had called me several times over the phone. I was in Delhi at the time. "Rajan! Where is Kalam sir now? I have been trying to reach him desperately! I even tried calling him at the DRDO guest house. I am in a crisis! Kalam must be in Delhi tomorrow evening. The Prime Minister has arranged a farewell party for him. Now only they informed me. Our minister Dr. Joshi will also be present. His office staff are also asking about Kalam's whereabouts," he said.

"Sir, I don't know what to do? I am not sure of his whereabouts. But I do know that he is not in any of the metros. He is in a small town. He went today morning or yesterday night. I think he will be back in only 2 or 3 days," I said.

V. S. Ramamurthy said: "I do not know what you have to do! But Kalam must be in Delhi by tomorrow evening. Otherwise, I will lose my job..."

There were no online bookings back then in 2001. Cell phones were emerging slowly. However, not many places in India had good cell reception. Moreover, there weren't many airports and aeroplanes as we see today.

Sadhana was an expert in press meet arrangements; Sheridon was an expert in booking flight tickets. Kalam would ask him to arrange some impossible flight schedules; there would be no time interval from one flight to the next! I have already written about this earlier.

Finally, I said to Prof. V. S. Ramamurthy: "I will ask Sheridon to help. Let us see!"

"Please do not give no for an answer. Ask him to bring Kalam somehow!" said the professor.

Sheridon undertook an impossible task. He had arranged for two consecutive flights. If there was no delay, then it would be possible for Kalam to be present for the farewell party in Delhi at least 10–15 minutes earlier. I told Sheridon, "This is fantastic! Let's do it!" Sheridon informed the travel plans to Kalam.

I informed V. S. Ramamurthy: "This is the only solution. Let us hope that the flight is not delayed. In case it lands on time, try to delay the PM's arrival by a few minutes..." V. S. Ramamurthy wouldn't have slept that night.

The next day, he repeatedly asked me about Kalam's arrival. People slowly started showing up for the farewell party. The rule was to be present one-one and half hours early. V. S. Ramamurthy kept checking with me: "Rajan! I have sent

S&T officials to the airport to receive Kalam. Let him come here directly! If he goes to his guest house, he will be delayed. It is your responsibility to ensure that Kalam comes here directly."

There was a slight delay in the arrival of Kalam's flight. Ramamurthy adjusted the PM's timings accordingly by speaking with the PMO officials. As soon as the flight landed, I spoke to Kalam: "Sir, please come here directly with the S&T officials. Please do not go to your guest house now. Ramamurthy's blood pressure is shooting up!"

Kalam said: "Why are they doing this? Had they informed me earlier about this farewell party, I could have rescheduled a few meetings. Somehow, you and Sheridon made me come here. Now I have not even washed my face.."

I said: "Sir, whether you wash your face or not, you will still be a hero! We have delayed the PM's arrival time. If we delay any further, it would become very difficult. Please come directly from the airport!"

After a few minutes of excitement, the PM decided to come early and wait for Kalam. However, it will not be correct as per the government rules. But, the PM arrived and was waiting in his chair. V. S. Ramamurthy was extremely worried. "Rajan! Is he coming here directly or not?" he asked me.

After a few minutes, Kalam arrived at the scene. All confusion ended. Celebrations began. The PM hugged Kalam.

Then began the speeches. Murli Manohar Joshi applauded Kalam. "One Kalam is not enough for the country. 100 such Kalams are needed. Kalam's interactions with our Indian children would make this definitely possible!" I do not know whether he meant this from the heart or if this was just a unique characteristic of the politicians!

The PM's farewell party to Kalam was a good thing. Now, the press reporters won't be able to write anything spicy or bitter.

The only thing left for Kalam to do now was to leave Delhi and occupy his seat in the Anna University in Chennai. He did not want anyone to come to the airport to send him off. He therefore did not inform anyone of his departure date. There are many opportunists in Delhi. They weren't bothered to go to the airport to send off Kalam. Afterall, what help could a professor in Anna University do for them!

The plan was that I should travel with Kalam. We were supposed to travel in the evening flight after office. We were to depart on December 4, 2001. Kalam would be in his room on December 5th morning and I would return in the night flight.

When I came home to get ready to go to the airport, my wife handed over a letter to me. It was an invitation to attend the kumbhabhishekam (crescent) festival in the Bhairava temple to be held on December 5, 2001. It was sent by the temple priest along with 'Vibhoothi prasad'. Earlier, I had sent my Bhairava poem to the priest (October 2001) who sent me a beautiful poem in reply. I lost touch with him after that. This invite letter from him was totally unexpected!

I told this to Kalam in the morning of December 5th. "Sir! It is your Bhairava, sir! You must definitely go! You will be able to reach there within 2-3 hours," Kalam said.

"Sir, I have come here to make arrangements for your stay. Lord Bhairava has given his blessings and the vibhoothi prasad. I can have his darshan without going there." I said laughing.

The function went well. Many from Anna University gave Kalam flower bouquets. He inspected the laboratories of his department.

Lunch was served.

Kalanidhi, myself and Kalam discussed his role. The name for his department was "*Technology for Social Transformation.*"

Kalam repeatedly advised me not to leave my job in TIFAC and in the PSA office. "Sir! Recall how much we struggled to establish the PSA office. You have a lot of work to do there. Only after Dr. R. Chidambaram is firmly rooted, you must think about quitting your job there. Work wholeheartedly. Anyway, we both will be meeting one another frequently." Kalam told me while we were both in Delhi...

But, I was not entirely sure about my future. I returned to Delhi. Even though Kalam was content with his new job, my heart sank. I felt that a precious gem was locked up inside an ordinary box. (Though I knew the circumstances in which I had to leave him there). I had a pressure in my mind...But I did not tell him.

Like Bharathi says, (I used to frequently say these words to myself..)
"Do you think that
I will die
Like many funny men
Who daily go in search of food ...."[3]

However, I did not have the mental strength on that day to say these words to myself; nor the mental skills.

It would be appropriate to describe it as a feeling of emptiness inside me.

No one even thought about major changes that were (destined) to happen in another six or seven months!

---

[3]*Translation of verses "Vedikkai Manitharai Poley-Naan Veezhvenendru ninaithayo" taken from 'Subramania Bharati Volume I poems' by Sahitya Academy; edited by Dr. Sirpi Balasubramaniam; Sahitya Academy, New Delhi, 2016.*

Kalam in Anna University

In Chennai, Kalam stayed in the guest house arranged by Kalanidhi. All his life, Kalam lived in guest houses in various places like Thiruvananthapuram, Hyderabad, and Delhi. He had bought an apartment in a multi storeyed building in Bengaluru. He had decided to stay there after he retired. Kalanidhi made provisions for Kalam to enjoy his home food rather than the food served at the guest house. There was a small dining table inside Kalam's room itself. As always, Kalam travelled frequently. He visited several schools and colleges in order to complete his target of meeting a million children. This interaction with children helped him in his later days and years.

Even though there were staff assistants in Anna University to assist Kalam, they all came to Sheridon for help to handle Kalam's complex time schedule. At the time, Sheridon was still working in the PSA office. Dr. R. Chidambaram asked Sheridon to continue there. However, most of the work that Sheridon handled was for Kalam. Since I was completely in charge of the PSA office, I told Sheridon: "Just do it; otherwise, he might find it very difficult!"

Kalam was keen on teaching college/university students. It would be difficult for him to teach according to the rules laid down by the University Grants Commission (UGC) and the AICTE; it required a special expertise. Since it would be difficult for Kalam (and also in order to accommodate the students' needs of completing the official syllabus), Kalanidhi arranged for a novel technique. He made Kalam speak in one of the audio visual film studios in Chennai. In 2001, the internet infrastructure was very poor, and so Kalanidhi made use of the intranet facility of Anna University and connected some 20-30 college campuses. A lot of college students had the opportunity to listen to Kalam's speech. Kalam enjoyed these lecture sessions very much; he spoke a lot about this during our frequent phone conversations.

Meanwhile, I got one of the greatest opportunities of my lifetime. Within 15 days of Kalam leaving to Chennai, he came to release my second Tamil poem collection, 'வற்றாத ஊற்றுக்கள்' *('Perennial Springs')*. The Devaneya Paavanar Hall in Chennai was flooded with people. Outside, there was heavy rain. In spite of that, there was a huge crowd. On the dais were Abdul Kalam, Vairamuthu, Sirpi Balasubramaniam, Ponneelan, '*Thamarai*' C. Mahendran, P. V. Indiresan, R. Natarajan (IIT Madras Professor).

Beautiful speeches interspersed with humour.

Then, Kalam gave a beautiful introduction to my English poem collection '*Agony & Harmony*'. It is a great honour to me that this was later translated into Tamil by Shri Sirpi Balasubramaniam under the title, 'துன்ப வீணையும், ஆனந்த பைரவியும்'.

I lost interest in working in the PSA office in Delhi. Even when Kalam was there, we were finding it difficult to approach the PM to approve our initiatives in order to put them to practical use. After Kalam left, the government did not show any special interest in the schemes. I don't think Dr. R. Chidambaram was interested either. To him, TIFAC and the PSA office became talk forums. He travelled all over India to deliver lectures. A few TIFAC schemes were still operating at a slow pace. PURA was completely stopped. Dr. R. Chidambaram wanted to initiate a 'special' project in the rural areas with his special stamp. I tried my best to help him.

However, deep inside me I felt that I couldn't continue to work there any longer as the 'funny person' as told by Bharati. Kalam too must have felt similarly. However, he was 70 at the time. I was just 58. We used to talk frequently over the phone.

One day he said: "Rajan, yesterday policemen came to my guest house with hunter dogs. They were searching for something. They said that there was some bomb threat!" He told this very calmly. It wasn't in the newspapers. Probably, the police took prior action.

"Please be careful, sir! Do not allow any strangers inside your room!" I said.

"Many do not like it that you have become a symbol of this nation's unity. What to do? Terrorism and divisive forces have penetrated deep within the country. Everyone talks about it; but no one has the courage to stop these forces," I said.

I wrote a poem which came in my third poem collection, அழியாத உயிர்கள்*('Indestructible Lives')* about this. I sent the poem to Kalam soon after I completed it.

The title of the poem is, 'கலாம் மனத்திலொரு பாட்டு' *('A Song in Kalam's Mind')*.

Because I am now an icon!
You came for my life in vain!
Do you know what I symbolise?
It is not that weapon that flies in the sky!
All of us are servants to Him alone
We shall love the whole of His creation,
This truth,
The Truth told by Him
Don't you know that I am a small man
Trying to put it to practice?

(13.3.2002)

Most of the songs in this collection depict my mindset after 2001. A few minor and major incidents within the country are also there. Some of them were about the horrible incidents that happened in Gujarat in the beginning of 2002. These were:

மக்கள் ரத்தம் *('People's Blood) 2.3.2002*
மகாத்மாவின் கண்ணீர் *('The tears of the Mahatma') 28,29.3.2002*
குஜராத் *('Gujarat') 2.3.2002*

Since my wife was born and brought up in Gujarat, she wrote a small piece after she read all these poems.

That has been published under the title, 'ஈசன் படைப்பு' *('God's Creation')*. They were also published in the '*Thamarai*' Magazine. Kalam must have been depressed looking at all this. But he never mentioned anything.

S. K. Sinha's death was a major blow to my career. Not only did he pave the way for the TIFAC 2020 initiatives, he also contributed immensely to several projects in many places like Bihar, Kanchipuram, Uttarakhand, Orissa etc after that. He was also instrumental in setting up the 'Soil Testing Laboratory' which served as the foundation of the NAF (*National Agro Federation*). This was the dream project of C. Subramaniam who died in November, 2001. We were consoled since he was already 90 years old. However, Prof. S. K. Sinha died at the age of 66. It was a major blow! When we gathered the next day in TIFAC to mourn over his death, something strange happened! Tears started to overflow from my eyes. Prof. S. K. Sinha was a good friend of Kalam. Kalam was very upset. My grief transformed into a poem that portrayed anger on Lord Shiva. It appears in the 'அழியாத உயிர்கள்' *('Indestructible Lives')* collection as 'மக்கள் உயர்வு' *('People's Uplift')* (19-3-2002). It was also published in the '*Thamarai*' Magazine. I never translate my poems myself. However, I translated this to English immediately. It gives a gist of all of 'TIFAC' initiatives towards the agricultural sector; Kalam was involved in all these projects.

Here comes my anger!
Boiling with anger,
I asked Lord Shiva

Why did you bring
Such a huge loss to our people?

Having taken
Subramanian already;
Now You have
Taken him;
——————————

And so it continues ...

After this huge loss, I completely lost interest in all of theTIFAC and the office of the PSA assignments. Since Kalam had advised me not to leave my job, I was holding onto it earlier. But I no longer had the interest to continue. Sinha's premature death impacted me greatly. I wanted to get away from everything. Kalam did not know about this.

But, there was a uniqueness in Sinha's death. Only the previous day, he had spoken with all farmers and had inspected their lands. While drinking his morning tea the next day, he collapsed... I wrote yet another poem on 23-3-2002 about this.

It comes in the 'அழியாத உயிர்கள்' *('Indestructible Lives')* collection under the title 'மு' *('Mu')*:

I'd like to depart
From this world
When I'm engrossed
In my valuable unfinished work
I seek refuge
In that infinite entity
To fulfil my wish;
——————————————

A long poem conveying the message of God to me. (It fully alliterates with The Tamil letter 'Mu' difficult to bring out in English)

Surprisingly, Kalam's death too happened in a similar manner!

Starting from 1999, even though I had too much work at TIFAC and CII, my mind was centred around economics, social science and composing poems. This becomes noticeable in my English and Tamil poem collections. I started writing a lot of poems in March-April 2002.

My poems, அன்னையின் சுமை'*('Mother's Burden')* written on 25.4.2002 and 'சிவனே என்று' *('That Siva')* written on 24.4.2002, clearly depict my fatigue. Two days before that, on 22/23-4-2002, I do not know what happened to me. Kalam's '*Bharat Ratna*' award ceremony held four years earlier in 1998 kept lingering in my thoughts. Especially the conversation I had with Mohammed Muthu Meera Maraikayar (Kalam's brother) was still fresh in my mind. I still do not know how they took the shape of a poem. Here's the poem:

Big Brother

(Pages 92-93 in the அழியாத உயிர்கள் (Indestructible lives) book)
Kalam (His brother, My big brother)
When my brother
Was awarded the Bharat Ratna
Hadn't your face
Glowed with brightness!
You flew on the sky
Your brother's favourite sporting ground
——————
You alighted from there
And landed upon earth
To look at admiration upon
Your beloved younger brother Abdul Kalam
And you
Mohammed Muthu Meera
Recalled your childhood memories
Fighting and playing fondly
You played it all
In your memory screen

That famous soil from
The southern Rameswaram seashore
Showered like flowers today and
Decorated the Rashtrapati Bhavan!

22/23/24/-4/2002

No one would have thought that Kalam would become the Indian President at that time. Only during the end of May, news about it spread. He became the Rashtrapati on July 25, 2002. Later, not only the soil of Rameswaram but also its people visited the Rashtrapati Bhavan.

I still do not understand the reason behind my poem.

Five months had passed since Kalam went to Chennai. We now frequently conversed over the phone even though we couldn't meet each other personally. Now, he had started reading Tamil magazines and newspapers too. He would share information from those. Funny incidents like constructing a temple for an actress were also part of our conversation. Kalam's favourite was '*The Hindu*' (English newspaper). Nellai S. Muthu's Tamil translation of *India 2020* was in its final stages at the time. The NCBH publishers were very worried since there was no reply from him. (Late) Megalingam Subramaniam told me over the phone one day: "Sir, can you please talk to Nellai S. Muthu about this? He says that he is consulting with Kalam. However, they have already been clarified by you and

Kalam sir earlier. We have sent the typed notes and now everything has come to a standstill!"

I spoke with Kalam: "Sir, I am hearing that you and Nellai S. Muthu have been speaking about the India 2020 translation..already the book is delayed by two months. You had already granted permission. Why are you holding it now, sir?"

Kalam replied: "I did not stop it.. During our regular walking routine in the morning, me and Nellai S. Muthu are discussing the topic, 'Are we bigger, or is the nation bigger?' He says that we could come up with a good book on that..."

"Sir, please ask Nellai S. Muthu to convey his approval to the already finalised book. It has been seen many times. He can discuss other future books with you later. If he doesn't approve within two more days, I will tell Megalingam Subramaniam to proceed further," I said.

Many such incidents. Overall, he was enjoying his job at Anna University. He especially enjoyed his interaction with the children.

Sometimes, I wondered whether he could spend even a whole year in this manner. Even for me, I got used to my work routine in TIFAC and the PSA office. I wondered what I will do after retirement. Besides, in order to accomplish the initiatives designated by them, we need approval from the government, the PM, and the Finance minister. The support could be obtained only through the *Office of the PM's Principal Scientific Adviser*. How could Dr. R. Chidambaram achieve something that even Kalam couldn't? Besides, it became clear to me that he wouldn't do it.

Once, Kalam had to visit the Tata Steel Company in Jamshedpur (2002 March 23). He asked me to accompany him. We discussed my retirement plan. Kalam said: "Ok! Let me speak to J. J. Irani..." I also knew J. J. Irani well. Kalam told him: "Rajan needs a change." J. J. Irani replied: "Tata would be happy to appoint you. I will inform the Tata headquarters." He spoke with me about it. He said: "Tata will be slow in replying. It would be better if you could visit him personally in his Mumbai residence.." I also knew Ratan Tata well. He frequently travelled abroad (2002).

Kalam asked me once or twice after this: "Sir, has there been any improvement after our discussion with J. J. Irani?"

"Yes, at a very slow pace. We have arranged for a meeting with the senior official there." I replied.

I wanted to tell Kalam to directly speak with Ratan Tata about my appointment. But I didn't. I was confused why he was asking me instead of directly doing this himself.

❑

Kalam Becomes a Candidate for the Indian President

Meanwhile, at the end of 2002, a few BJP party workers (the secretary of one of their important ministers and one other person) came to visit me. Around that time, there were rumours that Kalam could be announced as a possible candidate for the *Indian President* or the *Vice President*. The gist of what they said to me was: "If we announce Kalam as a candidate for the *Indian President*, would he agree to compete?" I said finally (our discussion was going around in circles): "Why should he say no? But you should ask this to him in a suitable manner. It should be asked by a big personality... he should be asked politely and with due respect..." I advised.

I informed Kalam of this incident.

A few days later, Chandra Babu Naidu had contacted Kalam regarding this. Kalam immediately told me over the phone: "Sir, Chandra Babu Naidu asked me whether they can announce my name as a candidate for the Indian Presidency. I have asked him to give me some time. What do you say?"

I told him: "If it is for the post of the Indian President, then please agree immediately. It would be difficult if it is for the post of the vice president since the Rajya Sabha proceedings would be tough! Please say 'yes' to them immediately.. Everything else could be sorted out later. Don't waste time unnecessarily by asking other people. All this is OK if it is for a job in the DRDO or the PSA office. But this is for the country's highest office. Many aspirants would be putting in their applications within a few minutes."

Within some time, Kalam called me and said.. "I have agreed as per your suggestion, sir. You forced me to accept, sir. However, I have not yet thought about it fully."

Our telephone conversation went back and forth. News of Kalam's candidacy was also printed in newspapers...

One day, Kalam told me: "Rajan! Some of my scientist friends are asking me not to compete! .. 'Kalam! We are hearing that you could be announced as a candidate. Please don't venture into politics blindfoldedly.' Some others are saying, 'Kalam, they will spoil your name and reputation..please do not accept!' I am receiving a lot of advice."

I asked him back: "Sir! Who are those friends? Big scientists?"

Kalam: "All big people, sir! Some are good friends!"

I replied: "Sir.. I know all about your friends. I also know about other science big shots.. You know what they will be thinking? 'Oh no! He is getting such a big opportunity!... But I am better than him; I am only eligible for the role and not him!' Everyone is jealous of you, sir! They are burning with envy and ego! After listening to everything they say, you simply respond: 'Ok, thank you. I appreciate your advice. I will think it over'. Do you understand, sir?"

Meanwhile, the *Industrial Economist magazine* (Chennai edition) released the photo of a scientist and suggested that he was the eligible candidate.

But no one seemed to have noticed. Things were moving quickly in Delhi. The then Prime Minister Vajpayee decided that Kalam should be the presidential candidate and got consent from Advani. I am not exactly sure of the proceedings that happened within the party. Finally, the BJP announced Kalam as the Presidential candidate. Finding no other way out, the Congress too accepted within a few days. It was reported in newspapers that the Congress was thinking of announcing the then President K. R. Narayanan for a second term.

All this happened at the beginning of June, 2002. Now, as far as Kalam was concerned, I needed to make sure that he responded sensitively to the questions put forth to him. I felt that it was my responsibility to take care that Kalam's replies or comments should not be twisted in wrong ways, creating problems for him.

All these years, Kalam had been the darling of the press. But those press people gathered information regarding S&T and defence. Now, he would be surrounded by the political media representatives who would pounce on him like a tiger! Their training is to look for places to scratch and bite!

"Sir! Going forward, you should be very alert! Your main national supporters are the BJP party workers. So far, they have only announced your name for candidacy. But you have not yet signed the nomination form which is important.

Also, the dates for signing the nomination forms and withdrawal are nowhere near. The political media might twist your statements. They could make it look like you are trying to create confusion for the government. You need not respond to all their questions. If possible, try to avoid meeting the press. To give you a bait , they might suggest that the questions would be about empowering India and PURA and might drag you somewhere else."

"First, you have to sign the nomination form. Then, there is a last date for withdrawal. The results would be announced on June 18th. On July 25, 2002 will be the swearing in ceremony. Till then, recall the quote from the Thirukkural: 'Whatever else you fail to guard, you must guard your tongue...' ('யாகாவா ராயினும் நாகாக்க...'). Remember, this is very important, sir!"

Kalam said, "Why are you tying me up like this, sir!"

I said: "After you become the *Indian President* on July 25th, do whatever you want. But until then, self-restraint is very important."

In general, Kalam did not speak about politics much. He was not really interested. But how will he answer such questions then?

For example, 'If he refused to answer about the Gujarat incidents which happened back then saying I don't know, it would lead to problems. If he gave his opinion on the matter, then also it would lead to other problems! Some might raise questions about him being a Muslim...'

We discussed several such possibilities.Where he should respond, and where not to. All these became a part of our discussion. Before submitting his form, we had to take care of other legal formalities. Some of the Supreme Court advocates who were my friends offered a few suggestions. Kalam should not be employed in any government job or in institutions that receive government funding, through which he could gain profits. It is a very complicated rule. (This became a big issue when Kalam was the *Indian President*; it was not about him; He had asked questions related to files sent by a few based on this rule. More on that later.) Sheridon made a detailed list of all the positions held by Kalam. We then sent resignation letters to all of them. We carefully collected and saved their acceptance for resignation letters. When we wrote a resignation letter to Anna University, Kalam refused. "No! Definitely I won't resign from this job!," he said. I said: 'Sir, we have a slight confusion about this job since this comes under the state government. It could be a 'office of profit'! Now you resign. After you finish your term as the Indian President, you could always go back there!" We tried several methods to convince him.

'But I am not receiving even a single rupee as my salary...' Kalam was adamant. He understood what we said as, 'receiving money'. However, the law is very strange. Even if he did not get his monthly salary, his assistants, his guest house stay etc could be considered as 'gains'!

There was just one more day left for filing the nomination forms. Kalam kept refusing to submit his resignation letter to Anna University. Finally, we got his signature that afternoon and sent it through fax to the Vice Chancellor of Anna University. We had already discussed the issue with Dr. Kalanidhi, the *Vice Chancellor of Anna University*. He immediately responded, 'We have accepted your resignation letter'. He put the official seal and signature and faxed it to us. We stored it in our file and breathed a sigh of relief.

As soon as his term as the Indian President was over, Kalam rushed to Anna University on 25.7.2007. I will talk about that later. I do not know what attraction he found in that job!

The process of filing nominations was over. I wasn't there. The BJP officials, and party administrators took care of the proceedings.

I need to mention something here. I still worked for TIFAC and the PSA office. Dr. R. Chidambaram stayed in Mumbai and came to Delhi for one or two days per week. He knew that I was helping Kalam in full swing. However, he never imposed any restrictions on me. This shows his good nature. Sometimes higher officials could impose unnecessary workload in order to create pressure. Even now when I think about this, I feel thankful to him for his kindness.

Soon after he filed his nominations, Kalam thought of something. He spoke with me.

"Rajan! The candidate applying for the election as the President should meet the chief ministers of various states and other members of the State Legislature soon after filing the nominations. They only elect him. We must also meet the Members of the Parliament. However, the people in the BJP and its coalition have told me, 'You need not do all that! Everything is already finalised! The Congress too has granted their approval. Only the Communist party has nominated Captain Lakshmi Sehgal (Netaji Subash Chandra Bose's military commander of the women's wing) against you. There will be an election for that alone. Otherwise, you are the unanimously elected candidate. Therefore, you need not indulge in campaigning!' That is a big relief. However, I need to visit a few places. I may not be free when I become the *Indian President*. You must also accompany me," Kalam said to me.

The places he wanted to visit were the Kanchipuram Mutt, Puttaparthi Satya Sai Baba Ashram, Vikram Sarabhai Space Centre in Thiruvananthapuram, and Rameswaram to see his family and his ancestral house. Later, he wanted to pray in the mosque where his family members normally offered their prayers.

I gave him some advice.

"Sir, you have planned well. These places are familiar to you. Even though you would like to offer prayers in the Rameswaram Dargah, you must also visit a prominent Islamic Holy Mosque. We should therefore commence our trip from the Ajmer Dargah," I said. Kalam agreed to my suggestion.

We started our trip on July 5 (2002).

First, Kalam offered his prayers in the Ajmer Dargah.

Next, we visited Kanchipuram. We met Jayendra Saraswathi Swamigal and discussed the TIFAC/PURA project which was initiated by Kalam. The people in the mosque (nearby Mutt) invited Kalam there. They had some time restrictions. Therefore, they kept reminding him. Kalam was interacting with the Sanskrit school students over there.

Swami Jayendra Swamigal told Kalam: "Kalam sir! Your people are asking you to come to the mosque. Please go there before the prayer time gets over. You can come here later. Take your friend, the bearded man, with you." He said laughingly.

Kalam finished his prayer at the mosque and returned to the Kanchi Mutt. When the 'Azan' for prayer in the mosque began, the Kanchi Swamigal stopped all noises in the Mutt like ringing the bell etc... till the prayer in the mosque was over. Kalam felt happy to hear this.

Later, we visited the *Vikram Sarabhai Space Centre* in Thiruvananthapuram (a really tiring schedule!). Everyone felt happy to receive Kalam. Kalam visited each and every corner of the VSSC. They had arranged for him to speak in a big auditorium. Everyone felt like they themselves had become the Indian President. Since Kalam was now one of the nominees for the Presidential elections, he was given extensive security. Besides the usual Z-security, the Tamil Nadu Chief Minister, J. Jayalalitha had arranged for more security. Thiruvananthapuram belonged to Kerala jurisdiction. However, while entering TN, we weren't stopped. The TN police force came with maximum protection including a medical van. They came to Thiruvananthapuram and followed the Kerala police vehicles.

While he was at the VSSC, Kalam wanted to visit Mahendragiri. He told me: "Rajan, please do not tell this to anyone. Today evening, we might go to Mahendragiri, and then to Madurai-Rameswaram."

He said, "I will confirm later!" and started to have lunch. The canteen was overcrowded.

I knew the security protocols quite well. For a Presidential candidate nominee, after crossing the Kerala border and entering inside Tamil Nadu, throughout the way, police force should be present enroute. They must have arranged security protection as per the usual route. But Kalam wanted to take a detour to Mahendragiri now. What will happen now? It would be difficult for them to gather the local police force on time. I did not want to compromise on Kalam's security issues. I knew the security protocol by heart; in 1983, I had to take care of security arrangements for the then PM, Smt. Indira Gandhi in Sriharikota. Later, when Rajiv Gandhi visited the place in 1986 also, I was in charge of security. I had taken care of many such security arrangements.

Even though Kalam had asked me not to inform anyone, I requested the Police official in-charge, who was having lunch there, to come to a lone place. I told him:

"Listen, just now Kalam sir told me this. He has plans to visit Mahendragiri in the evening. But nothing is certain now. You please arrange for your security men on both the routes just in case. Besides your local police force, you need not inform this to anyone else."

He was thankful to me for informing in advance and took care of the security arrangements. I did not tell Kalam about this. Finally, Kalam decided to go enroute Mahendragiri. Everyone else was surprised by this sudden change in plan!

We went to Mahendragiri. Overnight we travelled in the car. We arrived at midnight in Madurai. Kalam was surprised to see policemen everywhere. 'Why these many?' We stayed in Madurai. Apparently, Kalam had told one of the policemen not to come to Rameswaram...

After Kalam retired to his room, the policeman (I think it was the Superintendent of Police) came to me and said:

"Sir! Our VVIP guest is asking us not to accompany him to Rameswaram. He says the roads will be narrow there. He says just two policemen would be enough; what do we do now?"

I asked him: "Sir, do you know how to make a rocket?"

Hesitatingly he said, "Why are you asking me this, sir?"

I explained: "Look here! Kalam is a rocket scientist. You do not know about rockets. Fair enough. However, you are an expert in making security arrangements for important people. Neither he nor I know whether it would be one or ten cars.. Because it is your responsibility to give him utmost protection. Please follow your protocol. You need not worry over what Kalam sir said."

He felt relieved! "Thanks a lot, sir!" he said and left.

The next day, the entire Rameswaram was celebrating Kalam's arrival. The policemen were guarding from their designated spots. (Dr. Nazema Maraikayar has written about this in detail)

I went to the Rameswaram temple. Kalam accompanied me. The temple elephants blessed Kalam. After taking a few steps, Kalam said: "You go, sir! I will wait here!" The temple priests said to Kalam, "No, sir! You also must go inside!"

Kalam said to them: "Listen to me, please! As per the temple protocols, I am allowed to come only till here. You please take him and make him get a good darshan of God!" Kalam stayed there.

He must have left for his house. After darshan, I went to Kalam's house. People crowded inside the mosque to pray for Kalam. Kalam's brother Muthu Meera Maraikayar asked me to come to the mosque. I went to the mosque after washing my hands and legs as per their procedure. (I was not asked to come inside the Kanchipuram mosque; I waited for Kalam outside. So, I was a bit hesitant here.)

There were a few minutes left for the prayer to commence. Kalam and his brother were in the front row. Since many people asked me to come inside the mosque, I too covered my head with a kerchief and joined in the back row. My forehead was smeared with 'Vibhuti' and 'Kumkum' (since I just now returned from the temple), and I was praying inside a mosque. 'A very good reflection of India's good culture', I thought to myself.

We took some photos with his family. July 8, 2002 was our trip to Rameswaram; from there, we left for Trichy. On the morning of July 10, 2002, we rushed to St. Joseph's College. We went to all the places familiar to Kalam over there. We then left for Chennai on July 10 by the night train.

We reached Delhi on July 11, 2002. In this way, our hurricane journey which started on July 5, 2002 ended on July 11. Next, on July 13 we left for Bengaluru and visited the Puttaparthi Sai Baba ashram on July 14.

As he did earlier, Baba met both of us privately. We happily conversed for some time. Sai Baba felt extremely happy for Kalam. He pressed Kalam's hands tightly and said, " You tell me whenever you want.I will transfer all my spiritual powers (sakti) to you..." He repeated this twice or thrice.

We then left for Bengaluru after eating. On July 14, 2002 we were back in Delhi.

July 15, 2002 was the election day. Captain Lakshmi Sehgal stood against Kalam; all leftist parties supported her. Elections happened in Delhi and other capital cities. Even though we were sure of Kalam's victory, we were still tensed over the election results.

On July 18, 2002, the results were announced. As expected, Kalam emerged victorious. There were no big celebrations. Many people came to Kalam's DRDO guest house and congratulated him by handing over floral bouquets. Amidst all this, I continued to work for the TIFAC and PSA office.

I was thrilled. I composed a poem celebrating Kalam's victory. I saw his victory as a relief to the country. My conversation with Lord Shiva about the present state of the country...

Kalam's election

Oh! Lord Shiva!
You have taken the performance of

The Rudra Tandava dance
As your main work
Accumulating corpses
Adding hysteria
Promoting selfishness that
Destroys all penances

You have brought in a state
Where these are considered as dharma!

Shiva, today you have
Smiled beamingly!
Nation rejoiced as though
It heard the rhythm of a great poem!
Shiva, make this smile
An eternal one!

Destroy poverty
From the face of this earth!
Make all rogue partisans who divide us
As noble souls
By giving them new light!
Let peace prevail
Upon this lovely planet forever!

(22-6-2002)

Sheridon and a few others from the DRDO were brought in to assist Kalam. His guest house was given police protection. Many media people interviewed me. A few important questions were: "How can someone who doesn't know anything about the Constitution become the *Indian President*?" "How will he answer questions posed by different parties with different policies and varying manifestoes? Besides his S&T knowledge, he has no other political experience. What experience does he have in law and administration?"

Some were about him playing the Veena.

I had to answer each and every single one of them. Some of my replies were: "Look here! There is an entire team to give advice to the Indian President. He had worked in several large schemes before. Do not think that everyone over there was honest and simple. Different employees had different opinions, mindsets, and feelings over there too. Moreover, not everyone there was a saint. Just like all other ordinary men, they too were inflicted with anger, hatred, jealousy, and falsehood. This was the case within committees too. He has handled all these situations effectively. One of Kalam's biggest assets was that he listened to everyone patiently. After listening, he would analyse it thoroughly and then take appropriate action. That is the reason behind his success..."

Even in 2002, the press reporters asked several painful questions. We needed to answer them patiently. Further, we also had to ensure that they did not twist our answers. Once Kalam becomes the President, staff at the *Rashtrapati Bhavan* will handle all this. But from the 18-06-2002 result announcement to the 25.07.2002 swearing in ceremony, we had to be cautious.

Quite unexpectedly, a lady reporter asked me, "Sir, I understand that Kalam has a good understanding of scientific principles. He is currently working on a project in which physical disabilities are rectified by passing electric signals in the brain. Can you tell me your opinion?"

I did not know about that at the time. When I told her, the lady reporter kept on pressing me for a reply. She showed me Kalam's discussion related to the topic.

I was trying to avoid her. I escaped by saying, "He has discussed this as a long term project. By connecting electric sensors to the nervous system of the affected person they could perhaps be aiming to replace nervous system activities. Probably, Kalam could be thinking that this would become a possibility in some distant future!"

Several days passed. Many people were now asking me about the protocols inside *Rashtrapati Bhavan*. Some said that Kalam should take care of certain activities which were being performed by other staff. A few newspapers wrote about what my role would be in the *Rashtrapati Bhavan*!

The post of the secretary to the President was a major one in *Rashtrapati Bhavan*. Many people were putting pressure on Kalam for the job. There were a few recommendations from the PM's office too. In spite of our workloads, me and Kalam would sit together in his DRDO office room and discuss these matters. He asked for my opinion regarding everything. Even though I remember them all, I don't want to write them here.

The police made restrictions on Kalam's visitors. It was an important protocol. Therefore, many great men who were restricted would come to me for guidance. We had arranged a room in the lower floor of DRDO guest house to facilitate Kalam to meet such people.

I was relieved since Kalam's position has now become definitive. I was relieved of my mental pressure and the need for being in superalert mode . The DRDO staff took care of handling his visitors well.

Now, I started to think about my future. There were no improvements in the Tata job that we discussed earlier with J. J. Irani.

Many felt that my name would be recommended for the post of the secretary to the Indian President or as his adviser. However, my mind was blank. But, I definitely wanted to quit my TIFAC (full time work without payment) and the PSA office jobs. What next? My retirement money will not be sufficient to run my family. Just then, my son Vikram had finished his MBBS course and had joined the '*Indian Institute of Management*' in Lucknow for MBA course. I was 58 years old (59 as per government gazette); Kalam did not ask me anything about my future. He was perhaps trying to cope up with his new role.

These thoughts took the shape of a poem in Tamil. I wrote its English translation on the same day.

What do I need?

(*In Agony and Harmony*)

எனக்கு எது வேண்டும்? 20-7-2002

(அழியாத உயிர்கள் தொகுப்பில்)

❑

Kalam in Rashtrapati Bhavan

It became apparent that in another five days Kalam would become the *Indian President*. My life will be going in another direction. Where? What? How? I did not have an answer to these.

I did not think much as to who will be taken by Kalam for some special positions in the *Rashtrapati Bhavan* after he becomes the President. There are offices within the *Rashtrapati Bhavan* to take care of these. Besides, people in the Delhi administrative circle knew exactly whom to approach for such jobs. Also, I was upset over the petty politics being played already by a few people. Many tried to create a rift between me and Kalam!

Kalam talked to me especially about both our family members.

"Sir! I want your father and my brother to be seated together. We have to take a lot of new pictures which haven't been taken before (at the Bharat Ratna award day)... Many people will be coming from Rameswaram. My brother can handle all of them. He likes you very much. Please take good care of them."

"The head priests from the Rameswaram temple, church and the mosque will be there. Other than the formal protocols, I would like to allot time also for conducting prayers.. I also want to allot time to see my family members and other people from Rameswaram. There are huge auditoriums here."

"The *Rashtrapati Bhavan* staff and the security team of the President would be acting as per their protocols. However, it is your duty to take care of my wishes."

"You have to handle the security staff."

Other than this important task, we also had to prepare his Presidential speech. A few trustworthy people in the DRDO helped us with this. Sheridon was preparing one draft after another. He also took care of food, security and reception of Kalam's family members. Kalam's earlier private secretary R. K. Prasad also helped. Sheridon and R. K. Prasad became Kalam's chief private secretaries.

Kalam's brother took care of his family members and other people from Rameswaram. He wanted to ensure that Kalam's reputation was not spoiled due to any untoward incident.

Two days prior to July 25, 2002, Kalam's brother called me. "I know that you will be having a lot of work to do. But I need to speak with you for some 10-15 minutes privately," he said. We went to a separate room.

"Kalam has invited priests from the temple, church and the mosque. Everyone has arrived. However, no one has confirmed what they have to do here. Neither Kalam nor the staff from the President's office have suggested anything yet. It won't look nice if they do not perform a small ceremony. But if we inform them at the last minute, then it would lead to utter confusion..."

"You tell me...should we start from our muslim prayer..later, the other two groups can recite their prayers..."

I said: "Yes, you may. Kalam being a muslim, it would be apt to start from your prayer."

He said: "Yes, we could do that. But this is not our family function. Kalam is now going to become the leader of the nation...."

We were discussing various possibilities. Finally, Kalam's brother came up with a solution. He must have thought of this for quite a while.

He said: "Ok, listen to me. No one knows the time allotted for the prayer ceremony. I think it would take 10-15 minutes to recite our Al Fatiha prayer. I don't think the Hindus and Christians have a time restriction. So, around five minutes should be enough for those two..."

He continued.

"First, let the Rameswaram temple priest chant his prayers. Let him recite in accordance with the allotted time. Then, let the Church priest recite.. Finally, we will conduct our Islamic prayer; Al Fatiha should be enough!," he said.

After a few minutes of silence, he said: "If anyone asks about this, we will say that this was in accordance with this country's historicity (statistically). At first, the Hindus were there; then there were Christians; and finally Muslims.."

He convinced me. I was glad to see his intelligence and kindness. Moreover, he also satisfied his brother's desire to recite prayers from all three major Indian religions. He ensured that there was no further confusion over this.

"Very good," I said.

"In case anyone asks you, let them know that this is going to be the procedure. I too will say the same thing," he said decisively.

He was correct. The Presidential staff had not allotted any separate timings. Instead in the time sheet, they had just mentioned 'Family'. Kalam wanted to devote special importance to the prayer recitation by the three religious priests.

It was because of this that Kalam wanted my father (who applied 'Gopi Chandan' on his forehead) with his brother (with his black cap) to be seated in the first row.

I did not want to disturb Kalam about all this and so decided to take care of it the next day after office work.

Kalam wanted quotes from '*Thirukkural*' to be an important part of his Presidential address. He also wanted to discuss Vision 2020 and empowering India. Additionally, we added one quote from Kabir. (Since Kalam did not know Hindi, we chose a simple quote).

The swearing in ceremony went well. The new *Anna University Vice Chancellor* and a few of his friends were there. Since Kalam was fond of school children, students from the elite schools in Delhi were invited! This is the culture of the Delhi administrative circle. I don't think that many would have noticed this besides me. (Only big shots were present there!) Later, I was happy to conduct a programme on behalf of CII with school children from all backgrounds.(On November 14, 2002 for Children's Day).

After the swearing in ceremony, Kalam gave his Presidential address. Thirukkural echoed on all sides. There was intermission after the office programmes. From 3 PM onwards, time was allotted to the private function of the President. I hurried to the office of the PSA during intermission. I was carrying a huge burden on my shoulders. This was because political events were very tricky. For qualified politicians, it would be an easy cake-walk.

Confronting jealous people, careful understanding of the law, handling the media carefully...these were prerequisites which neither me nor Kalam possessed. None of us (including Kalam) imagined that such a major turning point would happen in Kalam's life.

Once Kalam becomes the *President*, there would be no need to worry further. It was beyond the reach of scheming politicians. Even the role of a *Vice President* is a tough one. Conducting the *Rajya Sabha* proceedings could become complicated. At times, the assembly could become a war front.

The files which arrive at the President's desk are strictly confidential. So, we do not discuss those.

Now that Kalam got settled down, I began to think for myself. What should I do after quitting TIFAC and the PSA office? I was pretty sure that I did not have a role in the Rashtrapati Bhavan. Sometime around the middle of June, right before Kalam's Swearing in Ceremony, I was upset over the conspiracy created by a few people. In order to create a rift between me and Kalam, many people stopped me from meeting him. It was only because of Sheridon that I was able to contact Kalam for a few important matters.

The fight for power within the *Rashtrapati Bhavan* won't stop. I sensed that many wanted to separate me and Kalam. Chanakya's rule on '*Human Nature*' was true even in the 21st century!

I went and saw Dr. R. Chidambaram at the PSA office after Kalam's swearing in ceremony. Luckily, he had not gone outside.

I told him: "Sir! I wanted to discuss this matter with you for some time now. I want to quit my post in TIFAC and the PSA office. I am thinking of quitting sometime in September this year."

He asked: "Do you have other plans? Oh yes! You might want to join Kalam, am I right?"

He immediately added: "I should not have asked about you joining with Kalam."

I replied: "Sir! I do not have an alternate plan. In case I was going to join Kalam, why would I hesitate to talk about that to you? I want to get away from everything. I want to start a fresh life. I am informing you so that you can find my replacement soon."

Picking up a piece of letter that was on his desk, Dr. R. Chidambaram told me: "Rajan! You can continue to work here. The retirement age for scientists can be extended to 64 years!"

As per my official gazette, my age was 59 at the time. I replied: "Sir, I know that; it is meant for only excellent scientists!"

That was a small 'dig' by me about the differentiation made between science and technology! The government rule was meant for science researchers. However, it was being used for science administrators. Initially, it was extended from 60 to 62 years. Now, in 2001-2002, it has been extended further to help an important S&T big shot (so that the person could get an apex role in S&T administration)!

I then informed him of the 3 PM programme in *Rashtrapati Bhavan* and left.

In that 3 o'clock programme (25-7-2002), Kalam met the VIPs. This was arranged by the *Rashtrapati Bhavan* staff. He then shook hands with people from Rameswaram, Ramanathapuram, and other places. Kalam came back and forth.

The prayer recitation by the three religious priests was getting delayed due to time constraints. Kalam's brother and my father took care of it. Amongst the Hindus, there were Shaivites and Vaishnavites. My father had to convince them to recite their prayers within 2-3 minutes. Kalam's brother took care of members of the Rameswaram Jamad mosque. I requested the priest from St. Joseph's college to finish their prayer too within 2-3 minutes.

Finally, Kalam arrived. Rameswaram people flocked around him. We had to control the crowd for some time.

The prayer recitation by the three religious priests got over smoothly. I do not know whether there are pictures of it in the *Rashtrapati Bhavan*. I did not visit the place after that. However, in case anyone is preparing a documentary, then these pictures would be totally worth it. A picture can be seen in this book. As a youngster in Rameswaram and an adult in the St. Joseph's College in Trichy... these are a testimony to Kalam's unifying spirit. Kalam saw himself to be a symbol of this unity.

Kalam had a very strong belief in God. He always ended his talks with "God Bless You!"

It was becoming impossible to control the crowd. They were not allowing us to take a family picture. Time was running out. I had to bring an order to the situation. Chairs were arranged for seating Kalam's family members. However, people from the crowd were trying to get in. I asked the staff to make a public announcement: "Only family members must be seated in the chairs arranged for them. For the current group photo, we require only them. All others, please stay away! Everyone will get a chance to take a picture with the President! Please..."

Even after announcing this several times, it was becoming difficult to manage the crowd. Kalam was smiling pleasantly and chatting as if nothing happened. If we cross the time limit allotted by the *Rashtrapati Bhavan* staff, then they will take Kalam with them! Kalam's family members would then become upset. Even though Kalam had promised his family members, he hardly said a word! Kalam never spoke harshly with anyone. This was his nature.

I asked Kalam's brother's daughter Nazema to help me. "Nazema, you point your fingers at who should be in and who should be out of the family group photo. I will take care of the rest," I said to her.

Quickly, I made them sit for the photo. Next to Kalam sat his brother. Then, an empty chair for Nazema was kept. Suddenly, an old man shouted that he was the eldest member and sat on the empty chair next to Kalam's brother (it was just an ordinary chair!). Now, Nazema did not have a place to sit. Hurriedly, we brought an empty chair for her and placed it at the far end of the first row. Everyone, including Kalam's brother, wanted me to sit for the picture.

"No! I can't do that! Even though we are close, I am not a family member. The rule for Rameswaram people that was announced earlier applies to me too!" I said and signalled the photographer to take the picture. That picture can be seen in this book.

The family people would have blessed me. It was a special feeling to be a part of the President's family after all! Even if I wasn't there in the picture, I would have gained a permanent place in their heart. Same with Rameswaram people, I think. Even today, when I visit Rameswaram they treat me with great respect. Then, we took small group photos.

They then took the President to his room. Everyone went to their respective rooms.

I came to my house in Moti Bagh. Kalam had come there while working as the *Principal Scientific Adviser* (2000). Our grandson Aditya built an aircraft with lego pieces (these lego pieces were not meant for aircraft. These were meant for 2-3 year old children). Aditya built one using his creative imagination. Kalam asked us to take a picture of the model and save it. "He is going to become a space scientist one day!" Kalam appreciated him. That was the day when Kalam tasted my wife's '*Poli*' for the first time. Kalam said: "Koma amma. Your poli is just like the one made by my mother; thin and soft. The poli in our town is thick. What did you do?" He asked for the recipe. He relished it with freshly melted ghee.

"Koma amma, today you have reminded me of my mother!" Kalam kept repeating these words. I mentioned this incident to a press reporter once. Later, after Kalam became the Indian President many people offered him '*poli*'.

He had a deep attachment towards my family. Soon after I returned home from the President's office on July 25, 2002, I received a phone call from Kalam. After speaking with me for some time, he said, "Give the phone to Koma amma, please!" This was his usual practice.

Kalam wanted to speak with us on the night of his swearing in ceremony. (He knew that we both slept early). He also enquired about Vikram who was in Lucknow at the time. We both felt very happy towards his affection for all of us. We informed our children (Vijay and Anu in America, and Vikram) about this. They too felt happy.

These incidents I recalled from my memory which may sometimes cheat me. However I have mentioned them in my letter to Kalam on 26.07.2002. I have a copy of that letter. It conveys it in greater detail.

I wrote a poem on the President's swearing in ceremony on 25-07-2002 after it got over on the same day. I sent a copy not only to Kalam, but also to Radha Krishnamoorthi (NCBH) and C. Mahendran (*Thamarai*).

Ceremony of the People's President

Within a fraction of a second
  We witnessed with our own eyes
The exit of the old
  And the entry of the new;
They conducted the show
  Like acrobats;
My dear old friend
  Is now the Indian President!

———————

"அழியாத உயிர்களில்"
(In Indestructible Lives)
(25.7.2002)

On 26.07.2002, I sent a long letter to Kalam containing four pages.

"To my dear respected Kalam sir,

Salutations!

Yesterday was a very happy day in my life. Everything went well...

....

I started writing a poem in which a President was blessed by three religious communities under the title, 'மனங்களின் ஒற்றுமை' *('Unity of Minds')*. If I finish it now, it could be published as a book. (It is still incomplete!)

My letter continues... "I pray to God Almighty to bestow upon you many more successes. I shall pray that you work tirelessly as always and for him to strengthen your words, actions, health, peace of mind...fame. In the days to come after July 24, 2007, the vehicle of God will be decorated with even more beautiful wings. We will know about that later."

....

We were happy to hear the voice of the Indian President over the phone on 25.07.2002.

He had asked me to write an epic on astronomy several times (from 1999). He has seen my writings occasionally. I have described what I wrote on 25.07.2002 in that letter.

Some important episodes: "We were engrossed in our work in TIFAC, PSA office, and other activities close to our hearts before 25.07.2002. I couldn't visit you in Asiad due to several painful incidents I encountered there. It was also becoming difficult to get in touch with you. Only after that, I realised how painful a man's life could become! With the mercy of God, I found solutions with the assistance of Sheridon. I prayed to God sincerely that nothing should come in the way of our friendship. (Asiad was the place in which Kalam's DRDO guest house was located)."

In the letter, I had also mentioned my conversation with Dr. R. Chidambaram about leaving my job in TIFAC and the office of the PSA. I also had mentioned that I would be quitting my job at the end of September 2002.

Kalam called me over the phone and said: "Rajan! Please do not leave your current job until you get another job elsewhere." He was worried!

Goma and I left for Baroda to attend the wedding ceremony of my wife's niece Shilpa.

❑

A Few Notes About our Gujarat Trip

Even though I spoke with Kalam everyday over the phone, I never visited him in the *Rashtrapati Bhavan*. I did not have the time to go there. Besides, I did not want the senior officials over there to unnecessarily misinterpret me. I knew how the race for power works in the Delhi circles. I have seen it for nearly fourteen years. Every single officer wanted to keep one of the ministers under his control. They engaged in spreading many fake rumours to their leaders!

Under these circumstances, in the first week of August the *President* Dr. Kalam called me to his office. "Please come to my room," he said. I rushed immediately. I had permission to enter through a special entrance (at the north gate). I did not have to sign in the daily attendance register.

Kalam spoke to me privately: "I am planning to travel to Ahmedabad on August 12, 2002 to visit Dr. Sarabhai's family members. In my office, they are asking me to also pay a visit to Gujarat where riots happened recently. What is your opinion? Please do not discuss this matter with anyone else."

"Sir, Dr. Sarabhai is a great person for all of us. However, not many people in the country might know about him. You should definitely visit Sarabhai's family. But that alone is not enough."

"I think you will remember. Even though we prepared a very good speech for your Presidential address, we made one major mistake; we had not included the name of Mahatma Gandhi in your speech. There was a criticism of it in a few newspapers too; luckily, they left it at that. No one knows of our deep respect for Mahatma Gandhi. Many people talk of him in big stages and misuse his name at times! Even in our *India 2020* book, for the '*Developed India*' concept, we have described Mahatma Gandhi's '*talisman*'. Somehow, we forgot to mention him in your Presidential address. We need to correct it in a big way so that the entire nation can see."

"Therefore, instead of being in Gujarat on August 12, 2002 alone, you must stay longer. You have to spend some quality time in the Sabarmati Ashram and pay respects to the Mahatma. Then, you can spend some time with the Sarabhai family members. Next, after visiting the places where the riots happened, you must visit the Bhuj-Kutch regions the next day. You must visit the colonies which we built while working for TIFAC."

"It would be good if you plan your itinerary like this. Your first visit after becoming the Indian President should be to pay respects to Mahatma Gandhi. Next, your professional guru Dr. Sarabhai, and finally to the quake-affected regions in Gujarat. Since you weren't able to answer many questions on Gujarat riots which were asked before you became the President, it will be better if you can go and speak with the affected people personally."

Kalam said: "Sounds like a good plan to me. They have given a list of areas where riots happened in Gujarat. It was given to them by the NGOs there. The state government is afraid that there could be security issues in a few of those areas."

Back then, many tried to create tension and turmoil to disrupt the rule of Vajpayee's NDA coalition. I knew that most of them would try to use Kalam (the President) as their instrument to accomplish this. Moreover, it was uncertain whether all *Rashtrapati Bhavan* staff (including those selected by Kalam personally) would be faithful to him or the country. The power politics in Delhi has always been a mystery as described by Chanakya.

Kalam should not get caught up in all this. It would look bad if it created confusion to the Chief Minister's (Narendra Modi) leadership. It will reflect on PM Vajpayee's leadership very badly. Only the Central and State governments decided the travel itinerary for the President. This was because it was very important to offer complete protection to him. If any unforeseen unpleasant incident happens in this Kalam's first trip after he became the Indian President, it could become very ugly. It would be a bad indication of Kalam's leadership skills. Actually, Kalam could have completely avoided the Gujarat trip. However, he wanted to meet Sarabhai's family. Besides, even before consulting me, they had started making arrangements.

On the other hand, this was also a significant trip. He could start by paying respects to Mahatma Gandhi first. Then, he can inspect the riot-stricken area of Gujarat. If everything goes well, it will be a great start to Kalam's Presidential career. Therefore, all other problems must be minimised.

I told Kalam: "Sir, whatever be the case, the State Government alone is fully responsible for your protection. Your office staff may not know of the ground realities there." All NGOs would have prioritised the areas where they have done work.

"You ask them to hand over the list to the ruling state government. The state government staff would have prepared their own list. Ask them to finalise by looking into both of them. Inform them that at least a few areas mentioned by the NGOs must form a part of your itinerary. Your aim is not to create any unnecessary tension or confusion for the ruling state government.."

Kalam told me: "Okay. I will do as suggested by you. But, you should definitely accompany me. Isn't Gujarat Koma amma's place afterall?"

"Alright sir," I said.

He was talking about my wife Gomati. She was brought up in Gujarat. Her first language is Gujarati while studying in the local school over there.

Kalam accompanied us in 2001 when we went to Gujarat to implement our TIFAC activities for the quake-affected region. Everyone over there called me '*Jamai*' (Gujarati son-in-law). I know how to read Gujarati; I can understand Gujarati well; I spoke a bit of the language too.

As told by him, they also added my name to the list. This was Kalam's first trip as the *Indian President*! As per the list prepared by the Presidential staff, I was one of the President's friends; Dr. Sivathanu Pillai was the other.

There was a big reception at the Ahmedabad airport. Kalam and the then Gujarat CM Shri Narendra Modi were supposed to travel in the same car as per the government rules. The proceedings like serving tea, some pleasantries , giving flower bouquets, introducing guests and so on were happening at a slow pace. But Kalam was in a hurry. He had only crossed his 70 at the time.

Before going to the *Sabarmati Ashram*, Kalam spoke to me hurriedly in Tamil; "Please get into our car."

In the back seat of the Ambassador car only two people could be seated viz. The President and the Chief Minister with a hand rest divider I therefore sat with the security officer at the front seat. I was squeezed into the seat and managed somehow. Kalam spoke with me in Tamil. He was asking a few questions. I was feeling uncomfortable. Not only was I travelling along with the *President* and the CM, but also I was speaking in Tamil which was a language unknown to the others besides me and Kalam!

Kalam visited the *Gandhi Ashram*. Many Gujarati leaders, big shots, and officers had come there to meet the *Indian President*. Their photographers were waiting to take their photos with the President. This photography business had a huge market!

Many of them could not cope up with Kalam's speed. I could hear some of them muttering in Gujarati: "*Rashtrapati Dhowde Che!* (Rashtrapati is running!)" I informed this to Kalam later and we both had a hearty laugh.

Later, while going back in the car, Kalam asked me to be seated between him and the CM. They both spoke to each other. Kalam asked me a few questions in between.

There is so much to write about this. However, in order to hasten my narrative let me skip a few of them.

When Kalam visited the regions of riot, the chief minister spoke to him kindly and said: "You please go and talk to them personally. If I am also present with you, they might hesitate to speak out their mind. You have a good discussion with them. I will come and join all of you later." This shows Modi's magnanimity.

Everywhere we went (the state government and the NGOs had given their details earlier to Kalam), Kalam spoke kindly and patiently to the people. All of them were muslims. They all spoke in Gujarati. I therefore served as their translator to Kalam.

Kalam would convey his message in Tamil to me. I translated it to Gujarati. They replied in Gujarati and I translated it back into Tamil for Kalam. In spite of time constraints, Kalam spoke to all of them. In some places, small group meetings were arranged with the Q&A sessions. They found some peace of mind since the *Indian President* himself came to visit them after all their turmoil. Some of them conveyed their problems directly to me. They told me what they wanted. "I will inform the President," I replied.

Then we continued our journey to Bhuj and Kutch from there. The TIFAC colonies had become a famous landmark there. As I had mentioned earlier, since the TIFAC colonies were built very robustly, the people living there refused to go elsewhere. Kalam became one with the people in spite of the security issues. I went with him to translate the messages of those who did not speak English.

Our Gujarat trip was immensely successful. The *Chief Minister* too must have felt the same way. I could make it from his face. Initially, there were several rumours that this trip could lead to public criticism or bad reputation or unrest among the general public. However, Kalam handled it all with his own trademark approach and brought a lot of positive outlook. Wherever he went, he spread his positive aura that lasted long.

While returning back from the trip, Kalam told me:

"Rajan, please prepare a detailed write up of our Gujarat trip. Please write them as individual statements giving a short summary of each and every single one of them. You must specifically include the statements made by the people suffering from the riots."

Accordingly, I prepared a handwritten summary containing four pages (16/8/2002).

I did not ask him what he did with it later. The news of me travelling with Kalam spread all over India through newspapers and TV channels. Pictures of me and Kalam close together were published. I only saw a few. (I later heard after a few years that all these caused jealousy in the minds of the Secretary to *Rashtrapati* and other high officials). They did not know at the time that I had decided to quit. They were worried that if I was in Delhi, I might weaken their influence on the Indian President.

I spoke with J. J. Irani on August 8, 2002 as per Kalam's advice. After listening to everything patiently, he said: "The Tatas did not treat you well in the way I expected. If I were you, I would be looking elsewhere for a job." I wrote a brief letter about this to Kalam. So, I wrote to Kalam that we could start a big national water project on 16-8-2002 as per his suggestion. He might have wanted to do this as a big movement in order to encourage me.

I wrote to him that I should get a decent job by October 2, 2002.

Then there were the Independence day celebrations. The President must arrange for a party in his house. I have attended all these parties organised in the President's house (At Home reception) starting from 1988 onwards (as I was an additional secretary level officer in Govt.). Those who participate in such events would get to meet higher officials, industrialists, and senior administrators. While working for the DST and TIFAC, I had to take care of promoting DST/TIFAC and I used these opportunities.

However, this one was very special. Kalam looked glorious on that day. A small interesting incident happened to me. I will talk about that later.

But before that, I need to disclose a letter sent by Nazema on behalf of Kalam's family members. It soothened my racing heart that was going through a rough patch as I was uncertain of my future prospects. It served as a prayer for my well being on behalf of Kalam's family members.

20.8.02

To our beloved Rajan sir,

We got the group photos which were sent by you. We were thrilled to look at all of them that were taken in the President's House. We also got the album which was sent to us as per your advice. We keep turning those pages over and over again.

I got the details about the 'Gandhi Institute of Computer Education & Information Technology' book.

Rajan sir, in spite of your excessive workload, we are grateful to you for remembering us and sending all these.

We saw on all TV channels how well you protected my father's younger brother (your friend Kalam) during your Gujarat trip. Saleem recalled how you waited for Kalam in the doorsteps of his college while you were here.

We are glad to see the real affection you have for your friend. We pray to God Almighty that this relationship should continue forever and reap enormous benefits for all people. Ameen!

Please convey our regards to your father; my father and others wish to convey their enquiries to you.

Rest in next.

With friendly affection,

Nazema Maraikayar,
House of Kalam,
Rameswaram

❑

New President, New Changes

August 15, 2002. On that day, I had a whole new experience. Many people voluntarily came up to me to introduce themselves. This was something I had never witnessed all these years. This is an open invitation for me to become a part of mighty administrative circles. Most people would wait for such an opportunity.

Friends greeted me. "Why are you greeting me, greet the President instead," I said.

I met my beloved friend M. D. Nalapat and his wife Lakshmi there. M. D. Nalapat belonged to the Kerala Royal family. He is a great journalist, an expert in geopolitics, an instructor and an excellent scholar. He became very close to me after the release of our *India 2020* book. I have interacted once or twice with his wife Lakshmi during these gatherings. She is a poet.

When I had met her earlier once, she jokingly told me: "You are a scientist. I am a poet. The name of my poem is '*Madness*'." She teased me thinking that scientists weren't great lovers of poems. I immediately told her an English poem:

A Poem to Poetess Lakshmi

(In the book Jumping Genes, NCBH)

"Poet sees beauty in madness;
Scientist searches for method in madness;
Manager tries to use the madness;
Journalist creates instant madness!"

Aug 01, 2001

The last line was meant to tease Lakshmi's husband M. D. Nalapat.

That incident happened a year ago. At that time, Kalam was the *Principal Scientific Adviser*

They came to Kalam's Independence day celebration party in the President's house.

M. D. Nalapat interacted with me for a while. He wanted to know my opinion on a few topics, if I supported or opposed them. To the journalists, this was the feast! While leaving, Lakshmi held my hands and said:

"Rajan, very rarely do we get to see a great man in this *Rashtrapati Bhavan*. Now, he has arrived. Starting from today, for another five years, it is your duty to ensure that he stays this way!"

"Why are you saying this to me, Lakshmi! I do not work here. I come here whenever he wishes to see me. That's all! Why are you holding me responsible?"

Lakshmi replied: "I have thought of this thoroughly. That will be your only responsibility from now onwards. I think you are the right person for the job! See you later!" She cannot inform Kalam of all this. But why me? However, I couldn't see her before 2007 after that.

However, after nearly one and a half years, our close family friend and poet Sirpi Balasubramaniam handed over a poem to me after Kalam's event in Coimbatore. (It is a great fortune to have Sirpi sir as our family friend). He asked me to hand over the poem to Kalam. I did. I made a copy of the poem so that it doesn't get lost. Poet Sirpi describes Kalam in a manner similar to that of poetess lakshmi. A certificate of merit indeed!

Leader

Obeying his Order
The three seas could become turbulent
The skies could become cataclysmic
The earth could cause quakes

For he is the commander
Of the three armed forces
But he is seated
On a peace pedestal
Holding a Sceptre of peace
He lives in the hearts of people
Surrounded by sweet children

He is our leader
Our unplated pure gold
Kalam.

26.01.04

Handed this to Y. S. Rajan in Coimbatore (In S. V. Balasubramaniam's House)

After the Independence day celebrations on 15-8-2002, I heard some good news. In continuation with our *Vision 2020* initiatives, I prepared separate project proposals in accordance to the needs of various Indian states for TIFAC. I met the respective state government officials for the purpose. I did it for states like Uttar Pradesh, Uttarakhand (Uttaranchal), and Goa. Likewise, Kalam met the then CM of Tamil Nadu, Kalaignar Karunanidhi earlier while working for TIFAC to explain our initiatives in detail. I proposed an initiative to the newly elected Punjab CM, Amarinder Singh.

Joint secretary, DST, Amitabh Pandey was also the IAS Officer of Punjab cadre. I became friends with him at DST. He spoke with me a few days after Kalam became the Indian President. He asked me about my future plans. I told him that I was going to quit my job in TIFAC and the PSA office. I also told him that I will not be working in the Rashtrapati Bhavan.

He immediately suggested: "The Punjab Chief Minister is a good friend of mine. He will agree to accept you as one of our ministers."

I responded: "I do not want a ministerial job. If there are any other suitable openings, kindly let me know."

He said: "Ok!"

Within a few days, he called me and said: "He has decided to appoint you as the Punjab CM's Scientific Adviser as well as the *Vice Chancellor* of the *Punjab Technical University* (PTU). The PTU is struggling with no proper leadership. We need someone like you urgently. How soon can you join us?"

"As soon as I get my appointment letter. I have already informed Dr. Chidambaram about my resignation."

I heard that it was under process.

I informed Kalam. Kalam insisted that I should quit only after I got the appointment letter in my hand. I agreed. A heavy burden has been lifted from my heart.

I continued working as usual in TIFAC and the PSA office till I left. I got used to it.

Kalam brought several new formalities to the Rashtrapati Bhavan. There were several rooms inside the Rashtrapati Bhavan. Earlier, the family members of various Presidents would become permanent guests there. However, Kalam stayed there all alone. Kalam's wake up time, his sleep time and his food time were also unique! He was a strict vegetarian and preferred the Tamil Nadu cuisine!

Kalam was very particular about his speech preparation. He needed review teams and powerpoint presentations just like the way he had them in ISRO, DRDO and other S&T offices. During that time in 2002, email facilities were also slowly picking up. These were arranged in his office and home (President's house). These were quickly setup by G.Sivakumar (who came from Anna University). The *Rashtrapati Bhavan* staff couldn't keep up with his pace! He was brilliant! Therefore, Kalam announced in his public gatherings: "Please send an email; I will reply within 24 hours!"

Traditionally, Indian Presidents looked into files, met a few visitors in their office, shook hands with famous international leaders in formal meetings, hosted dinner parties for them, and travelled occasionally to foreign countries. However, Kalam was not like that. Wherever he worked—be it ISRO, DRDO, PSA office, or Anna University (for a few months)—he had to travel in flights at least twice per week. His work centres were all over India. He went from one place to another. He travelled non-stop. He never retired after a small meeting to take a rest. Working tirelessly was his mantra! Sometimes his office meetings went on till 10.30 PM. Lunch, tea, dinner... all would be served in between the meetings. Meetings happened even after dinner at times.

Delhi offices operated in an entirely different style! Everything happened slowly. Only in the PSA office, a few employees worked at night. The staff in the President's House worked even more lethargically!

Kalam cannot be like that. He decided to visit all the Indian states within a year. I have not done a detailed research of the Indian and international travel itineraries of Indian Presidents. I have not even read an essay on that.

He wanted me to travel with him everywhere. Since I had to do my job, I couldn't accompany him to all places. However, Kalam insisted on my presence while going to a few places. "Please make a note of these dates in your diary!" he would say.

Several books would be required to describe each and every single place we visited together and the events that happened there. But I have written a poem either in English or in Tamil about these experiences. In மறக்காத தேடல்கள்*('Unforgettable Quests')* (NCBH) till mid-2004; in *'Jumping Genes'*(English) (NCBH) till mid-2005; in *'Ode to the Earthworm'* (NCBH) during various other years, and குதிக்கும் குழந்தைகள்*('Jumping Children')* (NCBH-*Thamarai*), all my compositions will be there. There are many poems about him. A few others, I wrote to him while we weren't travelling.

A few others that I wrote later haven't gone to print. I reduced my frequency of writing poems.

I wrote a lot of poems and other books during 2002, 2003, 2004 and 2005. I am not going to discuss them in detail here since this book is about Kalam. I will only mention those that are related to him.

After his Gujarat trip, Kalam visited North-East India. Usually, many Indians are not concerned about the north eastern states. They think that those people are 'uncivilised'. Kalam's visit to the north east was of political significance.

Kalam went to Manipur on 5th and 6th of October, 2002. There too he spoke about empowering India and projects related to those regions. The President's speeches are carefully documented in the Rashtrapati Bhavan Museum. Those who are interested to know more on the topic, can make use of it.

In my poem on Manipur in the 'மறக்காத தேடல்கள்' (*'Unforgettable Quests'*) book, the following lines appear...

In a developed India
    Where Manipur gleams
Work hard tirelessly
    Restlessly fearlessly
So says our
    Honourable President.

Terrorism of Separatist rebel groups in Manipur were at their peak. They had announced a 'Bandh' ('Strike') on the day of the President's arrival. There was heavy security. Men and women police officers guarded both sides of the road very carefully. Kalam's main aim was to strengthen the minds of the local people there.

When I returned, I got my appointment letters (from the Punjab state government) for the Vice Chancellor of PTU and the head of its *Board of Governors* (BOG). They were written on October 3, 2002.

I informed Kalam the next day. I told him that after retiring, I will reach Jalandhar on October 17, 2002 to take charge as VC, PTU and Chairman BOG of PTU. Kalam said: "Hearty Congratulations and best wishes!"

Within a day or two, Sheridon informed me that Kalam wanted to travel to Arunachal Pradesh's Tawang and wanted to know whether I wished to travel along with them. Kalam's birthday was on October 15, 2002. He wanted to get away from Delhi on that day. Otherwise, everyone will be showering him with floral bouquets from morning to evening on that day. Kalam did not like all that. There are many beautiful Buddhist monasteries in Tawang. There are not mere heritage sites. The Buddhist monks are preserving the place to this day.

Kalam could be all alone, enjoying the beautiful scenery and the sanctity of the place without any disturbance. Nowhere else in India could he get peace of mind. Be it in Chennai, Rameswaram, Thiruvananthapuram, or Hyderabad, he would be surrounded by people in power. Some might even fly from Delhi.

It was very difficult to travel to Tawang in October during the winter season. His travel is also geopolitically significant since the Chinese disputed that many parts of Arunachal Pradesh belonged to them. (The situation is similar even today!) If the *Indian President* Kalam visits Arunachal Pradesh, it would be a clear signal to the world that Arunachal Pradesh was a part of India. Kalam wanted to celebrate his first birthday (after becoming the President) over there.

I couldn't go. But I was extremely pleased for Kalam. I was a bit upset that I won't be able to wish him on his birthday, since the cellphone connections were not that great back then. There could be a separate one for the President for emergency purposes. It won't be nice to call on that. I thought of something. Occasionally, I sent him birthday poems like '*Kalam's sixty*'. Now, he will be completing 71 years.

I recalled one of his wishes that he had made earlier. After looking at all my poem compilations, Kalam once told me: "Rajan, one day you have to write an epic. You have written poems on several incidents in my life and also about a few of my relatives. I am a '*Seafarer*' and a '*Spaceman*'. Using your imagination, create an epic with sea on one side and desert on the other."

I started writing something intensely on 26-08-99. It stopped on the eighth page. He looked at it and said: "What is this sir! You have brought lady, love and all that inside my epic!"

"Sir, how can there be an epic or a poem without women and love? Aren't these natural to it?" I replied.

Likewise, if I mentioned ladies' breasts in any of my poems, he teased, "What is this , sir? All poets are naughty. All they see are just ladies' breasts!"

"Sir! You take a look at Manikkavasagar compositions. Have you forgotten the segment on love ('இன்பத்துப்பால்') in *Thirukkural*?" I replied.

Kalam was trying to accomplish several great tasks in 1999. I was also busy with my TIFAC/CII activities. After going to the PSA office, there were other new tasks in 2000. Therefore, there was no time to write an epic. Besides, I was not a great poet! But since Kalam reminded me occasionally, I continued to write my epic from the ninth page on 31.12.2001. When Kalam went to his Chennai job, I wrote a few more pages. Later, on 9.2.2002, I wrote some more. Many 'S&T' matters entered the plot. Then I stopped for a while. Later I continued from where I left on 19.5.2002. Some fifty pages were completed in this manner. My space epic came to an abrupt halt. I had to work hard for him to become the President. There was no time to write further. There were a few short poems. Not all of them were on Kalam.

Even in my 26.7.2002 letter to him when he became the Indian President, I wrote that I would continue my space epic and finish it quickly.

It stopped abruptly.

While thinking of his Tawang journey, one thing crossed my mind. I will never be able to complete my space epic. That too, to complete it within four days was impossible. I therefore decided to write on important episodes of Kalam's life by October 10, 2002... I decided to include his Tawang trip as well, and then greet him for his special birthday. That alone is possible within the next three days. Due to my immense affection towards Kalam and with Goddess Saraswathi's blessings, I composed a Tamil poem describing important events in Kalam's life that took the shape of children's poetry. (பிள்ளைத் தமிழ் கவிதை). R.Bhagavathi in the PM's PSA office typed it in Tamil. Out of her affection towards Kalam, she compiled it as a beautiful book. The name of the booklet was '*Poems*'.

"Mind's garden"("உள்ளப் பூங்கா") was its title. I sent it to Sheridon and requested: "Sheridon, please preserve this carefully and hand this to Kalam first thing in the morning of 15.10.2002 whenever he calls you!"

He did accordingly. He informed me that he handed it over to Kalam on the morning of 15.10.2002.

The 56th and 59th paragraphs in the poem is:

56 His seventy first revolution
Makes him a youngster!
Like a ripe fruit he evolves
But never rots!

59 Proclaim that we shall
Win on Vijayadasami Day!
Unite the land, water
And the sky!

(Y. S. Rajan 8, 9, 10 October, 2002)

Later NCBH publishers released a small book containing this poem collection, and the ones I presented to him in Surat on 15-10-2003 adding them as the 60th and the 61st paragraphs. It was published in October 2004 under the title *"Mind's Garden" ("உள்ளப் பூங்கா")*. (Can be seen through my website www.ysrajan.com in the Google link given.)

There is a note beside the poem that I sent to him in October 2002. ("On 15.10.2002, Dr. Abdul Kalam was there in Tawang in Arunachal Pradesh to celebrate his birthday. It was a Vijayadasami day as well. It was his first birthday celebration after he became the Indian President. This poem was sent by me to him on the morning of his birthday. I was in Delhi."). Even though I couldn't finish my space epic as promised to him, I was glad that I could send at least this poem to Kalam.

I couldn't see him after he returned. I could have gone with him otherwise. My Punjab trip started on October 16, 2002. I became the Vice Chancellor of PTU and the Chairman of BOG (Board of Governors) on 17.10.2002. I went and prayed in a Gurudwara in Jalandhar. I paid my respects to the Sikh Gurus.

I started my new job.

❑

The Beginning of Village Services in Uttaranchal

Soon after Kalam returned to Delhi, he congratulated me. "Have you joined? Excellent poem, sir! How were you able to send this within a short span of time?" Kalam asked me. (He was talking about my Punjab job and the poem I had sent to Tawang)

I said: "That is a secret, sir! I am glad that you liked it. You will be coming to Uttaranchal on October 19th. I will be with the 'Mobile Diagnostic Centre' staff. Let us meet then."

October 19, 2002 was a special day for me. On that day, one of TIFAC initiatives in association with the Uttaranchal government was inaugurated by President Dr. Kalam. It was the inauguration of the 'Mobile Diagnostic Centre' which was one of the pioneer projects for our country's health sector. It is important to discuss it here. It was formulated as one of the TIFAC Vision 2020 projects.

All of us say that our villages need good hospitals. We all want to send good doctors to work in villages. Some even insist that working in villages should be mandated for doctors. Politicians talk inspiringly on the dais. Officials say: "We are giving huge sums of money to the Primary Health Centres (PHC) in villages."

Many of them forget the practical realities. Doctors cannot function with just a stethoscope and a BP apparatus. In order to diagnose a patient thoroughly, he needs at least the following instruments:

1. Apparatus to test blood/urine/faeces.
2. Ultrasound facility
3. A good X-ray facility

It would be difficult to diagnose the disease without a minimum of these. But these equipment are very costly. Total cost would amount to nearly 30–40 lakh rupees. In order to function well, they require electricity. Even in big cities, hospitals are unable to make use of these due to lack of good electric supply. The patients suffer. The doctors also feel helpless.

Therefore, besides the above mentioned equipment, a 15KW generator is a must.

It will be difficult to arrange for all of these in each and every village. They might not be required for more than an hour since the population in many small villages is just 1,000–2,000. Also, appointing a doctor and a technician to each of these villages is difficult.

A doctor with a M.D. degree (be it a man or a woman) would have started his/her education at the age of five and would have completed his/her degree at the age of 30. If they are appointed in such small villages, then they won't be able to gain enough experience. They too are human beings; they have to take care of their parents, spouse and children. It is reasonable for them to think that their children receive a good education.

Therefore, after consulting several experts, TIFAC proposed a reasonable initiative. It is not necessary for everyone to see doctors everyday. So, it would be reasonable to arrange a roaming medical facility once every 8 or 10 days. A male doctor, a female doctor, a technician, and a pharmacist could then test and diagnose people in these villages and supply suitable medication. (Free for the poor and others have to pay for the medicines). Emergency patients could be sent with reports to the nearest hospital.

Even if this *Mobile Diagnostic Centre* visits each village once in every ten days, it would have covered several villages. The doctors could stay in a town nearby (to the villages) for these ten days. After that, they could take rest in their homes for the next four days, and then head back to work.

The Uttaranchal state government understood the significance of this project and agreed to work in association with TIFAC.

I was sure that this project would be very useful. We were lucky that the Indian President himself inaugurated the event by waving the flag.

Even today (2018), it is functioning well. The US-AID (*United States Agency for International Development*) understood its significance and provided funds to one or two of them. A few other states also accepted this scheme. The *National Rural Health Mission*(NRHM) accepted this model. The total cost of this project is approximately ₹ 1.5 crores. Private individuals can also fund it. However, our leaders are not concerned when it comes to helping the poor. They announce that they are willing to set up a big hospital foundation such as the AIIMS colleges that would cost at least ₹ 2000 crores. It would be difficult for our villagers to go to big towns for medical checkups. However, institutions like AIIMS can function only in big cities. Otherwise, doctors won't be able to come, and maintenance of instruments will also become difficult.

The cost to develop 1,000 mobile diagnostic centres would be around ₹ 1,500 crores. These could operate in remote villages in and around various states.

The first '*Mobile Diagnostic Centre*' was inaugurated by Kalam. Barnala was the governor. He then came to Tamil Nadu. He became a good friend of mine.

At the time of inauguration, I no longer worked for TIFAC. However, the Uttaranchal elites showered me with their affection.

Carrying fond memories of the event, I returned back to my work in Punjab. I heard shocking, sad news when I returned. The Punjab government arrested the former Vice Chancellor of PTU, the Minister of Technical Education, and another university official on corruption charges and imprisoned them.

Kalam was shocked to hear the news: "Rajan! What is happening there? Did you know about this before?" he asked me.

"No, sir! I did not know about this. Here, they are arresting many people on corruption charges. What can I do? I have started my work sincerely!," I said.

"Please take care and stay safe!" Kalam fondly told me.

On October 26, 2002, I became the scientific advisor to the Punjab CM that was equivalent to a minister of state role. Kalam congratulated me.

❑

Kalam, the Children's Man

I had the opportunity to arrange the meeting of the Indian President Kalam with school children. In the press meet held in November 2001, Kalam had said that he wanted to meet at least 10 lakh children. Even after he worked in *Anna University*, he was only able to meet a few children. This was because he wasn't in any major government job back then. But now that he is the *Indian President*, his wish could be fulfilled. Wherever he travelled, the respective state officials arranged for interaction sessions with the local school children.

The director general of CII Tarun Das was a good friend of Kalam. I had mentioned earlier, how Kalam was introduced to the Indian industrialists through him. He was also my friend. Tarun Das told me: "Rajan, I would like to arrange a big event with school children on behalf of CII on November 14, 2002 (Children's Day). What is your opinion?"

I told him that I liked the idea. I knew that the CII always conducted their programmes very well, in a grand manner. Tarun Das wanted to conduct this event in the Vigyan Bhawan auditorium which was a massive hall meant for conducting big government events.

"I am going to request the President. You too must inform him."

Tarun Das and I met Kalam in September 2002. Kalam agreed.

I then told Tarun Das: "It is customary to bring children from elite schools in Delhi, whose parents are powerful persons. It would be easy for CII to conduct their event with only the elite children. However, this time we must also bring poor children from the government schools. They must also participate in the event!"

Tarun Das said: "Excellent point! I agree with your idea."

The event got confirmed. CII made all preparatory arrangements. My Punjab posting got confirmed and I had to leave in October 2002. Tarun Das told me: "My best wishes to you for your job in Punjab. However, you must stay in touch with Rekha who is in charge of conducting the November 14 event. You have to be here at least two days prior to the event! This is very important!"

Rekha Sethi is a talented coordinator. She organised many big events. But she sent an SOS to me in November 2002: "Rajan, you must come here. All arrangements are in full swing. However, the Sarvodaya school people won't cooperate with me. It is a government school and they won't do anything."

Me: "Rekha! You are an excellent coordinator. Why don't you speak to the headmaster of the school?"

Rekha: "Rajan, I am meeting her everyday and wasting my time unnecessarily. She is the reason for this confusion. Only if you come here, the problem can be resolved. It is a government school; maybe you can help as you are more experienced. The headmaster won't talk to me."

As soon as I reached Delhi, we went to the school. Rekha told me: "A. R. Rahman will create a musical event based on Kalam's English poem 'Empowering India'. A few school students will be acting."

Rekha continued: "The headmaster won't even tell who will be performing from this school. There is only one music teacher here. He is specially challenged (visually impaired). The headmaster is not allowing me to meet him. Every time she says that they have not yet decided. How do we resolve this?"

We spent several minutes trying to convince the headmaster. She finally allowed me to meet the specially challenged music teacher Kedarnath Mukherjee.

I went to see him. I told Rekha: "You take care of other responsibilities. I will handle this one." She felt relieved. The music teacher was sitting in his chair. The children had taken off their shoes and sat down in the room. They had great respect for their teacher. I too tried to remove my shoes before entering. When the children told this to their teacher, he asked me to enter without removing. I insisted that I will also remove mine like the rest of them. The children brought me a chair as per their teacher's instructions.

"I have translated the English poem into Hindi. However, I cannot proceed without the headmaster's permission. I wanted to teach them the Raveendra Sangeeth methodology! However, due to lack of time, since there are just seven days left, it would be difficult to train the children. I therefore am thinking of teaching it to them in a familiar tune."

He then showed me both the methods by singing. To me, everything sounded good.

I told him: “Listen! Everything sounds good to me. You are a genius. I am a layman when it comes to music. So, please decide for yourself...”

He also told me that since Kalam’s poem was too long, it would take up a lot of time if done fully. He said that it would also be difficult to compose musical notes for a few lines.

“Alright! You have the ultimate authority! Please teach the children whatever portions can be sung in whichever raaga possible. You need to train them fast. You decide what works best!” I said.

“Listen! After you decide everything, just tell everyone else that Rajan sir only chose this method. Then they won’t trouble you any further!” I said. He was relieved.

I enquired about him before leaving. He was not born blind. He was beginning to lose his eyesight a few years ago. “Now, I can see some light; within a few years, I will become completely blind!” he said. It must be Glaucoma. He also talked about his life.

I congratulated all the children and went to the headmaster’s room. I immensely appreciated the headmaster for her commitment and dedication, to satisfy her ego. I then informed her that the school children must come in their usual uniforms. Otherwise, the school management would trouble their poor parents to buy costly attire.

I stayed in *Vigyan Bhawan* from October 13th onwards. I informed the CII officials to allow Kedarnath Mukherjee, the headmaster and the Sarvodaya school children to enter the building. *Vigyan Bhawan* premises was a high security area. There will be stringent protocols since the Indian President would be presiding over the event.

I informed Kalam about Kedarnath Mukherjee and the Sarvodaya children. I told him: “Sir! Please speak with the specially challenged music teacher for at least a minute. It won’t be there in the event schedule. However, when he comes down from the stage with his children, you must definitely meet him.”

“Certainly!” Kalam said.

I came several hours early before the start of the event as I had to make several initial arrangements. Children from various schools were there. The *Sarvodaya* school children were also there. Such a difference between the school uniform, and shoes of the *Sarvodaya* children from the other school children! This is India! (Even after 55 years of independence, there is no improvement!) I spent some time with the Sarvodaya school children, Kedarnath Mukherjee and the headmaster. Then, I had to run back and forth to complete all the other arrangements.

Senior CII officials and other big shots from Delhi started to come. Rekha and her team were responsible for their seating arrangements. There would be a big commotion on who should be seated front and who should be seated behind! Rekha and her teammates knew how to handle all this.

I am not going to describe everything fully here. My seat was next to A. R. Rahman in the front row. I gave my Tamil poem books "நெஞ்சக மலர்கள்" *("Blossoms of the heart")* and "வற்றாத ஊற்றுக்கள்" *("Perennial Springs")* to him. He went through my poems when he was sitting idle. When I returned back to my seat, he said: "Whatever be the case! It is always refreshing to read Tamil words." At that time, he was busy in the Hindi and English music industry (2002).

A. R. Rahman's music composition was sung by a few selected students. It sounded good. The *Sarvodaya* students under Kedarnath Mukherjee sang the Hindi version with minimal orchestra. It also sounded good.

Then it was time for the speeches. Kalam's big speech was followed by the photoshoot and video shoot of the TV and the press crew. It was a big event. I was not on stage. However, I had made arrangements for Kedarnath Mukherjee to stand near Kalam's exit spot. I ensured that the security people did not shoo him away.

Once Kalam gets off the stage, it won't look nice if he gets back on stage to congratulate the blind music teacher. Thankfully, he did not forget. Kalam held the hands of Kedarnath Mukherjee and spoke with him for a few minutes. Everyone in the auditorium including important officials saw it. It was a clear statement made by Kalam. It was otherwise one of Kalam's natural traits!

I felt happy. Kedarnath Mukherjee and his Sarvodaya children received special applause from the President himself.

Tarun Das was extremely happy. Many others also felt happy. Kalam spoke to me over the phone that night about the event.

The CII was prepared to organise many such events. They arranged for one in Guwahati. Later, the *Rashtrapati Bhavan* officials insisted that the state government officials used this as a model. Everyone followed suit.

Kedarnath Mukherjee's joy knew no bounds! He felt upset that I was working in Punjab. He saw me as his guardian. He spoke to me after a few days and said: "Our school headmaster got upset that the President only spoke to me. They are trying to transfer me elsewhere." I informed retired major general R. Swaminathan in Kalam's office to take care of this issue.

Even today, Kedarnath speaks with me at least once every year. The event took shape as an English poem which can be found in my "*Jumping Genes*" collection under the title, '*The Prayer for India*' (January 27, 2003) which is centred around Kedarnath Mukherjee. I sent a copy each to Kalam and Kedarnath Mukherjee.

I frequently conversed with Kedarnath Mukherjee over the phone. But, I couldn't meet him personally after that. He passed away on July 16, 2017. I am occasionally in touch with one of his students Sandeep even today.

I had made all preparations for the PTU board meeting before leaving for Delhi. I managed to complete the arrangements using a cell phone (even though reception was fairly poor in 2002). Since Kalam had scheduled his event for 22nd and 23rd November, I arranged for the PTU board meeting (after I became a senior board member) on 20th November. It was a big success. I got permission to execute the schemes I had proposed for the institution.

I helped in the preparation of the minutes and then left for Delhi on 21 November.

❑

Meeting with Baba Once Again...

I was to travel to Bengaluru with the *Indian President* on November 22nd. R. Bhagavati is a Sai Baba devotee. She does free service in Puttaparthi for 15 days every year. However, she could never meet Sai Baba personally even once. She handed me a letter and said: “Sir, can you please give this to Baba?” I came to Rashtrapati Bhavan on November 22 early in the morning. I was half asleep. It is my habit to be a little earlier so that I am not the reason for any delay. Suddenly, I remembered her letter. I searched everywhere, but couldn’t find it! Me and a few others had to go to the airport in the first vehicle well ahead.. The Rashtrapati would come only after the plane got ready for take off.

Many programmes were scheduled for November 22 in Bengaluru. It was Baba’s birthday on November 23 and the *Indian President* was the chief guest. I went in the helicopter with the President on November 23.

The President was directly taken to his room in the guest house by the Ashram people. Me, Sheridon and others went to the guest house later. “Kalam is in his room; you all please stay here,” the Ashram people told us.

Five minutes went by. Then it was ten minutes. Sheridon got confused and knocked on the President’s room. As there was no reply, he went inside. Kalam was not there. The Ashram staff arranged this trick since they wanted Baba to meet Kalam privately.

Sheridon panicked: “Sir is not here...let us run!” It was his duty to be with the President.

We ran helter skelter. Sivakumar with his pot belly was exhausted. Sheridon and Sivathanu Pillai ran with him. I too joined them.

We ran upto the room where Baba was supposed to meet Kalam. No one questioned us since we held our special identity cards while running.

Kalam saw me, looked and he asked me in a complaining voice: "Where were you, sir? Baba will then ask me your whereabouts!"

When Baba approached us, Kalam said twice to him: "Now Rajan is a Vice Chancellor!"

Baba looked at me and said, "I have read that letter."

At first, I was confused. Then I realised that Baba was talking about Bhagavati's letter. I was searching frantically for it on November 22nd. I found it in my hand baggage while boarding the helicopter. Later, I kept it inside my pant pocket so that I would not lose it. But how did Baba know about that letter? I was surprised! I forgot all about it in our confusion. I handed the letter to Baba.

He then spoke with all of us and the President.

I wrote seven poems in the Ashram. They were later published in my "மறக்காத தேடல்கள்" *("Unforgettable Quests")* collection. I handed copies to Kalam and the others as per my usual practice. The title of the poems are:

1. காவல்துறை அழகி (The beautiful lady police)
2. இரு பெரும் ஆத்மாக்கள் (Two great souls)
3. மன மகிழ்ச்சி (happiness of the mind)
4. புட்டப்பருத்தி நிலா (The moon in Puttaparthi)
5. நம்பிக்கை (Hope)
6. புகைப்படம் (Photo)
7. கலாம் (Kalam) (22, 23 November, 2002).

These were written about the events on 22 November, 2002. Some could have been added later. I normally mention only the dates in which I wrote my poems.

The நம்பிக்கை *(Hope)* poem was about the way in which we ran and met Baba:

To give meaning for hope
To grace the sweat drops
Baba blessed all four and
Fulfilled their desires!

———————

இரு பெரும் ஆத்மாக்கள் *(Two great souls)* is when Baba and Kalam shared the stage and delivered their speech. The last few lines in the poem are:

———————

Oh protectress of the Universe!
Bless our country

To become a developed one
To be a holy one and shine!

காவல்துறை அழகி *(The beautiful lady police)* is about a lady police woman who was trying to control the crowd when we came to see Baba. She was performing her duty with elegance. I have also described her in this poem. Kalam laughed at it and commented on our way back while we were in the flight. "I also noticed; you have described it well," he said.

After reading my poems, Sivakumar commented while we were in the flight: "Sir, you have such keen observation. It would be better if there was a camera."

I instantly told the poem புகைப்படம் *(Photo)*.

Later, while travelling back to Delhi with Kalam, he said that he was thrilled to see the affection of the crowd. I told him: "Sir, you have now become an icon! It is pleasing to note that. However, you need to fulfil your ambition of empowering India using various S&T initiatives. Do not forget that. Becoming an icon and affection from the crowd alone are not enough."

The poem கலாம் *(Kalam)* was meant for that. The poem:

Kalam
Kalam with a deep truth inside
An iconic symbol Kalam
If these two merge
Then we shall prosper!

Kalam was also eager to fulfil his dream. But how much could he possibly accomplish single handedly? The Delhi writer Penneswaran interviewed me in Delhi. He asked all about my lasting friendship with Kalam (November 28, 2002). Theeranathi published a few episodes. Later while publishing my book "சிந்தனை சிதறல்கள்" *("scattered thoughts")*, he published the entire interview. It reflects all my opinions about Kalam until 2002. All that I felt, spoke, and expected about Kalam are mentioned there. Even while reading it today, I could feel them realistically. Have all those expectations been fulfilled? More on that later.

❑

Endless Journeys

It is time to shorten my narrative now. Even though I did not attend many of the events inside India, all of them were very inspirational and intellectual. A few are reflected in my poems:

"பாலைவனப் பயணம்" *("Desert Journey")* written on 23.12.2002 is about the President's visit to Barmer in Rajasthan. It appears in my "மறக்காத தேடல்கள்" *("Unforgettable Quests")* collection. The city was hit with drought and the people were suffering. The entire picture can be seen in the poem.

Yet another event was the music concerts that were arranged regularly by Kalam in the *Rashtrapati Bhavan*. Many Indian musicians were invited. Kalam invited my family members to all these music concerts. Me, Koma, and her mother (my mother-in-law) were permanent guests. Tiffin was served after the concert. Kalam knew my mother-in-law well. She was extremely cautious about her calorie intake. Kalam filled up a plate with all delicacies and forced her to eat. Likewise, he interacted with all the guests casually.

I composed a poem while Pandit Jasraj was singing. I showed it to Kalam.

Kalam loved it. He mentioned it to Jasraj during the tiffin break. Jasraj told me later: "Your Kundalini is always on the rise!" Highlights of this programme were published in the *Rashtrapati Bhavan's 'Indradanush'*. My poem was published in yet another book of my poem collection.

Meanwhile, my thoughts were still about India's state of development, discourses of the elites, the indifference shown by important dignitaries (in both ruling and opposing parties) towards the development of the downtrodden and so on. I felt that nothing can improve if Kalam alone speaks up.

I wrote a poem "எந்த இந்தியா?" *("Which India?")* (2002 September) (it appears in my "மறக்காத தேடல்கள்" *("Unforgettable Quests")* collection). I sent it to Kalam like all others.

Then, one of exhilaration. While discussing various issues with Kalam, I have teased him several times. Some of them took the shape of poetry. I am not giving all of them here. One such poem is:

Innovative love (January 4, 2003)
In making the rockets
That he flies, he
Felt a woman's grip
And saw her gaze.

Kalam would laugh out loud when I recite such poems. He told me of a question asked by a girl student (I had not accompanied him to the trip): "Kalam! What will you do if India becomes a developed nation in 2020?"

I told him a poem in response; "செவ்வாய்க்கோள் வாழ்வு" *("Living on Mars")* (2.1.2003). I told him that he could respond like this to such queries.

He was very happy when he heard this poem. Space related works and imaginations always gave him a lot of joy.

When I read this poem, I feel miserable that he did not live until 2020. I do not know whether I will be alive in 2020. Had he been alive, he would have been 89 years old in 2020!

President Kalam never rested. Giving discourses on '*Empowering India*' and '*Vision 2020*' to the Indian people became his important job. He also liked to travel to the farthest corners of India. He stayed in the governor's house in the respective state capitals and met the intellectuals, politicians, and senior officials over there. He then visited the schools, colleges, and universities to interact with the children.

Travelling to farthest corners of India (like the way he visited drought-struck Rajasthan) became an important part of his itinerary. Visiting the north east Indian(NE) regions became his important travel mandate. Next, he went to Manipur and Tripura. In January 2003, he visited Assam. He especially went there to attend the festivities in its extreme eastern border. The name of the festival is "*Dehing Patkai*"—this festival happens in India's NE region. Many tribal people from NE gather every year to celebrate this occasion. It is celebrated according to their calendar system.

India's famous celebrity Sonal Mansingh came to attend the event. She was a friend of mine even before Kalam became the Indian President. Tribal dances were performed in the event. Sonal Mansingh who was seated on the front row became excited. She said that she too wished to dance with them in front of the President. "Rajan, I also want to dance. Can I ask permission from the President?"

I conveyed this to the President's military secretary. Everyone loves Sonal Mansingh's dance. Without any makeup, she danced for about ten minutes to a song played on the CD. (It appears as an English poem in my book Jumping Genes.)

I remember many such pleasant fond memories. Let me share a sweet incident that took place in the *Rashtrapati Bhavan*.

Right from his Hyderabad days, Kalam liked to walk. He walked either in the morning, evening, or at times in the afternoon everyday. He used to walk when he worked for the DRDO while he stayed in Asiad colony in Delhi. Many of his friends who accompanied him while walking, also saw him walk inside the Rashtrapati Bhavan premises. Kalam had told me about one "bird man" who brought one kilo of grains every day and fed the birds wherever he went! I think Kalam has mentioned him in one of his books too.

There are many walking paths inside the *Rashtrapati Bhavan* premises. Kalam invited me to walk with them. We conversed on a lot of topics while walking together. Sometimes, he called me over the phone while he walked alone.

One day, as I was walking with him, he said: "Rajan! There will be deers here. Can we go and see them?" We approached the place. A fawn had just been born. Kalam was happy to see it. He enquired the gardener about it and asked whether he was properly feeding its mother.

I noticed that the place was not properly maintained. I mentioned this to Kalam. As soon as he reached his room, Kalam spoke to the garden manager and asked him to place grass pots in five or six places for the deer. They had poured it all down in one place. The male head deer did not allow the other deers near the place.

He also arranged for a veterinary doctor to take care of them.

Out of enthusiasm, I wrote a poem ("மறக்காத தேடல்கள்") *("Unforgettable Quests")*:

"Little Fawn"
Sweet little fawn!
Not just Shakuntala
To hug and kiss you;
Even our great leader
Who won victory after victory
Though seated in an unreachable place
He works and spreads joy
Seeing you born as a little one
He melted today!

January 8, 2003

As they followed Kalam's strict instructions, the deer population increased. The ninth fawn was born. When Kalam informed this to my wife and her mother, they came to see it.

We searched everywhere. It was missing. Koma asked a worker in Hindi. Everyone said that one had died of sickness. After our search, before our breakfast we informed Kalam. He was upset. Then we came back to our place. Kalam enquired about the deer and told me all about it the next day. See in my poem...

"Koma asked
If he knew where
The President's
Twenty day old fawn was?
He is there
You may rest peacefully!
So said that
Great man!
The next day he
Announced over the phone
I'm still looking
At the little one's hopping
Do not write
Your sad song yet!"

February 23, 2003

This is under the title, 'புதுக் குட்டிமான்' *('The new fawn')* in my poem collection "மறக்காத தேடல்கள்" *("Unforgettable Quests")*.

Like this we saw many rabbits, tortoises and so on. They also were poorly maintained. Kalam secured their food and water. He regularly visited the places so that the workers would pay more attention to the animals.

There are many such tidbits. The Mughal garden was meant only for the elite. Others were not allowed inside. Beautiful roses of different colours bloomed during winter there. Kalam wanted all people to enjoy them. So, he made the Mughal garden into 'People's Garden'.

The internet services started by Sivakumar were successfully run by Ponraj later. Everyone including Sheridon and Prasad made use of the internet services. Since it would be difficult to stare in front of the computer screen for a long time, projectors were arranged. Kalam could read from them sitting in a comfortable chair. All these were arranged inside his President's house ("At Home").

"You were mentioning an email! Let us see that now!" Kalam would say and start to reply.

All his speeches would be displayed to him on a big screen in this manner. Kalam would discuss it with four or five people around him. We gave it the nickname "கச்சேரி" – *"Kutchery"* meaning "concert." Kalam knew about it.

While we prepared a rough draft or were finalising it, Kalam would say, "Has the kutchery begun? I will come now." He then would go to his room, get freshened up and come to us.

After I went to Punjab, I couldn't attend many of these 'Kutcheries'. I wrote my response and faxed it from the PTU office, colleges where I have meetings, or from my home. Even while travelling I sent my responses through good fax machines. The email facility was not widespread back then. Since my typing speed was slow, I wrote everything by hand instead of using typewriters. Only then, my thoughts and words will be synchronised well! "Sir, have you sent it?"Kalam would ask me. Some of my responses will also be in Tamil.

When the internet facilities improved, Kalam was absorbed in emails and web browsing. He described them to me. I replied to him (2003): "Sir, not many places in India have email facilities. You might be having it in big establishments and some schools. Besides, not all information given in the websites is true. Many places within India operate without these internet services." I mentioned this frequently to him.

I wrote a poem teasing him one day.
"Looking at the internet,
He forgot all about India!"

May 29, 2003

He did not object to my opposing views. I had the full freedom to discuss what was in my mind with him. During our phone conversations, we debated furiously at times. Teasing each other, sharing deep thoughts and discussing big initiatives were all part of our phone conversation.

A few examples. While Kalam was the defence minister's scientific adviser till he became the PM's principal scientific adviser, and even later when he became the Indian President, we both conversed over the telephone or the mobile phone. Kalam referred to big politicians, ministers, and other high officials using nicknames from our Puranas, or other Tamil characters. While talking, he used their nicknames. When I hesitated for a while, he would say, "What sir? Didn't you understand?" and then give me a clue. He never mentioned their names directly!

While discussing such matters, when Kalam was the President, he said:

"Rajan! They will be recording everything that we speak. Let us talk! Let them scratch their heads about what we are discussing!"

One day, we were discussing TIFAC and the people working for TIFAC. Kalam knew that I worked closely with the young team members and others from outside...

While we were engrossed in our discussion, Kalam suddenly asked me: "Rajan! How come you have not slipped in any of the curves?"

I got confused. I said: "I don't understand, sir! There was no curve in our discussion!"

"What sir! You are so dumb! Don't you understand what I mean by a curve?" Kalam said.

Looking at my confusion, he gave me a clue: "You operate closely with eight-year old girls to eighty year old grannies. Many slip in these! Don't you understand?"

I understood: "The reason for me not slipping is Komamma sir! She never suspects me!" I said.

"You are absolutely right! You are a good guy!" Kalam said.

Then we continued our intense project discussion once again. He frequently used the words "Good guy!"

He had one more habit. He spoke with me everyday. If he doesn't call me during our regular phone conversation timings, then I would call him. If the cell phone was not working, then it meant that Kalam was not in Delhi. Sometimes, he was out of station for three or four days in a row.

As soon as he arrived, he would call me.

"What happened, sir! I couldn't see you! Were you roaming around?" Kalam would say. "Sir! Offence is the best form of defence!… You went to roam around and you are now complaining about me?… Wherever I go, my cell phone would always be switched on, whereas yours was turned off! I would reply back."

"Ok, tell me sir. Where are you now?" He would ask.

"Where else I will be.....", I said and started to say a Tamil proverb. Before I could finish it, Kalam would complete my statement. "Kutti Chuvar…dilapidated wall".

Likewise, when I called him and he happened to be at the President's office, Kalam would say the same Tamil proverb to me. "Kazhuthai kettaal kutti chuvar…If donkey is missing it will be in a dilapidated wall."

After Kalam became the President, many religious leaders came to see him. Besides meeting him at the *Rashtrapati Bhavan*, they also strolled with him in the Mughal garden. Kalam made this his method of giving special respect for them. Likewise, he also allowed a few other guests to the Mughal garden. He described his interaction with them on the next day or a few days later.

Sometimes, he would be extremely delighted.

"Rajan, yesterday evening a saint came to visit me. We talked a lot. I felt extremely happy. How brilliant he was! He spoke about his ashram to me, and I even saw a few pictures. I think that I should leave everything right away and go with him..." Kalam said.

"Ok, sir…let's see after another week.. Yet another saint will come and you will feel like going with him. Where all will you go?" This has happened many times. This shows Kalam's mature mindset. I think that this was an indication that Kalam, as he has crossed his seventies, was attracted towards ascetic life.

He has told me several times: "Sir! We have to leave all this and be like those who chant on the streets in our hometowns! Do you know what I mean?"

"Yes sir. While doing that, it would be nice to recite a Bhakti song composed by Manikkavasagar. It has a beautiful tune..." I would say to Kalam and start to sing the song with its tune...

"Players of sweet-voiced Veena on one side; strummers
Of Yaazh on one side; reciters of Vedas
And praying devotees on one side; the holders
Of densely- woven flower-wreaths in their hands,
On one side; adorers, weeping devotees and those
That wilt on one side; those who joined their hands
Over their heads, in worship, on one side......[4]

(திருப்பள்ளியெழுச்சி மாணிக்க வாசகர்)

(Thiruppalliyezhuchi by Manikka Vasagar)

He enjoyed that composition very much.

"You seem to be readily keeping something for all items. Should we both then go together to beat chingi?" Kalam would ask. (Chingi—a simple instrument held in one hand to give rhythm to the singer).

When he was the Indian President, Kalam visited a lot of mosques, dargahs, churches, Buddhist monasteries, Gurudwaras, Jaina ashrams, and Hindu mutts. He spread joy wherever he went.

All religions are like beautiful islands. But instead of staying like isolated islands, all of them must be interconnected through a common bridge. He has spoken these words in several places. He established the '*Foundation for Understanding Religions & Enlightened Citizenship*-FUREC' with that intention in association with Acharya Mahapragya.

Smt. Sudhamahi Regunathan has written about it briefly in this book. Today neither Acharya Mahapragya nor Kalam is alive. Today, I wish that Kalam had strengthened FUREC further while he was still alive. It would have helped in building those bridges that he had mentioned. Those with true love and respect for Kalam could take it (FUREC) forward even today. If anyone who reads this book takes care of this initiative, it would be a great tribute to Kalam, India, and all Indian citizens.

---

[4] *Translation taken from the book Tiruvaachakam, Tamil Text and English Translation by T.N. Ramachandran, published by International Institute of Tamil Studies, Chennai (page 224)*

Kalam had one more big dream. He wanted all girl children in India to receive a good education and become pioneers in the intellectual field. He had visited several rural schools and colleges in order to motivate them. He visited the institutions which encouraged Muslim girls to attend schools and colleges in order to cheer them up.

"Please study well!" Kalam always advised the girl students.

I had written earlier that Kalam was wondering what to do after his term as the Indian President was completed. I suggested that he should establish an international institution for women. (My idea was supported by our other friends too). A few religions and a few societal elements do not encourage education of the girl child in a co-education school. Some girls are stopped abruptly from going to schools. An e-learning platform should be designed especially for such girls. It could be tailor-made to be acceptable to their respective religion and caste. It would be difficult to integrate science, maths, engineering, trading, law and so on with the help of the government since the project would get caught up in their cumbersome department rules and regulations. A private institution which only works for profit will not be bothered about such initiatives. Besides, our Indian private sector is not very well developed to fund such major projects.

I have therefore spoken to Kalam about this several times.

"Sir! When you speak with the King of Saudi Arabia or with the Sheikhs of the UAE, ask them to establish an international foundation with a huge investment (around 250 million US dollars). Let us first start from India and spread it to the rest of the world. There is no use in doing this for some 100-200 girl children. Several lakh girls require a good education. This requires a lot of money. The middle eastern kings and Sheikhs can help you out." I suggested this to Kalam.

"What sir! You are always talking about money. Some Indians would contribute around 5-10 lakh rupees sir!" Kalam would respond.

"Sir! Listen to what our Tiruvalluvar has to say."

"அருளென்னும் அன்பீன் குழவி பொருளென்னும்

செல்வச் செவிலியால் உண்டு"

(Sirpi's translation for the above verse: *"Love is the mother and her child is Grace. Wealth is the foster mother which nurses this child."* The meaning of this verse is that wealth should function in sync with love and grace.) (From the சிற்பியின் திருக்குறள் உரை (Sirpi's Tamil commentary on Thirukkural) book.)

Why I am stressing this is because without wealth, there is no love and grace!

"Sir! Your love and affection will be of no use. 5–10 lakhs rupees won't even last a year. That is why FUREC could never rise up. What could Sudhamahi madam do by herself! That is why! You should ask those who would donate huge amounts of money. If you ask them, then they won't even put any big condition!" I said to Kalam.

"Let's see," Kalam said.

This happened a few times. One day when I pressured him, Kalam said: "Sir! I do not know how to ask for money. I simply can't do it!"

I am writing this here to convey Kalam's mind. Kalam wanted that there should not be even a single girl child in India who did not receive a good education and skills that would help her earn a good income. I sincerely hope that those people who love Kalam and organise programmes in the name of Kalam would create a huge foundation to fulfil Kalam's dream.

❑

Successful Trips to Kashmir and Punjab

I accompanied Kalam on his Kashmir trip. I have written about it in my மறக்காத தேடல்கள் *(Unforgettable quests)* poem collection.

1. ஷிகாராப் பயணம் *(Trip to Shikara)*
2. ஒற்றுமைக் குரல் *(Voice of Unity)*
3. காஷ்மீர் சினார் மரம் *(Kashmir Sinar Tree)*
4. அஞ்சாவீரர் *(Fearless men)*

All these were written on June 28, 2003.

Of these, the fourth one was written from the Uri military camp. Uri is on the LoC between India and Pakistan. (Recently, a terrorist attack happened in Uri in 2016).

Kalam sang our National Anthem everywhere in Kashmir. They also sang along with him.

When he visited the Hazrat Bal mosque in Kashmir, there was a huge crowd. He prayed not only there but also at the Vaishno Devi temple which he visited later.

Earlier, he visited Punjab. Since Punjab was subject to terrorist attacks, none of the earlier Presidents visited the place. Kalam was the first Indian President to visit Punjab after 20 years! That too, he wanted to visit Punjab during the birth anniversary of Bhagat Singh. It became an added advantage to me. In our PTU BOG meeting (November 2002), we had decided upon one item. Even though the university was functioning nearly six years, a single convocation ceremony had not happened in the PTU. We decided to conduct the first one in March 2003. It was not known at that time that President Kalam would visit Punjab. He had made the decision to visit Punjab during Bhagat Singh's birth anniversary only much later. He told me: "Sir, I am going to visit your place!"

"Sir, in that case, you must come to the PTU first!" I said.

"Certainly," said Kalam.

Even though there were many colleges under the PTU and many students were studying there since establishment of PTU for the past six years, there weren't any proper buildings or halls within the campus. (This is the case even today with many of the newly established IITs and NITs by the Indian government.) PTU is a state university.

We did not want to conduct our first convocation ceremony in a rented hall. 100 acres of land donated by the Punjab state was the only asset of the PTU. We decided to put a tent over there and conduct the ceremony. Unusual rains had poured in March that year. But what can one do about uncertain climatic changes? At least the heat waves would be minimal because of this!

Though Kalam had said yes, now that Kalam had become the Indian President, we had to follow only formal protocols. The PTU cannot invite him directly. We had to go through the Punjab state government only. Also, we weren't allowed to disclose the news of the President's visit. Only the state government could make the announcement! Many such strict rules! For giving degrees there were some rules of the education department. We had to make all necessary arrangements. We also had to send invitations to the students to receive their degree certificates. Students who had passed out over six years had to be invited. We had made good arrangements. Even now, I remember all the pains we had to go through to make these arrangements.

Finally, the Rashtrapati came. As always, Kalam had tried to fit in several events in his itinerary. It was Kalam's nature to get engrossed in the event proceedings and lose track of time! This would delay his arrival to all the next events. Since there was enough space in the PTU campus to land the three helicopters of the Rashtrapati, Kalam had made the PTU convocation ceremony to be his last event for the day. After this, he had to travel to Chandigarh.

We therefore had to make up for the lost time! Yet another important protocol is that the helicopter of an important leader must take off and land before sunset. The President's military commander told me: "Rajan sir, you know this well. If your programme does not end in time, then we have to travel to Chandigarh by car."

I promised him: "You need not worry! How many times you have approached me under similar situations to safeguard our President. This is not my programme. The President's security will be our priority." We started the event. I informed the CM, Amarinder Singh, and the Governor General (retd.), Jacob.

The Punjab *Chief Minister* was very kind. He said: "Rajan, I will not give my speech. That way, we can save some time."

I said: "Please don't do that, sir. The *Indian President* has come to Punjab after nearly 20 years! Being the CM of Punjab, you must definitely speak. You take your ten minutes! I will make suitable adjustments."

I informed our event schedule to Kalam: "Sir! I will reduce my Vice Chancellor's report from 30 minutes to 10 minutes. The CM will speak for ten minutes. Then, you will address the gathering. But we will invite only the gold medalists on stage since the list of students for the past six years is fairly long. However, even the silver and bronze medalists have come here to see you. You must take a group photograph with them. They will feel very happy. Then allot two minutes of your time each for the college chairmen, academic council members, all other faculty members as per formal rules, and those who fund the colleges. I will come with you and introduce everyone!"

"Ok," he said.

I had informed the military secretary that I would take Kalam to the visitors section.

The students had informed me the previous day, "Sir! We have come from afar to take a picture with the Indian President Kalam! Please allow us..."

"I will certainly try. However, when he comes you shouldn't crowd around him. Otherwise, his security guards will take him back with them. When he comes, you all must be seated in your respective spots. We will take many pictures and ensure that all of you get covered."

After the convocation ceremony got over, group photos were taken with the silver medalists. Next, the President entered into the student crowd. Lots of group photos were taken. Everyone was happy. Kalam then took pictures with VIPs who were present and all other special guests. All important faculty members of the PTU were present. Kalanidhi who helped a lot was also there.

Five minutes before sunset, I said to Kalam: "Sir, thank you very much! Please go now. Otherwise, the military secretary will not allow your helicopter to take off."

"You are very smart, sir," said Kalam and left in his car.

I waved goodbye to him and mingled with the student crowd and faculty members. Before that, I sent off the CM and the governor. This was a major milestone in the history of the *Punjab Technical University* (PTU). Even today when people come up to me and say, "Sir, I am a student of the PTU. I participated in the first convocation ceremony," I feel excited.

It is even more exciting to think that it was Bhagat Singh's birth anniversary on that day.

Before coming to Punjab, Kalam wanted to know more about Bhagat Singh. He told me: "Sir, I know that you are an expert in telling stories (Kalam likes to pull my leg at times!). Can you tell me about Bhagat Singh so that I can use your tidbits in my speech?"

I read a few articles on Bhagat Singh. My heart melted and tears started to pour down my eyes when I read about him. I shared them with Kalam. "Look at the way these heroes have sacrificed their lives for our nation. And just look at the way our politicians and public servants behave today! The sacrifices of all our brave heroes have gone for a waste!" I lamented. I became emotional and wrote a poem:

"Hero's Tears" (in the *Jumping Genes* book). Even today when I read the poem, my heart boils. I think it is the fault of my heart only! It fails to understand human behaviour and expects the impossible to happen!

❑

A New Journey with Acharya Mahapragya

In 2003, President Kalam initiated something very new. Kalam, who only spoke of Indian security and Indian economic development, never disclosed his spiritual leanings. For the first time in 2001-2002 in his '*Ignited Minds*' book, Kalam has mentioned a few tidbits.

While writing about me in one of the segments of the book, Kalam has written about the unique cultural diversity of India. He appreciated India's unity in diversity. Even before that, Kalam had met Sai Baba, Sankaracharya, Brahma Kumaris, and many spiritual leaders. One such important spiritual leader was Acharya Mahapragya, the leader of Svetambar Terapanth Jaina sect. When Acharya Mahapragya became a Jain ascetic at the age of 11, Kalam was born. The three of us had interacted earlier. Acharya Mahapragya understands English but speaks in Hindi. I served as the translator for Kalam. Acharya Mahapragya was fond of me. Kalam and him wanted to unite the leaders of all the religions and establish a foundation. Acharya Mahapragya was keen in setting it up. The '*Jain Vishva Bharati University*' established by him was functioning in Ladnun, Rajasthan. Kalam and Acharya Mahapragya wanted the Vice Chancellor of the university Smt. Sudhamahi Regunathan and myself to take charge of this new initiative. We conducted a few seminars for that. An entire book can be written about it. Acharya Mahapragya was an intellectual genius with a sharp mind. He understood the modern world and India's present state very well. He was a fantastic poet.

Since he has travelled all over India by foot, he was familiar with the various religions and sects. He understood the mindset of the Indian people very well.

I became a messenger between him and Kalam. Let me condense an important event. On Kalam's birthday in October 15, 2003, Acharya Mahapragya wanted to gather the spiritual leaders of the Hindus, Christians, Muslims, Parsis, Buddhists, Jainas, Jews, and Sikhs under one roof and present him a declaration of unity signed by them and he was working on it.

Sudhamahi Regunathan, her husband Regunathan, M. L. Sethia and myself travelled to Surat two days before. We spent two days, 13th and 14th October to prepare the draft. My UN experience helped me here. Everyone kept making minor changes and we modified the draft accordingly.

President Kalam came on October 15, 2003. All of us, including various spiritual leaders who were seated around a round table, stood up for the President. Kalam went to each of them and spent some time with them.

In the end, there were brief statements by them. The typewritten draft copies of the Surat spiritual conference proposal were handed out to President Kalam. The spiritual leaders were also given a copy each. Everyone spoke one or two words about it. Then, it was read out loud.

Later, Kalam addressed the gathering. He said that unity of religions and intellectual wisdom of spiritually realised souls was extremely important for the growth of India. He said that all the spiritual leaders should spread the message conveyed by the Surat Declaration across all Indian villages and cities.

Acharya Mahapragya was extremely happy. Sudhamahi was appointed as the main person to take forward this project.

Sudhamahi was (is) very talented. At the time, she was the *Vice Chancellor* of the *Jain Vishva Bharati University* which was established by the Jainas. Acharya Mahapragya and Dr. L. M. Singhvi (he served as India's high commissioner in Britain and has served in several other capacities. He was an educationist. He introduced the Lokpal bill for the first time in the Parliament, and was a Jaina) wanted Sudhamahi madam to be the Vice Chancellor much earlier. She is an exemplary Bharatanatyam artist and a postgraduate in economics. She knows German and Sanskrit well. She wanted to be a journalist while she was writing columns for newspapers.. In order to introduce the Panchatantra tales to children she has introduced new Bharatanatyam techniques. She is a great English and Hindi writer. She speaks in Tamil fluently since it is her mother tongue. It was possible to make the Surat draft and hand it over to President Kalam only because of her talent and dedication.

Regunathan (IAS), M. L. Sethia (a small industrialist who traded high-tech products; he is a Jaina and a great devotee of Acharya Mahapragya), and myself helped her prepare the Surat draft for spiritual leaders. We were called as "*Chaturkon*" (Four pillars) by the Acharya since we helped in uniting the spiritual leaders, Acharya Mahapragya and Kalam. On June 15, 2004 during

Acharya Mahapragya's birthday, FUREC was officially inaugurated in the *Rashtrapati Bhavan*. Since Acharya Mahapragya was travelling by foot to other places in India, he could not attend it. Besides, he did not travel on flights. One of his elderly disciples represented him.

FUREC—Foundation for Unity of Religions and Enlightened Citizenship

A major part of Kalam's life was spent on rockets (1962-ISRO) and missiles (DRDO). After the 'Agni' missile was launched successfully in 1989, he had to perform the nuclear bomb tests by integrating them into the missile. He also had to develop and manufacture missiles. From 1992 onwards, DRDO became his full time responsibility; through that he took his nuclear test project forward. From 1993, his involvement with TIFAC increased; through the TIFAC initiatives he wanted to get rid of India's poverty and modernise our industrial sector.

After he successfully performed the nuclear tests in 1998, the launch of *India Vision 2020* book, his *Bharat Ratna* award, along with all his previous achievements made him an Indian icon. During all these phases, Kalam understood that humanity was more important than S&T, defence or economics. He therefore started meeting various spiritual leaders. His spiritual inclinations reached their peak when he left the DRDO to join as the Principal Scientific Adviser.

Out of the maturity in his mind, Kalam felt it necessary to unite everyone and promote social harmony. The seeds were first sown by him when he established FUREC in association with Acharya Mahapragya. Smt. Sudhamahi Regunathan who is the CEO of FUREC nurtured it well with her immense talents. I had mentioned about her earlier here. Impressed with her efficiency, kindness and mental maturity, Acharya Mahapragya appointed her to head FUREC. Kalam used to address her fondly as "Sudhamahi Amma!"

Whenever we discussed FUREC, Kalam would tell me: "If you have anything for FUREC, first talk with Sudhamahi Amma. In case she adds some more details, kindly let me know."

FUREC is an important symbol of social harmony. Kalam laid the foundation for this organisation. I therefore felt that Smt. Sudhamahi Regunathan should give a brief introduction about it here. Here is her essay:

"One afternoon when he was taking his siesta, he heard loud conversations from outside the palace and it disturbed him. He enquired what the matter was even as he looked out of the window. There were men of great dignity and learning engaged in animated discussion. Some had raised their voices. Some were looking very angry. They did not even see the king glaring at them.

They were discussing whose religion was better and each thought his was. The irritated king got all of them arrested and imprisoned them. 'You will stay in this dark dreary dungeon,' he declared, 'till you all come to one common form of religion.' So the religious men sat looking at each other, each wondering how to make the others see sense and agree that his religion was the best.

A great seer also lived in the same town. Hearing of the events that had come to pass, he sought an appointment with the king. 'Blessed sire, I am at your service,' declared the king. "Son and Lord of the kingdom, you are a wise king. I am going back to my Master and thought I would take from you a concise description of your town so that I can describe it well.'

The king was pleased. 'Sire, I have 84 palaces and 84 market places, with each market having 24 types of shops...'

Even as the king was going on, the monk interrupted and said, 'But king, why so many different shops? Bring them all together as one. That would be wise.'

'Oh learned sire, how can that be? Just imagine how crowded a single shop would be if it were the only one. And since people have different tastes and desires, how can one shop satisfy all of them? Being an ascetic, you are not able to visualise those problems.'

'Exactly what I want to say, O King. You are an administrator and are not able to understand the subtle difference between two different philosophies. When you cannot bring into one shop products of the same kind, how can you gather the aspirations of many different types of people into one religion?' The king then saw his mistake and allowed freedom of expression and faith."

The Genesis

Acharya Mahapragya, the tenth spiritual head of the Jain Swetambar Terapanth community told this story to prepare us for what lay ahead. What lay ahead?

He told us of how Dr. A. P. J. Abdul Kalam, the then President of India had met him late one night. They had a conversation. Dr. Kalam was disturbed, "by the divisive forces and religious fundamentalism that were disrupting the unity and bonhomie among our countrymen." His vision was for ".a fully developed beautiful India with prosperous and harmonious life for its citizens especially the youth."

The Surat Spiritual Declaration

Acharya Mahapragya agreed with him and felt that conduct was the true reflection of all and any learning. So at his behest a conclave of fifteen spiritual leaders from nine different religions came together at Surat to deliberate on the problem. A Surat Spiritual Declaration was signed and presented to Dr. Kalam. It reiterated the need for peaceful coexistence and mutual respect.

The conclave, held on 15th of October 2004, was in itself a beautiful experience. All the spiritual leaders said one thing in common: for the first time the

President of the country came to each one of us and presented us with a bouquet... that is true respect accorded to spirituality. The declaration drawn up was also symbolically like a flower, envisaging five garland projects. The emphasis of four of the five was on celebration of interfaith festivals, undertaking multireligious projects, healthcare and employment, imbibing value based education in school and encouraging interfaith dialogues among religious/spiritual heads. In order to pursue the above in a sustained manner and to coordinate all activities, a national level independent and autonomous organisation managed by religious/spiritual leaders was set up.

The spiritual leaders who came together were Archbishop Stanislaus Fernandes, Bishop Thomas Dabre, Brahma Kumari Sudesh Didi, Dr. Homi B. Dhalla, Dr. J. S. Neki, Jagadguru Sri Sri Sri Shivarathri Desikendra Mahaswamiji, Mahathero Rahul Bodhi, Maulana Wahiduddin Khan, Prince Husaifa Moyiuddin, Rev Ezeikiel Malekar, Sadhvi Kanakaprabha, Sri Sri Sri Balagangadharanatha Swamiji, Swami Jitatmanandaji, Syed Jilani Ashraf, and Yuvacharya Mahashraman.

FUREC

Of the Surat Spiritual Declaration the organisation that was born was named Foundation for Unity of Religions and Enlightened Citizenship. Dr. Kalam and Acharya Mahapragya were its benefactors while the fifteen leaders were the Apex Body members and Sudhamahi was the member-secretary. Dr. Y. S. Rajan, Mr. M. L. Sethia, Mr. S. Regunathan, Dr. N. Radhakrishnan, and Sudhamahi Regunathan formed the Executive Committee members. Dr. Y. S. Rajan, then the *Vice Chancellor Punjab Technical University*, was the architect for the entire proceedings beginning with the Surat Spiritual Declaration. Mr. M. L. Sethia, an industrialist (*Elin Electronics*), was the pillar of support who symbolised Acharya Mahapragya's vision and desire. Mr. S. Regunathan, then the *Principal Secretary to the Chief Minister, Delhi Government*, was the administrative guide and advisor. Dr. N. Radhakrishnan who was *Director, Gandhi Smiriti*, stood for peace in every respect and he defined the purpose of FUREC. Sudhamahi Regunathan was then the *Vice Chancellor of Jain Vishva Bharati Institute (Deemed University)* which became the nodal organisation for coordination.

The First Year

The mood was buoyant because of mutual respect and willingness of each and every member to see the other's point of view and try to incorporate it in their vision.

The first year was devoted to creating awareness. More than 70 meetings were held across the country where local representatives of different religions got together to express their solidarity and commitment to the cause. This was done in many ways.

a) Functions were organised on important festivals of the different religions in which people from all religions partook.

b) Public functions were held and different religious leaders addressed the gathering.

c) Processions were taken out through the streets of the towns to visually tell the people that all religious leaders want betterment of humankind.

d) Developmental activities in rural areas like building water tanks for school children or a compound wall for schools were undertaken with participation from leaders and people of all faiths. Endal village in Tamil Nadu and villages near Adichunchanagiri in Karnataka and Ladnun in Rajasthan are some of the places where substantial activities were undertaken.

e) Round Table discussions were held in different parts of the country wherein the Executive Body met with the intelligentsia and a two-way communication was set up.

f) Students from all corners of India were addressed during most of the above events, in addition.

Activities of FUREC

Soon FUREC multiplied its activities.

EYE-C: Enlightened Youth Essay Competition

i) An All India Essay Competition was launched. Subsequently became an annual feature. FUREC organised four competitions. After the second year, the competition was also offered in two additional languages: Kannada and Hindi in addition to English.

ii) More than 25–30,000 students have taken part in it.

iii) All students receive certificates of participation.

iv) 7 Books of compilation of the essays have been released so far. These compilations carry the best essays received. EVERY essay is perused and a maximum number of children are included so as to encourage more numbers.

v) The books are illustrated, also by children.

vi) Principals, teachers and parents have appreciated the effort.

vii) Around the 15th of October, the schools distribute the certificate celebrating enlightened citizenship day.

viii) Two human interest stories:

A mother from Madurai called to say she had twins, the essay written by one of them had been selected in the compilation. Could the other also attend the programme wherein Dr. Kalam was to address the students. FUREC sectt. felt the twin whose essay had not found a place should not feel left out and so the staff went through the "rejected" pile of essays, retrieved the other child's essay, took an excerpt from it and included it in the book.

Perhaps the family would have been happier! The staff of FUREC definitely was. It is also evidence of FUREC's well organised manner of dealing with the contributions received.

The second story: There were two girls in the same class in a Delhi school who had the same first and last name. The Principal had awarded the book to the wrong child: that is not to the child who had written the essay. A parent of this child (who had written the essay) came to the FUREC sect. Asking for another copy of the book. We told them we had no problem giving her a book but the child should feel honoured and so traced the original essay and by matching the handwriting the Principal could prove who the girl was who had actually won the award and she was given the book in the Assembly the following day.

EY-AC: In 2007, an additional art competition was introduced only in Delhi. More than 5,000 students participated and their works were exhibited during the annual day celebrations.

PROJECT SUDEN: Sustainable Development through Training in Non Violence: More than 1000 workshops have been conducted in Delhi schools by volunteers to develop an understanding of peace and non-violence. It has been widely appreciated.

Some schools have even paid to hold the workshops. Many feedback forms were received from the schools lauding the effort.

PROJECT DESH: Development of Education, Skill Formation and Health Care.

This project is primarily carried out in rural areas.

In Adichunchanagiri under the aegis of Sri Sri Sri Balgangadharnath Swamiji:

A memorandum was signed with the Dept of Education in Karnataka to develop, assist 100 government schools in rural areas. 10 areas where collaboration could take place were identified: like compound walls, toilets, water facilities, kitchen, teacher training, etc.

All schools have benefitted.

14 skills were identified by Swamiji and training workshops have been set up in more than 11 villages where youth are being trained regularly in vocations like carpentry, welding, tailoring and so on.

A separate cadre of health workers was established by Swamiji and these young women would go to the villages, help people, particularly women to access medical health, maintain their dossier and bring them to the hospital, get them treatment and even follow up.

Rural health camps are regularly held across Karnataka. Today, they have built a huge multi crore centre for imparting skills and have retained the banner of FUREC.

In Ladnun, more than 500 students passed class eight through open school. All these children studied in their respective villages and most of them were girls.

PROJECT INTERFAITH: Many interfaith activities like celebrating each other's festivals are regularly being held.

A Distinguished Lecture Series was launched wherein 5 lectures of high quality have so far been delivered. One has been published into a monograph.

A Syncretic traditions series was launched wherein four lectures have been held. This was again a unique step where people born into one religion spoke of another in which they had equal conviction.

All the spiritual leaders supported the organisations with live and genuine conviction. Dr. Neki, Sri Sri Sri Balagangadharanatha Swamiji, Jagadguru Sri Sri Sri Shivaratri Desikendra Mahaswamiji, Dr. Homi Dhalla were all presidents of FUREC for two years.

An event in the life of FUREC was significant. Maulana Syed Jilani Ashraf Sahib opted out of the organisation with great dignity. The Sufi preferred not to articulate his compulsions but we all knew that he was only physically no longer with the organisation but his spiritual presence would always be with us. Brahmakumaris too expressed their inability to keep up and Prince Moyinuddin found it difficult to represent their community at the meetings.

Meanwhile Swami Jitatmananda and Dr Homi Dhalla were travelling across the seas with the message of FUREC. If Swamiji spoke on Science and Spirituality, Dr. Dhalla spoke of Peace as a necessity. Swamiji organised a fabulous meeting with students at the Ramakrishna ashram in Rajkot.

Even while there was much interest generated and activities were gathering momentum, the usual disease afflicted FUREC also: Paucity of funds.

With one of the benefactors being the President of India, much caution was exercised on where FUREC funds got and how. Once when Dr. Kalam was presented with the problem, he said, "But I have not asked anyone for money..." he said so, so humbly that it stole the hearts of the members of FUREC.

Then with the benefactors and Sri Sri Sri Balagangadharanatha Swamiji passing on, a setback that came was difficult to recover from. But, the spirit is not lost.

Hopefully, this dream of great people will find realisation now, after the small, perhaps rejuvenating nap it has taken. It will then be a living memorial for Dr. A. P. J. Abdul Kalam, lasting for centuries.

Before handing over the Surat draft to President Kalam on his birthday, there was an event arranged with one of the major spiritual leaders on September 26,

2003. I did not know about it. Two days before the event, President Kalam called me and said: "Rajan, you must definitely come there. They have included some events. Sheridon will let you know of them. I do not exactly know what to do with those. Can you take a look at it and let me know. It's urgent." Looking at the tone of his voice and his urgency, I understood that there was some issue. At the time, I was in Punjab. I spoke with Sheridon. The President's concerns were real. However, he already agreed to attend the programme. Big industrialists had been invited and major programmes had been organised. This must be the work of the higher officials in the Rashtrapati Bhavan. We found a solution to resolve Kalam's concerns without creating any confusion.

I too attended the event. More than 5 lakh people were there. Many of the programmes upset me. They appear in my "மறக்காத தேடல்கள்" *("Unforgettable Quests")* collection as 'கொச்சிப்பாட்டு' *('Dirty songs')*. Why do spiritual leaders behave like this? Why should they attach Kalam's name to such a bad event? Thankfully in Surat, there were no such extravaganza. It was an ordinary programme in line with the simplicity of the Jaina culture. It gave me peace of mind.

❑

Krishna who Came to Sudhama's House

I was working tirelessly in the PTU. I was working hard and fast to make good improvements to the university. There were a few setbacks as well. Overall, the university saw some quality improvements. M.Tech. degree was started to help the teachers to acquire higher qualifications. Many were B.Tech. qualified. We also increased the number of PhD students. I had to work for nearly 15 hours per day. I did not take a break even on weekends. I used to go and inspect the affiliated colleges of the PTU. These weren't the work meant for a Vice Chancellor usually. I did this to understand and encourage them. Each and every initiative was documented carefully as per rules. Even when I had to travel with President Kalam occasionally, I continued to manage my PTU activities from there. Such trips, though exhausting, were indeed thrilling.

I also worked as the Scientific Adviser to the Punjab CM that added to my responsibilities.

The Punjab CM asked me to help with investments in technology areas. I did my best. There were no developmental schemes in Punjab at the time. The CM wanted to abolish corruption and many persons were being arrested on corruption charges. There was absolute confusion since everyone was complaining about the others. Under these circumstances, no investors were willing to invest in Punjab.

There were confusions in the Centre as well. Many important projects were running at a slow pace. I had the same experience when I was in Delhi in 1988. Even in ISRO many of ISRO's welfare schemes (that actually benefited the society) were making no progress at all. No one seemed to be interested. Many of these welfare activities could have pushed India forward. Wherever Kalam went, he was spreading happiness and a positive vibe. However, nothing seemed to happen practically. It was similar to the situation he faced while working as the *Principal Scientific Adviser*.

That was when I realised that I should drop out of everything. A week ago, one of my friends, M. L. Sondhi who was an excellent idealist and action oriented, passed away. The Bharati poem which echoed in my mind at the time was, *"Why was I born in this miserable country?"* ("ஏன் பிறந்தனன் இத்துயர் நாட்டிலே?")

I wrote a similar poem beginning with the same lines and informed Kalam about it. "I have found a suitable successor for the PTU. I am sure that he would take it to new heights. Now, I need a change of place. As per my official gazette, I have crossed my 60 years now; actually, there are a few more months left. I therefore need a change..." I told him in December. On December 21, 2003, I wrote a poem on that, "ஒரு மனிதனின் பாடல்" *(" The song of a man")* (22.12.2003). It appears in the "மறக்காத தேடல்கள்" *("Unforgettable Quests")* book. There is a note below the poem about my discussion with the *Indian President*.

The President inaugurated a fresh project of PTU in December, under these circumstances. He told me something which was not in his official schedule while he was attending the Science Congress (January 2004), "I am going to come to your Chandigarh house."

"Sir, this is not mentioned in your itinerary. Koma is also not at home. She is here. We have all come to attend a programme. What will I give you to eat?" I said.

"You can give me whatever you will eat. It is not in my itinerary. But, I am definitely coming to your home," Kalam said.

I informed this to Kalam's military secretary so that he could make suitable security arrangements. Me, Koma, V. Raghuraman (Kalam knew him well), and his wife Geetha rushed out of the programme. The police had brought sniffer dogs to help with security at my Chandigarh residence. I can never forget that day. Kalam went to each and every single room in our house. We had kept beautiful pictures everywhere.

"Komamma, what do you have in your fridge?" Kalam said and opened the fridge. Koma and Geetha welcomed him with the 'arathi' earlier. Hurriedly, they both prepared something to offer to Kalam. Kalam relished their food just like how Lord Krishna relished Sudhama's (Kuchela's) beaten rice. Koma said, "Sir, in case you had informed us earlier about your visit, I could have prepared an entire lunch meal for you."

"Why? What is wrong with this? It tastes delicious," said Kalam and had a mouthful. His security guards were also forced to have the same food. They ate well since they were very hungry!

Kalam wanted to visit us since he knew that I would be leaving Punjab shortly. He came to our house out of affection towards us.

Kalam was happy about me leaving Punjab. We were planning to stay in Delhi with my son Vikram for a while. Kalam thought that I could get a job in Delhi. However, nothing like that has been confirmed yet. We were looking to rent a house in Delhi.

As I had introduced many new changes to the PTU and had made improvements to all its affiliated colleges, it was in good shape at the time. I made them follow stringent protocols and so there was good discipline in the university. I knew that it was necessary to relax some of these strict rules. If I had it relaxed in the beginning there is no end to such relaxations. As I had already imposed a rigid system, now my successor can function in a relaxed manner. I wanted my successor to be more flexible. That way it would help the administration. Fortunately three months after I joined the PTU, Dr. S. K. Salwan retired from his DRDO job and joined PTU. He became the university adviser in PTU. Kalam knew him well. Salwan spoke Punjabi fluently. I decided that Salwan should be made as my successor and therefore spoke to the CM of Punjab. I told him that this will help strengthen the foundation of the university. Initially, the CM refused my resignation. But after repeated insistence, he agreed to let go of me. On February 29, 2004, I quit my job and handed over my responsibilities to Dr. S. K. Salwan.

Kalam had an excellent opinion about Dr. S. K. Salwan. In many of our meetings, he commented on Salwan's exemplary leadership skills.

Kalam said: "While we were constructing the building for the Imarat Research Centre (RCI) in Hyderabad, Dr. S. K. Salwan was the director. We had to build it on an empty land. There was a big building with an office room inside. Everyone was there inside the room and were making arrangements for construction. While we turned, we saw a huge python lying in between the room exit and the building. There were no workers outside. All of us got scared. There were no cell phones in 1980. Moreover, since the building was still under construction, there weren't any landline phones either.

If we stayed there for too long, those who were inside might panic. We weren't sure about what might happen if we hit the snake with something. Salwan saw it lying down. He brought a big basket and covered the snake with it. He sat on top of the basket and asked everyone inside the room to leave the spot. He then got up from his seat and exited."

"This is the quality of a great leader," Kalam said.

Salwan had worked as a Brigadier in the Indian army too. He used to work in the northeast, and Jammu and Kashmir regions under difficult circumstances. He did his M.Tech. and PhD in Mechanical engineering at the IIT.

Therefore, the PTU got a good leader. Kalam felt happy to hear the news. He said to me: "You did a good job, sir."

When news of me leaving the PTU leaked, Tarun Das called me over the cellphone and said: "Rajan! Is it true that you are leaving the PTU? Remember that the doors of the CII will always be open for you." I replied: "Thank you very much, sir. However, I have not yet decided. I am in no hurry. We will discuss it when I come to Gurgaon next week."

Governor O. P. Varma who was the Chancellor of the PTU was a great man. I introduced my successor to him. All three of us took a group photo. That is, the governor along with the ex-Vice Chancellor and the new Vice Chancellor. I was happy to see the photo on TV channels and newspapers.

I now had to start my life afresh in Delhi. Myself and Vikram had hunted down a house for rent. It was in very bad shape since it was left unoccupied for a long time. It was covered with dust and termites. I was very worried since I had a lot of books, reports and other signed manuals. Gomati often said: "This is all your trash!"

Earlier when I was in Delhi, many of my important collections got destroyed by termites. This time I wanted to be more careful.

After speaking with Tarun Das, I decided to join the CII once again. My CII office was in Gurgaon itself.

It became easy for Kalam to get in touch with me frequently. Whenever he wanted, I would go and visit him in his President's house. My new CII job was not as tough as my PTU job. The CII wanted me to be associated with two important activities that might benefit our Indian people. It was to upgrade the education system in schools, colleges, and universities, and also improve the quality of primary education.

I travelled abroad with Kalam several times. Other than Kalam's trip to Dubai/UAE, I accompanied him everywhere. He would inform me several days earlier that I must join him. Two others who always accompanied us were IISc's Dr. R. Balakrishnan and the founder of the BrahMos mission Dr. A. Sivathanu Pillai.

I started to live in Gurgaon from April 2004. Occasionally, Kalam invited our family to stay with him in the President's House. Kalam said: "Komamma! You, Rajan, and Vikram must come and stay in my house! You will get some rest! You can also train my cook with your culinary skills... make some good pickles."

"Certainly! Your house is like my mother's house ('*Mai ke ghar*'). We will certainly come," Koma said. We would then stay for a week there. It was the first birth anniversary of our second grandson Ashwin in May 2004. Kalam agreed to Koma's request to celebrate the birthday party in the President's house. It is an unforgettable event. Dr. Sivathanu Pillai was there with his family and grandson. It was a big celebration. My entire family (me, Koma, Vijay, his wife Anu, our two grandsons, and Vikram) was present. Also, Koma had invited a few of her friends to the event. Everyone in the President's house said that they had never seen such a birthday celebration happening in the President's house before. My six year old grandson Aditya drew a portrait of President Kalam. He also drew pictures of all he saw at the President's house. He fondly referred to Kalam as "Kalam Thatha (grandpa)!") Since he was born and brought up in America, he spoke in English. My family members were very happy. Many pictures were taken.

Soon after I came, Kalam went to Siachen on April 4, 2004. I couldn't go. There were restrictions for travel. For the first time, an Indian President visited the place. Situated at the tip of the Himalayas, it is extremely cold; a place for India-Pakistan confrontation! World's highest warfront! I was a bit worried about the cold weather. I told Kalam: "Sir, please take proper precautions about your health as per the doctor's advice. Don't show your courage in this!" I was happy to see his pictures on TV. That happy song is there in my "மறக்காத தேடல்கள்" *("Unforgettable Quests")* collection.

Siachen Mountain (04.04.2004)
On the top of the mountain peak
That Siachen mountain peak
Came the one who is always excellent
And beyond many peaks;
He poured out his love
With beaming smile_rain
I saw our brave warriors
In that world's highest point;

———————

His hair too waved
Like flag in that wind
This news flashing on the television
Telling news in all directions
Mother India ascended further like a mountain!

Kalam, being the commander of the Indian defence forces, went to Siachen and he also gave the soldiers his signatures. He also wanted to cheer those brave warriors fighting at the front (Jammu, Kashmir, Uri, border regions, Siachen, and those in the Indian air force flights). He wanted to boost their courage, and enthusiasm. This was the specialty of Kalam.

Suddenly, one fine day, President Kalam developed a sudden interest in the upcoming new technology called nanotechnology. "Divide your height by 100 crores. It is that small!"

Multi colours in peacock's feathers
Is due to nanotechnology!
Holding each atom
Through scientific methods
Bending it and join it with other atoms
Thus creating new materials,
This is nanotechnology.

He arranged for a two day workshop at the *Rashtrapati Bhavan* by inviting many Indian expert scientists and technicians. Many were from big government offices and educational institutions. He insisted on my presence. "Sir! These people would get government funding for several crores using your name. What is the point of imitating foreigners, without thinking focusedly on creating new products indigenously? Don't you remember what they did with the Superconductivity research in 1980?" Kalam said: "No! You have to attend the workshop fully!" He too would take part for a while and leave.

The last step was to call several expert scientists to his room and prepare a final draft for the project proposal. He called me before that. I told him my opinion. "Research as per wishes of individual scientists is of no use!" Then, I suggested a few examples as to what should be done. "Let's see," Kalam said.

He then called all the S&T big shots. They talked about several schemes. All they wanted was government funding; they weren't bothered about the results coming from the research. Kalam wanted to please his S&T friends. He was always like that. After SLV-3, he stopped saying 'No!' for an answer. He never said: "This should not be done; this wouldn't be good to do." Probably, he became more mature after his 50. I have told him this several times. He would laugh. In order to please those S&T big shots, he said that he would recommend a 1000–2000 crore project.

Soon after they left, I showed him my poem which I wrote while they were discussing. He laughed out loud.

Nanotechnology* *(29.4.2004) (மறக்காத தேடல்கள்-***Unforgettable Quests***)

They know the scientific truth that
Nanotechnology is impossible
From just a single atom!
Why then aren't they interested
To unite together
Towards a common goal?
'Me', 'Mine'
Is all they say;
Should I call out
To my Shivashakti out loud?

(The word Me and Mine comes in Tamil as Naaney Enakkey. Naaney rhymes with Nano)

'Project planning', 'orientation', and 'teamwork' were Kalam's strengths. He was an excellent project manager. At least now, when he has become the Indian President, should he not put pressure on these S&T big shots? Let them mumble something while leaving! Teamwork and good planning are the key factors for development. Kalam knew this quite well. He always advised this to students during his lectures. Why not tell these big shots the same thing! Everyone knew about the government money wasted in the 'Superconductivity research' done earlier; these were the same S&T people! This is the reason why India's GDP (*Gross Domestic Product*) never sees any speedy increase. Countries with populations lesser than India have better GDP than us!

Instead of thinking all this, Kalam's main aim was to please everyone. This had become his habit after he became the President. Probably, as a President, he was compelled to act in this manner. The role of the *Indian President* is equivalent to that of the British Queen. All tough decisions must be made by the cabinet ministers and the *Prime Minister*. However, in Kalam's case, when it comes to S&T matters, the *Prime Minister*, and the *Finance Minister* might see him as a S&T leader!

Kalam spent most of his time interacting with people and children. Unlike his predecessors, he travelled a lot, interacted with the people and gave lectures extensively. He was also going through his files. But that took him only about an hour to finish.

Kalam had to handle his job as the Indian President amidst all this. Vajpayee who was the Indian Prime Minister announced general elections. It became a popular topic on TV and newspapers. Discussions and debates happened everywhere. Even in our 'Kutchery' meetings, we discussed this issue as gossip. He was getting to know different opinions from us. In addition his officials would have given their researched analyses to him.

If it was an 'absolute majority', then the President would have no role to play. However, many people said that it would not be the case this time. Kalam had the opportunity to make a resolution for the first time.

The elections were over. The results were not yet announced. While we were discussing, we all said to Kalam: "Sir, your work starts now; it will be your responsibility!" In order to reduce the tension, I wrote a poem:

Lok Sabha Elections
(மறக்காத தேடல்கள்-*Unforgettable Quests)*

I have cast my vote
I have lit the fire of the cracker!
When will it burst

What confusion will our President have?
    (I have cast my vote...)
When will big heads roll
How will be many horse tradings ?
    (I have cast my vote...)
Isn't this only democracy-then
Why should I care for the government anymore?
    (I have cast my vote...)

May 12, 2004

(This comes as a folk song style in Tamil with a fine folk rhythm, difficult to capture in English)

As expected, the results were confusing. It was the NDA under Vajpayee's leadership which had proposed the name of Kalam. Even though they were the group with the highest numbers of victorious candidates (still short of majority), they were hesitant to form the government.

In case they had asked, Kalam would have had to allow them to form as per conventions. Still the critics would have commented that since it was the NDA which proposed Kalam's name for the Indian President, therefore Kalam acted partially towards them. As per the rules, Kalam was supposed to invite the coalition (formed before elections) which won with the largest number of seats.

The *United Progressive Alliance* (UPA) got the opportunity. Smt. Sonia Gandhi became the leader. Kalam has written about all this. Many might have noticed that Kalam handled such a major job elegantly and sincerely.

This silenced those people who had initially posed the question (at the time of appointing Kalam as the Indian President), "How could a scientist handle the role of a President?"

Kalam proved his competence and trustworthiness in the most important test which was given to him as the Indian President.

❑

A Big Heart with a Unifying Spirit

In september 2004, we went to Tanzania and South Africa. It was an excellent trip. Kalam attracted many people there with his charisma. He discussed many issues with Nelson Mandela. Because of Kalam, we too got an opportunity to shake hands with the great man. I composed some Tamil and English poems after this.

When Kalam spoke in the Pan-African Parliament over there (Johannesburg, South Africa), he said: "We will connect 53 African countries through a satellite; A satellite will be dedicated to Africa which will be used to improve many things such as education and hygiene here (in Africa)." He said that India will gift it to Africa.

India would donate 10 million US dollars. The TCIL (*Telecommunications Consultants of India Ltd*) which was a public sector organisation did this in association with various industries, universities, and hospitals. Part-1 was launched in 2009 and part-2 was launched in 2011. To know more about this, click on the google website '*Pan African e-network project*'.

It was expected that there would be big returns from this project, especially in the e-learning platform. It is not known whether it created employment opportunities in India and Africa using this initiative by promoting trading and e-commerce. I saw some funny news on google.

There it was mentioned that the African leaders were extremely pleased with the Pan African e-network project. I have not checked the authenticity of the news. It has appeared in Telegraph, Kolkata (Tuesday October 17, 2015).

A brief summary of this report on *Telegraph*:

The African leaders who attended the Pan African Parliament would be pleased to wear a 'wig' like Kalam's instead of Nehru's or Modi's jacket. This was because Kalam was deeply involved with Africa. This is because it was Kalam who had promised to give the Pan African e-network project that would save many African lives in 2004 as a gift.

This is very happy news indeed! Even after Kalam's death, the Indo-African unity will be preserved through this initiative. Let us hope that they will promote and develop it further.

I wrote a poem *'Pan African Bridge' ("In Jumping Genes")* on 14.9.04.

"Future is made in thoughts and words
But future unfolds with only actions bold
Actions need - steely biceps
Mighty will without hiccups"

I have been wonder struck by Kalam's vision in this poem.

I was happy to note that Kalam had been portrayed as the hero of the *Pan African e-network project*. Even after he left us, Kalam should be treated as the godfather of several major initiatives which he undertook. Sometimes, my heart burns to see the present state of our country. They let go of Kalam's charm and charisma. My heart weeps like a child crying over spilt milk.

Kalam travelled a lot within India than outside. The Indian President is the leader of the Indian states. Therefore, there were many protocols to be followed when he travelled abroad. Moreover, there are also sensitive geopolitical issues.

Kalam's first foreign trip was on October 18, 2003 for a week to the UAE, Sudan, and Bulgaria. After that, he travelled six times to various foreign countries. I travelled to these places with him. Since he clubbed two or three countries together in his travel itinerary, we visited 17 foreign countries. We discussed many issues; he acted upon a few of them. We observed many things in those countries as well. I had the opportunity to interact with many of the leaders. I wrote a few poems based on that. I am not going to elaborate more since it would become a book by itself.

Since all these happened during the age of the internet, everything has been archived carefully. Those interested can look in the *Rashtrapati Bhavan*'s official webpage under the section '*Archives on Kalam*'. Copies of Kalam's speeches can also be found in Kalam's webpage. It will also be in *Rashtrapati Bhavan*'s press releases. Newspaper articles can also be found. Some have been quoted in the *Wikipedia* site. Everything need not be necessarily authentic. However, a fair picture can be drawn by looking into all of these.

I therefore will not be elaborating on his foreign trips here. However, let me mention a few.

Trip to Russia: May 22-28, 2005.

Even though India and the Soviet Union were friendly nations, after the Soviet Union split into several countries, none of the Indian Presidents visited there. Kalam became the first Indian President to visit Russia officially. There were many formal official meetings. Vladimir Putin took part in the meetings enthusiastically.

Even though everything was proceeding smoothly in Russia, Kalam had to handle an Indian matter. Around midnight, Kalam was consulting me and Dr. Sivathanu Pillai. Even though he valued the feedback from his office, he sometimes invited us to his room to ask our opinion on a few matters. Suddenly, his secretary P. M. Nair appeared there, handed over a file and said, "Very urgent, sir!" Kalam moved away from our table to his side. He later told us: "A very urgent matter..the Prime Minister has sent some news...after having breakfast tomorrow, please come to my room. We will discuss more then."

Both of us went the next day. Kalam was getting ready for breakfast. It was unusual for him to get up early in the morning. He was probably thinking about yesterday's urgent matter. When we entered, Kalam said: "The PM had asked me yesterday if I could dissolve the Bihar assembly and impose President's rule."

Before he could finish, Dr. Sivathanu Pillai asked him: "Have you put your signature?"

Kalam: "Yes!"

Immediately, Dr. Sivathanu Pillai said: "Why did you sign it, sir? You could have waited for a day before signing!"

Kalam: "They said it was very urgent. They said that it could lead to law and order problems and violence!"

Pillai: "You made a big mistake."

What could we do now? We told him: "Leave this for now. The matter will go to court. So far, you were like the Dharmaputra. Your chariot never touched the earth while moving! Now, it has come down!"

Kalam was terribly upset. But nothing can be done now. Apparently, his secretary had asked him to take swift action.

At the time of the court proceedings, we asked him. He replied: "I asked many questions. Only after the PM answered me properly, did I sign the file." We asked: "Have you recorded them carefully then? Or have you asked your secretary to record the notings on them in the file at least?"

Even today, the matter can be looked up on the google website. Many great lawyers have given their opinions. There had been a hung assembly for several weeks since the election results which were announced on February 27, 2005. Why didn't they show the file to Kalam when he was in Delhi? Why disturb him when he was abroad? Moreover, they had insisted on settling the matter overnight. Why force him to sign so urgently? There are several questions in my head that need an answer. A big Chanakyan trick had been played, it appears.

I never saw these files; neither did I discuss them with Kalam. I was heartbroken that Kalam's good image had gotten spoiled because of this incident. The ruling UPA at the centre wanted to dissolve the NDA's rule in Bihar. Therefore, elections were held again in Bihar. Thankfully, the NDA won in the Bihar elections held again.

Besides this incident, since everyone had a good opinion about Kalam, the announcement made by the Supreme Court after nearly one year directly attacked governor Bhuta Singh. There were no comments about the Indian President Kalam. Kalam was upset for some 10-15 days after the court made the announcement. I have spoken to him personally, while discussing other matters.

There were debates over whether Kalam should resign from his post. It could be a major setback to the Congress party. However, the government protocols were not entirely clear. There was a time in India when Lal Bahadur Shastri resigned from his post during the Ariyalur train accident citing dharmic references. Governor Bhuta Singh who filed the Bihar report refused to resign!

Kalam was upset that all these happened because of his urgent decision. Later on, after several people requested him not to resign, Kalam agreed. He started to work as usual.

However, our Russian trip was not affected in any way. After discussing with us, Kalam continued his duty there. What I discussed in the above happened after about one year later in 2006 when the Supreme court gave its judgement.

Kalam and Dr. Sivathanu Pillai had worked for the BrahMos project with the Russian scientists and technicians earlier. They therefore worked cordially. Instead of behaving like the President of India, Kalam cheerfully participated in all discussions with them. He went and saw their latest technological innovations. He discussed some new projects. We all visited the beautiful churches in Ukraine.

I will skip the discussion about our Iceland trip and tell now about one of the projects that was close to Kalam's heart. After seeing a paper by a scientist in Iceland, Kalam believed that it is possible to predict earthquakes a few days before the occurrence. As per all accepted scientific understanding so far, something like this would be impossible.

"Maybe those above 40 might reject this idea. We only need youngsters who are less than 40. They will find a solution." Kalam repeated this several times.

Kalam insisted that the *Indian Meteorological Department* (IMD) should work along with that Iceland scientist. Kalam wanted to do this to resolve the problems faced by people in earthquake-prone regions. But this would lower his image with other good scientists who could think: "Look at the way he is using his position to indulge in a project that is completely opposed to science!"

A memorandum of understanding was signed a few weeks later. No significant scientific progress was achieved out of this initiative.

Later in 2007,we visited Greece, France, the European Parliament, and Socrates' prison (where Socrates was supposedly imprisoned). He met the Greek leaders. He gave a beautiful speech in the European Parliament and received a standing ovation. It was filled with quotes from the Purananooru, and the Thirukkural. Quotes like, "I belong everywhere, all are my people!"

He emphasised on unity of nations and world peace wherever he went.

Within two years of his speech came the world economic crisis. No one would have expected such a disastrous financial/economic situation in Europe (that is still happening).

Even the European multifaceted structure had to go through the crisis. Now, there is some scope for them to recover.

Therefore, the speech delivered by Kalam was like a divine nectarine to their ears. Many wanted to get his autograph too.

Kalam visited the CERN (*Conseil Européen pour la Recherche Nucléaire*) which is the European Council for Nuclear Research. The facility had provisions to conduct experiments on the "God Particle." Scientists from BARC (*Bhabha Atomic Research Centre, India*) designed a special magnet for it. They were very happy to speak with Kalam!

From January 31, 2006 to February 9, 2006, we visited Singapore, Philippines, and The Korean Republic (South Korea). He saw a lot of interesting S&T initiatives in South Korea and Singapore.

Between March 8-14, 2006 he visited Myanmar and Mauritius. There is so much to talk about the trips. Myanmar has beautiful Buddhist Viharas. Kalam enjoyed them all.

Wherever he went, he also interacted with university students and children.

In Myanmar, we went to Bahadur Shah Zafar Mazar. He was the last Mughal emperor. British rulers chased him away from India since he fought against the Britishers from 1857 onwards for Indian independence. He lived like a beggar there. They have built a 'Dargah' for him there. Many people worship him.

I will quote a small episode from our Myanmar trip. The Myanmar military chief (Myanmar was under military rule), and the head of peace and development of Myanmar, Senior General Than Shwe spoke with Kalam privately. None of his officers or ministers were there with him. Kalam took me along.

Kalam knew that Myanmar was very important for Indian politics and geopolitics. He therefore had asked me to prepare about it in advance. We also discussed a few specific plans. Since our north eastern states are isolated, it is difficult to bring in trade, technical infrastructure and investments to them. If we establish a 100 km link road, there are excellent ports in Myanmar. This will help boost the trade and economy.

Kalam discussed this with the *External Affairs Minister* and had collected all details of India's progress. Based on their feedback, we felt that the India-Myanmar connectivity project was happening as planned.

Senior General Than Shwe spoke pleasantries for a few minutes. Then he gave a big list. He mentioned the list of projects that Myanmar had undertaken with India. None of them were major ones. However, they were not yet started or were left incomplete. He then said that China completed all their projects on time or sometimes even within time.

A brief summary of what Than Shwe said that day: "Listen Mr. President. I have a special affinity towards India. My wife and I are strong devotees of Lord Buddha. We have visited the Buddha Gaya twice. As per our faith, if we visit there thrice, then we will get salvation."

"Many people here in Myanmar have a strong liking for India. However, none of the projects with India are ever getting completed. Why are we still begging India when China is working fast and completing projects on time?" Many people ask me this question.

I do not have an answer to them.

"It would be better if you could ensure that these projects with India get completed soon," he said.

Later, Kalam shared a few of his ideas with Than Shwe.

We left to complete other official jobs.

That night, when the External Affairs Ministry and other officials tried to give their explanation, Kalam openly showed his anger for the first time.

"You are giving me an explanation and I am trusting you completely. However, most projects are yet to begin or are left incomplete. Did you know about this? Or are you just getting the files from someone else?" Kalam asked.

As always, the officials were beating about the bush. "Sir, the respective committee should be given approval..for this one, the project plan is ready and it will be reviewed within a few months." They were giving many excuses like this.

Kalam intervened (which was quite unusual for him to do): "You need not give an explanation to me about how you move your files or how you conduct your meetings. I now want to know what all we have promised to Myanmar? When will they get completed? Can we or can't we? How long is it going to take further? I only need this information."

I was shocked to hear their responses!

They were not entirely to blame. Their supervising officers or the department ministers might have felt such initiatives to be irrelevant. Many leaders who visit other foreign countries sign memorandums of understanding. Even when President Kalam visited foreign countries, he signed such agreements along with the other foreign leaders. This has become a new tradition! No one is bothered about the details! Therefore, our external affairs officials also had the habit of finding some fault or other with other department officials. Their attitude is that we have signed the agreements in the presence of gig leaders; they are shown on press and TV; our duty ends here. Few are bothered to take action after that! They would move on and sign their next agreement.

If one or two such foreign agreements are pursued by some, their approach is "Let them do! It is not my responsibility!" This has been the general mindset of most of our foreign initiatives. Just like the promises made by electoral candidates before an election!

He asked me to write about what all must be done in Myanmar. I wrote and handed the document to him. I did not ask him after that since I am not a government official. He would have probably handed it over to his secretary and others to take care of it.

I therefore was pleased to hear about the *Pan African e-network project*. Something like that rarely happens!

Lastly, President Kalam visited France (Strasburg) and Greece (Athens) on April 24-28, 2007. I have briefly written about it earlier.

Kalam travelled within India and attended major events too.

Even though the Supreme Court judgement with respect to the Bihar assembly dissolution gave him some mental problems, Kalam continued to work tirelessly with a smiling face as always!

"He hid all his pain within himself."

❑

Kalam's Skillful Handling of a Tough bill

Before looking into the tough bill passed by Kalam, let me narrate a happy family incident.

Kalam's brother, Muthu Meera Maraikayar, was approaching his 90 in 2006. He wanted to visit the Ajmer Dargah and spend some time with his brother. Kalam therefore decided to stay in Delhi for a week to entertain his brother.

Kalam wanted to celebrate his brother's birthday on 16.5.2006 as well. One of the main reasons for the celebration was the completion of his Haj pilgrimage. From his side Nazema and many family members attended. From my side, Koma, her mother, Vikram and I were invited. He celebrated it as a family function with no big rituals. Kalam told me and his brother that he wished to celebrate his brother's hundredth birthday in a grand manner. It was to happen in 2016.

He wanted me to narrate my poem on that happy occasion. He then handed over a shawl to Koma and said: "Komamma you put the shawl for my brother!" My poem was based on a hymn from the Atharva Veda:

My big brother's big brother!

(Published in '*Thamarai*' magazine, Chennai in the "குதிக்கும் குழந்தைகள்" *(jumping children)* book)

A clear eyesight for hundred years,
A full life of hundred years,
Being with great intellect for hundred years
With growing prosperity for hundred years
Well nurtured for hundred years
Living with strength for hundred years

With fame and glory for hundred years
Pray we to You Allah, please bless
Muthu Meera Maraikayar with the above
My big brother's big brother
May he be blessed with all the above
Even beyond his hundred years

(16.5.2006)

When I was singing on the mic, Kalam was giving milk to one of his brother's granddaughters from a feeding bottle. He spoke with my mother-in-law and asked her to eat well.

As I narrate all these incidents, I feel like they are all happening right now. There are a few pictures of the celebration.

Kalam's happiness only lasted for a few days. He had to take one of the major decisions as the Indian President. This was something that was also a part of an earlier discussion. Officially, it is known as *'The Parliament (Prevention of Disqualification) Act, 1959'* that later on became a bill—*'The Parliament (Prevention of Disqualification Amendment) Bill, 2006'*. Several legal terms and our constitutional procedures need to be explained in detail to get a clear understanding of this bill. It can be looked up on Google. Various supporting and opposing views can be seen there.

It was about an important law to which a 'political colour' was given so that the truth would never be revealed. There was a lot of confusion.

In brief, as per the Indian Constitution, the members of the Parliament cannot hold positions in the central government or state government that yield profit (*Office of Profit*). If so, then they must be disqualified from their Parliament membership.

How could the Parliament decide that the members should hold no position? Therefore, using this small door as their chance, many such positions were exempted by the state governments and got them passed through the Parliament.

Those who have read the earlier sections of this book would recall that this was the reason why we insisted that Kalam must resign from his Anna University professor job. There was an uncertainty about what all must be considered as 'profit-making jobs'.

We wanted to ensure that Kalam did not face any problems on account of this confusion.

Since actress Jayapradha was holding a position in the UPA, a request was made to the election commission to disqualify her. The same thing could happen to others too. Major leaders like Sonia Gandhi, and the Marxist party leader Somnath Chatterjee were also there.

Therefore, the UPA government urgently amended the bill in 2006 and passed it in the Lok Sabha. The bill was then sent to President Kalam on May 25, 2006 for his assent. The bill was subject to examination. Eminent lawyers like Fali Norman suggested that the President should not sign the bill.

After reading many excerpts, Kalam sought opinions from many legal luminaries. He spoke with some of them privately. He also asked me. "Rajan, look here! Similar posts in two different states, but one is qualified whereas the other is not! Since many major political leaders could be affected, I am being pressured to give my assent immediately! What am I supposed to do now?"

He was correct. It was clear that the ruling governments were trying to change the rules at different times to suit their needs in those times. This amendment was one such.

"You are correct, sir! There is only one way out. To decide which are all qualified, you must make a list of all similar jobs. Let the central and state governments use the same list to decide. Then, no more changes need to be made any further," I said. He showed me a file in which many legal luminaries had advised that he should return the file to the government asking them to reconsider. They had quoted certain legal section numbers on which to reconsider.

"What do you think?" Kalam asked me. I asked him: "What are those numbers? What is their legal implication? Do you have any idea?"

"I read through them. Some of them can cause confusion. As far as I am concerned, let them do it for suiting any political leader; no issues. But it should be commonly applicable throughout the country. It should be transparent and in a generic manner. Only then will it be fair to all and a transparent process. It must be a single bill that applies equally well to the ruling and the opposition parties both in the Centre and in all the states."

"What you say is absolutely right! Write them down as small paragraphs in English. They might return the file with a statement that they have already looked into all that. If they do so then as per our Constitution, once amended, the Indian President has to sign for the bill to pass. You will also get some peace of mind that you have performed your duty well. It will also be saved in the archives properly!" I said.

I left from there. I heard that Kalam did as I said. I did not see the file since I am not supposed to see it.

They knew that Kalam would have learnt his lesson from the Bihar incident. However, they never expected him to give very clear references.

The details can be googled. I heard that he sent it to the Lok Sabha Speaker and the Rajya Sabha Chairman instead of sending it to the Prime Minister. All these are also mentioned in the website.

As expected, the Lok Sabha and the Rajya Sabha members made a few corrections, passed the bill and sent it back to Kalam for attestation.

Kalam did not mention all these details to me. Besides, I was not interested to know such details. I never asked him either since it was an important government secret.

The *'Midday'* newspaper published something funny about this incident. Someone gave a copy of it to me. To the question asked by the reporter: "Why is this bill taking so long to pass?" Apparently the President's secretary had replied: "This delay is not caused by the President's office. A bearded scientist who worked with the President on the 2020 projects is giving his advice to the President." I do not know whether he actually said these words. I was not interested. This was in the news. Kalam would have also noticed it.

Yet another funny incident happened on August 15, 2006 Independence Day celebration in the *Rashtrapati Bhavan*. Even now I laugh as I think of it. I have written about this yearly celebration earlier in this book. Along with the PM's first secretary T. K. A. Nair and the *National Security Adviser* Narayanan ran towards me.

I knew T. K. A. Nair earlier when he was working in the environmental department as the additional secretary (1994). We had been together in Beijing, China for official purposes for a few days. I have also seen him several times in Delhi in connection with my official work. I also knew Narayanan well since I used to attend meetings related to security.

"Rajan, we wanted to meet you personally and speak a lot of things. Do you have your card?" Both of them asked me at the same time.

"Sir, I have left Punjab and am currently working for CII, Delhi as the principal adviser. I had even written a letter to you. I even sent one to the PM's office," I said. I did not ask them why they wished to meet me personally. Both of them were in charge of many secret operations for our country. Just because they were my friends, it wouldn't look nice if I asked them here in the midst of so many strangers.

"Please give us your visiting card and cell phone number. We will call you either tomorrow or some day later." They both took my card and left. I was confused. Why would they want to meet me? Suddenly a thought flashed. The *Rashtrapati Bhavan* higher officials must have told them that I was only advising the President about the *Prevention of Disqualification Amendment Bill*. Kalam wouldn't keep the amended version with him for a long time since he had no use for it. He did not like to delay any proceedings. Kalam must have signed it. I never heard from both of them after that. They must have known that Kalam agreed to sign!

It was very hilarious. When I mentioned this to Kalam after a few days, he had a hearty laugh.

Many eminent Indian lawyers applauded the way in which Kalam handled this bill. They were surprised to see how someone who had worked in the science field till his age of 70, handled a bill with so many legal implications elegantly. This served as Kalam's fitting answer to the Bihar incident in which he had to act in a hurry.

A press reporter was repeatedly asking me a question when Kalam's name was proposed for the Presidential candidacy. He had asked me: "Sir, Kalam is an eminent scientist. He has performed his duties well in the field of science. However, how will he handle the post of a President with no experience in politics and law?"

I replied: "Superficially, what you said could be true. Does that mean that only a lawyer can become the *Indian President*? A President consults many people from many fields. We should only look at the following qualifications: Is he being just? Is he being partial? Is he open to receiving the opinions of others? Is he able to make his own judgement?"

"Kalam will perform exceptionally well in all of these. He had handled extremely tough jobs in ISRO and the DRDO and gained experience from them. It is not only about technical designing!"

"Kalam has the quality to learn from a new environment swiftly! Please wait and watch!"

I do not remember the name of the press reporter who asked me this question. But now I wanted to ask him how he felt! I was happy to see that my statement had come true!

❑

Political Games in Nalanda

Earlier we had seen how the Bihar assembly was dissolved in a hurry and fresh elections were held. In the election, the BJP coalition won with an absolute majority. Probably the people were not happy with the way in which the UPA government acted hurriedly to dissolve the state assembly. BJP announced Nitish Kumar as the Chief Minister of Bihar. Nitish Kumar wanted to bring several new developments to Bihar. One of them was to establish a new Nalanda University next to the old one, in the memory of the old one. He also wanted to establish a tech park with several IT companies next to it. He handed over the responsibility for doing this to the Principal Secretary, Education and Commissioner of Education Dr. M. M. Jha. He asked me to talk to him. I informed this to President Kalam who felt extremely happy to hear the news.

"Earlier we started this initiative when we were working in the PSA office. But it stopped abruptly! At least now, you must finish it, sir. The Bihar CM is a great man," Kalam said.

M. M. Jha and I met the Bihar CM several times. We created an excellent project proposal which extended to the national level.

CM (Nitish Kumar) said: "Ultimately, this university will come under the central government only. I have already spoken with the central ministers. But, if we send the proposal to them right now, it might take another 5-6 years. Therefore, I will pass this proposal through the Bihar state assembly and establish Nalanda University. There are also several lands under the control of the government in Nalanda and Rajgir. You take a look and let me know where to build the university."

"Also, we would like to invite Kalam sir as a lifetime Visitor of the university. Prepare your draft accordingly," he said. M. M. Jha was extremely sincere in his work. I have had the opportunity to work with him since 1998 for a lot of projects. He discussed with many state and central legal department officials to confirm whether President Kalam could be made the Visitor of the state university and obtained their opinions. They all said that it was possible but there are a few protocols to be followed.

Therefore, Nitish Kumar included this too in the bill along with the project proposal for construction and submitted it to President Kalam for acceptance. Me and M. M. Jha accompanied him. He explained the details of the proposal clearly to the President. He said that vacant land was available for construction and that all legal permissions have been obtained. He requested President Kalam: "You should be the first Visitor! Also, you should be a lifetime visitor!" Nitish Kumar said to President Kalam. He showed that portion in the draft bill. Kalam said: "I grant my approval wholeheartedly. Instead of making me a lifetime visitor, just mention 5 or 6 years. We will see later."

We then discussed developmental projects in Bihar. Then we returned.

M. M. Jha and I visited Bihar and selected the priority spots for building construction. Nitish Kumar told us: "I won't mention any place. Whatever is in your priority list, let that be the site for constructing the new Nalanda building."

He wanted us to start immediately.

"Rajan! You can ask M. M. Jha to appoint you in whatever post you require. It could even be made equivalent to that of a cabinet minister! Besides erecting this campus, we must also initiate other activities. We must start small courses," Nitish Kumar told me.

I was not interested in taking up any post there. I was already working in CII as the principal adviser. I had an office. I even received a small honorarium. In order to complete the work related to the university in Bihar, they created a Nalanda University Board officially by making me the Chairman and the Chief secretary and Finance secretary and a few others as members, giving the Board the powers to take government decisions. They gave a small room in Delhi Bihar Bhawan also for this work.

We started our work. The most important one was to make a project report to seek aid from the Japanese government. By this time, a few Delhi officials wanted the Nalanda University job for themselves. Now when I think of it, I know for certain that it was a big conspiracy. M. M. Jha showed me the minutes of all they had discussed in their group meeting. They wanted the President's secretary to advise Kalam not to take up the role of Visitor.

President Kalam said to me: "Rajan! Please make changes to the Nalanda University bill; delete my name from the Visitors' list!"

I said: "But sir, you have already agreed to the CM. It will now go to the Bihar state assembly for approval! It is under final stages! We discussed with several attorney generals of the state and the centre before adding your name to the list. Now if we remove your name, it won't look nice." Kalam said: "Remove my name for now; after I complete my term as the Indian President, let's take a look at it once again. I am getting pressured by my people. Meanwhile, you continue to do your job."

I immediately spoke to M. M. Jha. We both went and saw the Bihar CM. Nitish Kumar was a practical person. "Alright! We will amend the bill accordingly," he said. We said: "Ok, sir! We will simply state that the first visitor will be appointed by the Bihar government. Then, you need not go again to the state assembly for further discussion."

The bill was passed successfully. Nalanda University started functioning. As per Nitish Kumar's request, we had mentioned in the bill that the authority will be passed to the centre from the state whenever they are ready for it.

The *External Affairs Ministry* created a 'Mentor Group' to guide this initiative. Representatives from Singapore, China, Japan and India (government people) were members of this mentor group. The main job of this group was to bring in ideas from all over the world, especially to raise funds.

They invited me as a special invitee. I was sending briefings to Kalam and the Bihar CM of the proceedings. The Mentor Group did not do what they were supposed to do. Several heart wrenching incidents happened. I think it would be better not to elaborate all that here.

Meanwhile, Kalam's term as the Indian President was about to come to an end.

Kalam told me: "Ask them to issue the order regarding the first visitor as soon as possible."

"We will do it, sir! Even if M. M. Jha started it today, it would take some time. First, it has to go through the Bihar cabinet," I said.

He was in a hurry. Dr. M. M. Jha got permission and the government order making Kalam to be the first visitor of the Nalanda University. The incidents that happened during the end of Kalam's term and immediately after he left the President's office will be described later.

I heard some very devastating news a few days later. Dr. M. M. Jha died a premature death. I recalled S. K. Sinha's death. S. K. Sinha headed the Vision 2020 Agro team. (Kalam always regarded him with great respect. He has helped villagers in places like Bihar through TIFAC). After his death, I lost my intimacy with TIFAC. Likewise, even though Kalam's name was announced as the Visitor, since Kalam did not prevent the formation of that 'mentor group', I realised based on my many years of administrative experience as to what would happen next. Had M. M. Jha been alive, we both would have at least worked out some ways out of the comlex problems that would be created. Once Kalam completes his term as the Indian President, he cannot accomplish anything merely as a Visitor! Yet, I was there in the Nalanda Board as per Nitish Kumar's advice. I attended the meetings conducted by the mentor group. I also went to Singapore, Japan, and America.

Soon after he was made Visitor, Kalam wanted to conduct a discussion about the university. He said he wanted to visit the land. Nitish Kumar was trying to delay due to the political situation in Bihar. However, since Kalam insisted, Nitish Kumar was forced to agree. He then told me: "Since Kalam sir wanted to come, let him come and see. I know that everything is happening smoothly for the Nalanda university. However, please arrange for a Board meeting before Kalam's arrival."

Kalam came there. When we approached the construction site, people started throwing stones at us. (Probably, the arrangement was made by the opposition parties.) We had gone there several times earlier. The CM had given lots of money as compensation to the land owners there. However, they knew that if they threw stones when Kalam was there, the news would be made public.

Later on, the CM told me: "Rajan sir, what to do now? Due to all these political constraints, please delay some jobs like erecting a wall, ground levelling and so on for another six months. I will inform you when to start later."

Then, the central government officials said that the mentor group members were ready with their proposal. They therefore asked the state government to hand it over to them. The Bihar CM happily agreed. Several months went by. The central government took over. As per the rules they framed, Kalam could no longer be the visitor!

The mentor group members appointed a Vice Chancellor through the Delhi high officials without informing Kalam. Long story! The mentor group members appointed themselves as the board of governors of the university. I left all this. Later one day, Kalam asked me when I had settled down in my Bengaluru house: "Rajan, they have sent me a file. They are pressuring me to accept their selection of the person for appointment as the Nalanda University Vice Chancellor."

"Have they also sent you any background papers and details of the selection procedure?" I asked Kalam.

"No," Kalam said. I requested his office and got the govt gazette notification of the new Nalanda University Act and got it by email. I compared it with the note they had sent seeking the approval of Kalam. I said: "You are the Visitor as per the law (from the new Act also, as they could not remove any one already appointed by the University earlier to be taken over by the Central government till their terms ended). If you do not approve it, then the appointment they made will be nullified. I don't understand how they were functioning all these months without making a legal appointment. If you sign it now out of their pressure, then it will be your responsibility. As long as you were the Indian President, when you were Visitor to several universities, you were protected since you were the President. But now it is not the case. Therefore, analyse the selection procedure very carefully before signing it."

Many other funny episodes happened after that. Without explaining the selection procedure, they visited Kalam and handed over many files. In order to get rid of all these, Kalam voluntarily left the Visitor's list. He sent his resignation. The relationship which began in 2000 came to an end in ten years.

❑

Refusal to Become as the President for a Second Term—The Background

An important incident happened in the beginning of 2007 (March). The *Indian Prime Minister* during that time was Dr. Manmohan Singh (UPA). The BJP under former PM, Vajpayee formed the opposition party. Vajpayee and a few representatives from BJP met Kalam. Only this much was mentioned in the newspapers. Later on, Kalam told me: "Rajan, Vajpayee sir came to see me. After talking for a while, he said while all other coalition parties were present, 'Kalam! All of us wish to support you for a second term as the Indian President. We will approach you soon after the elections in Uttar Pradesh are over.' I told him to consult with the current PM, Dr. Manmohan Singh about this."

I said immediately: "Sir, this is indeed good news. Why did you ask him to consult Dr. Manmohan Singh? This is not a government matter. It is related to the likes and dislikes of individual political parties. The BJP and its coalition made you the *Indian President* the first time. Now, they wish that you continued to remain as the President for another term. In case a majority of them win in the upcoming UP elections, then they could easily announce you as the Presidential candidate. It's all a play of numbers only!"

Kalam asked: "What should I do now?"

I told him: "Don't do anything now, sir. Just like Vajpayee, others too might approach you. Please do not utter a single word for now. Wait until election results of the UP election are announced in May 2007. We will decide after that."

Kalam too felt the same way. If not for the UP elections, the Presidential elections will also gain more importance in May only. Even during the earlier election when Kalam submitted his nomination, it was like that. More than 400 candidates will be selected from UP. They will then select the Rajya Sabha members. Kalam was not quite familiar with the UP leaders. When Mulayam Singh was the defence minister, Kalam was the secretary/chairperson of the DRDO. Kalam found it difficult since he couldn't speak Hindi. However, Mulayam Singh liked Kalam very much. President Kalam visited Mulayam Singh's constituency Etawah in UP. He conversed with the leaders from BJP, Congress and the southern states in English. He did not speak with Mayawati in UP. Therefore, it created a big rift. In case Mayawati's Bahujan Samajwadi party won in the UP elections, then the number of BJP candidates and their coalition in the assembly will be low. That could lead to problems in the next Presidential election. Kalam called me to the Rashtrapati Bhavan the night when UP election results were announced (May 2007). We walked in the Mughal garden for a while and sat down. We chatted a lot.

"You asked me to remain silent until May. What is your opinion now?" Kalam asked me.

I said to him: "The BJP and its coalition have won very few seats. The Bahujan Samaj Party (BSP) under Mayawati has won more than 200 seats in UP. Therefore, if only the BJP and its coalition support you for your next term, their count alone won't be enough. The UPA with Congress and their coalition won't support BJP's decision and so they will not nominate you for a second term. Even last time, they supported you since they had no other alternative. Back then, the BJP coalition and Chandra Babu Naidu supported you strongly. Therefore, you would have won even if Congress and its coalition did not support you at that time. Even when the left/communist party knew that they would lose, they announced another candidate's name during the previous Presidential election. However, now this is no longer the case. In case you had some contact with Mayawati, then this would be possible. However, we don't have the time for that anymore. Besides, since the BJP coalition opposed Mayawati in the recent UP elections, it is uncertain if she will support your nomination."

After speaking for a while, I told him one more thing: "Vajpayee is a very honest man. He has a special affinity towards you. He might probably inform you that they do not have enough numbers to support you for a second term."

Vajpayee informed Kalam just that after two days. "Please forgive us, Kalam! We do not have enough numbers to support you." Kalam told this to me.

Vajpayee did not want Kalam to succumb to any political games. In 2002, since he was very sure that Kalam would definitely win with the support of the BJP coalition, he nominated Kalam at the time. But now, it has gone beyond reach!

The UPA/Congress did not nominate any candidate for the Presidential election. Therefore, many names were being suggested. Kalam received many emails: "Kalam, please stand in the Presidential election for a second term. We want you!" But they did not have the eligibility to vote.

Meanwhile, Chandrababu Naidu (who withdrew from the BJP coalition in 2004) was trying to form a third front with Mulayam Singh. They had therefore suggested that the third front might nominate Kalam. They promised to Kalam: "If you give us your confirmation, then we will take care of the numbers!" Kalam asked them for surety of support.

He must have talked about it to many others. The news was in the press. He then invited the 'Kutchery' members for a discussion. It was his habit to discuss a topic with 4-5 people. Sometimes, he used this method to prepare a rough draft for his speeches. That is why it got the name 'Kutchery'. I have already mentioned this.

But now, he has called us to discuss a sensitive political matter. We might have to openly disclose our thoughts about a few political leaders and parties now in a blunt manner. Only then, we will be able to give a supporting reason for our explanation.

The talks were going on ups and downs. Those who were present there, said that if Kalam became the Indian President for a second term, the Vision 2020 initiatives, PURA and other welfare schemes could be completed successfully. There were also discussions that many youngsters liked Kalam and wanted him to become the President for a second time. It was also mentioned that several lakhs of emails supporting Kalam's nomination had come.

I was thinking of just one thing. "In case Kalam agrees to stand for a second term, would he get enough supporters to win?" I did not think so. The third front had no numbers.

Why would Congress or BJP support a candidate nominated by the third front who is opposing them?

"It is not about winning or losing. If he gets majority supporters, Kalam could win; otherwise, he would lose! Will Kalam be able to bear a loss?" I conveyed my opinion thus.

The topic was swinging in different directions. Since Kalam had several email supporters, and since many big leaders (who were members of the Lok Sabha, not Rajya Sabha) supported Kalam, he should not say 'no' immediately and wait for at least a week. The kutchery group persons felt that the parliament and state assembly members might change their mind on account of pressure from youngsters. Therefore, Kalam asked the leaders of the third front to see him after a week.

The email supporters were not willing to come out to the roads during that hot May month and insist they needed Kalam.

The people have no role to play in the Indian Presidential election. Only the MPs (Member of Parliament) and MLAs (Member of Legislative Assembly) elected by them decide the results.[5] Even these elected candidates cannot vote according to their conscience. They have to obey the instructions of their party whip while voting. Otherwise they might lose their Lok Sabha/Rajya Sabha seat! They therefore cannot vote for whoever they liked. As per the *Anti-Defection Law*, they have to abide by the rules of their party, failing which they could be expelled from their party!

Mocking all these, I wrote a poem:

Presidential elections

Caged parrots which
Take out the astrology cards
Fearing the house owner crows
Handed the cards to be selected
To the crows for them to handle
The caged parrots forgot what they learnt
And recited japa of the crows instead

(19-7-2007)

Only very few people understand the legal framework of Indian democracy! Very few people know that the party leaders are like dictators! This dictatorship begins right from the moment they are to be given an opportunity to stand in the election. They become caged parrots after their victory. Some might say, 'why not stand as an independent candidate?' But how many independent candidates have been chosen by the people? Can they become ministers?

If the Lok Sabha/Rajya Sabha members are allowed to vote as per their conscience, then people like Kalam could easily win even without any support from the party leaders.

As per the current tradition, without the support of party leaders, no one can win against a party with a clear majority. Kalam had to encounter such a situation. He called us to the kutchery after a week. He too had gathered a lot of information in that week.

This uncertainty was not only for Kalam, but also for others. Congress did not nominate any big leaders. Besides, Bhairon Singh Shekhawat who was the Vice President at the time was also interested in getting nominated as a Presidential candidate. "If the BJP coalition is not nominating Kalam's name, then make me as the nominee. Besides your support, I can bring in more supporters," he said. He was not scared of losing since he was a diehard politician.

---

[5]*The President of India is elected by the members of an electoral college consisting of the elected members of both the Houses of Parliament viz. Lok Sabha and Rajya Sabha, and the elected members of the Legislative Assemblies of States and the Union Territories of Delhi and Pondicherry using the proportional representation method by secret ballot.*

However, Shekhawat had a problem. If Kalam contested, then Shekhawat did not want to contest against him. He informed Kalam of this. Therefore, Kalam's delay in making an announcement was impacting his decision as well.

Kalam said: "In a short while from now, Mulayam Singh, Chandrababu Naidu and Jayalalitha will be here. I need to convey my decision to them. Without beating about the bush, tell me whether I should accept or not?"

He asked everyone to give their reply one at a time. He also said that I should give my opinion in the end.

Even though Kalam said that he was in a hurry, some of them debated over the issue. Finally, they all advised him to accept.

It was now my turn. "Sir, since it was felt that some change would happen within a week, we all waited for a week. With the passing of every single day, your reputation will go down. There is a huge difference in numbers. You therefore must thank them for their kindness and reject their offer for nomination."

Usually during these kutchery meetings, Kalam would state his opinion in the end. He ended with, "Let me do this? Am I correct?"

But on that day, Kalam did not say anything. All he said was: "They will be waiting downstairs. Please stay here till I come back!"

After a few minutes, he returned and said: "Everyone insisted, however, I rejected it!".. He felt relieved. The people over there were disappointed. I think this happened in the second or third week of June. As per the internet, it was on June 20, 2007. There is a record which says that Kalam said "No!" to the offer.

❑

No. 10, Rajaji Marg House

Due to the confusion of contesting a second term, Kalam had not yet decided what to do after July 24, 2007. Especially, he had not decided where to stay. It was the duty of the Indian government to give security to a Presidential candidate for a lifetime. They cannot be left in isolation! He/she should be carefully guarded with enough security personnel all around his/her house. Police personnel must be present with him/her 24×7 and they need to accompany him/her when he goes out of the house.

There are big government houses meant for this purpose alone in Lutyens' Delhi.

However, Kalam wanted to move out of Delhi. He said, "Let me go to Anna University." Sometimes he said, "Let me go to my Bengaluru apartment." When he was the PSA, he had taken me once to visit the place. He had discussed how to bring it into action mode along with others.

I raised major objections to both of these options:

"Sir, your Bengaluru house is in an apartment building. Because of your presence, all others over there will get disturbed. They could evacuate the neighbouring apartments due to security reasons. When you go up and down the building, they would be forced to stop the elevator. Therefore, after your tenure as the Indian President, you can no longer stay in the Bengaluru apartment," I said.

"There is a different kind of problem if you stay in Anna University. They could erect a building to give you suitable protection probably. However, let us remember that Anna University is a state govt university. The state government could interfere and create confusion; maybe in some years. They may not be able to throw you out but may give other troubles. Besides, one more important reason is that if you go there, then you may be tied up in Tamil Nadu forever. You can go to schools, colleges and inauguration ceremonies daily... and you can be happy talking in Tamil."

"However, you are now a national icon; an international figure too. It won't be good if you disappear in Chennai. You must therefore stay in Delhi. Hunt for a house in Delhi to stay permanently. In case you wish, you could also stay in other regions of India for a few days. The government can make some temporary accommodation and also give you security. For example, you could stay in Raj Bhavan, Circuit House and so on. You cannot make a compromise in this matter." I said.

Kalam refused to accept this for many days. He said he was not interested in staying in Delhi.

Finally, I fired a Brahmastra: "Sir! Just remember that so far you have been shuttling from one guest house to another. The house which the government will be allotting you this time is going to be for your lifetime. It would be best if you selected something while you are still the President. Later on, it will be difficult to change it. In Delhi, they don't worry about the person who has left his (govt) position!"

I left. Two days later, Sheridon called me: "Sir, he asked you to come immediately!" It was in July 2007. Two weeks were left for Kalam to leave his office.

I hurried to meet him. He sent three men with me. Each of them had different ideas. It was extremely hot in Delhi; since it had rained a few days before, there was some additional humidity. We came back to him after seeing the houses earmarked for allotment for Kalam by the ministry of urban development. Kalam mentioned his likes/dislikes to us. He said that he wanted to live upstairs on the first floor. He also mentioned his other requirements to us.

Finally, we came back to him. He asked to speak one at a time. When it was my turn, I said: "Sir, as suggested by everyone here. You must choose No. 10, Rajaji Marg. The two secretaries of the central ministry who are there will get a better place, since they do not live alone there..."

Kalam said: "So, all of you are suggesting the same place!"

Kalam loved to indulge the 'Kutchery' in debates. However, he did not have enough time to do it now. He must get a place before his term is over. Since I knew Kalam's method well, I made them discuss each and every place earlier before coming to Kalam. Everyone agreed to No. 10, Rajaji Marg!

Kalam was allotted the house. Until he could go there, we had to look for a house in Delhi where he could stay temporarily. The military allotted a special guest house for their commander-in-chief. I heard later that they renamed it as 'Kalam guest house'.

After making necessary arrangements for Kalam's stay, I breathed a sigh of relief. We selected a beautiful house for him to stay in after retirement. There is an open grassland at the front where he could deliver his speeches. Many vehicles could be parked inside. Many big shots who wanted to see him could come in Mercedes Benz, BMW and other expensive cars. Even Children's buses could be parked there. He will receive 24×7 security protection. His security guards were allotted separate rooms to stay. The security guard stayed near the entrance. The houses of the security officers were on either side of his house. The whole place was completely protected. As per Kalam's preference, his house was on the first floor which was massive. It had a big hall with wall shelves to keep his books. There were separate bedrooms where his family members could stay. He could have his office room downstairs so that he and his family members could get some privacy.

However, the maintenance work was still pending. Maintenance was usually done when one left and another came in. Now, Kalam had the opportunity to design the house as he wished.

Till that time, Kalam could stay safely with military protection for another 3-4 months in their guest house.

Now, his office staff must keep his things ready for shifting. They had to separate Kalam's books, his writings and other documents carefully. They had to prepare a list of other office formalities before that.

It must have been a tough phase for Kalam. Besides our usual phone conversation, I did not visit him at the Rashtrapati Bhavan at that time.

The new *Indian President,* Smt. Pratibha Patil took over the responsibilities from the ex-President Dr. Kalam on July 25, 2007. July 25, 2002, the day when Kalam became the Indian President was a very special day to all of us. 100 days earlier, I started working tirelessly to help him, literally flying with my foot fingers. He stayed in office for five years. During his term as the President, Kalam had to encounter several happy moments and those causing mental pressures. But overall, it was a great experience for him.

After his tenure for five years, Kalam was upset over a totally different issue. I also felt it was one with a difference. Like everyone else, Kalam also expected a few things. Conventionally, none of the earlier Indian Presidents were given an opportunity to run for a second term. It was considered as the final rule. For those in public life for a very long period it was the highest office (to aspire for). There were many eligible candidates all across the political spectrum. My only interest was that Kalam, who has earned the trust of the common people and has attracted them due to his good intentions and love towards them, should make use of them (trust and charisma) along with clear practical administrative methods, to bring about changes to be beneficial to the Indian people. After giving such a shape, it should be such as to be self-perpetuating and be permanent in their lives.

From 2005 onwards, Kalam kept talking about this. Within the first two years of his Presidency, he visited all Indian states. He visited several rural areas, small towns, places of common citizens, spiritual places, and so on... He went everywhere, spoke extensively, heard their complaints and did his best. All his speeches have been archived in the *Rashtrapati Bhavan* website on the same day. There were email conversations too. When Vajpayee was the *Prime Minister*, he spoke of the *Vision 2020* initiatives directly with him. They made a big announcement for the PURA project. However, they were employing the usual government official practices and instead of doing it as it was conceptualised in the PURA proposals, they were spreading thin in many rural areas (like mixing asafoetida to sea water). It was more like their earlier practice of allocation of paltry funds to rural areas.

Kalam also therefore would have thought as to what he can do something concrete.. When we met during our 'kutchery' meetings to make drafts for his speeches, he would tell us: "Aren't we grinding the same flour again and again? Shall we do something new this time?". However, it became a practice that all that was done was to rephrase what was spoken before and prepare a fresh speech. Everyone spoke about *Vision 2020*; they spoke in different ways. But no one bothered to look at what was said in Kalam's book! Without caring about 'What was told about methods of implementing them ?', they made whatever they had in their mind as pet projects to be a part of the *Vision 2020* initiative! Reflection of their old thoughts glamorously (as *Vision 2020* projects) became their main intention!

When I heard about these, I was really upset. When I was talking to him one day, I wrote a poem which still echoes within me:

2020

2020 has become a mantra!
Childish sweet talks of parrots!
With a heart devoid of any feelings or emotions
Talks about destroying poverty were like glittering coatings!
Only a few know that it is a clarion call
To give Indians knowledge and work skills
To take actions duly discerned
To win around the world!
Like a powerless good Veena
Will they too get spoiled and perish?
Oh! Dear Mother of India! Where are you?

Do you need a mantra? Don't you want your children
To rise up in the world
And enjoy many pleasures and prosper
With many skills in machinery, farming,
Services, trade and many arts?
Don't you know the way
To change with speed their state?
Or don't you have the mind ?
To change their state?

13-01-2005

(The reference to the good Veena....is a derivative of a great poem by Bharati praying to Sakti Mother to give him strength etc. It starts with Nallathor VeeNai cheithe.....).

I always sent him copies of all my poems. I sent this one too. After seeing it, he too must have felt that some changes need to be done. That was why he kept repeating his 'grinding the same already ground flour' statement in our Kutchery sessions repeatedly.

I wanted to talk about it after he shifted to his new house in Delhi. I therefore mentioned nothing before July 25, 2007.

I did not want to go to the Swearing in Ceremony on July 25, 2007. Kalam's responsibility will be handed over to the new President within a fraction of a second. After that, only the new candidate will be allowed to deliver the speech. I therefore decided to meet Kalam after the event. When I spoke to him about this, two days before 25 July 2007, he said he would be going to Anna University on the afternoon of the swearing in ceremony.

"Sir! Why are you doing this? Why this urgency? You could go there on the next day! Others could think that you are trying to run away. Besides, why do you want to stay in the Anna University guest house? You could stay in the government's Raj Bhavan instead," I said.

He did not reply properly. "I decided already," he said. I did not pressurise him any further.

The newly elected President decided to delay the event by a few hours; Kalam had to postpone his flight trip to Chennai until evening. Sheridon took care of rescheduling the flight arrangements. Kalam reached Anna University guest house on the same day. I did not know what security arrangements they had made there for the former Indian President.

I must be thankful to God for a few incidents which happened on that day. Since there was a complete power outage that day inside the Anna University campus, Kalam was forced to stay in Raj Bhavan. I did not know this from Kalam, but from others. I asked him about it during a later discussion.

He was embarrassed to answer me. He just said nothing like that happened. However, after that day, whenever he visited the state capitals, Kalam always stayed in Raj Bhavan. I am thankful to God for that!

Unknowingly, they had arranged an event for Kalam outside Delhi on August 15, 2007 when he had to be present in the new President's party that night.

"Sir, will you be attending the Independence day event on August 15th in the Rashtrapati Bhavan?" I asked him.

"I have agreed to attend an outside event that day!" he said.

"But sir, it won't look nice. People will talk behind your back about your absence," I said.

After a few moments of discussion, he said: "I will meet the new President privately." I said: "Sir, that is fine. However, when she has invited you for a public event, you must go there!"

Maybe he was worried that people might ask him about his response to a second term of Presidency. It took some time for Kalam to settle down to his new lifestyle. He later became his usual self. He visited many places during those months. He also decided to travel abroad. Many companies wished to give him honorary posts. He agreed to a few.

One day, he called me and said: "Rajan, I have agreed to accept these honorary posts. Please take a look at the list!"

I made a note beside many of them.

"Sir! You are no longer Kalam. You are the ex-Indian President now, and a representative of the States and the Republic of India! It won't look nice if you accept a post, even if it is an honorary post, in all these institutions. You can deliver your lectures, and inaugurate a few events. However, do not get involved with them!" I said. Then there were some problems in a few of them. We requested Kalam to resign.

The government did not pay for foreign trips of former Presidents. Within India, they were allowed to travel freely. Since the government won't fund their foreign trips, people who invited them abroad only can pay for their trip. Even then, the former Presidents must get formal permission from the central government to travel abroad. This is because their protection is the government's responsibility wherever they go.

Kalam decided to go on a foreign trip in 2007 itself. He asked me.

"Sir, what can I suggest? You are going there as the former Indian President. Besides, you are also a 'Bharat Ratna'. Who invited you? What topic have they asked you to speak on? Is it relevant to your personal and professional qualification? You must decide for yourself based on these questions," I said.

"Why are you talking like this?" Kalam asked.

"I cannot speak beyond this sir!," I said.

A few days later, during our phone conversation, he told me:

"Sir! Are you a voice recorder? Your friend Mr. Shivraj Patil was here. They had written about my foreign trip to the government to get their consent/ advice. He is a great man. He came and met me personally and said, 'Sir, you are now in an extraordinary position both at the personal and the professional level. What could I possibly suggest? Wherever you go, just think whether the event is suitable to your high stature. We would grant approval to whichever place you want to visit.' These were the exact words used by you!" Kalam finished.

I do not know whether all his foreign trips satisfied these conditions. I do not know whether programmes were conducted keeping Kalam's good qualities in mind. I was not with him. Only one or two people could travel with him. The people who invited him won't have funds beyond that. When Kalam was the Indian President, he was given a separate Air India flight. He had a separate room and a dining table where we all dined with him. He also had a private bedroom!

After he retired as the President, Kalam had to travel like everyone else. I wasn't sure whether people who arranged his foreign trips looked at his stature? Many might have used him to uplift their own personal status. Some of his trips within India were like that.

Kalam never lost his individuality and kindness in spite of all these. Once when he went to America, he had to go to a place near my elder son Vijay's house. Kalam felt excited to meet Vijay and his wife Mahalakshmi. He told them that he would come to their house for lunch. He even gave them a detailed list to prepare. After having lunch, he said to them, "Now I need to get some good sleep after this sumptuous meal!" He rested a while and took them along with him to attend the event.

Likewise, when we permanently shifted from Delhi to our own house in Bengaluru, Kalam said: "I would like to visit you there."

"Sir, we have not yet furnished the house," I said. "No, I will definitely come there," Kalam said. Due to Kalam's visit our entire street was crowded with people. The police found it very difficult to control the crowd. From then onwards, we received special attention in our colony!

After inspecting our house, Kalam said to my wife, "Komamma! Your house looks auspicious (Lahshmikaram is the word he used in Tamil)!" He was glad that we had settled down in a good place.

I had requested him to bring two plants. "For your memory, sir," I told him. Kalam brought a special hybrid lemon plant. I planted it the next day. It yields very good lemons every year. When Kalam visited us at the time of my father's death, I showed it to him. He was surprised. He took it in his hand and inspected it. Meanwhile, a crowd had gathered there. He asked me: "Rajan, what did you do to get such big lemons! In my place, we only get smaller ones!"

"That is my secret, sir!" I told him. Now, everyone around my house has named it 'Kalam lemons'.

Six months after July 2007, Kalam had invited some of our 'kutchery' members and a few from the Rashtrapati Bhavan to his No. 10, Rajaji Marg house. Chairs were put on the grass at the front of his house. We were all seated around.

He said: "Today we are going to discuss only one topic. Should I continue to do what I was doing all these years, or should I make any changes to my approach? If so, what change must that be?"

Kalam had informed me before of this. I therefore had given it considerable thought. Kalam had crossed his 75. Even though his mind was strong, his body wouldn't cooperate. However, his charm and charisma remained as such. In fact, they were even better than before. We must therefore use its full potential and bring about some enormous social changes. An institution must be formed which would develop well when he reaches 80. He can then hand over the responsibility to some knowledgeable person and offer his guidance and some training to the person and slowly relieve himself of its duties, just being only a supporter. However, the goal of his new initiative must be such as to effect changes across all generations.

I have spoken a lot over the phone about this to him. I have also spoken to him personally. He will make the idea as a part of his speech.

"Sir! Didn't you hear my speech that day? I have spoken what you said, sir!" Kalam said to me.

My reply: "You will speak nicely on the stage, sir! But who will take up the initiative? You must only take up one or two of those and do them. If you yourself won't get involved, who else would? You can establish two or three like Ford Foundation, Tata Trusts, Ramakrishna Mission and so on." I have told him this several times.

I therefore had some clear ideas about a few big plans which would suit him very well and the ways of initiating them. However, since it was an important meeting, and since there were 8-10 people around us, I felt that things might get drawn in different directions and get lost in the course of our discussions. I prepared a detailed list of all my plans for him. Even today, I have it with me. I made a copy of it so that I could hand it over to Kalam whenever he asked me.

Everyone suggested something or the other. The discussion and debate happened for nearly three hours. There were questions, cross questions; changes to some proposed plans. When he asked me to speak, I took out my list and read them one by one. I also explained as to which I liked and the reasons. I insisted on one thing: "Sir! Going forward, you need to focus your attention entirely on only one or two initiatives. You must act tirelessly to develop them into big ones and you should only concentrate on that path.. Only then will a big transformation happen."

Finally, Kalam stood up and summed everything up:

"Everyone here has suggested that I must choose only one or two initiatives and focus entirely upon them. Since there are several topics in that list, I have to carefully choose from them. Thank you everyone! You have all been very kind to me!"

I don't think he did anything after that. He was visiting several places and delivering speeches as before. Most people who invited him simply made use of his visit for their personal benefits. Whether they all deserved him, was a debatable issue. They would take a picture of themselves with Kalam and use it to further their own personal agenda to benefit their organisation and also make money for themselves. I later heard that some bad men also infiltrated into this process.I heard it from my other friends who felt worried about this. They were people who were concerned about the good for Kalam. They urged me to talk to Kalam. However, I did not have the facilities to examine and assess such cases and then inform Kalam. Even when he was the President, I have heard a few like this. I would respond to whoever conveyed the message: "Sir! You too are his friend only! Please go and tell him directly!" Besides, I felt that such bad men cannot hurt Kalam while he was still the President.

However, now that Kalam is all alone, he could get hurt on account of such bad influence. Occasionally, without mentioning any names, I conveyed only my message to Kalam: "Sir, please be careful on these matters! Those without a blemish get hurt the most! Even a single black mark would look enormously ugly! Please be cautious! They will let go of you once their job gets done!" I had warned him several times.

Many private companies approached him to write a good piece supporting them. Thinking that he could propagate a few good thoughts, Kalam also agreed. All this happened through the people whom he trusted! Those private companies were actually held up in a few legal proceedings involving the government. Kalam's picture tagged along with their company name would serve as a protective shield to them!

Kalam wanted some progressive changes to happen in India. He supported a few impossible theories to this effect. This surprised (and made him the laughing stock for) a few experts. A few examples: The way he insisted that earthquakes could be detected a few days before occurrence during and after his Iceland trip; he was keen in initialising this project. Next, he insisted that India's energy requirements could be fulfilled to a great extent from biodiesel produced from the Jatropha plant seeds. Likewise, he made some bizarre calculations and predictions on solar energy.

All these became a part of Kalam's populist speeches. One such speech of Kalam that became a subject of ridicule among NGOs was on the Kudankulam Nuclear Power Plant. This made atomic energy experts like Homi Sethna, comment against Kalam. Kalam's lectures on stem cells were also quite bizarre.

All these could be regarded as his mistakes. However, they did not tarnish his image. Actually, he was forced to talk on these by "famous" experts in the respective fields. It must be said here that in our country, the qualities and ethics of scientists, technologists, engineers and doctors are not upto the mark. When I complained about this to Kalam, he told me:

"Sir, you are commenting like this. These topics were given to me by these people (he then mentioned the names of a few experts)."

Then, I replied: "Sir, they are making use of their positions and are mentioning these in order to impress you. However, these are opposed to the truth!"

He was confused. "But those men are specialised experts in their field, whereas I am a general expert. They trust me to deliver their thoughts. But, why can't I accept something proposed by the head of such a big organisation?"

Therefore, some of his lectures and writings contained such few bizarre proposals and scientific errors.

The reason behind such errors was because Kalam wanted the Indians to think differently and innovate more and more new things. He did this out of his immense affection for them. Whenever he received such information, he failed to check for their correctness or otherwise.

Let me explain with an example. I have observed him closely right from his days as the defence minister's scientific adviser, then when he worked in the PSA office, until his final days...

"Fantastic!" Kalam said to some proposals. Naturally, the people who suggested the proposal would feel very happy and excited.

After observing many such similar incidents, I asked him once, "Sir, why are you saying 'Fantastic!' to even irrelevant matters?"

Kalam laughed and said: "Rajan, you do not understand why I say 'Fantastic!'. Check with the DRDO people about that."

I later understood that whenever Kalam said 'Fantastic!', it meant 'Cruel!', 'Horrible!', and so on! This was his treatment of statements made by some of the DRDO people. However, it would please those who suggested the proposal.

Such statements by Kalam only made the life of his secretaries H. Sheridon and R. K. Prasad very difficult! When Kalam was in the PSA office and later on when he became the Indian President, they were pressured. Those who proposed such projects even approached me at times and said, “We met Kalam. He greatly appreciated our work. He told us that we could meet him whenever we wanted. However, their office staff are telling us either that he is not in town or that we can’t see him! Why are they cheating us like this...” This is what happens to people serving under soft hearted leaders; they have to adjust!

However, Kalam’s kindness towards his employees would blow out their stress like a breeze.

For example, H. Sheridon who worked under Kalam as his private secretary, worked till the last days of Kalam’s life. Sheridon would like to share his experiences with Kalam here.

❑

A Life of Honour: Kalam's Private Secretary H. Sheridon Speaks...

A Noble Life

To many, it's just one year that has passed..... it feels like a decade to me. Withdrawing into a shell is not a choice once a dear person says goodbye. But it takes a lot of time to come to terms, live the dream and visions, advocate them and the hardest part is... to me... is talk or write about it because then it brings back every detail 'ALIVE' and 'REAL' which is more hurting actually. Any time is ripe for looking back and remembering the bedrock of a relationship or about a hero whose life and work spanned genres and generations and an impressive six decades.

I had known Dr. Kalam ever since 1991 and literally grew wise and old with him. The prime of my life began ever since he accepted me as an acquaintance. As any other friendship, I walked alongside him... the bonding and trust... mutual understanding only grew stronger. Today, if I feel sorry for myself which I shouldn't, then it's because I still need him to look upto, I go numb because am exhausted thinking if India's leadership would ever work on achieving greatness, to realise his visions and if I grope for the right words to describe him or my with him, words don't seem enough. The qualities I saw in him... by qualities I mean...qualities of a simple man minus a tag or designation, qualities of the most admired President, qualities of a beloved teacher, qualities of a passionate scientist.... yes qualities too many to note down, to admire, qualities that he showed us to follow... a legacy he left for us to emulate and grow.

Simple

To me he came as one who prized loyalty and honesty in his day-to-day associations, wherever he was and with whomever. This was known in many circles and this quality of his was what was called as 'GRACE' by almost all he knew. He never minced or mixed words. He just expressed himself with all honesty. A couple of years ago, when I sported a beard, he questioned me twice on why I needed one for which I had no good answer. His curiosity didn't surprise me because I almost always sported a clean shaven look, the best accessory for men to be taken seriously than the super intimidating look. Since I didn't take the cue from his questions, he simply said, "Remove it, I say" just as a father would say to a son who lost his marbles. The tone conveyed more than those four words I heard. He was just honest and frank... sometimes brutally frank... Throughout my association with him, I was entrusted with the tasks of planning his daily schedule that involved meetings, travels and lectures, thereby helping me believe that I too had an incredible amount of input into what I was moulded to be. The one quote that comes to my mind filled with gratitude is, "Trust men and they will be true to you; treat them greatly and they will show themselves great" (Ralph Waldo Emerson). I was trusted and treated with great regard. Thus, Dr. Kalam was a player of the game who valued his team as much as he valued Indians and his faith in God.

Motivator

Dr. Kalam was buckled down to whatever he did and motivated those with him to go the extra mile. Being with him as he penned his first book, INDIA 2020 : A Vision for the new millennium, was a moment of personal triumph and I felt privileged to share in his efforts. I understood he had an obligation to fulfil. His mission after all was to encourage future generations. As I typed every word he said in addition to sharing my thoughts and suggestions, he was forcing me to think as well because when I agreed on something I had to tell why and when I disagreed also I had to tell him why. Thinking hard became my forte only because I was fortunate to be with him, a seriousness of purpose. Then I was thinking for him, and yes or no should be supported by enough facts, credentials, reasoning and in rare cases with examples too. I mean, with him beside, nobody can pretend to navigate or bluff through conversations.

Clothed in Humility and Morality

Connecting with people was another zeal or regularity of Dr. Kalam, through his books and in person as well. Wherever he went, he never held back himself. Never had the slightest inhibition for he always took the initiative for a chat with people regardless of whom or what they are. Be it a pilot, a driver, a small child, a doctor, a nurse, a gardener, a guard or whoever comes face to face with him or he notices. A trait that won him millions of hearts. Many times Dr. Kalam himself chose to click pictures with people after an interaction, which came as a surprise to them... a pleasant surprise mostly to shy fans who yearn secretly for a picture. That is something VERY EXTRAORDINARY of a person of his stature. I guess we all know who made it to the Rashtrapati Bhavan for his swearing-in ceremony. His strength lay in treating others with morality and all the hearts of the people under the sky love him still. 24 years is a long lesson in humility. Still I have not got enough.

Dr. Kalam connected with people—young and experienced alike. Who other than Dr. Kalam could pull it off with charm and ease. The impression he left with every other visitor, both in and out of Rashtrapati Bhavan was a quiet, pondering sort of thought, one that echoes the sentiments of a personal fulfilment. The connection was immediate with no membranes of ego and fear in between. Around students he had a mixture of grandiosity, childlike excitement and curiosity—a recipe that led him to become the most popular President among children. With every opportunity, Dr. Kalam reclaimed his identity, clarified values and made memories with children and I was fortunate enough to take so many lessons on what love for humanity can achieve. During meetings with children, he could answer the very last question with utmost patience and enviable enthusiasm.

The endurance of Dr. Kalam's appeal is not simply the result of a crafted image but his integrity, personal charm, action and dynamism. If he is admired or adored to such an extent by the global community, then he precisely executed his varied, meaningful roles. The most amazing thing was—whatever be his belief or ideals, which are positive or beneficial to human growth—be they trans-humanism, humanism, rationalism, skepticism—he concluded with good morals as the law. Everything he did proceeded with thoughtful conviction and those convictions arose from an understanding of good. On a personal note, I don't exaggerate, I only remember BIG when I tell you that, many a time we not only shared defining moments, but also ideas about transcendental and non-transcendental matters. Our souls were always in close contact and I always found in him a warm and cosy spirit to rest and a bright mind to learn.

Personal Touch

The food I eat, looks, smells and tastes isn't the same anymore. We filled our plates and talked and laughed and ate. How he relished helping me eat what I liked and exactly wished to! Fond memories of Dr. Kalam, a strict vegetarian, doing his best to help me with non-vegetarian meals through Prasangam, when I joined him at Anna University, Chennai, for a two week stay after he was nominated as the Presidential candidate, still moves me to tears. He made sure any non-vegetarian giving him company should not be deprived of his/her favourite dishes which he christened as, 'funny stuff'. Refusing the 'funny stuff' would be nothing but a next-to-impossible task. The simple act of eating together was bigger than just food. In addition to some great discussions and lessons, there was this bonding that nourished my soul even as I joyfully lost myself in the sheer delight of tasty food. Winding up a meal with a few chunks of papaya was just his routine but this fruit stirs up emotions in me.

Oh what a wonderful feeling, what a sense of liberation, when he called me the 'Funny Guy' because that meant something to both of us. I was his 'Funny Guy' when I said a right thing at the right time, when I took a great lesson from him, when I willingly unlearnt stuff, when I differed with him and backed it up with a convincing and logical reason and especially when we were strengthened by the most perfect feeling a person can ever have bonding. He also gave me an image, as worthy as our friendship, with a title, "My Guy." Everyone in our circle knew what it meant.

Dear friends, we lose a part of ourselves when we lose a person, a dear one... even though their thoughts remain... their dreams propel us... the person we once were while being with our beloved is gone too.

A Poet

Dr. Kalam wrote poems for everyone to understand. At times he was the near-invisible observer and archivist of the unutterable mysteries that underlie everybody and it is visible in most poems penned by him. Morning walks with him at the Mughal gardens during his 'Beautiful and Eventful years' left me in awe of his capability to commune with nature. He created Herbal garden, tactile garden, spiritual garden and a bio-diversity park, when he was in Rashtrapati Bhavan. Reading his poems always slows time down, leading me to places where beauty meets eternity—a subtle and elusive combination. Since the 1990s, Dr. Kalam has moved into the imagination and fascination of many poets and writers.

He is celebrated by international poets. Poems of celebrated poet, Dr. Yu Hsi of Taiwan, celebrates Dr. Kalam's nobility and virtues by comparing them to nature and the galaxy in a unique way. Poet Yu Hsi's poems are flawless to the last detail in his sense of honour and integrity for Dr. Kalam. Every concept of his, captures at least a part of Dr. Kalam's truthful whole.

Developed India

Dr. Kalam gave utmost importance to the idea of *India 2020*—a great Indian mission. Beneath his kind smile and soulful eyes were great depths of wisdom and knowledge. He never displayed his grand oracular voice when he convinced students of the urgency of dreaming BIG. The books he wrote, the lectures he gave, the students he met before, during and after his presidency, the missions he initiated.... What more do we need to salute this great man for! He grasped the need for a vision, a change... he didn't stop with dreaming or talking about dreaming but his objectives he backed up with commitment, action and results. He just didn't lecture.... He was way too cautious about messages he conveyed.

The preparatory sessions we had were something so tiring... tiring to me and it was visible. So, Dr. Kalam would make us understand that visions are absolutely crucial for our growth.

Can we transform India! Probably, we as a nation intend to be good, clean, engaged and self-sufficient. We cannot solve problems single handedly. But, we as individuals can surely serve as a FULCRUM for change and a pivot point for peace. We should remember that peace is the foundation for any kind of change or transformation.

Symbol of Hope

Dr. Kalam is a powerful symbol of hopefulness. We as a nation will surely succeed in escaping the darkness that has engulfed us through the loss of this noble soul and we shall definitely carry his dream India forward with an indomitable spirit. For the ignited minds of our country, the successive years will be a series of milestones, changes and transformations. It takes a unique mind to inspire many in many interesting ways. Dr. Kalam did just that, much to the appreciation, admiration and adoration of his fans around the world. Hundreds and thousands of curious, excited eyes that followed him, people who lined up for his autograph and fans who clicked photos with him have their own stories to tell about a great man who was accessible, acknowledged love without fear or fuss and will take strength from his quotes and thoughts to dream big. Is there an iota of doubt that Dr. Kalam lived his life to uplift our country.

Dr. Kalam believed that politics could speak to society's moral yearnings. Dr. Kalam was a believer of children as saviours. Almost all his works retrace his ideas, his certain optimism that children on the right track would light up this world. Everything Dr. Kalam wrote and did is sufficient proof of this.

Dr. Kalam practised what he preached and that too boldly because he not only talked of himself or claimed himself to be a world citizen but believed it to be true, made others believe it and also accomplished his purpose as a world citizen. He opened his address at the golden jubilee of the European Union Parliament with poet Kaniyan Poongundranar quote "*yaadhum oorey yaavarum Kelir*'' which when translated to English goes like this, "To us all towns are one, all men our kin." He was such a force, in his own gentle way, through his ability to seamlessly interact across the various age-groups and other man-made barriers to make us feel as a part of one large family of the world, despite many differences and difficulties.

YES, he believed in goodness too. He believed that for every raindrop that fell, a flower bloomed, he believed that somewhere in the darkest night, a candle glowed, he believed that for someone who went astray... somebody came to show the way.

Spirit of India

Every experience I had with him, part of travelling to lectures across the world, just being around in a team, early morning walks, discussions and private talks all form an entire picture of my life. They are simply picture pieces if put together would create a beautiful bond called friendship. Both of us knew each other differently than anyone else. Just as I mentioned earlier, now one year after his passing away, I realise I can never be the one I was with him because I can't relive those memories with anybody else. A little more than two decades seem such a small time for me that I've got even more joys to discover, jokes to crack, meals to share and curious endless things to be discussed.

More determined than ever we find ourselves so absorbed in our conviction to celebrate Dr. Kalam's life, his easy spirit-a result of understanding himself leading to self-containment that set this great personality apart from every other being out in the world. Of all his redeeming qualities, including intelligence, ambition, work ethic, and spirited sense of humour, his kind heart and compassion made him stand out amongst the crowd. He never wanted the '*Bharat Ratna*' prefix to his name.... He wanted to be remembered as a good human being throughout the world. In fact, he deserved much more but his gentle nature and a strong sense of modesty did not allow him to chase awards and rewards but only dreams of a beautiful, empowered, self-sufficient India.

Our journey together has been eventful, with many ups and downs. A journey is better measured in friends, than miles.... It's more than true. As far as the multiple roles I adorned as Dr. Kalam's chosen friend, I am more than conscious of my responsibilities to uphold the ideals Dr. Kalam represents and shall strive to live the life he chose to live. I find no greater way to honour him. Do you not know that a person lives as long as his name and deeds are spoken of with hope, love, satisfaction, happiness and gratitude! He lives as long as we gather to work on his dreams and visions, he will live.

❑

Presidential Elections Once Again

It was time for Presidential elections once again in 2012. Unlike 2007, there were members from several small parties within the Lok Sabha and Rajya Sabha. It would therefore be difficult to predict the outcome this time. Elections are all about numbers! Neither me nor Kalam had any idea about the election results. This was because I left Delhi permanently in 2009. Only my second son Vikram lived there at the time. Kalam was not in touch with persons who had some knowledge of the various parties, what they thought etc. Some floated 'kites'.

Since many people were asking him to come back this time, Kalam asked for my opinion. In 2007, Kalam did not stand a chance due to shortage of numbers. He wanted to check if chances of his victory were higher this time.

We first had to count the number of representatives from each party in the Lok Sabha and the Rajya Sabha. My second son Vikram googled this information and we both worked on this together analysing different possibilities, to help Kalam.

Both of us were thinking, "Why is Kalam trying to participate this time?"

Unlike 2007, there were only three people around Kalam in 2012 in his office. Therefore, he couldn't engage in the usual 'kutchery' discussions like before. However, many people passed many different suggestions to Kalam.

Some suggested that he must deliver a big speech in case he decided not to participate. Some others opined that he must participate even though he feared losing and that he must deliver a speech about all his proposals to the public.

I had to go to Delhi for some official work. Kalam wanted to meet me then. After I finished my work, I went to his No. 10, Rajaji Marg house in Delhi. Normally, the place would be deserted. But on that day, it was crowded with press reporters. They allowed my car to enter inside. I was confused. I remember seeing a similar gathering around Kalam's place in 2002 when he participated in the Presidential elections for the first time.

I was also worried that someone from the press could comment on "the bearded man's" entry. I never expected such a huge crowd; neither did anyone from Kalam's office inform me of this earlier.

I went to see him in his room on the first floor.

Kalam looked very pale and tired. Two youngsters in his office were typing something furiously on their computers. Kalam conveyed the matter.

- Should he participate in the Presidential elections?
- What statements should he release in case he wishes to/wishes not to participate?

He said that he had compiled a list of everything and asked me to check and give my opinion.

Those items were read out loud to me. I listened silently. The intentions expressed therein were genuine. However, there were many complicated issues involved. He wanted to take part in the election due to the requests made by millions of Indians from many states of India. He wanted to stand in the election because he wished to create a movement to empower India by 2020.

Yet another report was prepared to convey that Kalam will not be participating in the upcoming elections. The report conveyed the message that many Indians wanted to see Indian empowerment within 2020... Even though Kalam will not be standing in the election, he will still run the Indian empowerment movement.

My opinion was short and clear: "Sir, even though these reports have been prepared with a good intention, they seem to convey the message that India could be empowered by 2020 only by you. Why should you become the Indian President for this? It would only lower your reputation. Besides, the numbers are against you. In case you do not wish to participate, then what is the necessity for a detailed report? You could merely announce your decision."

The two youngsters over there opposed my opinion about not making any big statements. Even Kalam seemed to be unconvinced. He cited a few reasons on why he should make them.

I too had to say this: "Sir, legally there are no restrictions for an ex-Indian President to enter into politics, create a new party, and participate in different elections. However, in the Presidential elections where the vote bank is dictated by various parties, your chances are quite low. They might misinterpret your participation. You could start your own party later. However, now your statement has to be crisp and clear."

Many youngsters who had worked hard to prepare these statements did not like my opinion.

I left after drinking my coffee. While I exited, I noticed that Sudhindra Kulkarni was entering inside. I knew him well. I didn't even wish him. Nor did I want to be with him. However, I quickly got into the car and left the place in my car. He entered Kalam's place.

Later, I heard that Kalam announced that he wouldn't participate.

I felt relieved. As far as the political parties were concerned, they were now free to announce their choice for the 13th Indian President.

❑

Fertile Field for Dreams—
An Epitome of Simplicity

Kalam became 81 years old. One of the best qualities of Kalam was that he knew how to come out of tough situations. He knew how to forget and forgive any unpleasant memories. Not once have I seen Kalam in a depressive mood. He continued to live like before.

His walks, travels, and conversation with friends continued as before. We both conversed over the phone like always.

The Penguin publishers wanted him to write a book, *'Beyond 2020'* as a continuation of our *'India 2020'*.

"Rajan! The *Penguin publishers* asked me. I have asked them to contact you. In case they contact you, please go ahead and start. We will discuss it in detail later," Kalam said to me.

I had to write so much at the time. The most important one was to write a monthly article for the '*Kisan World*' magazine as per the request of *Arutchelvar* Dr. N. Mahalingam. I had to do so much research work before writing each and every single article. It widened my intellectual horizons. The Penguin publishers never approached me.

A few months later, I told Kalam: "Sir, no one from *Penguin publishers* approached me. I think they only want to talk to you."

Kalam said: "It's ok if they don't call you. You have to start only if they ask."

An executive of *Penguin Publishers* contacted me in May 2014. He said: "You have to finish this quickly."

"Why are you telling this to me now? I thought that you lost your interest in this book after the elections," I said.

"No, no, this is very urgent now!" he said.

I started to write it with Kalam. We speeded up our work, made necessary corrections and it got published in October 2014. Kalam said he got a copy of the book on October 22, 2014.

Kalam was extremely pleased. He told this during our regular phone conversations several times: "Sir! We have finished a very important job!"

I told him: "Sir! That is your birthday present to our country."

He sent copies of the book to the *President*, *Prime Minister*, *Finance Minister* and so on.

Excerpts from the *President's* message to Kalam after reading the book:

"This book is an excellent continuation to your '*India 2020*' book. Many congratulations! Your book lays a strong foundation to prepare India to compete globally. You have pointed out the missed opportunities and delayed schemes. Now is the right time to use the latest techniques in the fields of agriculture, industrial manufacturing, education, health and infrastructure.

I felt happy to read the book. It could serve as a good reference manual to our experts and policymakers. My good wishes for your continued good health."

(December 3, 2014)

Excerpts from the *Prime Minister's* reply: "Your vision and initiatives boost the confidence of many people. This recently published book of yours will serve as the biggest asset to those who wish to empower and modernise India, thereby contributing to her prosperity."

(November 06, 2014)

Kalam mentioned these happily to me. He also sent me copies of their responses. He spoke frequently about it: "Sir, we finished it!"

This last book of Kalam was translated first into Tamil by Shri Sirpi Balasubramaniam and published by *Arutchelvar* N.Mahalingam Translation Institute. Sirpi had mentioned this to Kalam during the final stages of its translation. Kalam felt happy. However, Kalam did not live to see the Tamil edition.

No one could have even imagined that Kalam won't be there next October. He himself wouldn't have known. We wanted to celebrate Kalam's 85th birth anniversary in a grand manner.

My father passed away in my Bengaluru house on the night of December 7, 2014. He was born in April 1917. Kalam felt happy to know that my father and his brother were of the same age. Kalam has spoken with my father several times. I informed Kalam and all my relatives of his death.

Even though Kalam had other plans on that day, he said: "Rajan, I will come to your Bengaluru house."

He felt that he should be with me and Koma at that time.

"Sir, we would be completing the cremation on December 8 itself. There will be several rituals to be followed after that. I do not have a problem with you coming to my house. However, everyone in the vicinity might want to meet you. The streets would become crowded as before. They will also feel uncomfortable entering the house of a dead person. Besides, we are not supposed to welcome anybody, including you! I think it would be better if you come here on day 13. That is the day when we will be allowed to receive visitors and offer them a feast. Even though I am not a firm believer of all these rituals, it would be better to satisfy the beliefs of others. If you come on the 13th day, everyone could meet you and have some sweets. See if this is possible..."

Kalam knew of all these rituals already. He therefore came to our house on December 19, 2014. He wanted to spend some time with us. We therefore had asked only a few friends to come to our house. However, the local politicians and other members of the municipality also entered. There was a huge crowd outside. Kalam showered flowers on my father's picture and spoke with my wife Koma. All others were standing around him. He ate after that.

I wanted to show him something. I said: "Sir! You must see something before leaving!"

He asked me about it before leaving.

There was a huge lemon on the plant he gifted us. It was inside our compound wall.

He held it in his hand and was wonderstruck.

"Rajan! What did you do? In my Delhi house, there are only small lemons. What did you do to make it this big?" Kalam enquired.

"Sir! It is my secret! I will do it for you when I visit you in Delhi," I said. Looking at Kalam inside my house, the street became flooded with people.

Kalam left us. Even though we spoke several times on the phone after that, this was the last time we both interacted personally. Kalam was his usual enthusiastic self on that day. Neither me nor Koma imagined that he would leave us all soon. Within one month of Kalam's visit to my house, there was a burglary incident on January 18, 2015. My wife Koma had gone to Delhi to stay with my son Vikram. I was at home alone. I went to an event after receiving an invitation from Prof.

U. R. Rao in Hubli. As per the usual practice, I had asked the watchman who took care of the ISRO colony to keep an eye on my house. However, when I came and saw, a burglary had happened. I do not know why this happened.

Kalam was unhappy to hear this. "Let me tell somebody here," he said. But I knew that he couldn't do anything from there (from Delhi). The local police force helped us. Ever since Kalam visited us, we had gained more respect in our vicinity.

Everyday Kalam asked me: "Have they caught the thief?" Within two weeks, there was some good news. They found some of our stolen goods.

Kalam felt happy. "Have you taken them back?" he asked.

However, there were many legal formalities to complete before that. I had to sign some surety documents and go to court whenever they called me. Many such legal procedures!

During our daily phone calls, I mentioned this to Kalam: "Sir, may I give surety?" Kalam asked.

"No, sir! First they have to book our case in the court. Next, we have to get the surety attested by a notary…" By the time I finished Kalam said: "What are all these legal formalities, sir? Are you the culprit? Or are the people who got released on bail the culprits?"

I replied: "Sir! You were the head of our Indian Constitution once upon a time. All these formalities are only a part of it. The thieves caught by the policemen are out on bail happily. Only we have to run here and there."

A few months later, I got back my stolen goods recovered by the police. Kalam felt happy to hear the news.

❑

Kalam's Food Habits

Now about Kalam's food habits.

Kalam's phone conversation with me lasted between 30 minutes to one hour. Of that, he spoke about food for at least some ten minutes.

"Sir! What did you eat today?"

"Do you know what all I had today?" He would then elaborate on how the food was prepared and what all must be done to improve upon the taste.

"Sir! In freshly prepared rice, you must add melted ghee... my mother used to make it like this...add some drumstick leaves, or curry leaves to the ghee... mix it with rice and have it! Sir, it tastes so divine!" Kalam said.

I also like it. My aunt (periamma) prepared it that way. Koma also prepares it likewise.

Kalam loved white rice.

Kalam visited us around the 1990s or in 2000. Koma had prepared fresh soft '*poli*' (an Indian sweet dish). Kalam tasted it with freshly melted ghee and said with teary eyes: "Komamma, you have reminded me of my mother today. She also prepares poli like this... soft like a sponge!"

While speaking about dosa, he said, "I like '*pothal dosas*', sir!"

He ate the ones prepared by Koma.

Kalam loved fried vegetables, especially spicy potato fries. He did not like brinjal. I like brinjal.

"How are you even eating that, sir?" Kalam would ask me.

Kalam enjoyed spicy pickles. He enjoyed the pickles made by Koma and her mother (my mother-in-law). When he was the Indian President, he asked Koma to train his cooks. Pickles prepared and bottled by Koma have gone to him several times. When he spoke last with Koma on July 25, 2015, he said to her: "I will definitely come to meet all of you in August or September 2015." He had given her a detailed menu on what all to prepare.

He then told me: "Sir, I have given a detailed list to Komamma including pickles."

Now, how are we ever going to serve him his favourite dishes? This will prick the conscience of me and my wife Koma forever.

I consumed food from all over the world, be it vegetarian or non-vegetarian. I also make a note of how to prepare them. I would explain the method of preparation while eating.

"Sir! You are such a glutton (Chaappaattu Raman in Tamil)!" Kalam used to tell me often.

However, I never ate more than I could digest. Kalam, on the other hand, would eat more sometime and suffer.

"Sir... you are like my brother...if you don't want it, you won't take it. But I consume a lot upon the insistence of others," Kalam would tell me.

One other matter which happened frequently. While we travelled, when we ate in places which were not formal occasions, everyone would be seated together while eating. Mostly, my chair would be next to Kalam's. Because his travel itinerary was rather hectic, the time by which he came for food would be late. He would be extremely hungry!

Even if they prepared many rich delicacies, most of them were not in the habit of informing the menu in advance. They will make us all sit together and start serving. Kalam will begin by eating everything they put in from the start. Even when I ask what was all there they won't reply. Whereas, I waited patiently and would refuse in case I did not like the items being served. While everyone else would be eating, my plate alone would be empty. They would try telling me to eat something. Sometimes even fifteen minutes went by in this manner. Kalam would look at me and say: "Rajan, please eat..." I would reply: "I will eat after sometime, sir!"

A few minutes later, all good items would be served. I will ask them to serve me now. Meanwhile, Kalam's stomach would be already full. I knew that Kalam liked the food item which was being served. I will signal him to eat. However, he wouldn't be able to eat much.

After our meal, Kalam would say to me: "Sir, you are very clever! I really loved the delicacies which were served later. However, those people served everything else earlier. I did not know how to refuse like you did! After my stomach was completely full, they started bringing in good food items."

"Sir! It is your stomach and your taste buds. If you don't say 'no' to unwanted stuff, then you will have to face the problem!" I said. This has happened many times.

Kalam did not like to hurt the feelings of others by refusing to eat. He would suffer in the end!

Even though Kalam was a pure vegetarian, he asked his cook to prepare non-vegetarian food for others. He asked his Rashtrapati Bhavan cooks to prepare non-vegetarian food for me. However, those would not go well with me. I therefore refused to consume them since my body can't accept those items which do not match (in combination).

"Why aren't you eating, sir? I specifically asked them to cook these non-vegetarian items for you today..." Kalam said.

"Sir... they don't match well. Your vegetarian food is superb. From next time onwards, I will inform Sheridon about my non-vegetarian menu," I said.

I later ordered some non-vegetarian food through Sheridon. They were very tasty. I happily ate them. Kalam would be pleased.

"What sir! You are eating well now! Sheridon is an expert in all these..." Kalam said happily. Likewise, he also ordered for my second son Vikram. I do not know whether Kalam did it for any others too.

Sometimes, he called me over the phone after his official meetings after 10 PM. (I did not attend such meetings since they were highly confidential meetings meant for the Indian President. I had been invited once or twice though, for example, when President Bush was there).

"What... have you slept already? Just now my official meeting got over and I have returned back to my place..." Kalam said.

"What sir! Is this your second feast for the day?" I asked him.

"Not like that... in that official meeting, all I could eat was just soup. I was having it slowly till the meeting got over. I did not like anything else there. I feel very hungry now. I will have my feast now..." Kalam said.

He would talk while eating his dinner. Sometimes he gave a running commentary of what all he ate.

❑

Kalam's Big Departure: Dr. Nazema Recalls

Kalam uncle sent money for Ramzan in July 2015. He spoke with us everyday. His main concern was his brother's health. What did he eat? Did he get good sleep? These were the questions he usually asked. He would ask my father if he attended the Jummah prayer on every Friday.

On the evening of July 26, 2015, Kalam uncle spoke with us for a long time. He said that since he would be travelling he won't be able to speak with us for a few days.

It dawned as always on July 27, 2015. My father Maraikayar finished his evening Isha prayer. He finished his dinner by 8 PM and went to sleep.

Nazema's cell phone rang. "Abdulkani-what is the matter?" Nazema asked. Amma, it seems Kalam grandpa is very sick. "This has become a regular habit nowadays! I do not know who is spreading all these rumours," Nazema said in disgust. "No amma, this time it is for real," said her son. Nazema stood up anxiously. "Ok! Let me enquire and get back to you," Nazema said and turned off her phone.

Nazema did not believe this because such news had reached them many times before. When she came to the hall, she saw that Salim was crying. She asked him why.

When she immediately contacted Sheridon, he said: "Yes, they are saying that it is very serious this time. I came to Tirunelveli on some business. Now I am heading for Delhi. Please pray for him."

Later, Prasad who was in Delhi picked up his phone and said: "Madam, sir is quite critical. Let me call you back."

Next it was Chellappa: "Chellappa, where is my uncle Kalam?" Chellappa responded: "Madam... right now sir is..." He couldn't talk beyond that.

Nazema was shocked to hear Chellappa's response. Her hands and legs started to shake vigorously. She sat next to her father when her cellphone rang. It was Prasad. He said: "Madam, Kalam sir is no more. They asked me to inform his family." Then Nazema realised that they had waited this long for an official announcement to be made.

She screamed, "Chinnappa!" and her hand accidentally touched her sleeping father. He asked her why she cried. Nazema told him: "Vappa! Chinnappa is no more!" He got up from his bed and started crying. All he could say was "My dear brother! Oh my brother!..."

Nazema asked the elder sisters Arabu Nachiyar and Meharaj to come there. Brother Jainulabdeen ran to their house with tears all over.

Friends, relatives and townsmen crowded the house. Brother Dr. Chinnadurai Abdulla who was in a rotary meeting in Rameswaram rushed to 'House of Kalam'. Nazema couldn't see beyond that. Her eyes were flooded with tears.

The phones were ringing non-stop. When Salim said that they were asking how many family members would be coming to Delhi, Nazema said to her father, "Vappa! They are asking us to come to Delhi!" Chinna Maraikayar said decisively: "Let my brother come here. Ask them to send him here."

They kept insisting that we come to Delhi. "No, please send his body here. That was Kalam uncle's wish too!" Nazema said.

Sheikh went from Chennai to Delhi. Ghulam went from Bengaluru to Delhi. Salim also wanted to go to Delhi and pressed his aunt. However, Nazema refused since he had to take care of the formalities in Rameswaram.

People flooded from all sides. They stayed there even after midnight. They slowly started dispersing the next morning.

Someone had turned on the TV. We heard that Kalam's body had been dispatched from Shillong. They showed the entire sequence on TV. "Uncle!" Nizamuddin cried out loud.

Sheikh reached Delhi and informed us: "We will come with Kalam Vappa to our town on Wednesday." "Where is our Kalam Vappappa now?"—No one knew the answer to this question!

Meanwhile, the Tamil Nadu government allowed us to bury Kalam in a place chosen by his family members. The district collector Mr. Nandakumar went and inspected several places with Salim for Kalam's burial. They finally chose 'Pey Karumbu'.

People were entering and leaving '*House of Kalam*' to console us. Meanwhile, Chinna Maraikayar refused to eat or drink anything. When Dr. Joseph Rajan came with his wife Vani, Nazema told him, "You at least talk to my father and tell him to eat, sir!" He was in tears.

When Nazema went to receive her elder son Shahul Hamid, his wife and their daughter Roja, she saw press reporters outside. Nazema said to herself, "Whenever you came, the camera people came before you... but now..."

Saleem took Nazema and Roja with him on July 29 to bring Kalam Vappappa's body.

In the first helicopter were the central ministers who had come there to participate in Kalam's burial. Kalam's body was there in the next one. Sheikh ran from the helicopter and held Nazema's hands tightly and screamed, "Aunty!" Ghulam, Sheridon and Prasad followed him.

A vehicle was kept ready to transport Kalam's body for public viewing. People were waiting patiently to see Kalam one last time. With tears in their eyes, they formed a line and folded their hands respectfully in front of Kalam's body.

People kept coming till 8 AM. When they were informed that it was time for burial, they gave way.

The body was taken to Mohaideen Andavar Mosque at 9 PM. Relatives of Kalam couldn't control their tears. On behalf of the Jamats, Janasa prayer was conducted there. Kalam's brother and all relatives participated.

Next, the body was transported using the military vehicle at around 10:40 AM from there to a place called '*Pey Karumbu*' that was 6 kms away. With a heavy heart and teary eyes, people flocked from all directions to pay respects to their beloved leader. Without any difference, the young and the elderly, the men and the women, specially challenged people—everyone was present. They silently marched on. The island whose population was less than one lakh saw nearly 4 lakh people that day.

It was announced that schools and colleges would be closed. However, even courts, theatres, petrol bunks, and shops remained closed for the day. The fishermen did not go to the sea.

Government and private buses were arranged from all major cities to Rameswaram. Some private buses operated for free. Even special trains were arranged.

Those who had seen Kalam before and those who wanted to see him but couldn't—everyone had gathered there.

People showered flowers everywhere and bade farewell. At 11 AM, Kalam's body reached the '*Pey Karumbu*' burial ground.

Kalam's brother followed it along with his daughter Nazema, son Jainulabuddin and grandsons.

In the place where Kalam's last rituals were meant to happen, separate sections were allotted for different people. One section was reserved for the *Prime Minister* and the central ministers. Other state ministers were allotted another section. Two other sections opposite to the place of burial were allotted to Kalam's relatives and the defence officers.

More than 300 press reporters and journalists took pictures from a distant spot allotted to them.

When Kalam's brother sat in the spot reserved for him among Kalam's relatives, Prime Minister Narendra Modi sat next to him and consoled him.

Next, the military soldiers kept Kalam's body down for burial. *Prime Minister* Narendra Modi paid his last respects to former President Abdul Kalam. Congress *Vice President* Rahul Gandhi, *Governor* Rosiah, the *central ministers*, other *state ministers*, *chief ministers* of various states, Tamil Nadu ministers and major dignitaries paid their last respects to Kalam.

Soldiers from the army, navy and air force paid respects to Kalam and removed the Indian national flag. They removed Kalam's body from there and handed it to Kalam's relatives. 21 gun salute was given.

Kalam's relatives and the town Jamats dug the ground to bury Kalam's body. Under the leadership of Ahmed Kanima's brother's son Naina Mohammed dug a square pit in the middle. Kalam's body was placed there and covered with palm planks and palm leaves. Finally, it was covered with sand.

When the body was covered with sand, relatives, townsfolk and everyone around screamed out loud.

We all prayed that Kalam should go to the highest gate of paradise known as *'Jannathul Firdhouse'*. We further prayed that Kalam's dream to empower India should become a reality one day. We prayed that the next generation Indians would work smartly to achieve Kalam's goal. Let Kalam's wishes come true. Ameen!

Since all shops within the city were closed, free food was supplied by Ramakrishna Mutt and other such people for the outsiders.

After Kalam's body was buried, people came to the burial spot. They took some sand and flowers from the place to their homes in memory of Kalam.

On the days that followed, people came from all over the world to see Kalam's burial place. They also consoled Kalam's elder brother Chinna Maraikayar.

As per the Rameswaram Maraikayar family tradition, we recited the Holy Qur'an for forty days and prayed for Abdul Kalam.

Only pure vegetarian food was served on all forty days since Kalam only liked it.

Everyday people came from all directions filled with Kalam's memories to our house and poured out their tears.

On the fortieth day, special prayers were conducted in the Mohaideen Abdul Kader Andavar Mosque. Many of Kalam's friends and relatives participated in this prayer event.

Dhotis, towels, and money was given to the Alims who conducted prayers by reciting the Holy Qur'an for Kalam on all forty days. With a foreword from revered Thengai Sharabuddin Misbahi, the Holy Qur'an's central portion known as 'Yaseen' was handed out to everyone.

In the afternoon, Kalam's favourite vegetarian dishes were served.

On the first year of Kalam's death anniversary, the central ministers laid the foundation stone for Kalam's Memorial. With the tireless participation of the DRDO people, it was completed. It was inaugurated by *Prime Minister,* Shri. Narendra Modi during Kalam's second death anniversary.

The location of Kalam's memorial is such that those who wish to pay their respects to Kalam can do so while entering as well as leaving Rameswaram.

Some 40 lakh people from all over the world visited Kalam's Memorial within a year of his death.

❑

World Famous Chinnappa Kalam— My Prayer

Chinnappa had huge respects to female personalities who withstood the test of time. Whether he had seen them or not, Kalam Chinnappa greatly appreciated them. A few such female personalities who accepted the challenges of life and emerged victorious as mentioned by my Chinnappa to me were...

Chinnappa's Vappamma (father's mother) Sultan Beevi Fatima, Ummamma (mother's mother) Hasanachiyar, Umma (mother) Asiamma, sister Aṣim Zohara, Machi Ahmed Kanima, Mother Teresa, Indira Gandhi, Amritanandamayi, M. S. Subbulakshmi, Vangari Mathai, Sudha Murthy, Jayalalitha, Gomati Rajan, Dr. Shanta Krishnamurthy, Mrinalini Sarabhai, Kalpana Chawla, Dr. Nachiyar Namperumal Sami, Smt. Saroja Sampath Kumar, Dr. Fatima, Chinnadurai Abdulla, and granddaughter Nagoor Roja.

My elder sister Arabu Nachiyar and Mubarak's only son Gulam Haja Moinudeen stayed with Chinnappa in Delhi in the beginning and spent his time laughing and teasing him. When he got transferred to Chennai, he was with his wife and children. He developed a severe illness.

Chinnappa too was in Chennai to attend an event at the time. That night, Gulam was critically ill. Upon hearing the news, Chinnappa rushed to the hospital. He said to her that her son would get better if she asked her father to come and pray for him. He asked if she could ask her father to come on the next day itself.

As soon as her father heard the news, he spent a sleepless night praying for his grandson to get well. Early next morning we went to Madurai and from there to Chennai.

Both the brothers prayed for him to get better. He was in the special ward in Apollo Hospital, Chennai. Their eyes were in tears when they saw their beloved grandson lying on the bed like this. They blew from head to toe and prayed desperately for his health to improve.

We then went inside the room allotted to us. I felt sad to see my Vappa (father) like this. He hadn't slept. He had travelled a long distance too. Gulam's office friend Mahesh offered him something to eat for lunch. I was very worried since Vappa hadn't eaten anything. I mixed rasam with rice and fed my Vappa forcibly. Looking at my eyes overflowing with tears, Vappa opened his mouth to eat. I rubbed his back and chest and fed him spoon by spoon as if he were my child.

I felt satisfied after he ate a little. Suddenly, I heard someone clapping at the back. It was my Chinnappa. He appreciated me for being caring and kind towards my father.

"Amma, you are taking care of your father so well. Will you also take care of me like this?" Chinnappa Kalam asked me in a soft tone. "Definitely! Both of you are like my two eyes. Should I feed you now?" I asked him.

I was wiping my Vappa's mouth and giving him water to drink. "Do you want to eat now, Chinnappa?" I asked. He said: "I will go and eat by myself. You please take good care of your father." He left.

An hour later the doctors said that Gulam's health had improved. We were all thankful to God.

Even today I am taking care of my father. However, I won't be able to take care of my Chinnappa who asked me whether I would take good care of him anymore. I am just an ordinary woman and I have lost such a wonderful opportunity to serve my beloved Chinnappa.

Chinnappa had been reciting the Holy Qur'an since childhood. He therefore knew all 114 episodes thoroughly. If he asked about an episode over the phone, I must definitely say that during our next phone call. Sometimes I wondered if he did this to test my clarity.

Chinnappa was very fond of the beginning section of the Holy Qur'an known as the Al Fatiha. After recurring the Arabic verses, he would instruct me on its meaning: 'We shall worship only you. We seek only your help. Please lead us along the right path.' After telling this within himself, he would ask me to say it.

I used to think then that Chinnappa was so successful due to his will power, hard work and trust in God.

One day, Chinnappa had a doubt in *Silappadikaram*. He asked me: "Amma... you are studying Tamil grammar and literature. I have a doubt in this section. Can you please clarify it?" He approached me like a student.

Whether I knew it beforehand or not, I would find out the answer for Chinnappa.

Amidst my routine work everyday, I will be eagerly anticipating the phone call from my Chinnappa. I am like his daughter, a student and an Indian citizen to him.

Chinnappa could easily identify my tone, and voice modulation. It was because of him that I am able to speak with clarity.

Some people had invited Kalam Chinnappa to deliver a lecture. He was not sure whether to accept it or not since they could create some controversies out of his lecture. He then asked my opinion. I gave him two reasons for why he should attend it. First of all, he was a public figure. Secondly, as per the preachings of Prophet Mohammed (Peace be upon Him), we should always accept an invitation to an event. "Good, now please ask your father about his opinion," Kalam Chinnappa told me. My father explained even more clearly why Chinnappa must go.

I felt like laughing. Why was Chinnappa asking my opinion about all this? Chinnappa said: "Listen to me, amma! When we share information and ask for an opinion, we get more clarity."

In this manner, he acted like my teacher. I am thankful to God for blessing me with such a person in my life.

Once we both were discussing the love and attachment of people like U. V. Swaminathan and G. U. Pope to Tamil, and about their contributions to Tamil. He asked me to gather information about them and send it to him. He delivered a lecture in an event conducted by the '*Dinamani*' magazine in Chennai based on my submission. That night he told me that he had spoken a few points from what I had shared.

Chinnappa shared what all he read and he would also discuss what was in his mind everyday. He would explain about Prophet Mohammed (Peace be Upon Him). Whenever he spoke of Khalifa Umar Ali (Ravi), he said with pride that he was an honest statesman.

Since Chinnappa was employed as a space scientist, he had many good friends. Of these, Rajan sir came first. He is like a family member to us. Next came Balki (Shri. Balakrishnan) sir. His relationship with Chinnappa extended beyond the professional level. Balki sir told me, "Kalam sir is like a mother to me. He always asks me with affection whether I have eaten or not." Even today, he is very close to our family. (Son-in-law Sheikh Dawood had worked under Balki sir for a while).

The head of the Madurai Aravind Eye Hospital Dr. Namperumal Sami, and his wife Dr. Nachiyar were very close to Chinnappa and my father.

Sampathkumar-Coimbatore, Dr. Joseph Rajan, Dr. Sivathanu Pillai sir, Dr. Salwan sir, Dr. Vijayaraghavan sir (Bengaluru), Dr. Vijayaraghavan sir (Paterson Cancer Centre, Chennai) and his wife Dr. Usha, Coimbatore doctor couple—Chitra and Guhan, Dr. Chinnadurai Abdulla and Dr. Fatima Chinnadurai of Ramanathapuram Syed Ammal Hospital faculty, the Chancellor of Thanjavur SASTRA University Sethuraman and his sons Vaidya and Swaminathan, Madurai Chamber of Commerce Ratnavel, dear friend Raji, Karthikeyan IPS, Madurai Nagendran, family lawyer Devarajan and his son-in-law Somasundaram, younger brother Ratnavel, elder brother Ravichandra Ramavanni, Karate Pazhanisamy, Nellai S.Muthu, Anantha Krishnan, Shanmuga Rajeshwaran, Somanathan, M. R. M. S. Ramanathan, Pon. Radhakrishnan, Muralidharan, Nisha Thotta, Bala Shanmugam, Shenbagavalli, Kavi Kalidas, and Rajkumar—all these people continue to maintain cordial relations with our family to this day.

Chinnappa liked the Ayatul-Kursi section of the Holy Qur'an. He would always ask me to recite the section. Chinnappa mentioned that the Prophet Muhammad (Peace Be Upon Him) preached that by reciting these verses health and wealth would flourish in a family.

Chinnappa was a huge fan of Mahakavi Bharathi. Many of Chinnappa's lectures contained quotes from Bharati. Chinnappa knew by heart Paanchaali Sabadham, Kuyil Pattu, and other segments of Bharati.

Everyday he would convey something new to us. One day he would elaborate upon Mughal architecture. The next day he will talk about how King Ashoka changed his mind and followed the path of Ahimsa. Chinnappa respected Gandhi's Ahimsa movement. He greatly admired the way in which Nelson Mandela fought for justice.

He appreciated *Vallalar* who sang that '*whenever he saw a withered crop, his heart withered*'.

By nature, my Chinnappa was a very kind man. He would tell us not to stick glass pieces in the compound wall for security since it could hurt the birds which sat on them.

One of the fawns in the *Rashtrapati Bhavan* had a leg injury. Chinnappa immediately arranged for a good veterinarian and took good care of it till it completely healed.

Chinnappa not only worked hard for the development of the society. He also showered his love on all living entities equally.

To this day, I cannot bear the loss of my Chinnappa. On the days immediately following his death, I would go to my dad after he finished his morning prayers. I told him, "Where is my Chinnappa, dear Vappa?" He remained silent for 2-3 days. After that my Vappa said, "Is this what you learnt from your Chinnappa? Go and take care of your duties."

I felt sad that I upset my father who was already lamenting over his dear brother's death. When I approached him once again, he told me: "Amma, birth and death are in the hands of the creator. Pray that your Chinnappa should go to heaven. Never forget to help others. You need to get back to your life."

After Chinnappa's death, I visited his No. 10, Rajaji Marg house in Delhi along with Sheikh and Salim. We went all around the place, wherever my Chinnapa had been. His favourite plants, his favourite Arjuna tree, parrots, mynahs and all other birds seemed to maintain silence to honour his death. Sheridon and Prasad too remained silent.

We went to Chinnappa's office in the front hall. They had removed his desk and it now looked bigger than before. There was a garlanded picture of Chinnappa hanging on the wall. Visitors had to sign in the bulky register in the front desk. The fan was rotating slowly.

Chellappa who had followed us told me: "Madam, I have turned on the fan so that our Kalam sir doesn't sweat! Everyday I pluck his favourite flowers from the garden and decorate the place."

Sheridon invited us upstairs. We went to Chinnappa's library. There was a wooden box. "He brought a present for his brother from Uttar Pradesh. Here is the key," they said and handed it over to us.

Chinnappa had kept everything ready to celebrate his beloved brother's birthday. Only he is not there anymore...

I entered Chinnappa's private bedroom where he slept. From the end of his Presidential term right until his Shillong trip, this was his bedroom.

Even though I had gone to all other rooms in the house, this was the first time I entered his bedroom.

I peeked in and saw everything: a small wooden cupboard, a few books on the table, the *Holy Qur'an* book—along with *Tarjuma* (translations in Tamil and English) there was a *Holy Qur'an* book exclusively in Arabic. Then there were a few papers for writing, three pens and a picture of my Vappappa (father's father).

Right in front of this desk was his bed. On the opposite wall was a metal plate with verses from *Ayatul Kursi*. My entire body trembled when I looked at it.

Chinnappa probably wanted to read those *Ayatul Kursi* verses everyday after waking up... he probably read them whenever his eyes fell upon them. Tears started pouring down my eyes.

How much of an impact *Ayatul Kursi* had upon him! Great people who never reveal anything about themselves probably never reveal their spiritual identities as well!

We left from Delhi on our flight. I recalled Chinnappa's smiling face. Everytime we left, he would come out and wave goodbye. Now he is no longer there... As I observed the fluffy passing clouds in the sky, I recollected Chinnappa's poems. Suddenly a thought flashed.

Everytime Chinnappa visited us in Rameswaram his father and later my father wrote the verses beginning in *'Innal lazee'* which meant that "Whoever accepted the preachings of the *Holy Qur'an*, God will bring you back (alive or dead) to your house."

That was the reason why Chinnappa who lived in Delhi and died in Shillong was brought to his house in Rameswaram for the final rituals. How powerful were these verses indeed! God is great!

My Chinnappa, Avul Pakir Jainulabdeen Abdul Kalam had lived following the footsteps of his ancestors all his life. The name and fame of our family spread far and wide because of him. Whenever I think of this.....

As a dedication to my Chinnappa who regarded me as his daughter and a friend, I promise myself to make my life more meaningful and useful. I pray to God to fulfil this wish of mine. Ameen.

❑

Eternal Memories: Dr. Y. S. Rajan Continues...

I take great pleasure in writing this book on Kalam. This is also my duty. Kalam's achievements made him a great man. He lived a humble life. If we write about him without quoting any personal experiences as a mere documentary, it will not be correct. Many books on Kalam that were written after he became the Indian President are mere exaggerations. This happens to all great men! In order to get publicity, they quote all that these great men never said and did. Many information shared on social media, press and books regarding Kalam are false narratives. Kalam hardly commented about others or their actions. He never used sentences like "I do not like..." He never said anything negative about anyone. He only spoke about what he liked. He would then stop with that. Not once did he speak about his dislikes. In other foreign countries, they always reviewed the works of great leaders, and writers with the help of computers to check for their authenticity. That way, they would be able to isolate information written/ spoken by them from those that weren't. However, in India nothing is researched thoroughly.

Under these circumstances, I have tried to write about that great man based on what all I saw, felt and experienced with him. I do not think that Kalam would fit within my description fully.

These are just portions of light scattering from that brilliant diamond. I have written here about all we discussed. That doesn't mean that Kalam never discussed anything with others.

Many people say and write that we both are like Krishna and Arjuna. I have nothing to say about that. It is true that Kalam was very close with me and my family. Indeed, it is a great honour for us! Kalam's family members (starting from his elder brother, his elder brother's son, daughter-in-law, daughter Nazema, his grandsons and so on) are also close to us.

I do not like to compete or compare. Like a pleasant breeze and a welcoming rain shower, our mutual intimacy and affection for each other was born naturally.

Our relationship with Kalam was always simple and casual. Sometimes, I have fought with him during the course of our discussion. I have been harsh and angry. Then I would want him to forgive me the next day. Even before I spoke, Kalam would speak casually with me as if nothing had happened.

During our 'kutchery' meetings or other conversations, I gave my opinion frankly. I have seen others swaying here and there. If Kalam insisted upon something, then they would either tell him that he is absolutely right or they would give their advice supporting his point of view. During these circumstances, I would explain clearly what would happen if he acted as he wished. I would explain the possible complications he would have to face later. All these responsibilities fell on my head. Sometimes I felt bad about it. Other kutchery members used to say, 'Only Rajan can speak frankly'. I do not know if they were applauding me or were trying to pull my leg.

Sometimes, the kutchery members discussed and decided upon something before me and Kalam entered. Then they would tell me: "Rajan! You only have to convey this to him; Periyavar (that is the word we used for Kalam, a word with great respect in Tamil, literally meaning Big Man, actually gender neutral plural) won't listen!"

I do not know whether the other kutchery members spoke privately with Kalam. I am not interested either. Therefore, when everyone said that the relations between me and Kalam are (were) special, I cannot be entirely sure. Others could say whatever they liked. I did not research it.

However, I did worry about people who made use of Kalam's name for their personal agenda. I would get worried that Kalam would lose his reputation. Some of his intimate kutchery friends (who were also my friends) would ask me to talk about such persons to Kalam. That would be very difficult (dharma sankatam) for me!

Having worked in ISRO and the science and technology field for a long time from a very young age, I never got involved in the "palace politics" matters surrounding big men. Here too it could complicate my relationship with Kalam. However, out of affection for him, I always worried that he shouldn't fall into the trap of such evil men.

A few weeks before July 2015, Kalam would often repeat his great appreciation for my 'assistance' to one of his closest work partners, Dr. Sivathanu Pillai who worked closely with Kalam right from his SLV-3 days and went with him to the DRDO days. Many initiatives undertaken by the DRDO stagnated without reaching the stage of large scale production. The BrahMos initiative launched by Kalam was an exception. This is a joint venture by India and Russia. Under the able leadership of Dr. Sivathanu Pillai, this supersonic missile was manufactured in large numbers and supplied to the Indian army, navy and air force. Those who used this weapon in the defence forces appreciated the precision and usefulness of this missile.

It is very rare in the Indian science and technology field, for someone to encourage and to boost the capabilities in the high tech manufacturing sector.

Kiran Kumar who took charge as Chairman ISRO in January 15, 2015 felt that the manufacture of the PSLV on a large scale like this should be done; if ISRO alone manufactured it, then technologists and scientists will be wasting their time unnecessarily instead of making new innovations. He therefore felt that Dr. Sivathanu Pillai was the right choice and decided to appoint him as an honorary distinguished professor for ISRO.

I knew about that. I could have extended my role as the honorary distinguished professor for ISRO. However, my work in ISRO was over. Still, I was provided with excellent office space and staff. I could go there anytime I wished. But Dr. Sivathanu Pillai's new role is very important for India. Once our manufacturing sector starts manufacturing PSLV, it would be good for India (not just for prestige alone). In ISRO, there were not many such excellent office spaces to seat such persons. I therefore decided to hand over my seating place to Dr. Sivathanu Pillai and took necessary steps for doing so.

Dr. Sivathanu Pillai started to work from July 2015 onwards in my room. Kalam knew of his role in manufacturing PSLV. He also knew the significance of this major initiative. He also knew that the job had been handed over to the right person. When Kalam learnt that I had allotted my work space and staff to assist Dr. Sivathanu Pillai so that he can start the work the very first day he joined, he was happy and was extremely pleased with me.

"Rajan, you handed over your office space to accommodate Dr. Sivathanu Pillai so that he could start immediately. No one else would have done this, sir..."

He told this several times in July. But Kalam didn't even last till the end of July, 2015. Never did I imagine that me and Dr. Sivathanu Pillai would be standing one behind the other and showering flowers over Kalam's cemetery on July 30, 2015. Had Kalam heard that Dr. Sivathanu Pillai successfully accomplished his job at the PSLV within 18 months, he would have been very pleased. I frequently visit Dr. Sivathanu Pillai in ISRO. Me and my wife Koma received special wishes and blessings from Dr. Kalam on July 25, 2015. That was the most important day of my life.

I had great ambitions about Kalam; and angst as well... He led a life which made all to say that he was a great man; he accomplished so many things in his life. He was a pioneer for many things in India. By becoming the eleventh Indian President, he attracted the hearts of people; he brought in front of people of our country the role of children (as wealth) (at a time when the political leaders who were fully engrossed in the voting based electoral democracy, media and all had forgotten about children). He is the reason why many people comment today that the future belongs to our children! It can be said that it is because of him that today's politicians compete to donate laptops and cycles to the school children.

Still I feel that Kalam could have used his charm better. I have spoken to him about it playfully and seriously.

For example, FUREC which Kalam co-founded with Acharya Mahapragya. The CEO Sudhamahi Regunathan is also a competent lady. Such situations don't arise often. He could have made some arrangements for funding it. It would have grown into a big institution by world standards by now. India could have led by looking at all religions in an equal way and by creating a feeling of unity between the religious leaders and people.

Likewise, Kalam could have established a Global Trust for educating girl children as described earlier, by getting financial aid from the middle eastern countries. It could have developed into a big world organisation today.

Had he done these two, Kalam could have become an international icon. The world could have benefitted from these two organisations for at least another 200–300 years.

This was my angst with Kalam. I have told this to him several times. "Sir! One day God will ask you this... I blessed you with charm and charisma. Did you make use of its full potential? How will you reply to him?"

Why am I saying this here? Long after he is gone, his charisma has not faded away. It is in their hearts and outside. There could be those who use his portrait and his name for their own benefits; in some places, such attempts have multiplied like mushrooms. However, in many places I go, I have myself seen that love for him in ordinary people has spread widely, even after his passing away. This is not limited to Tamil Nadu alone. Even discounting it, it is possible to see it. People could say that it is because Kalam was a Tamil man and a Tamil leader. But, Kalam belongs to the world.

I went to Kolhapur in Maharashtra for an event. Since Kolhapur Mahalakshmi temple is world famous, we tried to go there. However, there was not much time with us. Since there was a big programme over there, many policemen were stationed to control the crowd. The people who arranged for my visit were in trouble. If we got inside, their men would be there to take us. But how to get past this crowd! They were trying to inform that I am a friend of Kalam. Meanwhile, one of the policemen over there gave me a big salute and was informing the others in Marathi, "Kalam Sahib's friend!" He probably might have seen me on TV with Kalam! He helped me to get inside speedily.

Even in the ISRO layout in Bengaluru where we live, traders, workers, street vendors, and all others have great respect for us since they knew that Kalam visited us. Many of them did not even see this personally. They only got to know of Kalam's visit to our house through their friends. In this way, Kalam is in the heart of those who never saw him even once. People shower their love and affection towards us since we are Kalam's friends.

I have seen similar incidents in North India too.

This affection might last for a few more months or a few more years. They might celebrate Kalam's birth and death anniversaries. However, we all know how people let go into air the ideals of many great men, who were elevated to great heights.

I am concerned that this should not happen to Kalam.

Today, many schools, colleges and DRDO laboratories have been named after APJ Abdul Kalam. In Delhi, one of the big streets is named after him. Many memorials are being raised to honour him. All these might help to propagate Kalam's name to the future generation. Those now present could see this as duties and responsibilities of India and her people towards Kalam. Museums showcasing his life history will also be along similar lines.

My angst is that all these must not vanish like footsteps on the sand.

My wish is that a permanent living organisation, working to serve the society in ways that are relevant to the times, should be established in his name to honour him. I have spoken several times with him of this. Kalam had a special interest in promoting social harmony. In a way, Kalam's life itself is the greatest example of this. Social harmony will be a very great asset for this century and beyond. It would be valuable not just for India, but also many countries.

Would it be possible to establish a big organisation in each and every Indian district, with Kalam's name, keeping his initiatives like FUREC and others in mind so as to promote social harmony? The branches of such an organisation should never be in the virtual world (internet) only. An organisation formed with Kalam's goals in mind should be blended with the people. It should be a practical achiever, and not merely a lecture hall for elaborate speeches. It must help the people. It should be the one which helps Indian people to be in the upward movement for their socio-economic status.

Those who love and respect Kalam must work towards such an initiative. If they succeed, I will consider it as a very great outcome of this book.

Once such organisations have been established well in India, they could be extended worldwide. People who are born in India and settled abroad (PIO's, NRI's: *Persons of Indian Origin, Non-Resident Indians*) could help in a great way. They could invite people living there to take part in this prestigious project and help promote social harmony.

Today, Kalam is no longer with us. The rare memories of being with that great man come again and again not only in my mind, but they are also filling the minds of people .

Kalam's magnificent life story is extending to be a part of our history; the memories that don't leave us are living with us.

Memories have no death...

❑

Key Words and their Abbreviations

1. *AICTE* : *All India Council for Technical Education*
2. *AMTI* : *Arutchelvar N. Mahalingam Translation Institute*
3. *APPLE* : *Ariane Passenger PayLoad Experiment*
4. *ASLV* : *Augmented Satellite Launch Vehicle*
5. *ASSOCHAM* : *Associated Chambers of Commerce and Industry of India*
6. *ATS* : *Applications Technology Satellite*
7. *BARC* : *Bhabha Atomic Research Centre*
8. *BEL* : *Bharat Electronics Limited*
9. *BOG* : *Board of Governors*
10. *CAG* : *Comptroller and Auditor General of India*
11. *CAIR* : *Centre for Artificial Intelligence and Robotics*
12. *CCRD* : *Chief Controller of R&D*
13. *C-DOT* : *Centre for Development of Telematics*
14. *CERN* : *Conseil Européen pour la Recherche Nucléaire*
15. *CGDAST* *Consultative Group for Departments Applying Science and Technology*
16. *CGES* : *Consultative Group of Eminent Scientists*
17. *CII* : *Confederation of Indian Industry*
18. *CISF* : *Central Industrial Security Force*
19. *CMU* : *Carnegie Mellon University*
20. *CNC* : *Computer Numerical Control*
21. *DDP* : *Department of Defence Production*
22. *DDRD* : *Department of Defence Research & Development*
23. *DEA* : *Department of Economic Affairs*

24. *DIAT* : *Defence Institute of Advanced Technology*
25. *DMRL* *Director of Metallurgical Research Laboratory*
26. *DRDL* : *Defence Research and Development Laboratory*
27. *DRDO* : *Defence Research and Development Organisation*
28. *DSIR* *Department of Scientific and Industrial Research*
29. *DST* : *Department of Science and Technology of government of India*
30. *ECIL* : *Electronics Corporation of India Limited*
31. *ESCES* : *Experimental Satellite Communication Earth Station*
32. *FRP* : *Fibre Reinforced Plastics*
33. *FUREC* *Foundation for Understanding of Religions and Enlightened Citizenship*
34. *GDP* : *Gross Domestic Product*
35. *GOM* : *Group Of Ministers*
36. *GSFC* : *Goddard Space Flight Centre*
37. *GSLV* : *Geosynchronous Satellite Launch Vehicle*
38. *HAL* : *Hindustan Aeronautics Limited*
39. *HGT* : *Home Grown Technology*
40. *IAF* : *International Astronautical Federation*
41. *IAS* : *Indian Administrative Service*
42. *ICSSR* : *Indian Council of Social Science Research*
43. *IGMDP* *Integrated Guided Missile Development Programme*
44. *IHC* : *India Habitat Centre*
45. *IIC* : *India International Centre*
46. *IISc* : *Indian Institute of Science*
47. *IMD* : *Indian Meteorological Department*
48. *INAE* : *Indian National Academy of Engineering*
49. *INCOSPAR* : *Indian National Committee for Space Research*
50. *INSA* : *Indian National Science Academy*
51. *INSAT* : *Indian National Satellite*
52. *ISRO* : *Indian Space Research Organisation*
53. *ISSP* : *Indian Scientific Satellite Project/Indo-Soviet Satellite Project*

54. *ITR* : *Integrated Test Range*
55. *LCA* : *Light Combat Aircraft*
56. *MBT* : *Main Battle Tank*
57. *MIT* : *Madras Institute of Technology*
58. *MLA* : *Member of Legislative Assembly*
59. *MP* : *Member of Parliament*
60. *MPS* : *Main Project Supervisor*
61. *MTCR* : *Missile Technology Control Regime*
62. *MTCR* : *Missile Technology Control Regime*
63. *NAF* : *National Agro Federation*
64. *NASA* : *National Aeronautics and Space Administration*
65. *NAS* : *National Academy of Scientists*
66. *NDA* : *National Democratic Alliance*
67. *NNRMS* *National Natural Resources Management System*
68. *NRHM* *National Rural Health Mission*
69. *NRSA* : *National Remote Sensing Agency*
70. *NSG* : *Nuclear Suppliers Group*
71. *NTRO* : *National Technical Research Organisation*
72. *PMO* : *Prime Minister's Office*
73. *PRL* : *Physical Research Laboratory*
74. *PSA* : *Principal Scientific Adviser*
75. *PSLV* : *Polar Satellite Launch Vehicle*
76. *PSU* : *Public Sector Undertakings*
77. *PTR* : *Pokhran Test Range*
78. *PTU* : *Punjab Technical University*
79. *PURA* : *Providing Urban Amenities in Rural Areas*
80. *RCI* : *Research Centre Imarat*
81. *REX* : *Re-entry EXperiment*
82. *RFF* : *Rocket Fabrication Facility*
83. *RPP* : *Rocket Propellant Plant*
84. *RS* : *Rohini Satellite*
85. *RSR* : *Rohini Sounding Rocket*

86. *S & T* : *Science & Technology*

87. *SACC* : *Scientific Advisory Committee to the Cabinet*

88. *SCC* : *Space Centre Council*

89. *SETS* : *Society for Electronic Transactions*

90. *SHAR* : *Sriharikota Range*

91. *SITE* : *Satellite Instructional Television Experiment*

92. *SLV-3E1* : *SLV-3 Experimental flight-1*

93. *SLV-3E2* : *SLV-3 Experimental flight-2*

94. *SSTC* : *Space Science and Technology Centre*

95. *STAND* : *Science and Technology Agenda for National Development*

96. *TCFC* : *Technology Committee Finance Committee*

97. *TCIL* : *Telecommunications Consultants of India Ltd*

98. *TDB* : *Technology Development Board Technology*

99. *TERLS* : *Thumba Equatorial Rocket Launching Station*

100. *TIFAC-CORE* : *TIFAC Centres of Relevance and Excellence*

101. *TIFAC* : *Technology Information Forecasting and Assessment Council*

102. *UGC* : *University Grants Commission*

103. *UNDP* : *United Nations Development Programme*

104. *UPA* : *United Progressive Alliance*

105. *US-AID* : *United States Agency for International Development*

106. *VSSC* : *Vikram Sarabhai Space Centre*

❑❑❑